Moral Knowledge
and Ethical Character

Moral Knowledge and Ethical Character

‗

Robert Audi

New York   Oxford   ●   Oxford University Press   1997

Oxford University Press

Oxford   New York
Athens   Auckland   Bangkok   Bogota   Bombay   Buenos Aires
Calcutta   Cape Town   Dar es Salaam   Delhi   Florence   Hong Kong
Istanbul   Karachi   Kuala Lumpur   Madras   Madrid   Melbourne
Mexico City   Nairobi   Paris   Singapore   Taipei   Tokyo   Toronto   Warsaw

and associated companies in
Berlin   Ibadan

Published by Oxford University Press, Inc.
198 Madison Avenue, New York, New York 10016

Oxford is a registered trademark of Oxford University Press

Library of Congress Cataloging-in-Publication Data

Audi, Robert, 1941–
[Selections. 1997]
Moral knowledge and ethical character / Robert Audi.
p.   cm.
Includes bibliographical references and index.
ISBN 0-19-511468-X
— ISBN 0-19-511469-8 (pbk.)
1. Ethics.   I. Title.
BJ1012.A93   1997
170'.42 — dc20   96-36703
CIP

1 3 5 7 9 8 6 4 2
Printed in the United States of America
on acid-free paper

Preface and Acknowledgments

This book presents a large-scale position in ethical theory through twelve interconnected essays on four of its major dimensions. The first is moral epistemology, which concerns the possibility of knowledge and justification in ethics; the second is the ontology of ethics, which addresses the nature of moral properties and concepts and their relation to the natural world; the third is moral psychology, which concerns the nature and scope of moral motivation and judgment, their internalization in character, their influence on the will, and the extent of our responsibility for them; and the fourth is the foundations of ethics, which (in this book) concerns particularly the question of how motivational and valuational elements may be basic for moral reasons for action. The overall ethical theory I present combines four elements, each addressing one of the dimensions of ethical theory just sketched: a moral epistemology that is internalist, qualifiedly rationalistic, and moderately intuitionist; an ontology of ethics that is realist, pluralist, and non-reductively naturalistic; a moral psychology that countenances unconscious motivation and cognition, posits a good measure of control and moral responsibility for aspects of character, and describes how morality is internalized in us and reflected in action; and an account of value that posits a plurality of intrinsic goods and evils and yields a theory of how they provide objective reasons for action.

Five of the essays, comprising nearly half of the volume — chapters 3, 6, and 10 through 12 — have not been previously published. In each part of the book, the essays are ordered chronologically. This order is appropriate to their content, and the same holds for the ordering of the four parts. Many chapters build on accounts, ideas, or distinctions introduced earlier. My aim has been to order the essays to provide as much cumulative development of my position as possible while also making each essay and each part of the book essentially self-contained. This should be a significant convenience to readers interested in some one part or a selection among the essays. The previously published essays have not been altered apart from minor changes chiefly intended to put the notes into a uniform style, and there is some overlap. This is mainly among chapters 2, 4, and 5, but where overlap occurs it is generally developmental, and it yields some gain in the depth or comprehensiveness with which important questions are treated.

Those considering the book for teaching ethics may find it useful to conceive it in terms of *clusters* of essays, including a number of groupings not precisely corresponding to one of the volume's four parts. Among the essentially self-contained clusters are (1) *intuitionism* (or ethical rationalism), particularly chapters 2–5 and 12; (2) *moral psychology*, chapters 6–11; (3) *moral epistemology*, especially chapters 1–4; (4) the *foundations of ethics*, chapters 2 and 9–12; (5) *virtue ethics*, chapters 6–8 and perhaps 11; (6) the *metaphysics of ethics*, mainly chapters 4, 5, and 11; (7) *general metaethics* (objectivity, realism-anti/realism, moral explanation, justification in ethics), chapters 2, 3, 5, 10, 11, and perhaps 12. The concluding, synoptic chapter is appropriate to any of these clusters.

For permission to reprint previously published material I thank the editors of *Logos* for chapter 1, which appeared in vol. 10 (1989), 13–37; *Southern Journal of Philosophy* for chapter 4, which was published in the supplement to vol. 29 (1991), 1–24; *Ethics* for chapter 7, which appeared in vol. 101, no. 2 (1991), 304–21; *Mind* for chapter 8, published in vol. 104, no. 414 (1995), 449–71; and *Pacific Philosophical Quarterly*, for chapter 9, which appeared in vol. 72, no. 4 (1992), 247–71. I am also grateful for permission to reprint chapters 2 and 4, which were published in collections by two university presses; the former in Walter Sinnott-Armstrong and Mark Timmons, eds., *Moral Knowledge? New Readings in Moral Epistemology*, Oxford University Press (1995), 101–36, the latter in Steven Wagner and Richard Warner, eds., *Naturalism: A Critical Appraisal*, University of Notre Dame Press (1993), 95–115. Chapter 6, "Self-Deception, Rationalization, and the Ethics of Belief," though not previously published, draws much from one I contributed to Brian McLaughlin and Amélie O. Rorty, eds., *Perspectives on Self-Deception*, University of California Press (1988), entitled "Self-Deception, Rationality, and Reasons for Acting."

In working out the positions taken in this book, I have learned much from other philosophers and from my students. I cannot name all who should be thanked, partly because of their number but mainly because I cannot remember all the many times I have benefited from comments. The people in question include both audiences responding to my papers and authors of papers presented at conferences, in my own department, in the National Endowment for the Humanities Summer Seminars and Institutes I have held, particularly the Institute on Naturalism I directed in 1993, and in seminars in ethics codirected with my Law School colleague, Stephen Kalish, during alternate summers from 1988 through 1994. This book has also benefited from my reading, and sometimes talking with, a number of the authors referred to in the notes (and many not referred to or discussed because of limited space).

I especially want to acknowledge Richard Brandt, the late William Frankena, Jorge Garcia, Bernard Gert, Stephen Kalish, Walter Sinnott-Armstrong, Mark Timmons, and Mark van Roojen. I have also been fruitfully discussing ethical issues intermittently over a number of years with Kurt Baier, Norman Bowie, Dan Brock, Panayot Butchvarov, Norman Dahl, Stephen Darwall, John Deigh, Michael DePaul, Berys Gaut, Gerald Dworkin, Allan Gibbard, Brad Hooker, Philip Kain, Robert

Kane, Christine Korsgaard, Craig Lawson, Joseph Mendola, Michael Meyer, James Montmarquet, Michael Moore, Paul Moser, Jeffrey Poland, Nelson Potter, William Prior, Elizabeth Radcliffe, Peter Railton, Amélie Rorty, Bruce Russell, Geoffrey Sayre-McCord, Robert Schopp, Stefan Sencerz, Michael Slote, James Sterba, Nicholas Sturgeon, Laurence Thomas, Judith Thomson, William Tolhurst, Nick Zangwill, Michael J. Zimmerman, and, especially in relation to action theory and moral psychology, Michael Bratman, Hugh McCann, Alfred Mele, and Raimo Tuomela. Through their writings, and in our occasional discussions, I have learned from the work of Philippa Foot, Richard Hare, Alasdair MacIntyre, Thomas Nagel, John Rawls, Thomas Scanlon, and Bernard Williams. Comments by two anonymous readers for the Press were helpful in the later stages of revision. Significant proportions of this book have also benefited from my interactions with the faculties and visiting philosophers at the University of Notre Dame, where I held a fellowship in 1987–88, Dartmouth College, where in 1994 I served as the Senior Fellow in the College's Institute on Moral Knowledge; and at Santa Clara University, where in the same year I served as Fagothey Distinguished Visiting Professor.

Lincoln, Nebraska   R. A.
January 1997

Contents

Moral Knowledge
and Ethical Character

Introduction

Four Dimensions
of Ethical Theory

In the field of ethics the integration between theory and its everyday applications has commonly been close, and all the great moral philosophers have proposed both normative standards for day-to-day conduct and theories of the foundations of ethics. This book is written in the belief that ethical theory should not be isolated, either from concrete questions about what is right or wrong or from other parts of philosophy. From the rise of positivism in the 1930s, however, and at least into the 1960s, moral philosophy was preoccupied not only with ethical theory but, for the most part, with a fairly narrow part of it: the logic of moral concepts and, correspondingly, the uses of moral language. By the 1970s the tide had turned, and at least in the Anglo-American world applied ethics burgeoned in and outside academia and began to occupy a large part of the ethics curriculum in most departments of philosophy. But applied ethics requires theories and principles to apply, and at least since the early 1980s ethical theory in the broadest sense has regained strength and wider interest in the general field of ethics and particularly in philosophy.

A distinctive feature of ethical theory now is its self-conscious realization that other areas of philosophy — especially epistemology and metaphysics, philosophy of mind and action, and philosophy of natural and social science — have much to contribute to it. This book is intended to advance ethical theory in a way that does full justice to the integrity of moral philosophy as traditionally understood but also brings to bear on its problems a perspective drawn from extensive work in epistemology and the philosophy of mind and action. The four areas of ethical theory to which the parts of the book are mainly addressed are moral epistemology, the metaphysics of ethics, moral psychology, and the foundations of ethics. What follows is a sketch of the territory covered.

I. Ethical Knowledge, Intuition, and Moral Skepticism

Part I develops a position in moral epistemology. It explores the moral epistemology of some major ethical views, most notably those of Kant, Mill, and W. D. Ross; it

3

constructs a theory of the nature and grounds of the justification and knowledge that moral judgments, at their best, can express; it develops an account of ethical intuitions and their place in moral theory; and it shows how moral skepticism can be met by some of the arguments effective in dealing with skepticism about non-moral matters.

Chapter 1, "Internalism and Externalism in Moral Epistemology," shows how a major division in general epistemology applies in ethics. Epistemically *internalist* epistemologies ground justification and knowledge in elements accessible to reflection, such as sensory states and memory impressions; *externalist* epistemologies ground justification and knowledge in elements not thus accessible, such as the objective reliability of the processes causing belief: roughly, the relative frequency with which those elements lead to truth. Kantian ethics is argued to be internalist, in part because it grounds knowledge of basic duties in a priori reason; utilitarian ethics is externalist, grounding such knowledge in evidence concerning the consequences of acts. On one count, internalism is shown to be preferable: it better explains the importance of internal factors, such as motives and ideals, in appraising character. Good character is not a matter of what one's behavior causes; it is more nearly a matter of what causes one's behavior.

The task of chapter 2, "Intuitionism, Pluralism, and the Foundations of Ethics," is to develop an internalist, fallibilistic ethical intuitionism that can merit a serious place among contemporary ethical theories. The point of departure is Ross. In part through developing a more fine-grained account of self-evidence than Ross or other intuitionists provided, a reconstructed Rossian intuitionism is shown to be viable without some of the objectionable features Ross apparently attributed to it. As compared with his view, the more comprehensive intuitionism developed allows wider scope for moral reflection and inference as both correctives and systematizers of our moral standards. It is also free of some often alleged defects of intuitionism: arbitrariness, dogmatism, and an implausible philosophy of mind.

Chapter 3, "Skepticism in Theory and Practice," consolidates and defends the results of the first two chapters by articulating and, so far as possible in a single essay, meeting the challenge of skepticism. Just as skeptics about theoretical reason find a logical gap between our evidence for factual propositions and their truth, skeptics about practical reason find a logical gap between our moral reasons for action (or other reasons for action) and the overall moral goodness (or overall justification) of action. If we can vindicate common sense against theoretical skepticism (as I have tried to do in a series of epistemological works), we are at least in a good position to vindicate it against skepticism about the justificatory force of reasons for action. Skepticism about our behavioral realization of goodness has much in common with skepticism about our cognitive realization of truth, and important points responding to skepticism about the latter can be adapted to respond to skepticism about the former.

II. Moral Concepts and the Natural Order

Part II is devoted to a theoretical (mainly ontological) profile of moral concepts, such as those of justice, virtue, and obligation, and to appraising the view that moral concepts and properties merit a realist interpretation. Its results support the moral epistemology of part I. Ethical concepts are shown to be understandable through a certain kind of reflection on them and to figure in principles for which intuitions are the most important single source — though not the only source — of evidence.

The first chapter of part II, "Moral Epistemology and the Supervenience of Ethical Concepts," concentrates on the implications of the special dependence (the *supervenience*) of moral concepts on non-moral ones. A person is morally good, for instance, on the basis of non-moral, psychological features, above all basic desires, governing beliefs, settled intentions, and other elements of character. Does this imply that we can know such moral truths as that someone is a good person in the same way we can know psychological truths about the person? I argue that it does not, although it does imply (on plausible assumptions) that there is an objective, "factual" route to justification of certain moral propositions. Being governed by altruistic intentions is excellent evidence of one's moral goodness. This defense of objectivity is a positive result for ethical theory, but it is neutral between empiricism and rationalism and indeed can be interpreted so as to be compatible with non-cognitivism.

Chapter 5, "Ethical Naturalism and the Explanatory Power of Moral Concepts," picks up where the previous chapter ends: given the dependence of moral concepts on non-moral ones, are the explanatory uses of moral concepts essentially like those of (non-moral) explanatory concepts employed in the sciences, or are they perhaps sui generis? In answering, I explore the most widely held and most important naturalistic version of moral realism. On this realist naturalism, the reality of moral properties is shown by a proper account of their causal role in explaining human conduct. My own position accommodates what is most important in this one but yields a different kind of realism: I accept a naturalistic, broadly causal account of moral explanation but argue that this account can be cogent even if it does not construe moral properties themselves as natural. My strategy is to naturalize moral explanations without naturalizing moral properties.

III. Moral Psychology and Ethical Character

Part III concentrates on problems of moral psychology. It is devoted to extending, to a wider range of human conduct, the internalist, objectivist perspective on moral judgment and moral epistemology laid out in parts I and II. At one end in human behavior there is the generally regrettable conduct associated with self-deception, weakness of will, rationalization, and compulsion; at the other end there is virtuous action in its many forms.

Chapter 6, "Self-Deception, Rationalization, and the Ethics of Belief," shows how moral appraisal can reach below the surface of behavior and even of consciousness, where reasons for action can operate unnoticed by the agent. Explanation — naturalistically understood as in chapter 5 — is contrasted with mere rationalization. A broad picture of rational action is presented, in which moral conduct has a place even when it is not a response to the agent's moral judgment or grounded in the agent's moral reasoning. The chapter serves in part as an antidote to the intellectualist idea that moral appraisal and responsibility belong only to conduct that is grounded in explicit practical reasoning, consciously performed, or at least motivated by conscious factors. The ethics of belief is shown to be one domain in which moral standards reach beyond reasoned conduct and even below the surface of consciousness.

In Chapter 7, "Responsible Action and Virtuous Character," the conception of moral responsibility set out in chapter 6 is extended to character. To be sure, we do not have direct control over our character, and even our indirect control over it is limited, particularly in childhood. But there are several respects in which we can control it. I describe these and distinguish three major kinds of responsibility for elements of character. Here internalism again appears, this time in clarifying the basis not of justification but of responsibility. The idea, in outline, is that one is responsible for conduct only if it either traces to something internal, such as an underlying intention or decision, or there is at least some appropriate internal element accessible to the agent, such as a decision to check to be sure the fire is out, which would have altered that conduct. One might be responsible for a fire either because one decided not to check or because one *could* have decided to and did not. If moral responsibility is ultimately internal in this way, that is some confirmation of the general view, developed in many parts of the book, that moral concepts are in the main internally grounded.

The concluding chapter in part III, "Acting from Virtue," brings virtue ethics into the perspective of the internalist objectivism and multilayered moral psychology of the book. In the ideal cases, moral conduct is not merely acceptable on the surface but grounded in some virtue of the agent, as where a promise is kept not from fear of reprisal but from fidelity. But what is it to act from virtue, as opposed to merely doing what a virtuous person does? And can such action be explained in terms of reasons, in the way suggested by the explanatory account outlined in parts I and II? Moreover, can such action be understood in relation to rules or general standards of conduct, as Kant and Mill and the intuitionists believed? In response to these questions I develop an account of acting from virtue that represents it as a kind of action for reasons — reasons appropriately connected with the agent's virtues as elements in character. These reasons can be viewed both as virtue-guided and as rule-governed: there is no incompatibility here. This is not in the least to say that virtue ethics is dispensable in favor of rule ethics. Far from it. The concluding section shows how, if we distinguish (as is often not done) between the theory of moral obligation and the theory of moral worth, we can see that virtue concepts can be absolutely fundamental in the latter even if they are not fundamental in the former.

IV. Reason, Judgment, and Value

Part IV, drawing on the first eight chapters, presents an account of reasons for action, with the central focus on normative reasons, the kind in virtue of which (as where a child will be burned to death if one does not act) one in some sense *ought* to do the deed those reasons support. Normative reasons may also, in a broadly causal sense, explain conduct, but this explanatory power is not their defining feature. Chapter 9 connects normative reasons above all with desire; chapter 10 connects them with moral judgment; and chapter 11 connects them with values. On the theory of the foundations of ethics presented in these chapters, values are experientially realizable ends that, in autonomous agents, can yield guiding practical reasons: reasons for both desire and practical judgment.

Chapter 9, "Autonomy, Reason, and Desire," explores autonomy as a test case for both instrumentalism and objectivism. For instrumentalism, the proper function of reason is to serve desire: its role is instrumental. But autonomy implies governing oneself in accordance with reason broadly conceived. This suggests that reason should guide our desires and thereby motivate us to act rationally. But how can reason, as a capacity for discerning truth — and in that sense an intellectual faculty — motivate us? A broadly Kantian answer is that reason provides its own motivational power independently of desire. I find neither this position nor instrumentalism fully satisfactory. I argue that desire can be educable by reason even if reason does not automatically govern it by independent motivational power. Autonomy is neither mere efficiency in satisfying one's unbridled basic desires nor an automatic result of properly using a priori reason; it requires an integration between reason and desire.

Chapter 10, "Moral Judgment and Reasons for Action," like chapter 9, brings together issues in moral psychology with questions in the foundations of ethics. It reinforces the idea that rational agents exhibit an integration between reason and desire, but it also shows how deficiency in such integration can impede moral motivation even where the use of reason issues in accepting a moral judgment that would ordinarily produce motivation. This deficiency is a challenging case, since moral judgment is in some sense action-guiding and has been widely (and plausibly) taken to entail motivation. A main task, then, is to assess *motivational internalism*: roughly the view that some degree of motivation is internal to moral judgment. In doing this I distinguish a range of motivational internalist positions, and I show how motivation can support moral judgment even if it is not internal to such judgment. If, however, moral judgments need not motivate, how can they be essentially practical, action-guiding cognitions? The answer is in part that they can express normative reasons for action even if they do not express motivational reasons; they can point our way and in that sense direct us, even if they do not by themselves push us along the path. This answer is developed in relation to an account of moral judgment and practical reasons that places both in the context of a theory of the relation between intellect and will.

Chapter 11, "Intrinsic Value and the Dignity of Persons," reinforces a major result of chapter 10. If the latter and several earlier chapters are correct in the view that there are objective reasons for action, then we might expect some of these to reside in things of intrinsic value, for instance in elements constitutive of human flourishing. Naturally enough, I begin with Aristotle, constructing an analogue of his argument to the effect that if desire is not to be endless and futile, then there is something good in itself. I proceed to explore various concepts of the good, such as Mill's hedonism and a more pluralistic view on which various non-hedonic experiences can be (intrinsically) good or bad. With some concrete examples in place, I argue for the possibility of knowledge or justified belief about value. Given this anti-skeptical result, together with the plausible assumption that if there is anything of intrinsic value, then there can be objective reasons for action, I argue that there can also be knowledge or justification about reasons for action. Some of this knowledge or justification is specifically moral. If, however, there are potentially competing values, such as one's own pleasure and service to others, then knowledge of one's overall moral obligation may be at best difficult to achieve. I argue that practical wisdom is indispensable in approaching this problem.

The concluding chapter, "The Moral Justification of Actions and the Goodness of Persons," summarizes and further defends the overall theory of the book, makes additional connections among the chapters, and outlines a normative ethical view that extends the moderate intuitionism suggested in chapter 2. This Kantian intuitionism is shown to have significant advantages over Ross's position (though that remains among the best intuitionist views in the field) and to provide an interpretation of how a Kantian normative ethics can be made more concrete and plausible than it is if its first-order ethical principles are taken to be deducible more or less directly from the categorical imperative. The overall ethical theory that emerges from the book combines a version of moral realism with a moderate intuitionism: it is epistemologically internalist, normatively objective, valuationally pluralist, and qualifiedly naturalistic.

I

Moral Epistemology

1

Internalism and Externalism in Moral Epistemology

A major division has recently come to the fore in epistemology. On one side are internalist theories, on the other, externalist theories, most notably reliabilism. The distinction has proved fruitful in understanding justification and knowledge, but its bearing on moral philosophy has yet to be systematically explored. If internalist and externalist views can provide general accounts of justification or knowledge, they may be expected to apply to the justification of moral beliefs and to yield criteria for moral knowledge. There is reason to think, however, that internalism and externalism in epistemology have even wider implications, for they reflect broad assumptions about normative status and may thus apply not only to beliefs but to other propositional attitudes and to actions. If so, we should be able to formulate not only internalist and externalist accounts of justified moral belief but also parallel accounts of moral rightness, moral obligation, and other moral notions applicable to actions. This paper will develop such accounts, contrast them, and compare them with other views, including *motivational* internalism and externalism, the positions commonly given those names in the literature of ethics. The final section will briefly assess the two moral epistemologies as candidates to serve among the basic premises of ethical inquiry.

I. Internalism and Externalism in Epistemology

We must start with an explicit understanding of internalism and externalism in epistemology. To simplify matters, I shall first focus only on justification. Justification has, in any case, been central in the controversy between the two positions. The reason is not that knowledge is felt to be less important but that internalists and externalists differ in their accounts of knowledge primarily *because* of differences over justification conceived as a central element in knowledge. Moreover, if we can understand the controversy in relation to justification, we can readily consider its application to some aspects of the notion of knowledge, and I shall indeed do so later.

Accessibility

No simple characterization of either internalism or externalism has emerged from the recent literature as acceptable to all the major writers on the subject; but there is a tendency for the former to bear the conceptual weight and the latter — which is historically a much more recent theory — to be described in contrast with it.[1] There is also a tendency — sufficiently widespread to give us a good starting point — for internalism to be characterized by appeal to some notion of introspective accessibility. Roughly, the central internalist idea is that what justifies a belief is internal to the agent in the sense that the agent is aware of it or can become aware of it by introspection or introspective reflection, where the relevant kind of awareness grounds knowledge of, or justified belief about, the justifier, or at least provides a ground for the capacity to arrive at such knowledge or belief on the basis of the awareness. Consider a paradigm case of justification conceived along internalist lines. My sensory experience of a white expanse might justify my belief that there is something white before me; and clearly I am aware of this experience, or at least can become aware of it by introspection. The implications of 'introspection' should not be exaggerated: to achieve the appropriate kind of awareness I need only attend to my visual consciousness; neither elaborate reflection nor inward searching is required.

Internalists need not require a capacity to become aware of the justifier under any particular description or concept, such as the sophisticated concept of sensory experience. All the agent needs is some notion of the justifier such that, understood in terms of that notion, it can be plausibly thought to justify. By contrast, an externalist view takes what justifies a belief to be something *not* introspectively accessible, and in *that* sense external to the subject. The most common candidate is (causal) sustenance or production of the belief by a reliable process, such as perception, which — with certain qualifications — may be held to generate more true than false beliefs. Such generation is not only something inaccessible to introspection; to know or justifiedly believe that a belief possesses it would take high-level psychological knowledge based on considerable experience.

There are, of course, stronger and weaker conceptions of the appropriate kind of accessibility. Hence, there are stronger and weaker forms of internalism, and correspondingly purer forms of externalism, depending on *how much* of what yields justification (if any of it) is or is not accessible in the relevant sense. Regardless of the strength of an internalist or externalist view, a plausible account of either sort should observe two distinctions. One concerns the closeness of accessible elements to consciousness; the other concerns the difference between justifiers that are *possessed* and thereby accessible and, on the other hand, justifiers which, though *obtainable* through reflection, are not actually possessed. Let me develop this contrast.

Internal Justification

The first distinction holds between justifiers present in consciousness and those which, while not present, are internally accessible because they can appropriately reveal themselves in consciousness. In the first category are occurrent memory impressions that might justify a belief — say that I have met a certain person now mentioned to me as a former acquaintance; in the second are beliefs one holds, such as might supply me with premises for some view I maintain but do not now have in mind. The memory impressions, like visual ones, are actually *in* my consciousness now, while the beliefs are simply such that I can *become* aware of them should I need to indicate what justifies the view I hold for which they express premises.

Phenomenologically, the difference here is between the way occurrent conscious elements justify and the way dispositional elements do so. The case is also instructive because it illustrates that introspective reflection need not be explicitly concerned with facts about oneself but may take the form of a search for grounds, where the *target* of the search is propositions that might be evidence, rather than any beliefs or internal attitudes. This evidential targeting is as it should be. When a belief one holds is what constitutes one's internal justification for another belief, the best way to become aware of this justifying belief can be to search one's memory for a premise for the belief whose justification is in question. Often, we can best call up our beliefs by considering appropriate content categories, such as that of reasons for holding a certain view, rather than by scanning the cognitive field directly.

The second distinction is between *justified belief* and merely *justifiable belief* (for the agent). Suppose I am confronted by a mathematical problem which I do not want to trouble to solve. Imagine that I believe it has a certain solution, *x*, but hold this unjustifiedly, on the basis of Tom's testimony, which, given my past experience with him, I should not accept. In disparate strands, I may nonetheless *have* evidence that *would* justify my belief if I thought about the matter and thereby saw how my several unintegrated evidential beliefs support the belief. Here introspective reflection might *produce* a justification for believing the solution is *x*; but it would not *reveal* a justification already possessed. Call the first kind of reflection *generative*, the second *revelatory*.

Both notions belong in an overall internalist account of justification; but our main concern is with actual, not potential, justification: with justification one *has* (or at least has quite readily accessible), not with mere justifiability, that is, justification one can *get*. For instance, we want to act *with* moral justification, so that we *have* a justification for the action at the time we act; we are not content to act with only the capacity to find a justification if we reflect on how to piece one together from our relevant beliefs. The deeds characteristic of a moral agent proceed *from* the agent's moral virtue or sense of moral duty; they are not merely capable of being shown to be consistent with morality by retrospective reflection. Though the distinction is not sharp, I want to concentrate on actual moral justification rather than on justifiability. Externalists as well as internalists can make this distinction. An externalism would express it in terms of what *does* reliably generate a belief, as opposed to what *would* do so under appropriate conditions, such as carefully reflecting on possible grounds for it.

II. *Internalism and Externalism in Ethics*

In extending epistemic internalism and externalism to ethics, we might begin with the case of moral beliefs, even though action is ultimately of greater moral interest.

If we assume a cognitivist view, how should we characterize the two positions with respect to, for instance, a justified belief of what we might call the promising rule: that people should generally keep their promises?

The Epistemic Internalism of Kantian Ethics

To focus the problem, consider Kant as apparently an internalist in his epistemology.[2] He might hold that by reflection — conceived as an internal even if not an introspective process — I can become aware of an a priori principle I believe, namely the categorical imperative, and my introspective awareness of its apparent self-evidence, or at least of my beliefs of certain premises for it, can justify believing the imperative. Now the categorical imperative *is* a justification of the rule that one should keep one's promises, or at least is so together with premises which, on internal grounds, I also justifiedly believe. Thus, I have justified beliefs of premises that justify the promising rule, and on the basis of those beliefs I justifiedly believe the rule.

Some internalists might go further: even a child not yet in a position to be justified in believing the categorical imperative might have an accessible and adequate ground for believing the promising rule, namely, a belief that all its elders have taught this (or perhaps simply a memory *of their having done so*). Nothing precludes an internalist from allowing the authority of testimony to justify in these ways, even when the belief is of an a priori principle. Indeed, if testimonial generation of a belief may be considered reliable, an externalist may also allow testimony to justify believing the promising rule. In the full-blown adult case, however, a natural line for an externalist to take would be broadly utilitarian: beliefs of the promising rule might, on a utilitarian externalism, be justified by virtue of being sustained by beliefs to the effect that generally promise-keeping conduces to happiness, where this is a reliable process because by and large such beliefs are *true*, in which case following the promising rule does indeed tend to have good consequences.

Supposing it is clear in outline how epistemic internalism and externalism apply to moral beliefs, there is no obvious extension to the notions of obligation or rightness. These, after all, apply primarily to actions, which are not truth-valued and hence not appropriate objects of knowledge or belief. Nonetheless, the extension is quite possible. Suppose we think of morally right actions as morally justified and of (morally) obligatory ones as such that no alternative to them is morally justified. We can then try to fill out the idea that justification *in general* is an internal or external concept, so that behavioral justification is parallel, in the sense that what justifies an action is, or is not, appropriately accessible. Once again, it is instructive to work with Kant and Mill.

For Kant, what is obligatory upon me is what I have a duty to do. But as Kant saw, having a duty to do something is one thing, doing it in fulfillment of that duty quite another. For him, at least the paradigms of acting morally — that is, of performing acts having moral worth — are deeds done purely *from duty*. If I keep a promise to Jack in order to fulfill my duty to him, my action in so doing is morally justified. It is justified by its being my duty. Now, what kind of access do I have to *what* justifies it? Can I, by introspective reflection, be aware of it as my duty or perhaps know, or at least justifiedly believe, that it is my duty? A Kantian might well say that I have all these capacities. I can, for example, call to mind some memory of my promising to do it. I am also aware of my belief that one must keep one's promises; and Kant might well argue that normal adults can become aware of beliefs they hold which express premises adequate to justify that principle in turn.[3] Clearly, then, on a Kantian view one has appropriately internal access to what it is that justifies one's morally justified actions.

It might be objected that these points only show that an action's *conformity* with duty is accessible, not its being justifiedly performed, that is, its being done *from* duty and thereby having moral worth. To assess this objection, consider what is relevant to my justifiedly keeping the promise when I do the promised deed. This is determined by three factors: first, the *content* of my will, as reflected in what I *intend*, say to keep my promise as opposed to avoiding trouble with the promisee (something I may also take the deed to accomplish); second, my sense for the moral appropriateness of that content, for example of keeping my promise being a *duty*; and third, my actually keeping the promise *as* an expression of that content and from that sense, say *in order to fulfill my duty*, as opposed to acting on some self-interested purpose.[4] It will not do if, for instance, I unwittingly — and so merely in accordance with, and not from, the content of my intention — give Jack the money owed him, unaware that he is masquerading as the carrier collecting for my newspaper subscription, for which I happen to owe the borrowed amount. Now, a Kantian may plausibly claim that when I act with moral worth, I have access to the grounding elements, for instance the sense of my duty to do the thing. Granted, I may not have access to the fact *that* my sense of duty grounds the action, say through this sense's suitably sustaining it in a broadly causal sense. But to require that is to require access not only to *what* justifies my action but also to *how* it does so. A first-order internalism need not require that we have this more extensive access.

The Epistemic Externalism of Utilitarian Ethics

For Mill, on the other hand, an externalist account is a better fit. Indeed, it is not clear how any truly consequentialist view *can* be internalist (unless, implausibly, the relevant consequences are themselves suitably internal). What I have a duty to do, in the sense of what I morally ought, on balance, to do, is to contribute optimally to happiness (for the sake of argument let us make it simply the happiness of people now in the world and include reduction of suffering under the general notion of contributing to happiness). Thus, what justifies keeping the promise is the total consequences of the act, something that is certainly not introspectively accessible to me. To be aware of these consequences, or to know or form justified beliefs about this totality, I need external evidence about the world.

One implication of this consequentialist position is that I can fail to do what is right, and indeed do something seriously wrong, even when from my point of view there is no reasonable alternative. It must be said immediately, then, that no sensible utilitarian would consider me blameworthy if, on excellent evidence, I kept a promise expecting good consequences and brought about disaster, for instance by returning a car to someone who then went berserk with it. But this does not entail that what I did was right or obligatory after all; it simply makes my act morally *excus-*

able, as opposed to culpable. One might also protest that there must be two senses of 'right' or 'obligatory' here. But a utilitarian need not multiply senses, so long as a doctrine of excuses is at hand to do the relevant work.[5]

Note, too, that a truly utilitarian doctrine of excuses would itself be externalist; for instance, a lapse from duty would be excusable only if it stemmed from traits, in a very broad sense including sets of desires and beliefs as special cases of traits, which in general conduce (sufficiently) to happiness. Negligence, for example, would not be excusing, whereas trusting a credible but mistaken witness often would be. It might be thought that a utilitarian should hold that for agents to be praiseworthy, blameworthy, or excusable is, roughly, for praising, blaming, or excusing them (respectively) to be optimific. But even from a utilitarian point of view, this assimilates being praise*worthy* to being *worth praising*. Specifically, it conflates criteria for *having* an optimific character with criteria for justifiably *ascribing* it. It might be argued that utilitarianism makes the conflation natural; but even if that is so, the theory need not carry such baggage.

On Mill's view, then — or at least on the moral epistemology to which a Millian utilitarian seems committed — the consequences of an action are parallel to the reliable production of a belief. Both are external in a similar way, and justification is grounded in the respective causal processes: truth-conducive generation in the cognitive case, happiness-conducive tendency in the behavioral case. Beliefs are justified by what produces *them*, actions by what *they* produce. The direction of causation is different, but justification is external in both cases.

It is true that Mill allows us to take commonsense moral principles for granted; but that is only because, through collective human experience, they are justified by their consequences. For Kant, the consequences of my action do not matter to its moral justification — though this is easily misunderstood. The point is that if keeping the promise is my duty, then the moral justification of my doing this does not depend on its consequences, including even my friend's doing evil with the returned car; but internalism does *not* imply that *calculation* of consequences is not relevant to what I should do. If I have *reason* to believe the friend will go berserk, I may have an internal ground, related to consequences, for breaking my promise. At least on one reading of Kant, his principles need not be construed in the rigoristic way he apparently interpreted them, and an *assessment* of consequences, as opposed to consequences themselves, can be a properly internal ground of moral justification for action.

If a Kantian internalism can be stretched to allow consideration of consequences, it can also be contracted. Suppose that through no fault of my own I am made to hallucinate keeping my promise to Jack, and that the incident is so vivid and so ostensibly normal that I justifiedly believe that I have kept the promise. Any plausible moral theory would say that I am excusable; but a strongly internalist theory might go further: in the circumstances, it might be claimed, I willed, or tried to do, something which I conceived as keeping my promise. Morally, then, I might be thought to do all I could. Certainly my volitional act was both justified and obligatory. The only question is whether I have done my duty. We should not say I have if such duties attach to the overt behaviors we undertake to perform or if, when I regain my senses and discover the car still in my possession, I will have the *same* duty I originally had. But it would be consistent with both internalism and some of

Kant to say that we should conceive our basic actions, and hence our basic duties, *internally*: on this view, what we directly undertake to do in promising is to move our wills toward the promised overt act; whether we perform that overt act, and thus fulfill our secondary duty, is up to nature. Thus, I promise to do what I shall justifiedly take to be, say, a return of a car; if I am unlucky and only hallucinate returning the car, that is unfortunate, but it counts nothing against my moral character. If I then discover the car, I acquire a new obligation, namely, to do what I shall justifiedly take to be returning *it*. This view is not quite Kant's; but, in a way that seems quite Kantian, it makes morality wholly internal, a thing of the mind and will.

Virtue Ethics

It should also be instructive to comment briefly on the application of epistemic internalism and externalism to virtue ethics, conceived generically as the view that what makes an action morally right is its appropriateness to some moral virtue of the agent. Thus, a just action, in a given set of circumstances calling for justice, is to be characterized not as one which (say) treats similar cases similarly (even if it may turn out to be equivalent to such an act) but as one that is the sort of thing a just person would do in those circumstances. Now clearly, the notion of a virtuous person, say one who is just and kind, can be characterized either in terms of what is introspectively accessible, say the agent's beliefs, desires, and settled intentions, or by appeal to such external factors as traits whose manifestation in action tends to conduce to happiness.

It might be argued that we cannot be introspectively aware of, or know introspectively that we have, a *trait*, since this is a long-term feature a person can be known to have only through inductive behavioral evidence. A virtue ethics, therefore, must be externalist. But even if, on internal grounds, one cannot have knowledge of one's traits, it would not follow that one cannot, on such grounds, justifiedly believe one has a trait, as opposed to knowing this. Moreover, a cautious internalism in virtue ethics might only require that, for an act to be right, the agent is capable of being aware of a relevant underlying trait in a suitable way, for instance through an awareness of beliefs and intentions that manifest it. This might be conceived as an awareness of one's character *at the time*. Thus, if, as part of one's just disposition, one acts in fulfillment of an intention to treat two people equally, the moral rightness of the action may be grounded in the intention *as* manifesting the disposition, even if one cannot (as in the case of a very young child) *see* it as such a manifestation. One may need some rudimentary moral concepts, but perhaps not the concept of justice itself. Being just seems possible, in a minimal sense (and in ways described in chapter 8), for agents not yet capable of conceiving themselves as just, rather as — to recall Aristotle's point — habitually acting justly as a young adolescent may, is in some sense prior to becoming a just person.[6]

III. The Range of Internalist and Externalist Moral Theories

We can better understand both internalist and externalist theories in ethics if we explore their connections with certain other important general categories. I have in mind especially the bearing of the distinction on six issues: the contrast between objective and subjective interpretations of moral concepts; the debate between internalism and externalism in the theory of moral motivation; the rationalism-empiricism controversy; the problem of reductive naturalism; the question of noncognitivism; and the priority of moral reasons over other kinds. It would take a great deal of space even to describe these issues in detail. My aim here is simply to work with the issues in outline, providing only the amount of detail needed to clarify internalism and externalism in moral epistemology.

Subjectivism

It is important to see that internalism is not necessarily a kind of subjectivism, in any of three important senses. First, it does not imply *psychologism*, the view that a moral judgment, such as that one must help one's aging parents, is about oneself, say about one's settled distaste for neglecting them. Second, it does not imply, and in plausible versions disallows, the *rejection of moral supervenience*, construed roughly as the view that (1) if two people are alike in their non-moral properties — especially in beliefs, wants, and experiences — neither can have a moral reason for a certain action which is not equally a moral reason for the other to do the same thing, and (2) they have such moral reasons in virtue of having certain non-moral properties. And third, internalism does not imply *subjectivistic relativism*: the view that there are no external moral reasons, in the sense of reasons for people to do certain things whether or not they are motivated, directly or indirectly, to do them — and thus subjectively so inclined.[7] An internalist might hold that there *are* reasons for us to keep our promises, even if nothing we want makes that seem to us to pay off; for we might have internally rooted justification for believing that we should keep them (whether we do believe it or not). A plausible internalism might hold that the existence of such a reason implies that we *can* be motivated to act accordingly; but this is a weak motivational requirement which seems plainly fulfilled by normal persons with respect to anything plausibly considered an external reason. An externalist, of course, can also hold these things. But externalism does not naturally take the form of a subjectivist view in any of the three senses. An externalist could, however, treat rightness as a matter of external facts about oneself, such as one's attitudinal and behavioral tendencies under complex hypothetical conditions, and could also deny that there are external reasons for acting. But the natural positions for externalists are not subjectivist and do not deny that the moral justification they are at pains to ground provides at least some degree of external reason for action in accordance with it.

Motivational Internalism and Externalism

One might think that there should be more than a terminological coincidence between epistemic and motivational internalism, but there is little reason to believe so. The term 'motivational internalism' has been used in numerous ways, and here I take it broadly, as designating the view that believing (and so, normally, assentingly judging) that an action is one's overall (moral) obligation non-trivially entails having some degree of motivation to perform it. Minimally, the degree of motivation is such that if one does the thing in question, this action is explainable as performed at least in part on the basis of the agent's belief that it was obligatory.[8] It is *natural* for an internalist about moral justification to hold this; for the thesis is especially plausible if one notes that the kinds of factors which morally justify an action — such as an awareness of one's having promised to do the deed — are well suited to motivate it and often *cited* in explaining it. But it is open to an internalist about justification to hold that the agent, particularly if not assumed to be rational, *need* not be so motivated. For an externalist about moral justification, on the other hand, motivational externalism may seem the likelier option. For what renders an action morally justified need not be in one's ken at all; hence, one could fail to be motivated to perform it. But this is poor reasoning if taken to show that *believing* one is obligated on balance to do something need not motivate one to do it; it argues only that *being* so obligated need not be motivating. Consider also an externalist, quasi-internal notion of excusability, a notion applicable where, though the action would do great harm, one believes, for excellent reason, that it is an overall duty and thus that one *must* do the thing. Doubtless a motivational internalism finds support in this sort of case, but the view is not required by anything in the (epistemic) externalist's premises. This is not to deny that motivational internalism is plausible on other grounds (not relevant here); my point is simply that neither internalism nor externalism in moral epistemology commits one to it.

Rationalism and Empiricism

If Kantian moral theories are leading candidates for epistemically internalist accounts of moral justification, one might wonder if the distinction between these and externalist views of moral justification is neutral with respect to rationalism and empiricism. Doubtless it is not unnatural for an internalist about moral justification to be a rationalist, and (for reasons that will become apparent below) it is even more natural for a rationalist to be an internalist; but one could be an internalist or externalist virtue theorist without being a rationalist. Even a rule theorist might maintain that knowledge of the relevant rules is not a priori — either because no knowledge of non-formal principles is, or because moral knowledge (and justified moral beliefs) depend on experience, possibly including the deliverances of a moral sense conceived as an empirical faculty. Here we would also do well to consider Hume. In some passages, he seems to hold a psychologistic naturalism, on which moral appraisals of actions are really a kind of self-ascription.[9] Now one could be epistemically either internalist or externalist about what justifies the relevant self-referential beliefs, and so correspondingly internalistic or externalistic about what justifies moral action itself. Thus, my being morally justified in doing something might be a matter of my having appropriate grounds, internal or external, to believe that it would produce the appropriate moral feelings in me. Suppose, on the other hand, that we combined a Humean instrumentalism about rational action with an account of moral justification. On one version of this combined view, an action is morally justified when it is in one's long-run self-interest judged according to one's stable intrinsic desires viewed through one's own beliefs. Since one's beliefs and intrinsic desires seem accessible in the appropriate way, this could yield an empiricist, internalist egoistic standard of rational action and thereby of moral conduct.[10]

Reductive Naturalism

From the examples given so far, it should be plain that strictly speaking both internalist and externalist accounts of moral justification are neutral with respect to reductive naturalism, conceived generically as the view that the rightness of an act *just is* some natural property, such as conducing optimally to human well-being conceived in terms of pleasure and pain (hedonically). One might think that a utilitarian must in the end be such a naturalist; but Mill need not be so read, and certainly one can treat hedonic optimality as necessary and sufficient for rightness without taking it to constitute what rightness *is*. A utilitarian in normative ethics need not hold a utilitarian, reductivist metaethics. Nor, I think, must any other plausible externalism in moral epistemology be a reductive naturalism. Clearly, an internalist will incline against this reductionism, since it is not plausible to take the bases of moral justification, on such a hedonist naturalism, to be appropriately accessible. But recall the psychologistic case: if what morally justifies an action should be its tendency to produce a subjective response in the agent, there might be appropriate internal access to the ground of that justification, say to a felt inclination to do the deed. Similarly, if moral justification can be identified with being in one's interest where that interest is understood by appeal to what one wants and believes, again there might be internal access to the relevant kinds of properties. Reductive naturalism is consistent with justification, and normative properties in general, supervening on natural properties. But supervenience on natural properties does not entail identity with them or even analyzability in terms of them. Thus, internalists and externalists alike can affirm such supervenience without commitment to reductive naturalism.

Noncognitivism

When we come to noncognitivism, our first question is how the view provides for moral justification at all. For on this view, to say that action is morally justified is to express a certain attitude, not to make a true or false statement. It would be a mistake, however, to conclude that the notion of justification is thereby inapplicable; for attitudes themselves can be reasonable or unreasonable, justified or unjustified, and the like. Thus, an action might be appropriately said to be morally justified, not in the cognitivist sense that it truly has a *property* of justifiedness but in the sense that one is justified in holding the attitude one expresses in saying this. The way is then open to give either an internalist or externalist account of the justified attitude in question. If the relevant kind of justification is moral, one repeats the procedure, explicating what it is to say appropriately (but not truly) that the attitude is morally justified; if, on the other hand, the attitude expresses, for instance, a positive nonmoral valuation of, say, treating people with respect, and this attitude is based on one's informed desires and one's justified beliefs about how to realize them, then one has a non-moral, instrumental justification for holding the attitude. This may seem roundabout, and one may wonder why a cognitivist account of justified attitudes should be given if one is a noncognitivist about moral justification. That is a fair question; perhaps the answer is in part that noncognitivists want to attribute whatever moral justification there may be to items, such as attitudes or emotions, without truth value. In any case, there is surely no inconsistency in proceeding this way, and it seems to some philosophers to find support in the argument that since moral notions have in themselves no explanatory power, they do not correspond to real properties and so do not figure in true or false attributions.[11]

The Supremacy of Moral Reasons

One further issue remains in this section: do either internalist or externalist theories imply what I shall call *the primacy of moral justification*, that is, that in any conflict between moral justification for an action and any other kind of justification — say, prudential — for doing otherwise, the moral justification yields the better overall reason for action? Again, Kantian internalism may make it appear that the internalist's options are foreclosed. But I cannot see that this is so.[12] Above all, an internalist may take us to have introspective access to *other* kinds of grounds for acting, and internalism by itself is not committed to the normative predominance of any one kind. A similar point holds for externalism. Even a utilitarian, despite characterizing moral justification so broadly that everyone's happiness is in principle relevant to what one should do, is free to construe, as *rationally* overriding, those of one's reasons that bear on one's own future, and these could dictate an immoral action. Rightness could thus be characterized in terms of everyone's happiness, while rationality, taken as the overriding normative notion, is understood in terms of self-interest.

What this section shows, then, is that internalism and externalism in moral epistemology leave one a great deal of latitude. Logically, one may, but need not, be an objectivist, a motivational internalist, a rationalist, a reductive naturalist, a noncognitivist, or a moral supremacist. In arguing for this latitude, I do not mean to imply that choice between the two approaches is solely an epistemological matter, or that it has no bearing on how one is likely to view these further issues. Indeed, I now want to show that there is much at stake.

IV. The Moral Appraisal of Actions and Agents

In epistemology, externalist views have enjoyed much popularity — though they are currently under siege[13] — and I shall begin with a major ethical externalism, namely the act utilitarian view on which an act is morally right, and in that sense justified, if and only if it contributes at least as much to the balance of happiness to unhappiness in the world as any available alternative. This is a vague rendering, but my points will be quite general, applying to rule utilitarianism and to other forms of act utilitarianism, and nothing important in what I say will turn on inadequacies in this formulation.

A Problem for Consequentialist Externalism

I have already argued that utilitarianism would have us classify as wrong, and in that sense objectively unjustified, an act with far worse consequences than its alternatives, even when the agent has excellent reason to think the act will optimize happiness. Suppose, for instance, that I give a daughter an airline ticket as a graduation present, knowing it is the gift by far most likely to please, but unaware that the flight in question will be hijacked at the cost of agony for all its passengers. The natural utilitarian diagnosis is that the act is subjectively justified, but a mistake. Granted. Still, was it the morally right thing to do? To say so is plausible on the ground that the act is precisely what one would expect of a moral agent using the information available in the situation. But this cannot be correct by externalist consequentialist standards. To admit it is to grant in effect that what I *really* ought to do is a matter not of what would in *fact* optimize happiness but of what, from my accessible *internal* perspective in the situation, would optimize happiness. It is the former, however, that is required by the utilitarian theory of *value*: only actual happiness, and not the justified pursuit of it, is intrinsically good.

Suppose that the externalist acknowledges that what is really right, and thus what one really ought to do, is optimize happiness, and that anything less is only subjectively right or, say, excusable. This has a disturbing implication for any such consequentialist externalism, namely that what makes one a morally good person is *not* doing what, by consequentialist criteria, one ought, nor even doing that for the right reasons, but something that is apparently an internal matter: doing what one justifiedly believes is right (at least if one does it for the right reasons). This in turn can be given an epistemically externalist account; but even if, as I doubt, such an account will work for justified belief, there is still a disparity between doing what is objectively right — deeds that are morally justified — and being a morally good person. Moreover, the same sort of disparity arises in the purely epistemic case: a reliably produced belief might be one that the agent, as an epistemically responsible person, should not hold, since the agent might have excellent reason to believe the belief-producing process *un*reliable.[14] Call this general difficulty the *problem of normative cleavage*, though moral cleavage is the kind that will chiefly concern us. At a crucial point, the theory splits: it yields one kind of account of moral justification and obligation, but a very different kind of account of a morally good person.[15] And if the consequentialist tries to externalize the internalist criteria of good moral character by providing an externalist account of justified beliefs, the problem recurs in the epistemic domain, where the epistemic rationality of persons is again an internal matter.

It might be thought that the cleavage is not a problem: right action can be a matter of consequences, even if good moral character is a matter of acting on suitably justified beliefs, say beliefs about consequences. But surely there are both conceptual and epistemological difficulties with this reply. Let us take them up in turn. There are at least three important conceptual points and at least two major epistemological ones.

First, consider how actions figure in the concept of (moral) character. It is not a contingent matter that a person who again and again does the right thing in sufficiently various circumstances, and from a sense of moral duty to do it — say because it is keeping a promise or rendering aid or treating similar offenders equally — has exhibited good character. But on the consequentialist view, this must be seen as contingent, since such behavioral patterns do not necessarily optimize happiness (or any other plausible consequentialist objective specifiable in non-moral terms). For consequentialism, after all, there *is* no irreducible moral value; moral value is wholly determined by the contribution of actions or persons who have it to the kinds of consequences fundamental in the relevant theory of value, such as hedonism.

There is, second, a related problem for consequentialism: that assessments of character must surely be based on what an agent intends or tries to do (or both), as Mill granted. But for a consequentialist, good character is a means to the relevant consequences, *however it brings them about*. They alone have intrinsic value; goodness of character, like the rightness of action, is entirely derivative from its contribution to them. Some utilitarians have thought that being motivated by a sense of duty is in fact optimific; but the theory cannot construe this connection as necessary, and it may in fact not even be causally necessary that acting from duty *is* optimific.

A third conceptual point emerges when we consider the implications of character for action. It is not a contingent matter that a person of good character will tend to do certain sorts of things for a certain range of moral reasons, for instance to keep promises because one has promised, and to avoid lying because it is wrong. Such a tendency is part of what it is to have good character. By contrast, it is a contingent matter whether such actions performed for the relevant reasons are optimific; hence, a consequentialist view must take the relevant tendencies to be contingent features of a person of good character.

The epistemological difficulties encountered by consequentialism should now be easy to see. Again, begin with commonsense moral intuitions. First, right actions, performed because the agent believes they are right — for instance, acts of honesty or justice or rectification — non-contingently yield grounds for ascribing good character. Our everyday moral practices confirm this necessary connection again and again. But consequentialism cannot accommodate this point: it takes the connection to be only contingent, since such patterns are not necessarily optimific. Second, it is also a non-contingent truth that good character provides a reason to expect agents who have it to do what is right, or at least what they take to be right, for an appropriate moral reason. But consequentialism must also view this connection as contingent, since good character must be understood as a matter of possessing optimific dispositions.

A Unity Constraint on Moral Evaluation

If these conceptual and epistemological points are sound, they justify a *unity constraint* on moral theories: conceptually, epistemologically, and valuationally, right action and moral character must be explicated within a unified theory. A unified theory cannot, for instance, be epistemologically internalist about character and externalist about action, or hedonist about the rightness of actions and deontological about the goodness of character. It appears that, as in Mill's case, plausible consequentialist theories violate this constraint. They are grounded in a hedonistic or other non-moral account of intrinsic value, and their consequentialism requires externalism about right action; yet their assessment of character (if plausible) is epistemologically internalist and apparently deontological.

The problem of moral cleavage might seem soluble by appeal to a distinction between the objectively and the subjectively right. The former is, for a utilitarian, what is in fact hedonically optimal; the latter is what the agent has good reason to *believe* is hedonically optimal. It is true that only objectively right actions have optimal *value*, but it might be held that we now have a single standard — subjective rightness — for evaluating both the moral worth of actions and their agents' moral character. And this is an externalistically appropriate standard because subjectively right actions will *tend* to be objectively right.

One trouble with this move is that plainly there are possible circumstances in which, because of bad luck — or manipulation by an evil force — an agent's subjectively right actions do not tend to be objectively right and, over a lifetime, they are far from optimific and indeed do more harm than good. Still, if the agent's own reasoning is good by internalist standards, then these very actions are an adequate basis for attributing good moral character. It might be thought that they are merely excusable, but that is not so: it is questionable whether they even call for excuse, and in any case they count toward good character in a way the merely excusable does not. Thus, the utilitarian cannot claim that the cleavage problem is overcome because the basis of moral character is an objective *tendency* to contribute to what is of intrinsic value. Instead, moral character must be conceived as having a quite different ground: intending to optimize happiness may be crucial, but any objective, externally characterizable tendency to do so is not.

It is important to stress that the cleavage in question is normative, not semantic. A normative consequentialist might give an internalist analysis of the meaning of 'good character', by appeal to, say, dispositions to do the things normally taken as duties, for example keeping promises and abstaining from injuring others. But given a consequentialist theory of value, together with the thesis that contribution to valuable consequences is the *basis* of rightness, the normative cleavage is inevitable: for the sorts of reasons just given, if the assessment of character used by the theory is plausible at all, it will not be consequentialist. Given any of the ways in which consequentialists may plausibly define 'good character', they must *attribute* good character on the basis of the contribution the agent's character actually makes or tends to make to the relevant consequences, say happiness. To take the goodness of character to be based on the believed contribution, or even justifiedly believed contribution, that the agent's character makes to happiness, is to abandon the theory of value which motivates consequentialism in the first place. Semantic unification, then, is not sufficient to avoid normative cleavage.

Kantian Internalism and Moral Evaluation

Let us see if an internalist ethics can do any better. For Kant, read in one way, what I ought (overall) to do is simply what it is my duty to do, and I *may* do what I have no duty not to do. Moreover, the moral status of my character is determined precisely by my doing what I ought — provided I do it from the appropriate moral duties — and doubtless also by my being disposed so to act in relevant hypothetical situations. If I promise my daughter the airline ticket, I ought to give it, and so doing is justified by that duty regardless of the actual consequences of the act. There is no cleavage. The unhappy consequences of the act are bad luck, but they are not bad *moral luck* since my moral status is unaffected by them. On this kind of Kantian view, there is no moral luck, unless it is internal, for instance a matter of being fortunate in developing good will, from which one then builds one's character.[16]

It may seem that a Kantian view must also distinguish objective from subjective rightness and so must confront a cleavage after all. For instance, a kind of action one believes to accord with the categorical imperative may not in fact accord with it, and so cannot be the standard of what is really (objectively) right. This charge of cleavage confuses the subjectively right with the *doxastically right*: what the agent *believes* to be such. But the objection can be tightened by requiring that the agent's moral assessment of the action be justified. The assessment might still be wrong, yet the agent might be blameless. Would there then be a moral cleavage?

For a Kantian position, at least two lines are open here. First, we must consider the *degree* of justification. It is arguable that what one has *adequate* justification to think accords with the categorical imperative actually does: adequacy is simply understood in terms of the normal capacities of rational beings, and it is to them that the categorical imperative is meant to apply. It legislates *for us*. Thus, what makes actions right — their *consistency* with the imperative — is an internal matter. The second line is more cautious: granting that a perfectly adequate justification to believe that a kind of action accords with the imperative does not preclude one's being mistaken, the issue is at least resolvable by reflection. That is, sufficient reflection could in principle yield a correct answer. Moral rightness would thus remain an internal notion: though it could not be infallibly determined by a normal agent at any given time, it is accessible to competent reflection. Granted, if a maleficent neurosurgeon (or Cartesian demon) interfered with one's moral reflection, one could repeatedly err excusably in concluding it. One might, then, often harm others where one intends to help them. While this would not make the action one mistakenly decides upon right, it would not prevent one's exhibiting virtue in *trying* to act rightly; such trying would be constituted by acts, particularly such inner ones as deciding to help others, and on that score one might manifest good character. Both right action and good character, then, are internal matters even on a fallibilist interpretation of Kantian moral reflection.

If a fallibilist reading of Kantian internalism is given, however, could a maleficent neurosurgeon not prevent even one's *trying* to act rightly? Doubtless this is possible; but the right response would be pity that moral agency has been destroyed, not giving moral credit for doing as well as one can. Excusability is not praiseworthiness. Similarly, if I am repeatedly prevented from using the categorical imperative (or any other moral standard) correctly, I am excusable, but not admirable. It should not be objected, then, that Kantian views must also face a cleavage, since the basis of good character is the internal matter of doing the best one can, while the Kantian standard of right action is the objective one of conformity with the categorical imperative. An objective standard may be internal; that excusability for failure to meet it is also internal does not preclude this, nor does it imply a separate standard for good character. The only cleavage here is between blamelessness due to excuse and blamelessness due to virtue.

The internality in question, though sensitive to our individual capacities, is not subjectivistic and is in fact consistent with a kind of universality. For not only is the standard of rightness universally applicable; the wherewithal to grasp and apply it belongs to all rational beings. One even has access to the motives that give one's actions moral worth. Plainly one would be fallible about whether a motive of duty *is* what one acts from; this is particularly so, as Kant saw, when one has a different kind of motive, such as one of self-interest, aligned with it. But a first-order internalist need not require access to one's acting from the relevant motive. Much can be said for the second-order view that we have this, provided the access in question (which implies a capacity to be aware of causal relations) is taken to be fallible; but there is no need to discuss that view here.

One may wonder how a Kantian or other internalist view can take any account of the value of the consequences of actions, for instance allow me to break the promise to my daughter if I discover a significant chance of a hijacking. Here I think Kant's theory may be better than at least some of his interpretations of it. Specifically, I cannot see why the categorical imperative, in any plausible formulation, must yield an absolute duty to keep promises. It is true that neither Kant nor other internalist rule theorists provide a simple way to decide just *what* principles we should have for promising, veracity, distribution of goods, and so on. It is tempting to take this as a fatal flaw for the view *as* internalist. For it may seem that if I cannot formulate a precise maxim that generates my duty in a given situation, then I do not have appropriate access to what morally justifies my action. Kant's talk of acting on a maxim encourages this impression; for to act morally I must apparently act on a maxim, yet how can I act on a maxim which I could not, even on reflection, formulate?

There seem to be at least two lines of reply open here. The one closest to Kant is to maintain that an unselfconscious agent keeping a promise from duty is at least *tacitly* following a maxim which the agent could formulate on reflection, including reflection on the content of the intention with which the action is performed. If, for example, I give Jack money with the intention of keeping a promise — as opposed to the intention of avoiding his wrath — then my maxim will be one that prescribes promise-keeping, either categorically or, if I am more sophisticated, under certain conditions, where these are of a kind I take to obtain now. But another line is open, if not to Kant himself, then to a broadly Kantian internalist. If we stress the idea of acting from duty, we might argue that all one needs access to is one's awareness of the duty itself, provided this awareness is suitably anchored in one's overall moral outlook. This would require certain attitudes toward others, some degree of understanding of obligation in general, and a sense of relevant circumstances. But it would not require a *formulable grasp* of the relevant rule, much less of how to derive it from the categorical imperative. One has ready access to what morally justifies one's act — one's awareness of the duty from which it is done. One need not have access to awareness of the rule from which that duty is derivable.

One might defend this qualified Kantian line as follows. Granting that a formulable grasp of a principle of duty may be required for agents to *know* or to *show* they are morally justified, and granting that Kant appropriately stresses such a grasp in setting out his moral theory as a model for the self-conscious guidance of moral reflection, still, simply to *be* morally justified, one need only meet the general conditions for moral agency and be aware of the duty from which one acts. To take an epistemic analogy, to be justified in believing there is white paper before me, I need not believe, or even have a formulable grasp of, any epistemic principle but must simply be aware of the visual experience which grounds the belief. On this view, while the a priori framework of the categorical imperative and its subsidiary rules is a valuable heuristic for the ordinary moral agent, it is indispensable only in formulating rules or defending claims about moral justification, quite as beliefs of epistemic principles are not required for having justified beliefs, as opposed to the philosophical tasks of clarifying the notion of justification or trying to show a skeptic that one has justified beliefs. Ordinary agents can learn to use such principles; but a significant degree of moral character can be developed and exercised with only the potential to be led, Socratically, upward toward the general principles instantiated by the moral conduct typical of unreflective virtuous agents.

Internalist and Externalist Accounts of Moral Knowledge

The conclusion suggested by the cleavage problem is that insofar as utilitarian and Kantian views are typical of externalist and internalist views in moral epistemology, internalist views seem to give a better account of moral justification and related moral notions. But their ability to account for moral *knowledge* may be different. Except in the case of knowledge constituted by beliefs about oneself, knowledge (at least empirical knowledge) *is* external, since having it entails something about the external world, to which one does not have introspective access. It may even be possible for knowledge to exist without justification.[17] On the assumption that there can be moral knowledge, would externalism in moral epistemology give us better prospects for understanding moral knowledge?

There is no doubt that an externalist, consequentialist account of moral knowledge is prima facie more straightforward than the most plausible internalist accounts. Consider utilitarianism again. My belief that an act will optimize happiness may be reliably generated by good evidence that this is so and may in turn produce (in part) my believing that the deed in question is morally right. This moral belief is thus (indirectly) based on the facts in virtue of which it is true, and that is a prima facie good reason to call it knowledge. By contrast, an internalist must take what justifies a moral belief to be internal, while in some cases giving an externalistic account of that in virtue of which it is true. Do we have, then, a problem of *epistemic cleavage*? Does the internalist give us one kind of account of moral justification and an incongruous account of moral truth?

In pursuing this question, let us assume the plausible and widely held view that moral justification supervenes on natural properties. Thus, my overall duty to keep a promise to Carol, including my justification for keeping it, might supervene on my having sincerely made the promise in circumstances of an appropriate kind, say circumstances that include her wanting the thing promised and my capacity to give it to her. Now suppose my belief that I ought to keep the promise is reliably produced in part by those very events and circumstances; for I believe that I ought to keep it because I believe those circumstances obtain, which in turn I believe because they do in fact obtain. The truth of my moral belief can be thus externally grounded, while my justification for it is internally grounded in my other beliefs. A justified moral belief so grounded is a good candidate for knowledge. Even if these beliefs were false owing to hallucination, they might still be justified, though they would not constitute knowledge.

I cannot see that this approach yields a damaging epistemic cleavage, at least not if (as I am inclined to think) *non-moral* justification and knowledge are grounded in irreducibly different ways. Note, too, that truth and justification are quite different sorts of concepts, in a way that the notions of moral action and moral character — between which externalist moral accounts force a cleavage — are not. By contrast, the internalist view outlined here does not imply normative cleavage: my character is still assessed in terms of my moral justification, not my moral knowledge, except insofar as that implies justification. Thus, if I am mistaken in believing an action is my duty, but only because, through no fault of mine, I have been given highly credible misinformation, I may justifiedly believe it is my duty, do it from duty, and express moral virtue in so doing.

We should also consider knowledge of moral principles. An externalist account might deal with them in the same inductive, reliabilist fashion illustrated for believing that a specific act will optimize happiness. An internalist may also allow induction; for instance, if one held that morally justified acts are those the agent would approve of upon impartial reflection, one might use induction on specimen acts of truth telling to generalize to a principle about veracity and might justifiedly believe that principle, provided one's memory gave one access to a sufficient set of premise beliefs.

But what about a rationalist approach to moral knowledge? Here I suggest we begin by supposing that one has internal access to those a priori truths which one can understand to hold in virtue of one's understanding of relations among the concepts one has. The rationale might be this: if the truths are a priori, they are necessary, and if necessary then true in all possible worlds, including the inner world; and if one can understand them by reflection, one has some kind of "introspective" — and certainly an internal — access to grounds for them, such as the grasp of their self-evidence or of their entailment by what is self-evident, and one can justifiedly believe them on the basis of that understanding of them. The understanding may occur immediately upon considering them, or may come only through reflection; but in either case it is introspectively accessible. Kant might argue, along these lines, that we have internal access to moral principles (though to be sure we do not actually believe, but are only potentially justified in believing, many of them). If this line is plausible, then a rationalist internalism can account, on internal grounds, for *general* moral knowledge, and need appeal to external considerations only to account for such existential moral knowledge as that one has a duty to another person. Clearly, one cannot know one has a duty *to Carol* unless one knows or may justifiedly presuppose the external fact of her existence. This approach has its difficulties, but I cannot see that it should be rejected out of hand.

To conclude, we have seen in outline how to construct epistemically internalist and externalist moral theories. We have noted many options that are in principle available to both, for instance objectivism or subjectivism, rationalism or empiricism, naturalism or non-naturalism, and the supremacy or defeasibility of moral reasons. A paradigm of an internalist moral theory is Kant's; a paradigm of an externalist theory is utilitarianism. Particularly in view of the difficulties besetting externalist theories of justified belief in general, I have suggested that such theories do not give a plausible account of justified moral beliefs or morally right actions. A major problem faced by externalism in moral epistemology is a cleavage between what morally justifies particular actions and what counts toward the moral worth of their agents, or, more generally, a cleavage between externalism's account of morally sound actions and its account of morally sound persons. Internalist theories can achieve unification on this point. They do, however, need an externalist component to account fully for moral knowledge, particularly knowledge of concrete actions in the world. But this implies no normative cleavage, nor does it require reductive naturalism. It is simply a reflection of the irreducible difference between justification and knowledge. The general conclusion to be drawn at this point, then, is that the epistemological controversy between internalism and externalism is highly relevant to ethics, and that at present internalist theories seem to provide a more promising basis for an account of moral justification.

Notes

For helpful comments on this essay I thank Frances Howard-Snyder, Bruce Russell, Robert Revock, James Sennett, Mark Timmons, William Tolhurst, and especially Norman Dahl, who provided an extensive and valuable commentary on the penultimate version, given at the Santa Clara University Conference on Reason and Moral Judgment in April 1989. The general discussion at the conference was also beneficial, as was discussion of other drafts at Vanderbilt University and in a seminar at the University of Nebraska.

1. Extensive recent discussions of the internalism-externalism controversy include Laurence BonJour, *The Structure of Empirical Knowledge* (Cambridge: Harvard University Press, 1985); William P. Alston, "Internalism and Externalism in Epistemology," *Philosophical Topics* 14 (1986); Richard Foley, *The Theory of Epistemic Rationality* (Cambridge: Harvard University Press, 1986); Paul K. Moser, *Knowledge and Evidence* (Cambridge and New York: Cambridge University Press, 1989); Alvin Plantinga, "Positive Epistemic Status," *Philosophical Perspectives* 2 (1988); and my "Justification, Truth, and Reliability," *Philosophy and Phenomenological Research* 69 (1988). Leading externalists are David Armstrong, *Belief, Truth, and Knowledge* (Cambridge: Cambridge University Press, 1973); Frederick I. Dretske, *Knowledge and the Flow of Information* (Cambridge: MIT Press, 1981); and Alvin I. Goldman, *Epistemology and Cognition* (Cambridge: Harvard University Press, 1986).

2. Here and in the next page or so I develop ideas I suggested in "The Architecture of Reason," *Proceedings and Addresses of the American Philosophical Association* 62, no. 1 (suppl.) (1988), reprinted in my *The Structure of Justification* (Cambridge and New York: Cambridge University Press, 1993).

3. Here I leave open how *much* of the rationale for a duty Kant would think one needs to grasp to account for one's having that duty, in the way required to justify an action performed in accordance with it. I shall return to this issue later.

4. Kant's formulation of the three propositions of morality is especially relevant here.

The second is particularly pertinent: "Its [an action's] moral value . . . does not depend on the realization of the object of the action but merely on the principle of volition by which the action is done. . . . Where, then, can this worth lie, if not in the will in relation to its hoped-for effect?" Immanuel Kant, *Foundations of the Metaphysics of Morals*, trans. Lewis White Beck (New York: Liberal Arts Press, 1959), p. 16 (399–400 in the Akademie edition). Note that the effect of the action *is* relevant *as* hoped for, and hence internally rather than consequentially.

5. Mill's own exposition of his utilitarianism does not settle this matter. His initial statement of his central principle, in ch. 2 of *Utilitarianism* (Indianapolis: Hackett, 1979), suggests that he did not mean to introduce two senses of 'right'; his principle is that "acts are right in proportion as they tend to produce happiness; wrong as they tend to produce the reverse of happiness" (p. 7). And later in the chapter he says, "He who saves a fellow creature from drowning does what is morally right, whether his motive be duty or the hope of being paid" (p. 18), suggesting that the good outcome is what is morally crucial. On the other hand, in a note to the same passage he distinguishes motive from intention and declares that "[t]he morality of the action depends entirely upon the intention — that is, upon what the agent *wills to do*. But the motive, that is, the feeling which makes him will so to do, if it makes no difference in the act, makes none in the morality: though it makes a great difference in our estimation of the agent" (p. 18n.). The Kantian sound of this may be due to Mill's conflating the *rightness* of an act with its *morality* conceived purposively as what distinguishes moral from, say, prudential performances. Given Mill's hedonistic theory of value, which he tells us, immediately after introducing the utilitarian principle, is "the theory of life on which this theory of morality [utilitarianism] is grounded" (p. 7), he is apparently committed to taking the *actual* contribution of an act, or at least type of act, to happiness as the standard of rightness. In any case, I shall discuss the implications of bringing to utilitarianism a plausible distinction between objective and subjective interpretations of rightness.

6. Epistemic virtue conceptions have been proposed, though not often compared with virtue ethics. For an epistemically reliabilistic view, see Ernest Sosa, "Knowledge and Intellectual Virtue," *The Monist* 68 (1985); and for a conception of epistemic virtue that does compare it with moral virtue, see James Montmarquet, "Epistemic Virtue," *Mind* 96 (1988).

7. I take the term 'external reason' from Bernard Williams but may not be using it exactly as he does. See his "Internal and External Reasons," in his *Moral Luck* (Cambridge: Cambridge University Press, 1981).

8. I say 'non-trivially entails' because I want to leave open that a desire to do one's duty is a necessary feature of agents who are capable of moral belief and, in a highly complex way, believe that something is (on balance) their duty. Relevant discussion of internalism in various senses, and a number of references, are given in my *Practical Reasoning* (London and New York: Routledge, 1989). Notice that my formulation leaves open whether moral beliefs are intrinsically motivating or (if this is not equivalent to that) in some way guarantee the presence of an appropriate desire.

9. In the *Treatise*, e.g., he at times gives a psychologistic account of what we mean by certain moral judgments: "[W]hen you pronounce any action or character to be vicious, you mean nothing, but that from the constitution of your nature you have a feeling or sentiment of blame from the contemplation of it." A *Treatise of Human Nature*, ed. L. A. Selby-Bigge (Oxford: Oxford University Press, 1888), p. 469.

10. I have some sympathy with the view that even an enlightened egoism is not a moral theory at all; but if that is so, the point here can be illustrated by simply building into the internalist view in question the requirement that to qualify as having *moral* justification, the agent must have certain altruistic desires.

11. Something close to this argument is at issue between Gilbert Harman and Nicholas

P. Sturgeon. For relevant writings of theirs and other pertinent discussion see Louis P. Pojman, ed., *Ethical Theory* (Belmont, Calif.: Wadsworth Publishing Co., 1989).

12. For supporting discussions see William K. Frankena, *Ethics*, 2nd ed. (Englewood Cliffs, N.J.: Prentice-Hall, 1973), and for a generally contrasting (though in places similar) view, see Thomas Nagel, *The View from Nowhere* (Oxford and New York: Oxford University Press, 1986). Some of my reasons to doubt the primacy view are given in "The Architecture of Reason."

13. See, e.g., Carl Ginet, "*Contra* Reliabilism," *The Monist* 68 (1985), Foley, *The Theory of Epistemic Rationality*, and Moser, *Knowledge and Evidence*. But note the functionalist (and arguably prima facie theistic) twist given reliabilism in Plantinga, op. cit.

14. This is controversial, but there are many arguments supporting it in the works cited in note 1. Related difficulties arise for reliabilism in cases where a belief is unreliably produced, but *S* has excellent (internal) reasons to hold it.

15. Mill seemed willing to live with something like this, as with other problems in his position. In implicitly attacking Kant's view that the moral worth of an action depends on its motive, he said, in ch. 2 of *Utilitarianism*, "It is the business of ethics to tell us what our duties are, or by what test we may know them; but no system of ethics requires that the sole motive of all we do shall be a feeling of duty . . . the motive has nothing to do with the morality of the action, though much with the worth of the agent" (pp. 17–18). From a Kantian point of view, unless there is a utilitarian criterion for the worth of agents, this grants that moral value is not wholly a matter of utility; and if there is such a criterion it treats people as *means*, even though one is taken to be means only to human happiness, including one's own. For related discussion, see Norman O. Dahl, "Obligation and Moral Worth: Reflections on Prichard and Kant," *Philosophical Studies* 50 (1986).

16. For a valuable defense of a broadly Kantian view of the issue of moral luck, with discussion of various prominent views on the topic, see Michael J. Zimmerman, *An Essay on Moral Responsibility* (Totowa, N.J.: Rowman and Littlefield, 1988), esp. pp. 128–39. It may well be true that luck can figure internally as well as externally. If so, then dealing with moral luck is not a problem for externalist theories alone, but I see no reason to think the problem any more serious for internalist accounts.

17. Dretske's view seems to imply this, and I have argued for it briefly in *Belief, Justification, and Knowledge* (Belmont, Calif.: Wadsworth Publishing Co., 1988), ch. 7.

2

Intuitionism, Pluralism, and the Foundations of Ethics

Ethical intuitionism is historically important, widely referred to, and generally considered a major position in the foundations of ethics. But it is not widely discussed in depth. This is in part because, although it is held by some leading philosophers, its resources are often underestimated. It is certainly conceived divergently among ethical theorists, and those who find its central elements compelling may often think it easier and better simply to argue for their position under another name than to indicate what kind of intuitionism they hold and defend their position under that rubric. My aim here is to clarify intuitionism, to bring out some of its strengths and weaknesses, and to reassess the case for giving it a more significant place in contemporary ethical theory.

The timeliness of an explication and appraisal of intuitionism can be seen through examining the apparent tension between the almost unquestioned relevance of *intuitions* to philosophical method and the apparently easy rejection, by many who appeal to them, of intuitionism.[1] The appeal to intuitions is a pervasive and approved strategy in contemporary philosophical discourse. A good philosophical theory is widely taken to be one that gives an adequate account of our intuitions about the subject matter of the theory. A good ethical theory, for instance, should largely explain our intuitions about when we are or are not being unfair, when we must go out of our way to help others, and when we may or may not break a promise. But only a few of the many philosophers who appeal to intuitions as support for their ethical theories (or, similarly, to "considered judgments," to what "seems plausible," or the like) would maintain ethical intuitionism. This calls for explanation. One would think that in virtually any form, intuitionism in ethics is above all an approach which justifies generalizations in ethics by appeal to intuitions, as one might support the generalization "We should not interfere with the liberty of others" by considering judgments about cases, including cases in which one's own liberty is restricted. It might be said, for example, that our intuitions go against the view that those who can increase the sum total of happiness in the world by having children are obligated to do so whether they want to or not.

32

Many who oppose intuitionism make such appeals to intuitions in establishing a basis for their ethical views. Why, then, do so many ethical theorists strongly resist combining their appeal to intuitions with maintaining some form of intuitionism? Given the degree of evidential cogency commonly ascribed to intuitions, one would think that intuitionism might at worst be guilty not of building castles in the sky but of resting too much on intuitive foundations that cannot sustain the weight they are meant to bear.

To assess ethical intuitionism and the role of intuitions in supporting it, we need a clearer conception of what it is, an account of its relation to ethical intuitions, and a theory of how both are related to the distinction between rationalism and empiricism in moral epistemology. If this task of explication succeeds, it will yield more than a deeper understanding of intuitionism. It will provide the raw materials of a framework for moral theory that overcomes many of the difficulties confronting intuitionism, accounts for the role of intuitions in moral reasoning, and provides the outline of a moral epistemology. In the light of the conception of intuitionism that emerges from the first three parts of this chapter, I will briefly develop this framework. The concluding parts will appraise intuitionism as a restricted version of this wider framework.

I. Traditional Ethical Intuitionism

There are currently two main uses of the term 'intuitionism'. On one use, intuitionism is conceived as an overall kind of ethical theory; on the other, it is a moral epistemology held to be characteristic of such theories. My aim is in part to determine whether either of these common conceptions is adequate to the best intuitionist theories available.

In the former, overall conception, intuitionism has three main characteristics. (1) It is an ethical *pluralism*, a position affirming an irreducible plurality of basic moral principles. (2) Each principle centers on a different kind of ground, in the sense of a factor implying a prima facie moral duty, such as making a promise or noticing a person who will bleed to death without one's help. (3) Each principle is taken to be in some sense intuitively known. (1) and (2) are structural and conceptual; they affirm a plurality of basic principles affecting different kinds of conduct, and they thus deny, against both Kantian and utilitarian theories, that there is just one basic moral principle. (3) is epistemological; it locates the basic principles with respect to knowledge.

In the second, epistemological conception of intuitionism, the view is roughly the thesis that basic moral judgments and basic moral principles are justified by the non-inferential deliverances of a rational, intuitive faculty, a mental capacity that contrasts with sense perception, clairvoyance, and other possible routes to justification. A number of writers, particularly critics of intuitionism, conceive intuitionism as implying the stronger thesis that the intuitive faculty yields indefeasible knowledge of self-evident moral truths. One concern of this essay is whether this stronger conception is justified.

Rossian Intuitionism

The position of W. D. Ross is widely regarded as a version of intuitionism in both the overall and epistemological senses: as pluralist and as implying that we have intuitive moral knowledge.[2] My chief concern is intuitionist moral epistemology. This epistemology is, however, fundamental in intuitionism as an overall ethical view, and an examination of the epistemology will ultimately lead us to a discussion of the pluralism of the view.[3] We can best clarify this epistemology and appraise the adequacy of the formulation of it just given if we explore a representative intuitionism. Ross is at once an important moral philosopher and an excellent example of an intuitionist. We can learn much by examining the basic elements of his ethical theory. In the light of that examination, and building in part on a reconstructed Rossian theory, I will outline a general (though not a complete) account of justification in ethics. Intuitionism in various forms can then be seen as largely a restricted version of that account.

In what is probably his most important ethical work, *The Right and the Good* (1930), Ross proposed, as fundamental both to philosophical ethics and to everyday life, a now famous list of prima facie duties: duties of fidelity (promise-keeping, including honesty) and reparation, of justice and gratitude, of beneficence and self-improvement, and of non-injury.[4] In calling these duties prima facie, Ross meant to indicate that even when we acquire one, say by making a promise, the act in question need not be our final duty, since a competing duty, for instance to attend a sick child, might override the original duty.[5] This does not imply that a prima facie duty ever lacks *moral weight*; one should, for example, regret having to break a promise, and perhaps must make reparations for it, even when one did right in breaking it. The point is simply that a prima facie duty is not necessarily final, and to recognize such a duty as applicable to oneself is not sufficient for knowing what, all things considered, one should *do*.

A word of further explication is in order. Because it is only under certain conditions that a prima facie duty indicates a final duty — roughly, a duty "all things considered" — prima facie duties are sometimes called *conditional duties*.[6] This misleadingly suggests that we have prima facie duties only when they prevail, that is, express one's duty all things considered. Worse yet, it may suggest that the *content* of prima facie duties is conditional, as where you promise to pay a bill *if* your friend does not have enough money. Here there is a condition for your *having* the duty to pay, at all: your conditional duty becomes "operative" only if your friend does not pay. But whether, if you do have this duty, it is just prima facie rather than final is left open. Prima facie duties, far from being possessed only conditionally, are necessarily possessed when their grounds are present, and they are often not conditional in content. To illustrate both points, if you promise to pay the bill (period), then you thereby have a prima facie duty to do so; and you still have this duty even if a conflicting duty, say to save a life, overrides your prima facie duty to keep the promise. This is why one needs an excuse for not keeping the promise and may owe an explanation to the disappointed promisee. Without a satisfactory excuse, one is to some degree morally deficient.

The central idea underlying the Rossian notion of a prima facie duty, I suggest, is that of a duty which is — given the presence of its ground — *ineradicable but over-*

ridable. The presence of its ground (a notion Ross does not explicate) is crucial. If, for example, others could not benefit from our help, there would be no prima facie duty of beneficence, since our ground for the duty would be absent. A prima facie duty that is ineradicable given the presence of its ground is nonetheless *cancelable* by removal of that ground. Consider the duty to keep a promise. Where the promisee releases one from a promise or where the fulfillment of the duty becomes impossible, say because the person one had a duty to help has died, there is no longer any such duty. But overriding conditions do not cancel the duty they override. A duty's being overridden by conflicting prima facie duties implies that its ground is outweighed, but not that it is removed. A superior counterforce blocks, but does not eliminate, the force it overpowers.

Ross stressed a number of features of his position, and at least some of these have become part of the common conception (so far as there is one) of intuitionism. First, he insisted on its irreducible pluralism; he argued that there is no one thing, such as enhancing goodness in the world, that is our only direct, overall duty.[7] Second, he emphasized the self-evidence of the propositions expressing our prima facie duties. Here is the central passage:

> That an act *qua* fulfilling a promise, or *qua* effecting a just distribution of good . . . is *prima facie* right, is self-evident; not in the sense that it is evident from the beginning of our lives, or as soon as we attend to the proposition for the first time, but in the sense that when we have reached sufficient mental maturity and have given sufficient attention to the proposition it is evident without any need of proof, or of evidence beyond itself. It is evident just as a mathematical axiom, or the validity of a form of inference, is evident. . . . In our confidence that these propositions are true there is involved the same confidence in our reason that is involved in our confidence in mathematics. . . . In both cases we are dealing with propositions that cannot be proved, but that just as certainly need no proof.[8]

Third, Ross apparently intended this claim of self-evidence to hold for certain kinds of act, not particular deeds. He says, for example, "[W]e are never certain that any particular possible act is . . . right," and, clarifying this, that "we apprehend *prima facie* rightness to belong to the nature of any fulfillment of a promise. From this we come by reflection to apprehend the self-evident *prima facie* rightness of an individual act of a particular type. . . . But no act is ever, in virtue of falling under some general description, necessarily actually right; its rightness depends on its whole nature and not any element in it."[9] His positive point, applied to promising, is in part that when one thinks clearly about what it *is* to promise a particular friend to do something, one can see that doing the deed is called for and would be right barring special circumstances, such as a medical emergency. His negative point, in the Rossian terminology just introduced, is something like this: from a general description of the grounds that yield a prima facie duty, for example from the description of an act of mine as a promise, it does not follow that the duty (here the duty to keep the promise) is not overridden, nor is it self-evident that it is not overridden, however clear that may be in many cases. It is not self-evident, for instance, that no medical emergency will intervene and override my duty to keep the promise.

The fourth and final point here is that in explaining how we apprehend the moral truths in question, Ross appealed to something like what we commonly call intuitions. He said, for example, that if someone challenges

> our view that there is a special obligatoriness attaching to the keeping of promises because it is self-evident that the only duty is to produce as much good as possible, we have to ask ourselves whether we really, when we reflect, *are* convinced that [as he takes G. E. Moore to hold] this is self-evident. . . . [I]t seems self-evident that a promise simply as such, is something that *prima facie* ought to be kept. . . . [T]he moral convictions of thoughtful and well-educated people are the data of ethics, just as sense-perceptions are the data of a natural science. Just as some of the latter have to be rejected as illusory, so have some of the former; but as the latter are rejected only when they conflict with other more accurate sense-perceptions, the former are rejected only when they conflict with convictions which stand better the test of reflection.[10]

Ross does not make clear whether the imagined conflicts are ever resolvable by appeal to generalizations, such as one to the effect that promises to meet with students have priority over promises to campaign for political candidates. Suppose I discover that keeping a promise to comment on a long manuscript will take vastly more time than anyone could foresee. Something rather general may then occur to me (if I follow Ross): that I have prima facie duties of other sorts, arising, for instance, from duties of beneficence as well as from other promises, such as promises to my family or friends. As I think, in this light, about my overall duties, my sense that I must prepare the comments may conflict with my sense that I should fulfill other duties. Ross countenances this kind of conflict, but because he treats "the verdicts of the moral consciousness of the best people as the foundation on which we must build" and is thinking of judgments about concrete moral options, he seems to hold the view that ethical generalizations do not *independently* carry evidential weight in such conflicts. One should not, for example, appeal to a second-order generalization that duties of justice are stronger than duties of fidelity. Rather, one should focus on the specific facts and, in that light, determine what one's actual duty is.

The task of conflict resolution here is very much like that of using Aristotelian practical wisdom in dealing with a moral problem. It is possible, for Ross as for Aristotle, that a rule emerges *on the basis of the resolution* one reaches, but there is not necessarily any rule *antecedently* governing each particular case one may encounter. I may, through my reflection on such a conflict of duties, frame a rule for similar future cases; but I do not bring to every case a ready-made rule that, irrespective of my intuitive judgments about that case, will tell me what to do.

In this rejection of the view that there are always second-order generalizations available to resolve conflicts of prima facie duties, Ross seems to be, as regards judgments of overall obligation, a *particularist* rather than a generalist: he holds that we must attend to particular cases in order to determine what generalizations hold, even if it is repeatable features of those cases, such as their being acts of promising, that reveal the general truths we reach through reflection on the cases.[11] This is a point not about what *can* be known but about the order of knowing: our basic moral knowledge — even of prima facie duties — comes from reflection on particular

cases, especially those calling for moral decision, where those cases are properly conceived in terms of their repeatable features. Our basic moral knowledge does not
come from reflection on abstract, universal moral propositions. We do not, for
instance, grasp the Kantian categorical imperative a priori and then apply it to the
issue at hand with a view to formulating, on the basis of it, a "theorem" that resolves
our problem. That abstract, monistic approach is also precluded by Ross's pluralism.
But pluralism is not his only demand: he would also reject even a set of mutually
irreducible rules if they were abstractions imposed on particular cases in the way the
categorical imperative or utilitarianism might be, rather than derived from reflection
on particular cases.

An example of commitment to such a set of rules would be an a priori *hierar-
chism*, a view on which some of the prima facie duties automatically outweigh one
or more others. Ross would reject this because for him, as for intuitionists in general,
there is neither a *complete* ordering of duties in terms of moral weights (a ranking of
duties from strongest to least strong) nor even any *pairwise ordering* (a ranking of
some pair of the prima facie duties), as where the duty of non-maleficence, say, to
avoid killing, is always said to outweigh that of beneficence, for instance to save
life.[12] These points do not entail that *no* comparisons between strengths of (prima
facie) duties can be proper objects of intuition. Given a typical pattern of facts concerning a babysitter annoyed by a cranky infant, one might have an intuition that the
babysitter's duty not to flog the child to death is stronger than the duty not to give it
a heavy but non-fatal dose of vodka.

Self-Evidence and Defeasibility

We can now compare Ross's view with the common conception of intuitionism (in
moral epistemology) noted earlier. He fits that conception in holding that the basic
moral truths — which he takes to be constituted by his principles of prima facie
duty — are self-evident. But he does not posit a special rational faculty. He is not
committed to the existence of a "part" of the mind, or even "capacity of reason,"
required only for moral thought. He talks, to be sure, of moral consciousness and of
"apprehension" (roughly, understanding) of those self-evident truths (by 'apprehension' he often means a species of what is commonly meant by 'intuition', which will
be explicated in the next section). But in presenting his moral epistemology he
emphasizes that the prima facie moral duties are recognized in the same way as the
truth of mathematical axioms and logical truths.

Ross also speaks (e.g., in the same passage) of our apprehending the self-evidence
of the relevant moral and mathematical propositions. He does not always distinguish apprehending the truth of a proposition that *is* self-evident from apprehending *its self-evidence*.[13] This is an important point, since (if there are self-evident
propositions) it should be easy to apprehend the truth of at least some of them,
whereas the epistemic *status* of propositions, for example their justification or self-
evidence or apriority, is a paradigm source of disagreement. It should be noted,
however, that even apprehension of the self-evidence of propositions does not
require having a special faculty. But suppose it did. Does Ross's overall position
commit him to our having non-inferential knowledge of the self-evidence, as

opposed to the truth, of the relevant principles? I think not, and if I am correct then one apparently common view of intuitionism can be set aside as a misconception. Let me explain.

We might know that a moral principle is self-evident only on a limited basis, say from knowing the conceptual as opposed to empirical (e.g., observational) character of the grounds on which we know that principle to be true. We would know its truth *on* these grounds; we would know its self-evidence through knowledge *about* the grounds. For instance, if we take ourselves to know a moral proposition, say that there is a prima facie (moral) duty to keep promises, (1) on the basis of understanding the concepts involved in this proposition and (2) non-inferentially (roughly, without dependence on one or more premises as evidence), we may plausibly think it follows, from our having this kind of knowledge of the moral proposition, that it has the status of self-evidence. This way of knowing the status of a Rossian proposition expressing a basic prima facie duty requires having concepts of self-evidence, of non-inferentiality, and, in effect, of a priori knowledge. But *none* of these concepts is required simply to know that there is a prima facie duty to keep promises. It is, however, that first-order proposition, the principle that promise-keeping is a duty, and not the second-order thesis that this principle is self-evident, which is the fundamental thing we must be able to know intuitively if a Rossian intuitionism is to succeed. As moral agents we need intuitive knowledge of our duties; we do not need intuitive (or even other) knowledge of the status of the principles of duty.

This brings us to the last key point in the most common conception of intuitionism: the idea that it posits *indefeasible justification*— roughly, justification that cannot be undermined or overridden — for any cognition grounded in a genuine intuition. Ross is not committed to this general idea, even if he might have regarded some moral beliefs as indefeasibly justified. Once it is seen that the primary role of intuition is to give us direct, that is, non-inferential, knowledge or justified belief of the *truth*, rather than of the self-evidence, of moral propositions (especially certain moral principles), there is less reason to think that moral beliefs resting on an intuitive grasp of principles must be considered indefeasibly justified.

Indeed, even if self-evidence were the main element that is intuitively apprehended, Ross would be entitled to hold — and in fact stresses — that there can be conflicts of moral "convictions" in which some are given up "just as" in scientific inquiry some perceptions are given up as illusory (see the earlier quotation from *The Right and the Good*, pp. 39–40). If intuitions are sometimes properly given up in this way — and the convictions in question are apparently a species of what are commonly called intuitions — the justification possessed by intuitions is plainly defeasible (subject to being undermined or overridden); and so, at least with respect to moral judgments of particular deeds, defeasibility is to be expected.

This brings us to something that does not seem to have been generally noticed by critics of intuitionism and is at least not emphasized by Ross. The view that the justification of moral intuitions is defeasible, even when grounded in the careful reflection Ross thought appropriate to them, is quite consistent with his claim that the self-evident truths in question do not admit of proof. That a proposition does not admit of proof is an epistemic fact about *it* and leaves open that a person might have only poor or overridden grounds for *believing* it. This logical and epistemic fact does not entail that one cannot lose one's justification for believing it, or even fail to become justified in believing it upon considering it, or fail to find it intuitive.

It must be granted, however, that by putting us in mind of the simplest logical and mathematical truths, Ross's unprovability claim easily creates the mistaken impression that genuine intuitions are either infallible or justificationally indefeasible, or both. Nonetheless, there is nothing in Ross's theory as set out in *The Right and the Good* which is inconsistent with the rather striking disclaimer made by his great intuitionist predecessor, G. E. Moore, following his sketch of what, in his view, constitutes an intuition.[14] Moore says that in calling propositions intuitions he means

> *merely* to assert that they are incapable of proof; I imply nothing whatever as to the manner or origin of our cognition of them. Still less do I imply (as most Intuitionists have done) that any proposition whatever is true, *because* we cognise it in a particular way or by the exercise of any particular faculty: I hold, on the contrary, that in every way in which it is possible to cognise a true proposition it is also possible to cognise a false one.[15]

Apparently, for Moore as for Ross, even if the truth or self-evidence of a proposition can be apprehended by reflection, there need be no special faculty yielding the apprehensions; and whatever the basis of those apprehensions, it is of a kind that can produce mistaken beliefs, including some that one would naturally take to be apprehensions of self-evident truths.[16] Anyone who is aware that mistaken beliefs can arise from apprehensions or intuitions (or in any other way one can "cognise" a proposition) should be willing to regard intuitions as capable of being unjustified or even false.

II. Intuitions, Intuitionism, and Reflection

We have seen that if Ross's view is a paradigm of intuitionism, then a widely held conception of intuitionism is inadequate. Above all, he is (by his major views) committed neither to the existence of a special faculty of intuition — such as a capacity peculiar to ethical subject matter — nor to the epistemic indefeasibility of the "self-evident" judgments that reflection yields. The same seems true of Moore, for reasons I have suggested, but I cannot pursue Moore's views separately here. This section will clarify further what an intuitionist like Ross *is* committed to. I begin with a sketch of the notion of an intuition. I mean, of course, 'intuition' in the *cognitive sense*, a psychological state like (and perhaps a kind of) belief. We have not been discussing, and need not explicitly discuss, intuitions in the *propositional sense*, that is, propositions of the kind Moore (as quoted earlier) took to be unprovable, a kind supposed to be fitting objects of intuitions in the cognitive sense.

To summarize my negative points about intuitions, I have contended that they need not be infallible or indefeasibly justified deliverances of a special faculty that is distinct from our general rational capacity as manifested in grasping logical and (pure) mathematical truths, and presumably other kinds of truths, ethical and non-ethical, as well. What, then, is distinctive of an intuition? I shall suggest four main characteristics.[17]

Four Characteristics of Intuitions

First, an intuition must be non-inferential, in the sense that the intuited proposition in question is not — at the time it is intuitively held — held on the basis of a premise. Call this the *non-inferentiality (or directness) requirement*. Some intuitionists have emphasized this, and it is at least implicit in Ross and Moore.[18] If we do not grant it, we cannot explain why Ross and Moore should hold the stronger view that what we know intuitively is not provable; for if they took intuition to be potentially inferential and thus potentially based on premises, they would surely have addressed the question whether, for at least some intuitively known propositions, there might be premises to serve as a ground or a proof of those propositions and thereby as an inferential basis of the intuitions in question. I should add that despite appearances the *ungroundability thesis*, as we might call it — the view that what is intuitively known cannot be (evidentially) grounded in premises — does *not* imply that a proposition intuitively known is a priori or necessary. Ross apparently believed, however, that the universal moral propositions in question (notably his principles of prima facie duty) are both a priori and necessary; but it is doubtful that he regarded as a priori one's apparently primitive sense that one has a prima facie duty to keep *this* promise. If he held some such aprioristic, rationalist view regarding particular cases, it would presumably have been qualified so as to avoid empirical assumptions, as does the position that one apprehends the truth of a concrete generalization like "*If* one sees someone fall off a bicycle and can easily help with what appears to be a broken arm, one has a prima facie obligation to do so." Consider, by contrast, the unconditional proposition that I actually have this obligation; this presupposes both my existence and that of the injured person(s) and hence is plainly neither a priori nor a necessary truth. The conditional generalization, on the other hand, even if one grasps it in application to an individual case, is simply not about any actual case. I emphasize this point because while Ross was doubtless a rationalist in his epistemology, his intuitionism — taken simply as a pluralist view committed to intuitive moral knowledge, at least — does not entail moral rationalism.

Second, an intuition must be a moderately firm cognition — call this the *firmness requirement*. One must come down on the matter at hand; if one is up in the air, the jury is still out. In the contexts that concern us, intuitions will typically be beliefs, including cases of knowing. But the term 'intuitions' may include (sincere) judgments or other mental events implying belief. A mere inclination to believe is not an intuition; an intuition tends to be a "conviction" (a term Ross sometimes used for an intuition) and to be relinquished only through such weighty considerations as a felt conflict with a firmly held theory or with another intuition. Granted, a proposition one is only inclined to believe may be or seem intu*itive*; but one does not have an intuition with that proposition as its content until one believes the proposition. We might speak here of intuitive inclinations as opposed to intuitions, and the former need not be denied some degree of evidential weight, though it would be less than that of intuitions proper: the data, we might say, would be less clear, just as a view of an unexpected island in the fog is less clear than it would be in sunlight and provides less reason to alter one's map. The concepts of intuition and of the intuitive are not sharp, but nothing in what follows will turn on their vagueness.

Third, intuitions must be formed in the light of an adequate understanding of their propositional objects — call this the *comprehension requirement*. That they are formed in this light is doubtless one reason for their firmness, as is their being based on that understanding rather than on, say, inference from premises (I assume they are normally based on such an understanding). As to the required adequacy of this understanding, Ross, like Moore, insists that before one can apprehend even a self-evident moral truth, one must get precisely that true proposition before one's mind. In many passages (including one quoted earlier) Ross indicates that reflection is required to see the truth of the proposition in question. The more complicated the proposition, or the richer the concepts figuring in it — like the concept of a promise — the more is required for an adequate understanding of that proposition.[19] Intuitions are sometimes regarded as arising quickly upon considering the proposition in question; they need not so arise and in some cases probably should not so arise.

The fourth requirement I suggest is that intuitions are pretheoretical: roughly, they are neither evidentially dependent on theories nor themselves theoretical hypotheses. If this *pretheoreticality requirement* entailed their being *preconceptual* or, more broadly, uninformed, it would undermine the comprehension requirement: without at least a minimal understanding of the concepts figuring in a proposition, one is not even in a position to find it intuitive. But clearly Ross and other intuitionists intend our "convictions" (intuitions), including those of other people, to be used as data for moral generalization somewhat in the way sense perceptions are data for scientific theorizing. Given his understanding of this idea, not only will an intuition not be an inference from a theory, it will also not be epistemically dependent on a theory even in the general sense that the theory provides one's justificatory ground (even a non-inferential ground) for the intuition. This point does *not* entail that intuition has a complete independence of theory: an intuition may be defeated and abandoned in the light of theoretical results incompatible with its truth, especially when these results are supported by other intuitions. This is a kind of negative epistemic dependence of intuition on theory: the justification of the intuition does not derive from the impossibility of such untoward, hypothetical results, but it can be destroyed by them if they occur. Such defeasibility on the part of intuition is not a positive justificatory dependence on any actual theory; it is a negative dependence on — in the sense of a vulnerability to — disconfirmation by theories, whether actual or possible.[20]

In some ways, the perceptual analogy can mislead. For one thing, an intuition is more like a belief based on a careful observation than like an impression formed from a glimpse, though that impression is nonetheless perceptual and can produce belief. One could, however, speak of sensory intuitions in reference to cognitions that rest on observational sense experience in the way perceptual beliefs commonly do when they are formed under favorable conditions. Consider, for instance, visual beliefs, acquired in good light, about an island seen before one. From this point of view, my four conditions are probably too broad; but to build in, say, that intuitions are non-observational cognitions of a conceptual or at least classificatory kind would probably make the conditions too narrow, and the breadth of the characterization is appropriate to our purposes.

The perceptual analogy is also misleading because intuitions need not be about observables: rights are not observable, yet we have intuitions about them. We may see them in the sense of recognizing them, as where one sees a right to refuse feeding tubes, but they are not seen visually. If what is both non-observable and significantly complex is thereby theoretical, then we certainly have intuitions about theoretical entities; but such "theoretical" intuitions need not be epistemically dependent on any theory.

It is of course controversial whether, in either intuitive or perceptual cases, there *is* anything pretheoretical to appeal to. But if not — if, for instance, to have concepts sufficient for judging a theory one must be biased by either that theory or another one relevant to judging the theory — then it is not only Ross who has a problem. One would hope that even if every judge has some biases, there are some judges who at least have no biases that vitiate their decisions on the cases they must resolve.

Even if no cognition is entirely pretheoretical, perhaps some may be pre-theoretical *with respect to* a moral generalization needing appraisal. Granted, this would rule out only theoretical biases. Intuitionists apparently hope that no others are ineliminable, but absence of *all* bias is apparently not part of the concept of an intuition; the effects of biases may indeed help to explain how an intuition can be mistaken. Nor is it necessary, for purposes of working out a satisfactory intuitionism, that biases always be unavoidable; it is enough if, as Ross apparently thought, they are always correctable by further reflection. Such reflection may include comparison with the intuitions of others, just as in scientific inquiry one might compare one's observations with those of coinvestigators.

There are two points that may significantly clarify the sense in which intuitions might be pretheoretical. One point (implicit in what has been said) is that an intuition's being pretheoretical does not imply that it is indefeasible — not even indefeasible by judgments based on the theory we build from a set of intuitions including the one in question. Recall the case in which I see that keeping a promise is not my final duty because, reflecting on my general duties, I realize that other duties override my duty to keep the promise. Here, the basis of the other moral considerations is the same sort as that of the first duty. The second point is that an intuition that is pretheoretical at one time can evolve into a judgment grounded in a theory. A Rossian view is committed to the existence, at any time when our convictions provide the data for ethics, of pretheoretical intuitions; but it is not committed to denying that yesterday's intuitions can be today's theory-laden assumptions — or that they can be given up because they are undermined by the reflection of "thoughtful, well-educated people."

Let us suppose for the sake of argument that either there are no pretheoretical intuitions or, more likely, *some* of the intuitions needed for confirmation of basic moral principles are in some way theoretical. We can still distinguish between theories that bias the appraisal of a moral principle and theories that do not. If, for instance, a theory of the psychology of persons is needed for the capacity to have certain moral intuitions — for instance the intuition that flogging an infant to death is prima facie wrong — this need not vitiate the appraisal. The intuition may depend on a theoretical (psychological) understanding of the pains caused by flogging and of (biological) death, but neither the kind nor the level of the relevant theory undermines the justifiability of the intuition. We might, then, distinguish between what is *relatively* and what is *absolutely* pretheoretical: the former is simply pretheoretical relative to the issue in question, say the moral status of the act-type, flogging an infant to death. Perhaps a relative notion of the pretheoretical is all that intuitionism needs in order to meet the objection that theoretical dependence vitiates the justificatory role it claims for intuitions.

Conclusions of Reflection Versus Conclusions of Inference

If intuitions are non-inferential and pretheoretical, one might wonder to what extent they represent rationality, as opposed to mere belief or even prejudice. Here it is crucial to recall Ross's requirements of adequate maturity and "sufficient attention." I propose to go further: there is a sense in which an intuition *can* be a conclusion formed through rational inquiry. Consider listening to someone complain about a task done by a coworker, where one has been asked to determine whether the work was adequate. In a way that is impersonal and ably documented, Timothy criticizes the work of Abby. One might judge, from his credible statements of deficiencies in her work, that it was shoddy. This is a response to evidential propositions. Now imagine being asked a different question: whether there might be some bias in the critique. One might now recall his narration in one's mind's eye and ear, and from a global, intuitive sense of Timothy's intonations, word choices, selection of deficiencies, and omission of certain merits, judge that he is jealous of her. This is a response to an overall impression. Let us call the first judgment — that the work is shoddy — a *conclusion of inference*: it is premised on propositions one has noted as evidence. Call the second judgment a *conclusion of reflection*: it emerges from thinking about the overall pattern of Timothy's critique in the context of his relation to Abby as a coworker, but not from one or more evidential premises. It is more like a response to viewing a painting or seeing an expressive face than to propositionally represented information. One responds to a pattern: one notices an emotional tone in the otherwise factual listing of deficiencies; one hears him compare her work to some that he once did; and so forth. The conclusion of reflection is a wrapping up of the question, similar to concluding a practical matter with a decision. One has not added up the evidences and formulated their implication; one has obtained a view of the whole and characterized it overall.

It might be objected here that one is really inferring, from the tone of Timothy's complaint and of his comparison of Abby's work with a job he once did, that he is jealous; this is not something just "seen" on the basis of a careful, overall look. To say that the case must be so described is to confuse the grounds of one's judgment with beliefs expressing those grounds. Granted, if I *articulate* my non-inferential grounds, they will then be available to me as premises. If, for instance, I say to myself that his tone was quite emotional given the factual character of the deficiencies he listed, I now have a premise for the conclusion that he was jealous of her. But if this point implied that my belief that he is jealous of her is inferential *prior* to my articulating my ground and "basing" my conclusion on it, the same would hold for perceptual beliefs based on visual impressions whose evidential force can be articulated. We would have to say that since the statement that I have a visual impression of gold-lettered buckram before me is a premise for believing there is a book before me, I concluded that there is a book before me, on the basis of this premise, even when I merely *had* the impression, had not articulated my having it, and from it spontaneously formed the belief that there is a book before me. But surely my having a ground that is *expressible* in a premise does not imply that I must *use* that ground *in* a premise in order to form a belief on the basis of the ground.[21] I suggest, then, that this kind of conclusion can be an intuition in the sense just sketched. Not all intuitions are of this sort, but it is essential to see that particularly when a case, real or hypothetical, is complicated, an intuition may not emerge until reflection proceeds for some time. Such an intuition can be a conclusion of reflection, temporally as well as epistemically; and it may be either empirical or a priori.

This example and other paradigms of intuition might suggest that intuitions are always about *cases* as opposed to generalizations. They typically are, and arguably a generalization can be only *intuitive* — roughly, highly plausible considered in itself — as opposed to being the object of *an* intuition. The intuitive status of a proposition is consistent with its being inferentially believed, or with its being the object of an infirm cognition, or with both. But this restriction of intuitions to cases as opposed to generalizations is neither entailed by the four general conditions I have proposed as roughly necessary and sufficient for an intuition nor implicit in the history of the notion.[22]

A generalization can be intuitive in much the way a singular proposition about an example can be; and just as some intuitions can be better grounded and firmer than others, some generalizations can be more intuitive than others. It is true that an intuitive generalization can be supported by intuitions about examples, but it does not follow that its only way of being intuitive is through such support. Kant might have found the generalization that I ought to keep my promises more intuitive than the singular proposition that I ought to keep my promise (to my sister) to educate her daughter; Ross might find the latter more intuitive (and would reject the generalization unless it is understood to refer to prima facie duty).[23]

III. *Self-Evidence and the Systematization of Intuitions*

In order to appreciate the sense in which Ross's basic moral truths might be plausibly considered self-evident, it seems to me absolutely essential that we distinguish his actual case for them from his analogy to mathematics and logic. He knew full well that it takes more reflection and maturity to see the truth of the proposition that promises generate prima facie duties than to see the validity of a logical principle like the syllogistic 'If all As are Bs and all Bs are Cs, then all As are Cs'. On this score, the disanalogy between the moral case and that of logic and other domains of self-evidence both undermines the plausibility of Ross's view and gives ethical intuitionism a burden it need not carry. Logic can (let us assume) be axiomatized given a few self-evident propositions (e.g. that if (a) either p or q and (b) not-q, then p).

Their substitution instances, for example the proposition that if either Jim is in his office or he is home, and he is not in this office, then he is home, have a similar axiomatic self-evidence. Moral principles, by contrast, seem to many reasonable people neither self-evident nor comparably simple. Ross might have pointed out that self-evidence, at least of the kind in question, should not be expected in substantially vague generalizations. He might also have done more to distinguish different kinds of self-evidence, for it seems to me that only one of them need be claimed by intuitionists as possessed by some moral truths.

Two Kinds of Self-Evidence

Two kinds of self-evidence are especially relevant here. Let me first establish a general conception of self-evidence, and in that light we can distinguish them. I shall assume that the basic notion of self-evidence is this: a self-evident proposition is (roughly) a truth such that understanding it will meet two conditions: that understanding is (1) sufficient for one's being justified in believing it (i.e., for having justification for believing it, whether one in fact believes it or not) — this is why such a truth is evident *in itself* — and (2) sufficient for knowing the proposition provided one believes it on the *basis* of understanding it.[24] Two clarifications are needed immediately.

First, as reflected in (1), the self-evidence of a proposition does not entail that if one understands (and considers) the proposition, then one believes it. This non-belief-entailing conception of self-evidence is plausible because one can fail initially to "see" a self-evident truth and, later, grasp it in just the way one grasps the truth of a paradigmatically self-evident proposition: one that is obvious in itself the moment one considers it. Take, for example, a self-evident proposition that is perhaps not immediately obvious: if there never have been any siblings then there never have been any first cousins.[25] A delay in seeing something, such as the truth of this, need not change the character of what one sees. What is self-evident can indeed be justifiedly believed on its "intrinsic" merits; but they need not leap out at one immediately. In some cases one can see *what* a self-evident proposition says — and thus understand it — before seeing *that*, or how, it is true.

Second, the understanding in question must be adequate, as opposed to mistaken or partial or clouded, understanding. Adequate understanding of a proposition is more than simply getting the general sense of a sentence expressing it, as where one can parse the sentence grammatically, partially explain what it means, and perhaps translate it into another language one knows well. Adequacy here implies not only seeing what the proposition says but also being able to apply it to some appropriate cases, being able to see some of its logical implications, and comprehending its elements and some of their relations. If inadequate understanding is allowed, it will not be true that understanding a self-evident proposition provides a justification for believing it, nor that beliefs of the proposition based on understanding it constitute knowledge.

Given these points about (1) and (2), we may distinguish those self-evident propositions that are readily understood by normal adults (or by people of some relevant description, e.g. mature moral agents) and those understood by them only through reflection on the sorts of cases they concern. Call the first *immediately self-evident* and the second *mediately self-evident*, since their truth can be grasped only through the mediation of reflection.[26] The reflection may involve drawing inferences, but their role is limited largely to clarifying what the proposition in question says: as self-evidence is normally understood, a self-evident proposition is knowable without inferential grounds. One may require time to get it in clear focus, but need not climb up to it on the shoulders of one or more premises.

Immediately self-evident propositions are *obvious*; roughly, their truth is apparent as soon as one considers them with understanding, which is usually as soon as one is presented with them in a natural formulation in a language in which one is competent. The obvious need not be self-evident, however. It is obvious that there exists at least one person, but this is not self-evident: the proposition is not evident in itself; but if we consider a natural formulation of it in a language we understand, we have ample ground *in that situation* for seeing its truth (at least if we know we are persons). Moreover, there are *degrees* (as well as kinds) of obviousness, but there are *kinds* rather than degrees of self-evidence.

Granted, some self-evident propositions are more readily seen to be true than others, but this is a different point. Even immediately self-evident propositions can differ in obviousness, whether for everyone or for some people or for one or more people at different times. Consider the proposition that if all As are Bs and all Bs are Cs, then all As are Cs. This is "very intuitive" and very obviously true, or at least that holds for its ordinary substitution instances, such as 'If all cats are furry creatures and all furry creatures are animals, then all cats are animals'. It is also, for many people, more readily seen to be true, even if perhaps not in the end more intuitive, than the proposition that if no As are Bs and all Cs are Bs, then no Cs are As, or the proposition if there never have been any siblings then there never have been any first cousins. As these examples suggest, mediately self-evident propositions need not be (psychologically) *compelling*: they need not produce belief the moment they are understood, nor, even after reflection on them, in everyone who understands them.[27]

Once we distinguish between the immediately and the mediately self-evident, and appreciate that a self-evident proposition need not be obvious or even compelling, we can see clearly that an intuitionist — indeed, even a rationalist one like Ross — may be a fallibilist about the sense of self-evidence. He can thus make room for error even in thoughtful judgments to the effect that a proposition is, or is not, self-evident. He might grant, then, that a non-self-evident (or even false) proposition may seem to someone to be self-evident. Moreover, not every self-evident proposition need be "intuitive," just as not every proposition believed on the basis of intuition need be self-evident. If there are self-evident moral truths, the sense that one has grasped such a truth can be illusory, and at least the majority can be expected to be in the mediate category.[28]

Two further points may help here. The first is that particularly when a proposition is questioned, if only by a skeptic or by someone who wants a derivation of it in order to understand it better, then where the proposition is not obvious or immediately self-evident we may think that it is not self-evident at all, even if it is. Yet surely we can know a proposition to be true even if we cannot show it to be true, or even defend it by argument, as opposed to illustrating or explaining it.[29] This is how it is for most people with respect to the proposition that if all As are Bs, and all Bs are Cs, then all As are Cs. They can explain it by example but can find no prior premises for it and may not even be able to defend it by (non-question-begging) argument if confronted by skillful objections. The second point is that as I have characterized intuitions, they not only are justificationally defeasible but need not even be prima facie justified. Still, insofar as they are like certain perceptual beliefs, for instance in being non-inferential, "natural," and pretheoretical, and (perhaps more important) insofar as they are based on an understanding of their propositional object, there is reason to consider them prima facie justified (in part because in such cases one tends to find it at best difficult to see how the proposition might be false). This may be as much as a moderate intuitionism needs to claim, and it does not entail that an intuition, as such, is prima facie justified. It leaves open that, say because one believes a proposition on a basis other than one's understanding of it, the proposition could become the object of an intuition for one, yet, at the time, that intuition might fail to be prima facie justified.

The Possibility of Grounds for the Self-Evident

In closing this section, I want to bring out the importance of the distinction between the immediately and the mediately self-evident and to introduce a special case of the former. By comparing his candidate basic moral truths to the (elementary) truths of logic and mathematics, Ross wrongly implied that the former are of the first kind. Indeed, when he went on to say that proving them is impossible, he created the impression that he would place them in a yet narrower category: that of propositions which are *strongly axiomatic*, in a sense implying not only immediate self-evidence, which is often taken to be roughly equivalent to simple axiomatic status, but also the further property of unprovability from anything epistemically *prior*. Such unprovability is, roughly, the impossibility of being proved from one or more premises that can be known or justifiedly believed without already knowing or justifiedly believing the proposition in question.[30]

A different way to express the difference between self-evidence and strong axiomaticity is this. A self-evident proposition can function as an epistemic *unmoved* mover: it can be known, and can provide support for other propositions, without itself being seen to have (and perhaps without there even existing) a basis in something constituting evidence for it. But, unlike a strongly axiomatic proposition, it need not be an *unmovable* mover, one such that there cannot be further evidence for it, since the existence of that evidence would move it upward from the lowest possible foundational level.[31]

These points about self-evidence have far-reaching implications for intuitionism. I believe that Ross said nothing implying that there cannot be good arguments for certain self-evident propositions, even the immediate ones. What is evident "in itself," even if immediately self-evident, need not be such that it cannot also be evident in some other way. It need not be known through premises; but this does not entail that it cannot be so known. Let us explore this point in relation to a further problem concerning his view.

What is it that makes all of Ross's principles moral, and might their truth be known in terms of the same account that explains why they are moral? Ross probably thought that even if there is an answer to the first question it provides no answer to the second.[32] If there is just one fundamental obligation, and hence the property of being obligatory is (even if not by definition) equivalent to, say, that of optimizing happiness, then all moral principles can be seen as endorsements of behaviors that optimize — or condemnations of those that do the opposite. Ross rejected this view. Consider, by contrast, a Kantian unification of moral principles, including Ross's principles of duty. The intrinsic end formulation of Kant's categorical imperative is suggestive. Above all, it stresses respect for persons: it says they are to be treated as ends and never merely as means. Is it not plausible to hold that in lying, breaking promises, subjugating, torturing, and the like one is using people merely as a means? And in keeping faith with people, acting benevolently toward them, and extending them justice, is one not treating them as ends, roughly in the sense of beings with intrinsic value (or whose experiences can have intrinsic value)?[33] The point is not that Ross's principles can be deduced from the categorical imperative (though we need not rule out the possibility of an interpretation of it that permits such a deduction); rather, the intrinsic end formulation of the imperative expresses an ideal that renders the principles of duty intelligible or even expectable.

Ross apparently thought that the existence of a theoretical account of the prima facie duties is inconsistent with their self-evidence, at least if they are deducible from some more general principle. He may well have taken it to be also inconsistent with their plurality. But, to take the second point first, the existence of such an account would not entail that there really is just one duty, only that one moral principle can be a unifying ground for others. Unification of a set of principles in relation to a single one, say one that entails or explains them or both, does not imply that there is really only one principle. Nor does exhibiting several duties as serving a larger one entail that there is just one duty (as opposed to one basic duty). Regarding the first point — that unification of the Rossian principles of duty is not inconsistent with their self-evidence — the truth of a theoretical unification of the kind imagined would, to be sure, be inconsistent with the strong axiomatic self-evidence of these other principles. That, however, is not the kind of self-evidence to which Ross is committed by his account of how we know the moral principles corresponding to his prima facie duties.

If, then, we take that account, rather than Ross's analogy to logic and mathematics, as primary in understanding his intuitionism, we arrive at the surprising conclusion that a Rossian intuitionist — even construed as also a moral rationalist — can allow for *epistemically overdetermined moral knowledge*. There can be a moral theory that both explains and provides inferential grounds for moral propositions which, given sufficient reflection, can also be seen, non-inferentially, to be true. What is, at one time, only a conclusion of reflection — and in that way a candidate to be an intuition — can become a conclusion of inference. It can still derive support simultaneously from both the newly found premises for it and any remaining intuitive sense of its truth. An appropriately non-inferential, pretheoretical sense of its truth may survive one's inferring it from premises. Seeing a thing in a new light need not prevent one's still seeing it in its own light.[34]

To be sure, the categorical imperative is not immediately self-evident.[35] Indeed, it may not be self-evident at all, but knowable (assuming it is true) only on the basis

of a derivation from non-moral principles — or, as Ross might argue, as a generalization from more restricted, intuitively justified principles such as his own. That is not
the issue here. What unifies moral principles need not be self-evident; presumably it
need not even be a set of moral principles, but might come from a general theory of
practical reason.[36] The point is that once we appreciate that the kind of self-evidence
to which intuitionism is committed is only mediate, we can allow that intuitive
moral principles, even if they are self-evident, are knowable through premises as well
as by reflection on their content. We can also see that these moral principles can be
supported by their providing an account of our intuitions, and not just through a
direct intuition of their truth or self-evidence.

IV. Reflection as a Basis for Moral Judgments

If anything has emerged from this study as common to all the ways of knowing that
deserve to be called intuitive, it is reflection, above all reflection on the concepts
figuring in, and on the necessary implications of, the moral or other propositions
whose status is supposed to be knowable through intuition. The reflection may be as
brief as simply focusing clearly on the proposition, or it may require many sittings,
possibly spread over many years. It turns out, however, that what is knowable in
this reflective way — or can be at least justifiedly believed in this way — need not be
strongly axiomatic, in a sense implying that there cannot be epistemically independent grounds for it. What can be justifiedly believed "in its own terms" is not thereby
precluded from being justified by premises.

Intuitive Justification and Reflective Equilibrium

I have already shown how, from a broad moral principle such as the categorical
imperative taken as expressing respect for persons, one might try to derive the Rossian duties. Call this *justification from below* (from something plausibly held to be
"deeper"). I now want to argue that intuitionism — or at least the method of inquiry
that seems to be the core of it — can allow *justification from above*, in part by appeal
to what philosophers commonly call intuitions. We can then begin to articulate the
overall framework for moral theory that is a major concern of this essay.

In deriving intuitive moral principles from below, one does not presuppose
them, even for the sake of argument, but builds them from one or another kind of
supporting ground. By contrast, their justification from above proceeds by provisionally presupposing them and exploring the consequences one infers from them.
Above all, we do two sorts of things. First, we deduce from them what kinds of decisions we would make, and what kinds of lives we would lead, if we took the principles to be true and regularly acted on them. Second, we reflect on, as Ross would
put it, what we really think about these possibilities, that is, on our intuitions about
them. We might, for instance, contemplate a life in which we recognize duties of
beneficence versus one in which we do not, and consider whether, in the light of
what we really think about those lives and about the beneficent social practices they
would imply, the relevant duties still seem to be prima facie duties, as opposed to,

say, mere charities or even meddling with others. If we are satisfied by what we find, we regard the principles as confirmed, as we do scientific hypotheses borne out by predictions derived from them. Granted, we may *now* form an argument that seems to proceed from below: namely, that since the assumption of these principles has these "intuitively appealing" consequences (or best explains them), we may take the principles as likely to be true and to that extent as justified. But this mode of argument is not a route to discovery of its conclusion, as argument from below may be; and it need not proceed, like the latter, from epistemically independent premises, since some of the judgments we make about cases may be partly based on the principle we are testing.

Argument from above can also result in revising, rather than confirming, the principles we began with. We may find that if, for example, we restrict the cases in which promising yields a prima facie duty — say, to situations in which it is fully voluntary — we get a better principle. A Rossian view can surely countenance such a procedure, and using it may result in enhancing our justification as well as in our revising our initial view, whether that was justified or not.

We are now in a position to see something else. The use of reflection made by Ross is quite consistent with — and indeed seems to anticipate — the procedure of reflective equilibrium as described by (among others) John Rawls.[37] One can compare one's intuitions with each other, with those of people one respects, and with the results of applying plausible generalizations to the situations that the moral intuitions are about; and one can strive to get all these items — revising them if necessary — into a stable, coherent whole: this is the equilibrium resulting from one's comparative reflections. The intuitionist might, to be sure, use the procedure more to refine moral principles already accepted than to discover moral principles; but this is a contingent matter that depends on what principles are accepted at the start of the process and on how many new principles or refinements of old ones it produces.

How wide the appropriate equilibrium should be is also contingent, and is quite variable: whether, for instance, non-moral considerations such as psychological facts should be in equilibrium with a body of plausible moral principles is left open. Some styles of reflection might proceed from principle to consequence and back again; others, such as Ross's, from case to principle first. One might think about individual promises and thereby frame standards for promise-keeping, or instead posit initially plausible principles governing this activity and refine them by looking at cases.

In a moral theorist whose basic method is reflection of a kind we find both in Ross and in Rawls and others, the order of discovery can diverge, as it does in science, from the order of justification. We might, for example, first discover a principle on the basis of serendipity, by simply guessing at the truth about the subject we are investigating, and might later get justification, and pass from conjecture to belief, by doing confirmatory experiments; or we might both justify and discover a principle by deducing a new generalization from more comprehensive ones already established. But regardless of the kind of procedure by which we discover or justify moral principles, intuitions about cases should cohere with intuitions about the principles that apply to those cases. Inferential justification, moreover, can support intuitive justification regarding either cases or principles.

Ethical Reflection as a Justificatory Method

It is no accident that I have been trying to exhibit common ground between intu-itionism and some of its critics. It seems to me that when one looks closely at the best intuitionists, such as Ross, one finds something that transcends their own char-acterization of what they are doing. It is the *method of ethical reflection*: roughly, judiciously bringing to bear on moral questions, especially general ones such as what our duties are, careful reflection on what these questions involve. To take the case of promising as a source of moral duty, one reflects on what a promise is, on what a duty to keep it is, on what duties can conflict with that one, on what counts as a rea-son for action or — arguably equivalent to this — as an intrinsically good or bad thing, and on what human life would be like if we took certain kinds of acts to be duties, and regarded certain conflicts of duties as properly resolved in some particu-lar way. Facts, then, come into the process. Such reflection is what, more than any other method, seems to yield reliable intuitions (roughly, intuitions likely to be true), or at least intuitions we can rationally hope will remain credible as we con-tinue to reflect on them. Reliable intuitions may or may not be conclusions of reflec-tion.[38]

Inference of any kind, whether from below or above, can figure in the reflection that generates or tests intuitions. But the primary case of such reflection is that in which one arrives at conclusions of reflection or at (temporally) immediate intu-itions, not at inferential judgments. If no such primacy of non-inferential reflection were recognized, then we would have to ask what else might serve to ground one's premises for inference.[39] Factual assumptions can figure in such reflections — and must if the reflections concern what specific action to take under various future con-tingencies. But in the most basic cases, we consider what ought to be done *given* cer-tain factual assumptions, for instance the assumption that we have made a promise which the promisee expects us to keep, or that we can help someone and we have no conflicting demands on us. For purposes of justifying general moral standards, the most important epistemic element is our intuitions regarding cases with fac-tual assumptions built in, not those assumptions themselves. We may need to make observations to determine whether keeping a specific promise, say to return a set of car keys, will actually harm the promisee; but on the assumption that no harm will be produced, it will be intuitive that one has a prima facie duty to keep the promise.[40]

The framework for ethical theorizing I have introduced here might be called *ethical reflectionism*. Its major thesis is that the method of reflection is and deserves to be our basic method for justifying ethical judgments, especially general moral principles or general judgments of what has intrinsic value, and among our basic methods for discovering such judgments. Discovery is, as in scientific inquiry, less constrained than justification. If tea leaves help us think up hypotheses, we may use them; but we may accept the hypotheses we thus arrive at only if they pass certain rigorous tests. By attacking the most common conception of intuitionism — the infallibilist, immoderately rationalist, special faculty view — I have tried to make intuitionism more plausible, with reflection as its chief method.

It is not only intuitionism, however, that uses the method of reflection; the method seems implicit in any appeal to intuitions as a way of justifying, refining, or discovering general moral principles. Using it does not commit one to intuitionism. A non-intuitionist empiricist, for example, might hold that our intuitions reflect a sense, perhaps a quasi-perceptual one, of moral properties. There might, after all, be evolutionary reasons why injustice should be grasped directly, say by the application of conscience, conceived as an empirical moral faculty, even if injustice is a natural phenomenon and can also be inferentially known to exist. We respond non-inferentially and almost instinctively to the difference between happy and angry faces, yet this does not preclude their being characterized theoretically and known inferentially. In responding to Katherine's smile I do not and probably could not single out the lines and movements that produce my pleasure, but the psychology of perception could in principle describe the causal connections in detail. Ethical reflectionism allows for a similarly complex relation between morally sensitive observers and various moral phenomena. We can feel indignation over one person's slighting of another even if we cannot put our finger on what it was in the demeanor of the first that offended the second.

In taking reflection seriously as a ground of justified non-inferential judgment, then, one need not commit oneself to any particular account of why it succeeds. For similar reasons, one can combine it with various kinds of ethical theory. Ross may have thought, as is natural for a rationalist, that one grasps necessary relations between propositions or concepts, but one could also hold, as an empiricist might, that we simply regard deeds like lying and killing as causing pain — a contingent (causal) feature of those actions — and hence as prima facie wrong. This sense could precede, rather than derive from, hedonistic utilitarianism, just as the sense of duty to keep a promise of a certain kind one is reflecting on can — and Ross seemed to think does — precede, rather than derive from, the conviction that in general one has a duty to keep promises. He apparently was (as suggested earlier) a particularistic intuitionist, rather than a generalist: he took us to apprehend moral facts more basically in, or at least in the context of reflecting on, particular instances, whether actual or hypothetical, than in the abstract and universal propositions we know through (but not by ordinary inductive inference from) these instances. By contrast, there are places in which John Stuart Mill talks as if what is primary is the grasp of pleasure and pain as intrinsically good and bad, and from this, inferentially or otherwise, we see individual phenomena as good or bad, and right or wrong.[41] Use of the method of reflection does not commit one to either the particularist or the generalist view.

Similar considerations show that the method is neutral with respect to the controversy between naturalism — by which I mean roughly the view that nature is all there is and the truths of nature are the only basic truths — and non-naturalism. There may be a sense in which ethical reflectionism is *methodologically a priori*, for its major demand is that we think adequately about moral questions, using, above all, the concepts essential in their formulation. It does not imply that moral concepts are analyzable in any particular way; and, epistemically, it is compatible with various different accounts of the grounds of the justification that, in its non-skeptical forms, it takes reflection to yield. This justification can derive from an a priori grasp of conceptual relations or from an empirical sense of what sorts of acts have morally relevant properties, such as causing pain. Either approach is consistent with various forms of naturalism as well as with non-naturalism.

Different theorists may put differing constraints on the appropriate kind of reflection. At the extreme rationalist end of the reflectionist spectrum, where some forms of intuitionism may lie, we may need only to think of what rational beings are in order to see by reflection what general moral principles apply to them. At the empiricist end, it may be held that since only pleasure and pain are intrinsically good, only reflection that reveals plausible assumptions about how action affects them can yield general moral principles. Any plausible theory, of course, will require our making factual assumptions in *applying* moral principles to daily conduct, and so in reflecting on what concrete action is a duty or is otherwise morally appropriate. I cannot, from a sense of obligation to keep a promise, know that I should actually do the deed unless I have adequate grounds to believe that I in fact promised to do it; and I cannot know that I should, all things considered, do it, unless I can have adequate grounds to believe that it will not violate stronger duties I have.[42]

The method of reflection is also neutral with respect to ethical noncognitivism, which we may construe as roughly the view that in making moral judgments we do not perform the cognitive act of stating facts (or falsehoods) but express attitudes, typically of (moral) approval or disapproval. We are, in this way, being "prescriptive" (or evaluative), not "descriptive." Noncognitivism takes the objects of reflection to be in crucial cases non-propositional, but it allows for moral justification of the attitudes that one expresses in making moral judgments. We must often reflect on whether certain pro or con attitudes are appropriate, but we may bring facts and logic to bear in appraising them: inconsistency and factual error make an attitude objectionable, even though not false. This justification is potentially grounded in reflection, and presumably in intuitions of some kind, in a way analogous to the grounding that other theorists take to justify moral judgments construed as true or false. What cognitivists may take to show that I should keep a promise, noncognitivists may take to show that it is reasonable to have the positive attitude which I express in saying I ought to keep that promise.[43]

One might wonder whether any substantive view is ruled out by ethical reflectionism. Given its methodological character, it is not meant to rule out any particular ethical position. But an ethical view might be partly methodological and thereby ruled out. Ethical reflectionism seems inconsistent with a crude divine command view (perhaps never seriously held) for which an act-type's being commanded, or forbidden, by God, for instance as indicated in Scriptures, are — by definition — its only morally relevant properties: moral properties are grounded wholly, directly, and indefeasibly, in divine will. For here reflection with contrary results would be irrelevant; discovery of properties independently relevant to moral judgment is precluded. Reflectionism is not inconsistent with the theory that moral truths are ultimately (non-definitionally) grounded in divine will and knowable jointly through natural theology and Scripture — a view that can be argued to be supported by reflection of an appropriate kind. A second view ruled out by reflectionism would be an instinctual theory that grounds moral knowledge and justified moral beliefs — by definition — in a moral instinct, one that makes the kinds of brute deliverances sometimes thought to be characteristic of a faculty of intuition.[44] For here there would be no need for reflection and perhaps even no role for it: certain judgmental tendencies are simply built into us, whether by evolutionary factors, divine artifice, or some other power. It is quite otherwise with certain moral sense theories, or their contemporary successors that claim we have moral perceptions arising in moral experience and capable of conferring moral justification in a way similar to the generation of perceptual justification from vision and hearing.[45] For the relevant kind of perception grounded in moral experience is not only conceptual but requires the sort of sensitive understanding needed even to "intuit" a truth straightaway. Such intuition is the minimal case of reflection as I construe it.

V. Modified Ethical Intuitionism

I hope by now to have shown that there is good reason to think that ethical reflectionism is a framework of moral inquiry which is far more common than it may appear. Let me reiterate why it may seem otherwise and, in response to objections to the framework, cite some of its advantages. We can then consider intuitionism as a restricted case of reflectionism.

Because what is known through reflection is commonly taken to be a priori, moral empiricists, and even non-empiricists who stress moral experience, may reject ethical reflectionism. Because reflection (often) yields non-inferential judgments, which may seem indefeasible, fallibilists may also reject the view. Because, in its paradigmatic, cognitive uses, reflection appears to yield justification or knowledge regarding moral propositions, noncognitivists may reject the view. Because, in being neutral with respect to naturalism in ethics, it leaves open whether moral properties may be natural, non-naturalists, including the historically prominent intuitionists, may reject it.[46] And because the view allows that what is known non-inferentially and intuitively at one time may also be known, at another time, by inference from above or below, and in that sense "proved," traditional intuitionists in moral epistemology may reject it. But none of these theorists need reject ethical reflectionism. It is neutral with respect to rationalism and empiricism; it is, in its most plausible forms, not only fallibilistic but also easily combined with the procedure of reflective equilibrium; it is consistent with noncognitivism and with naturalism; and it can be combined with an overarching moral theory that unifies the disparate moral judgments which intuitionists have commonly thought to be incapable of justification by appeal to premises, yet it allows that those judgments can be self-evident and thereby non-inferentially knowable.

Ethical reflectionism is not as such a form of ethical intuitionism, but its truth provides the best explanation of what the most credible forms of ethical intuitionism are committed to. In these forms, I suggest, ethical intuitionism is, in outline, the view that we can have, in the light of appropriate reflection on the content of moral judgments and moral principles, intuitive (hence non-inferential) justification for holding them. Most of the plausible versions of intuitionism also endorse a plurality of moral principles (though Moore is notable for holding an overarching, ideal utilitarian principle of right action), and most versions are also rationalist, holding that there are a priori moral principles. But an intuitionist could be an empiricist, taking intuition to be capable of providing an experiential ground for moral judgments or principles. Intuitionists typically hold that moral knowledge as well as moral justification can be intuitive, but the major ones are not committed to the view that this justification or knowledge is indefeasible, and they tend to deny that it is.

If the arguments of this essay indicate how intuitionism as just broadly characterized can be plausible, they also show how an overall rationalistic intuitionist theory like Ross's can be strengthened. Moreover, if what is said earlier in support of reflectionism indicates how an intuitionist view in moral epistemology is compatible with empiricism — even if it also brings out why it is natural for intuitionists to be rationalists — it also shows how a rationalist moral epistemology can be freed of the apparent dogmatism and associated arbitrariness, the implausible philosophy of mind, and the immoderate epistemic principles often attributed to it. Let me comment on each of these points and in that light proceed to some conclusions by way of overall appraisal of intuitionism conceived, as it should be given the overall views of Ross and its other major prominent proponents, as a rationalist view.

I will be stressing the rationalism of the reconstructed Rossian intuitionism developed earlier — construed as the view that we have intuitive justification both for some of our particular moral judgments and for a plurality of mediately self-evident moral principles — because the controversy between empiricism and rationalism as epistemological perspectives is apparently very much with us in ethical theory, despite how few ethical theorists are openly committed to either perspective. I believe, moreover, that most of the plausible objections to a broadly Rossian intuitionism are either motivated by empiricism or best seen as objections, not to its appeal to intuitions but to the underlying rationalism of the view: roughly, to its taking reason, as opposed to observation, to be capable of supplying justification for substantive truths, such as (if they are indeed true) Ross's moral principles of prima facie duty.

Is intuitionism dogmatic, as some have held?[47] It might well be dogmatic to claim both that we have intuitive, certain knowledge of what our prima facie duties are *and* that we cannot ground that knowledge on any kind of evidence. But I have argued that Ross, at least, is not committed to our having "certain knowledge" here — where the certainty in question implies having indefeasible justification for moral propositions. Far from it. Despite his in some ways unfortunate analogy between moral principles and, on the other side, elementary logical and mathematical ones, he provides a place for reflective equilibrium to enhance — or override — our justification for an "intuitive" moral judgment. Nor does anything he must hold, *qua* intuitionist, preclude his allowing a systematization of the moral principles he suggests in terms of something more general. If such systematization is achieved, then contrary to what the dogmatism charge would lead one to expect, that systematization might provide reasons for the principles and a possible source of correctives for certain intuitions or apparently intuitive moral judgments.

From these points about the issue of dogmatism, it should be evident that intuitionism also need not be arbitrary, in the sense that it permits simply positing, as reasonable moral standards, any that one finds "intuitive" and then claiming to know them. Intuitionism requires that before one can be intuitively justified in accepting a moral standard, one must have an adequate understanding of the proposition in question; this often requires reflection. What reflection yields as intuitive is not arbitrary; and although products of prejudice or whim may masquerade as intuitive, this does not imply that they cannot be discovered to be deceptive. Reflection can correct its own initial results — or even its repeated results. In sophisticated forms, intuitionism may also require an appeal to reflective equilibrium as a condition of justified adherence to a set of basic principles. This procedure often provides justifying reasons for, or for that matter indicates a need for revision or withdrawal of, the posited principle.

Moreover (and this is something not noted earlier), given how intuitions are understood — as deriving from the exercise of reason and as having evidential weight — it is incumbent on conscientious intuitionists to factor into their reflective equilibrium the apparent intuitions of *others*.[48] Ross appealed repeatedly to "what we really think" and drew attention to the analogy between intuitions in ethics and perceptions in science. Intuitions, then, are not properly conceived as arbitrary. They normally have a history in human society and a genesis in reflection. Moreover, anything arbitrarily posited would be hard-pressed to survive the kind of reflection to which conscientious intuitionists will subject their basic moral standards. Thus, even if an intuition might arise as an arbitrary cognition, it would not necessarily have prima facie justification and could easily be defeated by other intuitions or those together with further elements in the reflective equilibrium a reasonable intuitionist would seek.

One might protest, in response to some of what I have said in arguing that intuitionism is not dogmatic or arbitrary, that if Moore and Ross claim strong axiomatic status for their candidate basic moral principles, one should take that claim as essential to intuitionism, at least insofar as they are paradigmatic intuitionists. I reject this principle of interpretation on the ground that the best theoretical classification of a philosopher's view comes not from simply putting together all its proffered theses but from considering its overall purposes and thrust. If, moreover, a view takes its name from a major phenomenon — such as intuition — and if, in addition, the relevant notion is pivotal throughout the development of the theory, there is some reason to take the overall operation of that notion in the theory as more important in characterizing the theory than relatively isolated theses which proponents of the theory advance about the notion. This certainly applies to what I have developed here in connection with Ross's view: a reconstruction of the theory intended to be among its most plausible versions, even if that means only strong continuity with its historical embodiments rather than a descriptive articulation thereof.

We can perhaps be briefer on the associated philosophy of mind, if only because the chief issue we encounter here applies to philosophy in general. Is there any reason to think that a rationalist epistemology, in ethics or elsewhere, entails an implausible philosophy of mind? Does the view presuppose either a mysterious mental faculty or a scientifically unlikely mode of access to entities that cannot causally affect the brain? It *may* be that there can be a priori knowledge or a priori justification only if we in some sense grasp abstract entities, such as the concept of a promise, where this grasp is conceived as something more than our having a set of behavioral tendencies, including linguistic ones, and requires some kind of apprehension of abstract entities that do not figure in causal relations. But if this is so, it is not obvious that the comprehension in question is either obscure or in any event not required for a grasp of arithmetic truths and other apparently a priori propositions essential for both everyday reasoning and scientific inquiry.

It is true that we will have a simpler philosophy of mind, at least ontologically, if we can avoid positing any "non-empirical" objects, such as numbers or propositions or concepts. But if properties are abstract entities, as many philosophers hold, then it is not clear that even empirical knowledge of generalizations about the physical world can be known apart from a grasp of abstract entities. I believe it is fair to say that there is at present no clearly adequate, thoroughly empiricist account of justification in general, applicable to logic and mathematics as well as to epistemic principles.

I turn now to the matter of epistemic principles, roughly principles indicating the bases or nature of knowledge and justification — say that if, on the basis of a clear visual impression of faces, I believe there are faces before me, then I am justified in so believing. There is no conclusive reason to think that Ross or other intuitionists are committed — by their intuitionism, at least — to implausible epistemic principles. I have already suggested that they need not, as intuitionists, hold the principle that if a proposition is self-evident, then it cannot be evidenced by anything else. I now want to suggest that Ross's basic principles of duty are at least candidates for a priori justification in the way they should be if they are mediately self-evident. Keeping in mind what constitutes a prima facie duty, consider how we would regard some native speaker of English who denied that there is (say) a prima facie duty not to injure other people and — to get the right connection with what Ross meant by 'duty'— meant by this something implying that doing it would not be even prima facie wrong. Our first thought is that there is a misunderstanding of some key term, such as 'prima facie'. Indeed, I doubt that anyone not in the grip of a competing theory would deny the proposition.

Imagine, however, a steadfast instrumentalist about practical rationality: someone who holds that one has a reason to do something only in virtue of its advancing one's basic desires, and then (let us suppose) insists that doing something can be wrong only if there is reason for one not to do it. Such a person would say that there *need* not be in anyone a basic desire advanced by not injuring others, so Ross's principle of non-maleficence is at best contingent.

Sophisticated versions of instrumentalism are quite powerful, and they are especially plausible in the current climate because they appear to be consistent both with empiricism and with naturalism, yet instrumentalists need not claim to reduce normative properties to non-normative ones.[49] This is no place to explore instrumentalism in detail.[50] But we should notice an implication of it: that either there is nothing intrinsically good or bad, including pleasure and pain, or, if there is, that the existence of things having intrinsic value, even things within our grasp, provides, apart from what we or someone else actually wants, no reason for action. This will seem to go against many intuitions, in the standard sense of 'intuition' that is neutral with respect to intuitionism. Is there not a reason why I should not burn a friend with a red-hot iron (and is this not an evil of some kind), even if at the moment, perhaps because my brain has been tampered with, I have no desires bearing on the matter? And even if I have lost all motivation in life, is there not reason, and indeed reason for me, not to burn myself? If the answer is, as it seems to be, affirmative, then there can be non-instrumental reasons favoring my action.[51]

I have granted for the sake of argument something intuitionists would generally (and I think plausibly) deny: that one could justifiedly hold that there are things of intrinsic value, yet deny that they provide, independently of actual desires, even prima facie reasons for action. Imagine that an opponent of intuitionism takes this route. What would justify holding that there *is* anything of such value? It is not obvious that one could have an empirical justification of this thesis. To be sure, there are things people *value intrinsically*, for example toward which they take a positive attitude directly rather than on the basis of believing these things to be a means to something further. But this psychological fact about human *valuation* does not entail the normative conclusion that the things in question actually *have* intrinsic *value*.[52] I believe that reflection will show that it is at least far from clear that justification for believing that there is anything of intrinsic value — including intrinsic moral value — does not have to rest at least in part on a priori considerations of the kind Ross describes. But I put this forward only as a challenge. The issue is highly debatable.

What is perhaps less controversial is that if we do not ascribe to reason the minimal power required in order for a moderate intuitionism of the kind I have described to be a plausible theory, then we face serious problems that must be solved before any instrumentalist or empiricist ethical theory is plausible.[53] For one thing, instrumentalists must account for their fundamental principle that if, on my beliefs, an action serves a basic (roughly, non-instrumental) desire of mine, then there is a reason for me to perform the action. This principle appears to be a better candidate for mediate self-evidence than for empirical confirmation.[54] This is not to say that a moderate intuitionism is true. The point is that unless reason has sufficient power to make that principle a plausible candidate for truth, then it is not clear that instrumentalist theories are plausible candidates either.

If I have been roughly correct in this defense of a reconstructed Rossian view, then intuitionism in moral epistemology, and in the foundations of ethics, should be a more serious contender for contemporary allegiance than it is. For many of the same reasons, there is more room for a rationalist moral epistemology than is generally realized. Once it is seen how reflection of an at least methodologically a priori kind is central in ethical theorizing, some of the major obstacles in the way of a rationalist account of the foundations of ethics are eliminated. There is much to commend a fallibilist, intuitionistic moral rationalism that uses reflection as a justificatory method in the ways described here, encompassing both intuitions as prima facie justified inputs to ethical theorizing and reflective equilibrium as a means of extending and systematizing those inputs. Whatever our verdicts on intuitionism and rationalism, however, when they are rightly understood they can be seen to carry less baggage than often attributed to them and to provide, in their best embodiments, a method of ethical inquiry that may be reasonably used in approaching any basic moral problem.

Notes

This essay has benefited from presentation to various audiences, especially at the 1994 Moral Epistemology Conference at Dartmouth College. I am also grateful for comments by Malia Brink, Bernard Gert, Christopher Kulp, Hugh J. McCann, Stephan Sencerz, William Throop, Mark Timmons, Douglas Weber, Patrick Yarnell, Nick Zangwill, and, especially, Walter Sinnott-Armstrong.

1. John Rawls comes to mind here, especially A *Theory of Justice* (Cambridge: Harvard University Press, 1971), p. 34. The following passage from a review of Rawls's *Political Liberalism* (New York: Columbia University Press, 1993) and Thomas K. Seung's *Intuition and Construction* (New Haven: Yale University Press, 1993) typifies contemporary attitudes toward intuitionism: "Intuitionism makes metaphysical claims and epistemological demands that run counter to modern thought . . . [W]hen science emphasizes observation and verification, can we still believe in a 'brooding omnipresence in the sky'?" See William Powers Jr., "Constructing Liberal Political Theory," *Texas Law Review* 72, no. 2 (1993), p. 456. (Seung himself defends a Platonic intuitionism; this passage is presumably meant to represent what Powell takes Seung to consider wrong with intuitionism of the kind found in Ross, to be examined later in this chapter.) For further critical discussion of intuitionism (and a good example of a theorist who often appeals to intuitions but rejects Rossian intuitionism) see Jonathan Dancy, *Moral Reasons* (Oxford: Basil Blackwell, 1993), esp. chs. 4–6.

2. See W. D. Ross, *The Right and the Good* (Oxford: Oxford University Press, 1930; reprint ed., (Indianapolis: Hackett Publishing Co., 1988), esp. ch. 2, pp. 16–39. Rawls finds the pluralism so important that he considers it the basic feature of ethical intuitionism, though he grants that intuitionism is usually taken to have other important properties. See A *Theory of Justice*, pp. 34–35. According to Bernard Williams, in the 1950s and 1960s "it was taken for granted that intuitionism in ethics was an epistemological doctrine . . . the kind of view held, for instance, by W. D. Ross and H. A. Prichard." "What Does Intuitionism Imply?" in R. Dancy, J. Moravcsik, and C. Taylor, eds., *Human Agency* (Stanford: Stanford University Press, 1988), p. 198. Williams credits Rawls with changing "our understanding of the term" so as to "restore an earlier state of affairs" (ibid.). For William K. Frankena, "[a]n intuitionist must believe in simple indefinable properties, properties that are of a peculiar non-natural or normative sort, a priori or nonempirical concepts, and self-evident or synthetic necessary propositions." See *Ethics*, 2nd ed. (Englewood Cliffs, N.J.: Prentice-Hall, 1973), p. 103.

3. I am not alone in so conceiving the matter; see Walter Sinnott-Armstrong's valuable account of intuitionism in *The Encyclopedia of Ethics* (New York and London: Garland Publishing Co., 1992), pp. 628–30.

4. See Ross, *The Right and the Good*, p. 21.

5. Ross often used 'actual duty' where I use 'final duty', but this is misleading: as explained later, even an overridden duty is actually possessed.

6. Ross himself spoke this way: "I suggest '*prima facie* duty' or 'conditional duty' as a brief way of referring to this characteristic . . . which an act has, in virtue of being of a certain kind (e.g. the keeping of a promise), of being an act which would be a duty proper if it were not at the same time of another kind which is morally significant" (*The Right and the Good*, p. 19).

7. He contrasts his view with that of "Professor Moore and Dr. Rashdall, that there is only the duty of producing good, and that all 'conflicts of duties' should be resolved by asking 'by which action will most good be produced'?" Ibid., pp. 18–19.

8. Ibid., pp. 29–30. Cf. H. A. Prichard, "Does Moral Philosophy Rest on a Mistake?" (1912), in his *Moral Obligation* (Oxford: Oxford University Press, 1949). The mistake is "sup-

posing the possibility of proving what can only be apprehended directly by an act of moral thinking" (p. 16).

9. Ibid., pp. 31 and 33. Ross's examples show that he is thinking of the possibility that an act has some properties in virtue of which it is prima facie right and some in virtue of which it is prima facie wrong, and in such cases "we come to believe something not self-evident at all, but an object of probable opinion, viz. that this particular act is (not *prima facie* right but) actually right" (p. 33). The note on p. 33 admits his overstating the no-general-description claim; his point could be taken to be a version of the thesis that no factual description entails an *actual* obligation, but might also be considered epistemic: no set of facts makes it self-evident, even if a set of facts does entail, that a specific act is one's actual duty. The crucial point is that Rossian intuitionism does not claim that intuition yields knowledge of what to do in conflict cases. For Ross it would be a mistake to say, "Intuitionism is so called because it says intuition is what tells us what duty prevails," as remarked by Joel Feinberg in *Reason and Responsibility* (Belmont, Calif.: Wadsworth Publishing Co., 1993), p. 445. Regarding what to do given conflicts of duty Ross cites Aristotle's dictum "The decision rests with perception," which he did not identify with apprehension or anything else plausibly taken as a kind of intuition (*The Right and the Good*, pp. 41–42).

10. Ibid., pp. 39–41.

11. The quotation is from p. 41; for the primacy of reflection on specific cases see, e.g., pp. 41–42. In *The Foundations of Ethics* (Oxford: Oxford University Press, 1939), he says, of "insight into the basic principles of morality," that it is not based on "a fairly elaborate consideration of the probable consequences" of certain types of acts: "When we consider a particular act as a lie, or as the breaking of a promise . . . we do not need to, and do not, fall back on a remembered general principle; we see the individual act to be by its very nature wrong" (pp. 172–73). Speaking approvingly of Aristotle, Ross said of right acts that while first "done without any thought of their rightness," when "a certain degree of mental maturity" was reached, "their rightness was not deduced from any general principle; rather the general principle was later recognized by intuitive induction as being implied in the general judgments already passed on particular acts" (p. 170). The reference to induction is not meant to imply that the knowledge of "basic principles of morality" is inferential. As the later intuitionist A. C. Ewing put it in referring to intuitive induction, it "is not reasoning at all but intuition or immediate insight helped by examples." See "Reason and Intuition," *Proceedings of the British Academy* 27 (1941), reprinted in his *Non-Linguistic Philosophy* (London: George Allen and Unwin, 1968), p. 38, note 1.

12. This is relevant to problems of euthanasia. I would stress that the absence of any a priori hierarchy does not prevent Ross's countenancing either prima facie generalizations to the effect that one duty is stronger than another or generalizations to the effect that under certain conditions a type of act, such as unplugging a respirator, is preferable to another, say a fatal injection. He says, e.g., "[N]ormally promise-keeping comes before benevolence" and then *roughly* specifies the conditions under which it does (*The Right and the Good*, p. 19).

13. This may be in part what leads R. B. Brandt (among others) to consider intuitionism as such committed to the possibility of intuitively grasping self-evidence, as opposed to truth. See *Ethical Theory* (Englewood Cliffs, N.J.: Prentice-Hall, 1959), ch. 8. Cf. Jonathan Harrison: "According to this view [intuitionism], a person who can grasp the truth of ethical generalizations does not acquire them as a result of a process of ratiocination; he just sees without argument that they are and must be true, and true of all possible worlds." "Ethical Objectivism," *The Encyclopedia of Philosophy* (New York: Macmillan, 1967).

14. I do not think that this point is contradicted by Ross's *Foundations of Ethics*,.

15. G. E. Moore, *Principia Ethica* (Cambridge: Cambridge University Press, 1903), p. x. See also p. 145. Cf. Henry Sidgwick, 7th ed. *The Methods of Ethics* Macmillan: (London,

1907): citing "an ambiguity in the use of the term 'intuition'," he says, "[B]y calling any affirmation as to the rightness or wrongness of actions 'intuitive', I do not mean to prejudice the question as to its ultimate validity. . . . I only mean that its truth is apparently known immediately. . . . [A]ny such 'intuition' may turn out to have an element of error, which subsequent reflection and comparison may enable us to correct" (p. 211). For detailed explication of Moore and an ethical theory in the Moorean tradition, see Panayot Butchvarov, *Skepticism in Ethics* (Bloomington: Indiana University Press, 1989). For further pertinent discussion and a number of helpful references, see Caroline J. Simon, "The Intuitionist Argument," *Southern Journal of Philosophy* 28 (1990).

16. Such fallibility is not strictly entailed by the defeasibility of the justification of the intuition in question. An intuition of a logical truth could be defeasible — as where one finds what looks on careful reflection like a disproof — without being fallible; one could thus lose justification for the proposition even though, objectively, one's intuition, being of a logical truth, could not have been in error.

17. I restrict discussion to *propositional intuitions — intuitions that*, intuitions of some proposition as true, as opposed to *property intuitions — intuitions of*, roughly, apprehensions of some property. Suppose, however, that the former must be based on the latter — e.g. an intuition that a triangle has three sides might have to be based on an intuitive grasp of the nature of a triangle (or, perhaps better, of the concept of a triangle). The points to follow concerning propositional intuitions will hold whether or not there is such an epistemic dependency.

18. A. C. Ewing is explicit on the point, at least for basic intuitions. See, e.g., *Ethics* (London: English Universities Press, 1953), p. 136, where he says that "propositions, particularly in ethics but also in other fields of thought, sometimes present themselves to a person in such a way that he . . . knows or rationally believes them to be true without having reasons or at least seems to himself to do so. . . . [S]ome ethical propositions must be known immediately if any are to be known at all." Cf. his *The Fundamental Questions of Philosophy* (London: Routledge and Kegan Paul, 1951), pp. 48–49.

19. Ross even comments on the difficulty of determining exactly what a promise is (*The Right and the Good*, p. 35).

20. An intuition may also be caused by commitment to a theory, as where reflection on the theory leads one to explore a topic and one thereby forms intuitions about it. But this causal dependence of the intuition on the theory has no necessary bearing on the justificatory status of the former.

21. To some readers this will need argument or further explanation; both are given in some detail in my *The Structure of Justification* (Cambridge and New York: Cambridge University Press, 1993), esp. ch. 4, "The Foundationalism-Coherentism Controversy: Hardened Stereotypes and Overlapping Theories."

22. Sidgwick, e.g., speaks of our discerning "certain general rules with really clear and finally valid intuition" (*The Methods of Ethics*, pp. 100–104).

23. Kant might not find the singular proposition intuitive *at all*, at least prior to one's grasp of the moral generalization applying to it. He stresses that it is a disservice to morality to derive it from examples — *Foundations of the Metaphysics of Morals*, trans. Lewis White Beck (New York: Liberal Arts Press, 1959), 408; this, however, apparently indicates a rejection of particularism and a view about the relative *priority* of intuitions about examples vs. generalizations, rather than a commitment to the view that we cannot have intuitions about examples.

24. Two qualifications will help. First, if the belief is based on anything *other* than understanding the proposition, that understanding must still be a sufficient basis (in a sense I cannot explicate now). Second, there may be a non-truth-entailing use of 'self-evident', which would allow for false and hence unknowable self-evident propositions; but I assume that any

such use is at best non-standard. What is more controversial about my characterization is that — apparently — only a priori propositions satisfy it. Note, however, that the analysandum is self-evidence simpliciter, not self-evidence *for S*. There is some plausibility in saying that it is self-evident, for me, that I exist. I leave open whether such cases illustrate a kind of self-evidence, but the relevant proposition asserting my existence is surely not self-evident.

25. Someone might argue that this is not evident in itself, since it is knowable only through knowledge that (1) first cousins are children of siblings and (2) if there never have been any siblings then there never have been any children of siblings. But (1) is a definitional truth, in a sense implying that (2) simply *is* the proposition in question — that if there never have been any siblings, then there never have been any first cousins — formulated with 'children of siblings' in place of 'first cousins'. Seeing its truth requires understanding what it says, but not separately believing a definition and inferring the proposition from that as a premise. Cf. the more complicated proposition that first cousins have at least one pair of grandparents in common.

26. Two clarifications. (1) Assuming one cannot reflect in the relevant way on the concepts in question without *some* kind of understanding of them, I take it that there is a level of understanding of mediately self-evident propositions, or at least of parts of them, not by itself sufficient for justification but capable of leading to that as the understanding develops by reflection. (2) The term 'normal adults' is vague, but that begs no questions here; the problem is largely eliminable by relativizing, making the basic notion mediately self-evident *for S*, or for adults with a certain level of conceptual sophistication.

27. The suggested characterization of an immediately self-evident proposition does not entail that such a proposition is compelling; but it would at least be true that for normal persons in normal circumstances it would be compelling. None of this rules out there being a notion of self-evidence *for a person*; but the concept we need is that of a self-evident proposition, and that is my focus. That concept has implicit *reference* to persons, or at least minds; but this does not make it *relative* to persons, in the sense that we cannot call a proposition self-evident except *to* some particular set of persons.

28. This paragraph and the remainder of this section overlap parts of ch. 4.

29. This is a broadly foundationalist assumption. I defend it in *The Structure of Justification*. For further defenses and relevant references see W. P. Alston, *Epistemic Justification* (Ithaca and London: Cornell University Press, 1989), and Paul K. Moser, *Knowledge and Evidence* (Cambridge and New York: Cambridge University Press, 1989). For a contrasting view applied to moral judgments, see David Copp, "Considered Judgments and Moral Justification: Conservatism in Moral Theory," in David Copp and David Zimmerman, eds., *Morality, Reason, and Truth* (Totowa, N.J.: Rowman and Allanheld, 1985).

30. Two comments are in order. First, while priority may suggest the Aristotelian notion of being "more easily known," that elusive notion is not the one characterized in the text. Second, I am taking the provability relation to be, unlike mere logical derivability, asymmetrical, so that the relevant premise is *not* provable from the proposition it can be used to prove, and is in that way prior to the latter). Third, some might require strong axiomatic status as a condition for being an axiom at all, but notice that a proposition can systematize a body of theorems even if derivable from some prior proposition, and even without being immediately self-evident. That it might itself be a theorem relative to something else does not change this, though it does suggest that an *elegant* system would put in place of the proposition a prior, strongly axiomatic one.

31. In *Posterior Analytics* 72b, where Aristotle introduced his famous epistemic regress argument, he seems to imply that the appropriate foundations for knowledge must be strongly axiomatic. But even what cannot be moved higher in the epistemic hierarchy of a person might perhaps be moved *out* of it: indefeasibility (the impossibility of one's justification's being overridden) is perhaps not entailed even by strong axiomaticity.

32. For a somewhat Rossian case against there being a correct answer to the second question by appeal to a derivation of moral principles from some overarching moral principle, see Bernard Gert, *Morality: A New Justification of the Moral Rules* (Oxford and New York: Oxford University Press, 1988).

33. Cf. Christine Swanton's point (noted after the previous passage was written), in a rigorous defense of intuitionism, that "there is no reason why an intuitionist could not appeal to such a conception in grounding both the first-order principles of the system and the second-order principles for resolving conflict. Such a conception may be a conception of human flourishing founded on an Aristotelian system of human virtue. . . . Alternatively, the underlying moral conception could be contractualist, involving an understanding of the point of morality as a system which renders possible co-operation amidst conflict of interest." "The Rationality of Ethical Intuitionism," *Australasian Journal of Philosophy* 65 (1987), p. 175. This line is not developed in relation to any account of self-evidence nor shown to be an option for Ross in particular. Moreover, the grounding is not said to be potentially deductive, though that is allowed and perhaps intended by the text. See also Sinnott-Armstrong, *The Encyclopedia of Ethics*, for a formulation of the consistency of intuitionism with a kind of derivability.

34. Perhaps in part because of the way Moore and Ross (among other intuitionists in moral epistemology) put their views, many philosophers have taken the intuitionist moral epistemology itself as a positive account of how general moral truths can be known noninferentially, to imply that these propositions cannot be justified inferentially. Speaking of Prichard, J. O. Urmson says, "Moral philosophy, regarded as the attempt to provide a basis and justification for common morality, was a mistaken enterprise because the essentials of common morality were immediately apprehended. . . . One can apprehend that to lie or break a promise is as such wrong, *so that any attempt to show that it is wrong . . . must be wrongheaded*" (italics added). See "Prichard and Knowledge," in Dancy, Moravcsik, and Taylor, *Human Agency*, p. 14. I maintain that the inference attributed to Prichard is invalid. Cf. Frankena, *Ethics*, p. 103.

35. Here and elsewhere I speak as if there were just one categorical imperative. Even if that is not so, the point here probably applies to all the formulations.

36. This possibility is explored by many writers. Plato and Aristotle surely explore it, as do Hume and Kant. Rawls's theory of justice explores it from a restricted, largely instrumentalist conception of rationality — only largely because, for one thing, he assumes that a rational person does not suffer from envy (*A Theory of Justice*, p. 143). Another approach, and relevant references, are provided in ch. 4. An examination of Rawls's assumption in relation to instrumentalism is given in ch. 9.

37. See *A Theory of Justice*, e.g., pp. 46–52. It is true that Rawls suggests that reflective equilibrium is a coherentist procedure, whereas Ross is a foundationalist; but Rawls is probably taking foundationalism to posit indefeasible starting points, as Ross need not do. A. C. Ewing is even more emphatically defeasibilist and fallibilist than Ross; see, e.g., "Reason and Intuition," pp. 58–63, and *Ethics*, ch. 8. If I am correct about intuitionism, then even if Rawls is right in saying that it is "not constructive" (p. 52), this limitation would be extrinsic. For discussion of Rawls's general strategy of ethical justification and of reflective equilibrium in particular (with an indication why it need not be viewed as a coherentist procedure), see R. B. Brandt, *A Theory of the Good and the Right* (Oxford: Oxford University Press, 1979), and Roger Ebertz, "Is Reflective Equilibrium a Coherence Method?," *Canadian Journal of Philosophy* (1993). Another valuable study of Rawlsian reflective equilibrium, with special attention to its use of intuitions, is Stefan Sencerz, "Moral Intuitions and Justification in Ethics," *Philosophical Studies* 50 (1986).

38. At least if we are realists, we will count intuitions reliable only if we believe we may

also hope they are true. For non-realists, reliability may be more a matter of, say, coherence over time. On either view, reliable intuitions may or may not be conclusions of reflection.

39. This point suggests that *some* kind of foundationalist assumptions underlie the method (as is certainly plain in Ross). That a moderate foundationalist approach is reasonable in general is defended in detail in *The Structure of Justification*. There is no implication, of course, that non-inferentially justified elements are indefeasible; and the method is fully compatible with the use of reflective equilibrium as a corrective and confirmational technique.

40. The notion of harm may not be purely "factual," but the factual components in it will serve our illustrative purposes. There may be other factors: perhaps if the promisee would, reflectively, no longer *want* us to keep the promise this would remove the very ground of our obligation; it would certainly weaken the prima facie obligation.

41. See esp. *Utilitarianism*, ch. 1.

42. This is a good place to note the relation of ethical reflectionism to R. B. Brandt's "qualified attitude" method for appraising moral judgments. We are to arrive at attitudes that are impartial, informed by an awareness of "relevant facts," not the result of an abnormal state of mind, and consistent and general. See *Ethical Theory*, esp. pp. 244–52. This method appears to be a (good) theoretical extension of the method of reflection, perhaps something like an application of it, and less basic. Would it not be by reflection that we determine (e.g.) what sorts of facts are relevant, what partiality is, and that partiality can vitiate moral judgment? It is arguable that reflection is not specifically moral if it does not take account of such factors as Brandt describes; but even if that is so, I want to leave open that the basic moral principles or standards might derive from the more general point of view of practical reason.

43. This higher-order proposition may be given either a cognitivist account as, say, a claim in metaethics, or a noncognitivist account as an evaluation, and what some cognitivists call self-evident propositions some noncognitivists might reconstrue as expressions of self-evidently rational attitudes. (I bypass problems about how 'self-evidently rational' might be characterized on such a view.)

44. Compare a reliabilism that says moral knowledge and justified moral beliefs can be produced by reliable processes to which we may have no access by reflection. This would not be ruled out by reflectionism so long as the results of the relevant processes can be validated by reflection (as is not the case for a crude divine command view), in which case we would have inductive evidence that moral beliefs of a certain kind, say those delivered by a moral sense, are true. Even if knowledge can arise in the former way, however, justification seems to require accessible grounds, as I have argued in *The Structure of Justification*. I am not aware of any ethical theorist's holding such a reliabilism about moral justification, but the position is a good foil for reflectionism.

45. For a specimen view of this sort see William Tolhurst, "On the Epistemic Value of Moral Experience," *Southern Journal of Philosophy* 29 (suppl.) (1991): 67–87. Cf. Michael DePaul, "The Highest Moral Knowledge and the Truth behind Internalism," and Adrian M. S. Piper, "Seeing Things," both in that issue (pp. 137–60 and 29–60).

46. I do not see the emphasis on non-natural properties that is so prominent in Moore as required by the core of Ross's view, and I therefore do not make non-naturalism a commitment of intuitionism in general.

47. See, e.g., Stephen C. Pepper, *Ethics* (New York: Appleton-Century-Crofts, 1960), p. 237.

48. On the importance of this in ethics see Margaret Urban Walker, "Skepticism, Authority, and Transparency," in Walter Sinnott-Armstrong and Mark Timmons, eds., *Moral Knowledge?* (New York and Oxford: Oxford University Press, 1996).

49. There is a temptation on the part of many instrumentalists to do this, as may be noted in places in Richard A. Fumerton's *Reason and Morality* (Ithaca and London: Cornell

University Press, 1990); for an indication of relevant passages see my review of this book in the *Philosophical Review* 101 (1992): 929–31.

50. Thomas Nagel's *The View from Nowhere* (Oxford and New York: Oxford University Press, 1986) and Bernard Gert's *Morality* are far-reaching critiques of instrumentalism; I have explored it in, e.g., *Practical Reasoning* (London and New York: Routledge, 1989) and "The Architecture of Reason," in *The Structure of Justification*. I offer an account and critique of ethical naturalism in ch. 5.

51. One might, as Walter Sinnott-Armstrong has pointed out to me, posit future desires as sources of reasons here, e.g. my future desire not to be a person who has burned a friend. But unless I now have — what I may lack — a second-order desire to give some weight to future desires, this move in effect gives us a significantly changed instrumentalism, as would the related move of giving weight to present desires I *would* have under various conditions, such as reflection on my options. Why should a real instrumentalist be interested in future or hypothetical desires? It is not as if, e.g., rational persons must give equal weight to all stages of their lives. That would be appropriate to an *overall* desire-satisfaction theory of reasons for action, but that is a different theory — and, I suspect, not plausible unless there is something intrinsically good about desire satisfaction. For detailed critical appraisal of instrumentalism, see Gert, *Morality*.

52. A point missed, I think, by John Stuart Mill in his attempted proof of the principle of utility in ch. 4 of *Utilitarianism*.

53. I neglect noncognitivism here; I believe that it encounters serious problems of its own, but it is a significant contender. See, e.g., Allan Gibbard, *Wise Choices, Apt Feelings* (Cambridge: Harvard University Press, 1990). For criticism of Gibbard's position, see Walter Sinnott-Armstrong's "Some Problems for Gibbard's Norm-Expressivism," *Philosophical Studies* 69 (1993). I also neglect R. B. Brandt's modified instrumentalism; see his *A Theory of the Good and the Right*. I have appraised Brandt's overall view of rationality in "An Epistemic Conception of Rationality," in *The Structure of Justification*.

54. Some empiricists might claim that it is analytic, say because to have a reason for action just *is* to have such a basic desire and set of beliefs. But this is at best highly controversial, in part because it simply begs the question against intuitionism and other prominent views.

3

Skepticism in Theory
and Practice

Justification and Truth, Rationality and Goodness

Skepticism is possible for any normative domain. Wherever there are purported reasons, there can be skepticism about whether they justify, render rational, conduce to knowledge, establish — in short, whether they do what they are supposed to do. Skepticism about theoretical reason is well-known. There is, for instance, the skepticism of the Pyrrhonians, there is Cartesian skepticism, and there is Humean skepticism. In the practical sphere, however — that (roughly) of reasons for action as opposed to reasons for belief — it is much less clear what constitutes skepticism and how one might reply to it. The most widely discussed kind of skepticism about practical reason is ethical skepticism. Often this is considered to be simply theoretical skepticism about knowledge of moral claims, rather than skepticism about the normative force of purported reasons for action, say the capacity of moral reasons to render rational the actions performed in their service. In other cases, skepticism about practical reason has been taken to be at least as much about its *motivational* power as about its normative force.[1]

There remains a need for a direct, clearly focused treatment of practical skepticism as concerning the normative force of practical reason. The central problem here, I take it, is whether there are reasons for action capable of rendering it rational and, if so, whether the reasons themselves are in some way objective, say in pointing toward something intrinsically good. Similarly, the central problem raised by theoretical skepticism is whether there are reasons for belief capable of rendering it justified and, if so, whether they are in some way objective, for instance in pointing toward something true. Broadly speaking, then, practical skepticism is the view that there are no normative reasons for action or at least none capable of rendering it rational and that there are therefore no rational actions. The best way (and certainly a good way) to approach the status of skepticism about practical reason is in relation to the analogy — which to my knowledge has not been much explored — between theoretical skepticism, understood in relation to justified belief and justificatory reasons for believing, and practical skepticism, conceived as just described. If pursuit of this analogy proves fruitful in understanding practical reason, that will confirm the value of epistemological reflection in clarifying practical inquiry — a perhaps unexpected benefit of a kind of thinking that some consider at best abstruse or unfruitful.[2]

I. Skepticism about Theoretical Reason

Perhaps the most general basis for theoretical skepticism — roughly, skepticism about reasons for belief — is the logical gap between experience and truth. If a deceptive Cartesian demon is possible, then my experience could be exactly as it is even though I am hallucinating all of the seemingly familiar objects around me. Thus, any experiential evidence I may have regarding the external world is logically inconclusive. Similar arguments can be brought against the purported cogency of evidence regarding the future, regarding any aspect of the past, and even concerning elements in my own character: again, none of my grounds in these territories logically rules out systematic error about the landscape I think I know.

Some skeptics might stop there. Others argue for the fallibility or defeasibility even of our beliefs about our own current mental life. After all, my believing that I am, say, imaging a wide blue sky, does not entail — at least does not self-evidently entail — that I am in fact imaging it. As to the bastion of a priori, skeptics may argue that even a priori grounds for believing a proposition do not self-evidently guarantee its truth.[3] An a priori ground, from this point of view, is just an experiential, though reflectional, ground and either does not guarantee the truth in question at all or does not do so in the *way* required for knowledge.[4]

Skeptics tend to think it obvious that the gap between experience and truth — the *truth gap*, for short — undermines the possibility of knowledge, at least of propositions lying on the far side of the gap, that is, those whose truth is not entailed by our experiential evidence for them. On this skeptical line of thinking, we have at best knowledge of our current mental life and of some a priori truths: perhaps of certain intrusive experiences or processes like being in pain or seeing a blindingly bright red, and of simple logical truths, for instance that if no apples are oranges, then no oranges are apples.

The case with justification is more complicated. Given the truth gap, skeptics tend to conclude that we not only do not know the propositions we tend to think we do but are not even justified in believing these propositions. And why, after all, should we repose conviction in propositions on the basis of evidence that does not rule out mistake? There is, of course, much controversy about whether this line of thinking is sound: some philosophers hold that mistake need not be ruled out absolutely; others think it can be absolutely eliminated, since experience sometimes provides "conclusive reasons."[5] This issue cannot be settled here. I simply want to put it before us and proceed to formulate the corresponding skeptical problems in the practical domain. In that territory I will try to sketch a partial solution.

II. The Practical Analogy to Theoretical Skepticism

Theoretical skepticism is unified by the concept of truth as a sort of target of the grounds that theoretical reasons are supposed to constitute: knowledge is of truths; evidence is for the truth of propositions; grounds of rational belief count toward the truth of the propositional object of the belief in question; and so forth.[6] Is there is any counterpart of truth in the practical domain that is sufficiently comprehensive to be the most general "target" of practical attitudes, as truth is of theoretical ones? If so, it is probably goodness.[7] One might argue, for instance, that (as Aquinas thought) it is "under the aspect of good" that we want the objects of our desires (in a sense of 'desire' wide enough to permit expressing any reason for acting we may have), and that, even apart from this aspectual view, goodness is the "point" of the practical attitudes, for instance desire and intending, in much the way truth is the "point" of the theoretical ones, above all belief and knowledge.

The Good and the True

The reference to a point here is, despite appearances, not best understood as one might expect from typical ascriptions of a point to actions, namely as referring to a purpose for which theoretical or practical attitudes are "adopted" or held; they are dispositions and not suitably under voluntary control to be taken up and aimed. Instead, talk of the point of (say) beliefs or desires is a way of indicating the applicability of certain critical standards. Wanting what we do under the aspect of goodness would be comparable to believing what we do under the aspect of truth; and just as discovery of reasons to think a proposition false tends to weaken or eliminate our belief of it, discovery of reasons to think an object in no way good tends to weaken or eliminate our desire for it.[8] In each case, what we discover using the appropriate theoretical or practical standards might be broadly described as showing that we are "missing the point."

To be sure, it is often held that to believe is to believe *true*.[9] This claim — call it *doxastic internalism* — is that the truth of a proposition, *p*, is internal to the very content of a belief that *p*. Perhaps there is no obvious, full-scale practical analogue of this phenomenon. Consider wanting, which seems to be the most fundamental practical attitude. Wants are certainly not true or false; and even if what one wants can be described as the realization of the thing one is said to want, 'realization' here does not seem part of the content of the want (its intentional object) itself, as, for doxastic internalism, truth is for a belief that *p*. Doxastic internalism takes believing *p* to have the content: *p* is true. Wanting to swim seems at best clumsily expressible as wanting the realization of a swim, for reasons similar to those that emerge when we consider differences between believing simpliciter and believing true. Granted, an analogy survives the contrast just drawn: just as 'true' is a status-indicator regarding the object of a belief, 'realized' indicates the status of an object wanted. But whereas a belief that is not true is thereby in a way defective, a want that is not realized is not thereby defective. The (prima facie) remedy for a false belief is to relinquish it and change one's belief system to reflect the truth; the (prima facie) remedy for an unrealized want is to retain it and change the world to reflect one's desires.

One might think that we can find the practical analogue of truth by showing that to want is to want *as good*. The good, then, would emerge as the counterpart of the true. But wanting in general is not wanting *as good*. Nor is intending — which entails wanting in the widest sense of that term and is the motivational attitude "closest" to action — necessarily intending the relevant deed or thing *as* good. So, on the assumptions that wants — of one sort or another — express the basic reasons for which we act and that intending is the practical counterpart of believing,[11] we apparently get a profound disanalogy between the practical and the theoretical.

I grant these points about wanting and intending; their objects need not always be conceived by the agent as good. Moreover, for similar reasons I think that the idea that to believe *is* to believe true (doxastic internalism) is mistaken. Once this is appreciated the analogy between truth and goodness can be seen to be significant. Here are two important supporting considerations.

First, the proposition that *p* is simply not the same proposition as the proposition that *p* is true. To see the difference between believing and believing true, notice that there are tiny children capable of believing propositions who do not possess the concept of truth, and so cannot believe a proposition to be true. Surely we form beliefs earlier in life than the time at which we acquire the concept of truth. Arguably, moreover, a rational adult might think the concept of truth is idle or incoherent and for that reason not form beliefs essentially involving it. Granted, one may believe that a concept is incoherent and tacitly use it anyway. But it is doubtful that skeptics about the coherence of the concept of truth who nonetheless speak in the normal ways with others need do any more than use some functional equivalent of the *term* 'true' in expressing themselves.

Second, the view that believing *p* is believing that *p* is true implies a regress. If the proposition that *p* is true is believed, so is the proposition that that *p* is true, is true (which, for doxastic internalism, is the same proposition), and so forth. The regress may be held not to be vicious, on the ground that even in our own language, we cannot express all the formulations of the propositions we believe, such as the full formulation of the proposition that *p* is true, is true . . . where the dots stand for what is expressed by the multivolume formulation we get by suffixing a trillion occurrences of 'is true' after *p*. Leaving that aside, surely in believing *p*, we do not automatically believe (say) the proposition that that *p* is true, is true. I understand this, yet I deny that I form a belief of this artificial kind each time I come to believe something.[12]

There may yet seem to be a profound disanalogy between the theoretical and the practical here. I cannot say without pragmatic contradiction that I believe (some proposition) *p* but *p* is not true: the latter statement abrogates the former. I apparently can say without such contradiction that I want *x* but *x* is not good. This disanalogy seems to me genuine, but how deep is it?

To assess the disanalogy, we should create parallel cases by construing the second imagined speaker as employing a broad notion of the good, as we understand the first to be employing a broad notion of truth — something we must do to get a genuine pragmatic contradiction from 'I believe *p* but *p* is not true', since there is no difficulty about believing *p* but not believing it is *logically* true, or not believing it is empirically true, or not believing it is scientifically true, and so on. Now take a similarly broad notion of goodness and consider whether one can, without "practical contradiction," say 'I want x but x is neither intrinsically good nor instrumentally good, nor even subjectively good — in (e.g.) answering to any interest of mine'. If, on the assumption that these are all of the modalities of goodness, I believed this were true of me, then in having the want in question I would be mysterious even to myself — perhaps just as mysterious as someone who believed p but also believed it is not true. The want in question would be (and would seem to me) a kind of motivational dangler, a sort of urge that, from the point of view of rationality, should not coexist with the defeating belief that its object is in no way good, rather as a belief that p, should not coexist with a belief that p is not true.

There are still other analogies lending some support to a parallel between the theoretical and the practical. For instance, each admits of non-descriptive uses: 'I want some water but don't give me any' can be inappropriate for reasons similar to those making 'I believe p but it is not true' inappropriate.[13] It may be, then, that the difference between pragmatic contradiction and practical contradiction is of quite limited depth.

Fortunately, we need not establish just how close the analogy between truth and goodness is in order to see that there is *some* significant degree of analogy. There is surely enough to enable us to formulate a practical counterpart of theoretical skepticism. Goodness is, for instance, just the kind of target a skeptic would tend to doubt we can regularly hit, and says we cannot know we hit. There is, after all, a prima facie gap between experience and goodness — the *value gap*, for short — analogous to the truth gap. For any plausible notion of (overall) goodness, our evidences of goodness, for instance disinterested pleasure in some state of affairs, or reflective approval regarding it, does not seem to entail (self-evidently, at least) that anything is in fact good. We can take pleasure, even disinterested pleasure, in an experience, such as the experience of punishing an offender, and we can approve, even reflectively, of a deed, without their being good. They may, for instance, be neither intrinsically nor instrumentally nor even subjectively good.[14] Sadism may underlie our pleasure in punishing someone and jealousy our approval of doing it; and even if the pleasure by itself is good and the punishment has good effects, it does not follow that either the experience or the deed is good, overall, any more than the truth of a proposition follows from the existence of good grounds for it, including some that are true. In administering the punishment, then, we thus neither realize an overall good nor acquire knowledge that we have done so.

It might be pointed out that the objects of such desires can still be subjectively good, good for the agent. But this holds only in the sense that one might *believe* they are good, and this kind of "goodness" is no better a candidate to be what is designated by a plausible conception of goodness conceived as the target of practical attitudes than merely believed truth is for what is designated by a plausible conception of truth conceived as the target of theoretical attitudes. Thoughtful non-skeptics quite agree with their skeptical opponents that if there is any truth or goodness at all, mere believing does not make it so.

Given the common tendency to think of ethics as the primary domain of practical reason, one may wonder how rightness and obligation come into our inquiry. It is arguable that rightness is minimal moral goodness (permissibility) and obligation is a kind of moral goodness on balance. I cannot appraise this idea now, but I find it plausible enough to accept for the sake of argument (it will receive some confirmation in chapter 11). Fortunately, there is no need to discuss rightness or obligation in detail here: if they are not kinds of, or in some way derivable from, goodness properly understood, at least the troubles with goodness are representative of those the skeptic raises for rightness and obligation.[15]

Practical versus Theoretical Skepticism about Rational Action

One might largely accept what has been said so far and still object that what is being presented as practical skepticism is really just theoretical skepticism applied to actions. The objection does not entail that there are no rational actions; the thrust is that it is *only* on the basis of the justification (or rationality) of the belief(s) underlying actions that they are rational or not. It is not rational, for example, to go to a park for a swim if one is patently unjustified in believing that there is water in the pond.[16]

I can accept a *qualified* version of the view that a kind of practical skepticism is implied by global skepticism about instrumental beliefs — for instance beliefs that going to a pond will enable one to swim. If there is no justification for instrumental beliefs, then arguably there are no rational *instrumental* actions. But notice the possibility of performing a *basic* action (one not performed by performing an instrumental action), such as reciting a sonnet to oneself, for its own sake. Presumably I can do this at will, just because I want to, *without* even holding any instrumental belief as to *how* I am to do it or what else it leads to. Thus, the rationality of my doing it — and surely it could be rational to do it — would not turn on any such belief. But if my wanting to do this provided no good reason to do it, it might *thereby* fail to be rational. These points are best explained on the hypothesis that wanting can express a crucial kind of reason for an action even apart from an instrumental belief regarding the action.

As this last point suggests, even if certain theoretical skepticisms entail practical skepticism, it is doubtful that practical skepticism is *equivalent* to any kind of theoretical skepticism. For surely, if there are no good *motivational* reasons for action — such as the kind provided by desires for something intrinsically good — then even if we have all manner of justified instrumental beliefs, we still lack adequate reasons for action, hence do not act rationally. Evaluative beliefs might seem sufficient as a substitute for motivational reasons; but if they are, this is apparently because believing, say, that something is intrinsically good implies the rationality of wanting it, even if one does not in fact want it.

What makes skepticism about the possibility of good motivational reasons for action irreducibly *practical*, then, is that the absence of rationality on the part of non-truth-valued, conative, or otherwise motivational, elements is what it conceives as precluding the rationality of actions (and even of adequate reasons for action). Practical skepticism could thus be true, even if theoretical skepticism were not.[17]

Practical skepticism, far from depending on theoretical skepticism, may also be quite consistently held without holding the latter. A practical skeptic who is a thoroughgoing theoretical *non*-skeptic could claim to *know* that there is nothing intrinsically good and that we are warranted in believing that there is nothing else in virtue of which there can be rational actions, or even reasons for action.[18] This skepticism is directed toward a proposition about reasons for action rather than for belief. Practical skepticism of any sort must, to be sure, *also* attack actual or possible *beliefs* about practical reasons and rational actions; but this shows only that its content is propositional and that it implies an element of theoretical skepticism. A practical skeptic need not affirm this content by deriving practical skepticism from a more general and theoretical kind, and the *content* of the skepticism can be carried by beliefs which practical skeptics, by contrast with their theoretical cousins, take to constitute knowledge.

Skepticism, then, is a problem in the practical domain as it is in the theoretical, and practical skepticism need not derive from any theoretical version. There is a value gap as there is a truth gap, and the former seems to call into question the cogency of apparent reasons for acting much in the way the latter calls into question the cogency of apparent reasons for believing.

This conclusion leaves us at least two problems relevant to reasons for action. First, how can we know practical propositions, such as that aesthetically enjoying a painting is intrinsically good or that avoiding injustice is a basic (normative) reason for action? Second, supposing we cannot, might we still have adequate reasons for action? Need we *know*, or even justifiedly believe, such propositions in order to have reasons to act? Might there be practical justification even if there is neither practical knowledge (of the cognitive kind as opposed to knowing *how* to do something) nor justified practical belief? I want to pursue these questions in the light of three major responses that might be proposed to answer skepticism. In each case, I begin with an outline of the theoretical response and proceed to a counterpart practical response. The overall skeptical view opposing the cogency of both theoretical and practical we might call *normative skepticism*.

III. Three Major Responses to Normative Skepticism

One kind of response to normative skepticism argues in effect that there is no truth or value gap: once theoretical justification and practical rationality are adequately understood, we have all we need to account for the grasp of truth and the realization of goodness. Another kind of response attacks the presupposition that truth and goodness are the "goals" of theoretical and practical attitudes, thereby eliminating the gap the skeptic argues cannot be bridged. Still other responses may embrace the goals as worthy but analyze them in a way that puts them as much within reach as other things, such as justified belief and rational desire, with respect to which we must deal with skepticism anyway. Let us consider these in turn, beginning with the theoretical case and proceeding from there to the practical.

The Epistemization of Truth and the Subjectivization of Goodness

The first response to theoretical skepticism derives from the sense that if our evidence is good enough, then we have done all it makes sense to expect of us in the quest for truth, and those who think there is something more are hypostatizing truth and would saddle us with an unreachable metaphysical absolute. The most plausible form this response takes is epistemizing truth: truth is simply a matter of, say, warranted assertability or some other category of sufficiently strong evidence. The category of truth is thus epistemic, rather than ontological: a belief is true provided it is appropriately assertable; it need not be conceived as, for example, corresponding with an external reality.[19]

To be sure, skepticism about when we have sufficient warrant is still possible, but at least there is now no truth gap that is ineliminable (at any rate none for those who do not insist that adequate evidence for p must entail its truth). At least when combined with pragmatism about epistemological matters, this epistemic approach can set the degree of warrant needed for justification at a level we can actually achieve in science and everyday life. But epistemizing truth is still not necessarily a pragmatic approach. The truth of propositions is defined in terms of adequate evidence for them; this can be a matter of correspondence with an aspect of "the world." It need not be defined in terms of appropriate results, in our practical enterprises, of our believing the propositions, as where acting on a belief leads to what seems to confirm it.

If the evidence crucial for an epistemization of truth is internal, say in depending on sense experience and phenomenal elements deriving from memory, then the closest counterpart among views of practical rationality is a similar internalization of goodness, for instance by taking goodness to consist in doing or experiencing something that, on one's beliefs, satisfies one's stable, considered basic desires. Such a desire-based theory of the good may be more or less subjective: at one end is the idea that goodness is simply the satisfaction, on one's beliefs, of one's basic desires, and at or near the other is the partly epistemic view that it is the satisfaction, on one's *rational beliefs*, of one's *rational* desires, where these are understood at least in part in terms of the impact on our overall desire system of certain kinds of theoretical rationality.[20] An intermediate position might be that goodness consists in satisfying desires one would have in the light of reflection on both what it would be like to realize them and on how this would affect the prospects of satisfying one's other desires. Those attracted to a highly subjectivistic view of justified belief may prefer the first conception of goodness;[21] those attracted to a more objectivistic view of justified belief may find it more natural to adopt the third conception of goodness. As against the satisfaction-of-actual-desire account of the good, the realization-of-rational-desire view seems to presuppose that there is theoretical rationality. But that is beside the point here, except in confirming a main thesis of this book — that practical and theoretical rationality are significantly parallel.[22]

The epistemic version of the desire-satisfaction theory of the good must be distinguished from two quite important positions. Both of them also take rational action as subordinate to desire, but one does this by connecting rational action with realization of the intrinsically good; the other makes no essential use of such goodness. The former can be seen as a subjectivist attenuation of Aristotle's view (discussed in chapter 11) that (roughly speaking) the good is what we desire for its own sake and never instrumentally; the second is a version of Hume's conception of practical reason (discussed in chapters 9–10).

The first view is a *simple subjectivism*, which says that the good is satisfying one's basic desires (regardless of what they are, apart from some consistency constraints). This view, unlike the subjectivist epistemic desire-satisfaction conception of goodness, requires no belief that the action or experience does this. The crucial thing is to "get what you really want" (though even here the 'really' suggests there may be a non-desire-based standard in the background). This view is akin to the idea that true propositions are those one believes in a kind of basic way (regardless of what their content is, apart from consistency constraints) and is only slightly more plausible. Just as a belief's merely being basic, in the sense of non-inferential, does not imply its truth or even its justification — as the case of wishful thinking amply shows — a desire's merely being non-instrumental does not imply the goodness of its object or its rationality, as the motivating power of posthypnotic suggestion indicates.

The second view to be contrasted with the epistemic version of the desire satisfaction account of the good is a plausible and widely held position in the theory of practical reason — *instrumentalism*: roughly, the Humean view that rational action is action that appropriately serves the agent's basic desires.[23] On that view, there *is* no intrinsic goodness. This is, at any rate, a reasonable conclusion to draw on the highly plausible assumption that if there is anything intrinsically good, then it can provide something Humeans deny to be possible: *non*-desire-based reasons for basic desires and thereby for actions. For on the Humean view, by contrast with Kantian and other objectivist positions, there are no such reasons for basic desires.[24]

Instrumentalism, in placing no substantive objective constraints on basic desires (as opposed to, say, the formal objective constraint that a desire for an obviously contradictory state of affairs cannot be a basis of rational action), is a kind of subjectivism. But as most plausibly developed, instrumentalism is less a response to the goodness gap than an *eliminativism* regarding intrinsic goodness: there is no such goodness to realize, and rationality must be understood in much less ambitious terms than those of realizing, or even tending in some way to realize, the good (at least where goodness of any kind either is or depends on intrinsic goodness). The theoretical view that perhaps best serves as a counterpart to instrumentalism construed as a subjectivism about rationality is the position that what we misleadingly call justified belief is not belief suitably connected with truth but, roughly, psychologically basic belief, together with those beliefs (actual or hypothetical) that we do or can arrive at by acceptable inference from the former.[25] The theoretical counterpart of eliminativism regarding goodness, however, is anti-realism about truth. This is the second broad response to theoretical skepticism I want to consider.[26]

Anti-Realism about Truth and Goodness

There are many forms of anti-realism about truth. One way to deny that there is anything clearly denoted by 'truth' is to hold that 'It is true that *p*' is simply a way of asserting that *p*. On this deflationary view, there is again no gap to be bridged between experience and truth, but only a series of diverse standards governing human assertion. Whereas the epistemization of truth reduces truth talk to epistemic parlance but allows us to treat 'true' as expressing a genuine property (or relation), the anti-realist, deflationary view says that truth talk commits us only to countenancing the predicate 'true' and to explicating the related standards of assertion. I do not see this approach as solving the problems of skepticism, since they can still be raised concerning the several standards of assertion that remain. But we need not pursue this: my aim is simply to get the anti-realist option before us for purposes of ascertaining its practical counterpart.

The closest practical counterpart of anti-realism about truth (at least of deflationist anti-realism) is probably noncognitivism about goodness, at least about intrinsic goodness (clearly there is no incentive to hold a noncognitivist view of claims to the effect that something is "good as a means" in a purely causal, comparative sense of that phrase). On one plausible version of this view, to say that, for instance, aesthetic experience of a beautiful painting is good is not to ascribe a property to the experience but rather to express a positive attitude toward it.

Noncognitivism may seem to open the door to irrationalism or rampant relativism. But just as, for anti-realists about truth — who may be quite scientifically oriented — some assertions may be justified and others not, noncognitivists may distinguish between rational and irrational grounds for attitudes and may thus contrast rational with irrational grounds of action insofar as rationally grounded attitudes provide good reasons for action (as, on the more plausible noncognitivisms, they do).[27] Thus, if a kind of relativity is implied by noncognitivism, insofar as (for instance) what attitudes people may rationally hold is relative to their circumstances and beliefs, there are limits to the relativity.[28] The least controversial point here is that attitudes based on obviously inconsistent beliefs are irrational; but it may also be argued that rational attitudes, especially in ethics, must reflect a strong disposition to treat like cases alike.[29]

Naturalistic Reductivism

A third approach to theoretical skepticism is naturalistic reductivism. This approach dramatically alters the experiential side of the truth gap by denying that justification is internally grounded in experience. Suppose instead that the justifiedness of beliefs is identical with the property of being reliably grounded, where this is roughly grounding in a belief-forming process most of whose cognitive outputs are true beliefs, as is the case, we may plausibly suppose, with ordinary perception. It appears to most of us, for instance, that by and large our visually grounded beliefs are true. Then, having justification can by its very nature at least *probabilistically* cross the truth gap.

What specifically constitutes reliabilist justification? This is a question left to the scientific (or at least empirical) study of the relation between the grounds of beliefs and what the beliefs in question are about. Skeptics, of course, will reject this approach. They will tend to claim that from the crucial point of view of our experience we cannot tell whether we have justified belief or not — precisely because we cannot determine the reliability of a belief-grounding process unless we can determine the *truth* of the beliefs grounded in it — so there is still a gap between experience and truth. There is a large range of issues here which I must set aside.[30] What I want to do is explore a parallel naturalistic reduction in the practical case.

To see what one of the more plausible naturalistic reductions in the practical sphere might be, think of the naturalization of the notion of justification as equating it with an objective tendency of belief-grounding processes to hit the relevant target — truth. The counterpart move would be to take the practical rationality of an attitude or action to be a similar grounding, where the target is goodness. Rationally wanting to rectify an injustice, for instance, might be a matter of having a motivational pattern that tends to promote goodness. The target, however, is arguably not natural and in that way unlike truth as naturalism understands it: naturalism characteristically takes the only basic truths to be truths of nature. Suppose, then, that in addition to (and in support of) the naturalistic reduction sought on the experiential side of the value gap, one tries to achieve it on the target side. One could take goodness to be ultimately a natural property. Then the value gap would be narrowed: where there was an ontological and evidential gap, there is only the latter, and even that is probabilistically crossed whenever the relevant justificatory processes leading to rational attributions of goodness are reliably produced, that is, produced by elements most of whose outputs are true attributions of goodness, just as most of the belief outputs of perception are true. Goodness may, for instance, be explicable in terms of a tendency to satisfy our needs, whether (say) biological, social, aesthetic, religious, or some combination thereof, where such satisfaction is interpreted in a broadly naturalistic way.[31] A good deed, for instance, is the kind that suitably contributes to satisfying social needs, which may include such biological and aesthetic considerations as preservation of the environment; and a good person is one who is sufficiently strongly disposed to perform such deeds and to abstain from the opposite kind.

One can imagine G. E. Moore asking here how goodness can be any such natural property given that, for any satisfactory thing of the relevant kind, we can ask whether it is really good (just as skeptics can ask, of any belief whose grounds are of the kind supposed to lead mostly to truth, how they can really justify any proposition given that they do not rule out its falsity). One response is that property identity does not require synonymy of the predicates in question: satisfying certain needs in an appropriate way, then, can *be* what having the property of goodness is even if 'good' does not *mean* any such thing. How, one might ask, could aesthetically viewing a beautiful painting with pleasure not be good? Would it not have to be good even if 'good', as applied to experiences, does not mean any such thing? This is among the kinds of questions we must explore.

IV. The Irreducibility of Truth and Goodness

I cannot assess in detail these three kinds of response to theoretical and practical skepticism. All I hope to do is point out some of the serious problems for them with a view to preparing the way for an approach of my own that, as developed in this and later chapters, may have significant advantages over all of them.

The epistemization of truth has a certain appeal, even independently of skeptical worries, especially to those inclined toward the verificationist view that a proposition's being true is equivalent to its being appropriately verifiable, as where we can all see an unidentified flying object under good conditions of observation, and hence agree that it is true that there is one. But the notion of truth stubbornly resists this treatment, as has been argued in detail by many philosophers.[32]

The most important single point, I think, is that in general the truth of a proposition is simply not entailed by any set of (the relevant kinds of) evidences for it or by the outcomes of verification procedures, however rigorous. Truth is not even entailed by what the scientific community would agree on in the "long run" (C. S. Peirce's notion) unless perhaps we both restrict the subject matter to scientific topics and build into the long run something like approach to infinitely long inquiry (and even these moves seem too weak to secure the entailment unless some question is begged). I believe, then, that this strategy is unlikely to succeed.

One might expect the counterpart view — the epistemic subjectivization of goodness — to fare better, at least insofar as one thinks of goodness as "softer" than truth, and perhaps it does fare better. But on any plausible view of goodness, we can achieve what we believe will realize what we basically want and nonetheless not realize genuine goodness.[33] It even appears that this can happen when our wants and beliefs have been "corrected," to the extent that they can be, by exposure to facts and logic and by any other procedures or reflections specifiable without presupposing in the first place that the desired object is good. Brain manipulation may surely control the content of our desires without controlling whether satisfying them is good.

A difficulty in understanding this object-of-corrected-desires view of the good is that "facts" may include propositions necessarily implying that something is in some sense good, such as propositions to the effect that someone is aesthetically enjoying a beautiful painting. Aesthetic pleasure surely is a strong candidate for an intrinsic good. These entailments are not the kinds of propositions the naturalistic view in question can appeal to, since they are neither empirical nor in the relevant sense logical.[34] If what necessarily *makes* an experience good is its being enjoyable (a possibility that, incidentally, does not by itself entail the truth of naturalism) then even if belief that it is enjoyable would yield or at least warrant an appropriate desire for it, this fact is not a naturalistic bridge across the value gap, but perhaps an indication that we are already crossing it. One correct result does not make a sound theory; and this result is also explainable by a competing theory, such as the intuitionism developed in chapter 2.

It might also be objected, by a certain kind of skeptic, that a person could have a belief of such a factual proposition — the kind of proposition implying the goodness of an object of desire or possible desire — without having a desire to realize its object, in which case the (normatively) practical *content* of the belief might fail to yield a (motivationally) practical reason for *action*, one that by its nature tends to lead the agent to act in some way supported by the reason.[35] The problem would be that, supposing for the sake of argument that one could specify a procedure guaranteeing that desires which pass the crucial tests are directed toward what is genuinely good, one could still not guarantee that *believing* that a desire would pass such a test would produce that desire.

Let us grant that believing that the satisfaction of a would-be desire would be good does not entail formation of that desire. Still, the objection imposes on attempts to cross the value gap a burden they should not have to carry: guaranteeing that motivation to pursue the good will arise upon one's discovering conclusive evidence that something one takes it one can pursue is good. This guarantee seems especially likely to hold where that evidence is at least partly constitutive of what goodness is, as pleasures of certain sorts may be argued to be. Our problem in this essay, however, is how to discover a practical analogue of adequate evidence, and we may leave open that just as people can fail to respond cognitively to adequate theoretical evidence, they can fail to respond conatively to adequate practical grounds.[36]

Even apart from the kinds of difficulties just noted, the best-developed version of subjectivism about practical reason seems unsuccessful.[37] There are certainly internal, and in *that* sense subjective, elements in goodness, but there does not seem to be a wholly satisfactory way to cross the gap between experience and (overall) goodness by appeal to corrected desires. Particularly because our desires can be manipulated — neurosurgically, for instance — in such a way that exposure to facts and logic does not "correct" them, even desires that have undergone as rigorous a correction process as subjectivists are entitled to devise seem at least as liable to "aim" at the wrong targets — non-goods — as justified beliefs are to "aim" at false propositions — non-truths.

As to anti-realism about truth, I suggest that it is a position of retreat. There are at least two possible reasons for its appeal. One is a conviction that foundationalism fails, thereby eliminating our only hope of experiential access to truth. The other is a verificationistic sense that if theories are in principle underdetermined by any supporting data we may have for them, then there really is no truth of the matter, as opposed to the empirical adequacy of one or another theory — roughly, its capacity to account for the relevant data. But first, the idea that if there is truth, we have "direct access" to it, in the sense of indefeasible, experiential justification for believing certain true propositions, is not a commitment of any plausible foundationalism. The thought that it is may arise from conflating direct access to truth with direct access to justification, in the sense of direct (non-inferential) justification, a much more moderate achievement, which foundationalism does take to be possible. Second, granting that our data do not uniquely determine the correct theory to explain them, surely the best way to account for how this is so is to note that theoretical *truth* does not follow from statements of supporting data — a point that also helps to undermine the epistemization of truth. The content of a truth commonly outruns the evidence for it.[38]

Similar points seem to me to hold for anti-realism in the practical domain, a position that I take to be well represented by noncognitivism. Goodness does not have to be a natural property, much less one to which we have direct access, in order to be a real property. Moreover, its not being entailed (at least formally) by any "factual" statements need not tell against its being a property either. This applies also to something's having shape: being, for example, square conceptually entails not being round, but it entails this synthetically and non-formally. There are also internal difficulties for noncognitivism, as a number of philosophers have brought out.[39]

Naturalistic reductivism is, in some ways, the most appealing of the three responses to skepticism just sketched. This is in part because normative properties appear to supervene on natural ones — a relation that at least firmly anchors them in the natural world — and partly because moral explanations (and presumably other explanations by appeal to normative properties) may plausibly be argued to succeed in just the way they should if they are natural.[40] But I doubt that this reductivism succeeds. A version of reliabilism might succeed for understanding knowledge, but even then it will not adequately deal with the problem posed by Cartesian skepticism on the basis of the truth gap; and I doubt that it succeeds in accounting for justification, as opposed to knowledge.[41] In my judgment, justification is an internal concept in a sense that reliabilism does not capture.

It should be stressed, moreover, that a naturalistic account of knowledge is one thing and the epistemization of truth, even in naturalistic terms of the kind crucial for justification, is another. Knowledge can be a naturalistic notion without truth's being reducible to any epistemic conditions for asserting it, even if the proper evidences of truth are naturalistically specifiable. Similarly, our evidences for goodness (which may yield knowledge of it) could be altogether naturalistically specifiable, as Mill, for instance, took them to be, without goodness itself being reducible to them. The targets of theoretical and practical attitudes do not have to be composed of the same kinds of materials constituting our grounds for believing we will hit them.

In the practical domain, the attempt to naturalize goodness may perhaps be as plausible (or implausible) as the attempt to naturalize justification. I will not try to appraise it here.[42] I do, however, want to suggest another analogy between the theoretical and the practical that may help us. Let us grant that if we believe that a process, such as observing the shape, color, and movement of the clouds in order to predict the weather, is a reliable producer of true beliefs, we tend to regard the beliefs it produces as justified. Similarly, if we believe that an experiential process, such as aesthetically studying a painting, more often than not leads to satisfaction of a kind of human need (or at any rate to a kind of universally desired activity), we tend to consider the experiences yielded by such processes to be good. May it not be, however, that the real theoretical justifiers of belief are elements in perception (such as sense impressions), in memory, and in induction, and that their occurrence is our criterion for ascribing truth, and may it not be that the real grounds for ascribing goodness here — the practical elements that count toward goodness — are not the evidence of satisfying of a need (or universal desire) but indications of the pleasure itself, and that the likely production of pleasure or some other good-making characteristic is our criterion for ascribing goodness to the experiences produced by the aesthetic process? Let us pursue this in terms of what most basically grounds ascriptions of truth and goodness.

Very roughly, the question is whether the reliable grounding justifies because it is reliable or because it is, say, perceptual, and whether the aesthetic experiences are good because they satisfy human needs or because they yield pleasure. The naturalistic approach here may gain undeserved plausibility because the natural processes it uses to account for justification and goodness entail phenomena that *independently* ground justification and goodness. Whatever one says in such cases, the naturalistic theories are not the only ones that may plausibly cross the truth and value gaps. Let me present an alternative.

V. *Internalist Objectivism and Reasons for Action*

Let us return to the gap problem in the theoretical domain. Must we grant skepticism about knowledge of the external world if we admit that our experience (internally construed) never entails any fact about the external world? If we distinguish the bare logical possibility that we *could* be mistaken in external world beliefs from the dubious epistemic claim that we *might*— realistically — be mistaken, and if we reject strong closure principles, such as the principle that if one is justified in believing that *p* and one sees or can see that *p* entails *q*, then one is automatically justified in believing that *q*, then I see no compelling reason to acquiesce in skepticism about knowledge of the external world.[43]

Moreover, even if we cannot refute skepticism about knowledge, it by no means follows that we cannot refute skepticism about justification. I am inclined to think we can accomplish the latter task, in part because justification is an internal concept and in part because there appear to be a priori epistemic principles usable without dependence on successful external observation, such as the principle that if one has a clear and steadfast visual impression of something green before one, one is prima facie justified in believing there is something green before one.[44] If I am justified, a priori, in believing this and also justified in believing I have such a visual impression, surely I have prima facie justification for believing that there is (in fact) something green before me.

This view is a version of rationalism,[45] but the most it requires is a quite moderate rationalism. For one thing, although reflection can yield substantive justification, that justification is defeasible. The idea, in part, is that the concept of justification is constituted by principles connecting justification, in the a priori way just illustrated, to certain basic sources. These principles do not simply give us criteria contingently connected with justification; they each express, in part, what it is.[46] In this context the best thing I can do to make the idea more plausible is to suggest how it may be extended to the practical domain. If it helps us there, this would be significant (though only partial) confirmation of it.

Basic Reasons for Action

Once again, I want to grant the gap that so stirs the skeptic about practical reason: the value gap. Suppose for the sake of argument that no experience of ours entails that there is anything objectively good.[47] Does this imply that we cannot know there is any such thing or, especially, that we have no adequate reasons for action? I cannot see that it does. Let us first look at the case of reasons for action in general and then proceed to the important special case of moral reasons. As before, I am taking it that if there is anything intrinsically good (or intrinsically bad), it provides a (basic) reason for action. The converse — that if there are reasons for action, then there is at least something intrinsically good (or intrinsically bad) that is a basis of those reasons — may also hold; but this is a more controversial assumption I do not need here and cite only because of its general importance in exploring practical reason.[48]

Could an experience's being painful fail to provide a reason for one to act, say to avoid it? If I am being shocked and frozen by the frigid water I have just fallen into, is there not a reason for me to get out of it? One can say there is only a psychological regularity here and that I merely *have* a (motivating) reason; but surely anyone who sincerely denies that there is a reason for me to act in such a case reveals a failure to understand reasons for action (or at least some conceptual failure).[49] Pleasure is a similar source of normative grounds, but of positive reasons: roughly, of reasons to seek, as opposed to avoiding. To be sure, we may be puzzled at what pains some people and at what gives pleasure to others; but we do not regard pain and pleasure as providing no reasons for action.

I do not mean to endorse (valuational) hedonism; pain and pleasure are simply clear cases of what seems to ground reasons for action in the way perception and memory, say, seem to ground reasons for belief. They ground those reasons, moreover, in a distinctively practical way. They make it rational to want the enjoyable experience (or be averse to the painful one) for its own sake. The practical value of such desires (like that of aversion to pain) is not derivative from the rationality of *believing* that the objects in question are (intrinsically) good (or bad). It is indeed doubtful that it *would* be (theoretically) rational to believe this of the objects if it were not (practically) rational to want or be averse to those objects on account of such properties as being enjoyable or painful. Imagine someone claiming that although listening to a symphony is intrinsically good on account of the aesthetic pleasure of the experience, it is not rational to want to listen to it *for* that pleasure. This is instructively absurd. Practical reason is not reducible to theoretical reason in the suggested way. Indeed, it would seem that no such reduction can be accomplished: the theoretical rationality of believing any (kind of) experience to be intrinsically good apparently depends in part on the rationality of wanting such experiences.

In very general terms, the suggested moderately rationalist, anti-skeptical approach views both theoretical and practical reason as based on taking certain internally accessible criteria for the attribution of truth and of goodness to be partly constitutive of justified belief and of reasons for action. Our basic epistemic evidence, for instance our steadfast visual experience, is itself partly constitutive of epistemic justification and can render certain of our beliefs justified despite the truth gap; our basic practical evidence, such as pleasure in an aesthetic experience, is itself partly constitutive of practical justification and can render certain of our actions rational despite the value gap.[50]

This approach does not completely dispel the worries raised by skeptics. It does assure us that we can have *reasons to act* and can even *act rationally* if we act entirely *for* those reasons. But in at least three respects — each parallel to a point about theoretical reason — elements of practical skepticism can still be forcefully raised. For one thing, certain alternative actions we face might produce *both* pleasure and pain, leaving us with a difficult balancing to do, and it might also be at best hard to tell what and *how much* pleasure and pain various actions produce. For another thing, we are fallible about why we act and perhaps cannot always know that we act *for* a reason we *have* for acting; thus, even when we do act rationally, we may be unable to know we do, just as even when we justifiedly believe a proposition, we may be unable to know that we do.[51] A third difficulty is that there may be (and I think are) non-hedonic goods to consider, and we then have the problem of balancing heterogeneous goods. Thus, it may not be clear to us what we have the *best* reason to do, even if it is clear to us what we have prima facie reason to do. This is comparable to the point that it may not be clear to us what we have the *best* reason to believe, even if it is clear to us what alternatives we have some reason to believe.

It might be thought that to admit that skepticism has this much room to worry us is to give up on grounding objectivity and rationality. I think this is the wrong approach. In my view, if an account of the notions of knowledge, justification, objectivity, and other central notions in the theory of rationality does not make clear why skepticism is at least plausible, it is missing something. Our normative practices are complex and subject to fallibility. It is folly or dogmatism or both to think that it should always be obvious what we ought, on balance, to do or believe. But to grant that this is not always obvious is by no means to grant that we never know it, or never even have justified beliefs to this effect, or never act for adequate reason. Again, why need justified belief, or good reason to act, occur only where it is utterly obvious what proposition to believe or what deed to do? And why cannot objectivity, of a high even if not maximal degree, be grounded in the a priori relevance of certain kinds of reasons, epistemic and practical, even if it is not always obvious how these reasons balance?

The Problem of Deliberative Composition

The internalist objectivism just set out readily allows for wide and sometimes rational disagreement on how competing reasons should balance: even rational deliberation on one's relevant reasons does not always make it clear how they may be so connected as to favor a unique choice among one's alternatives. This problem (also discussed in chapters 11 and 12) is serious but need not undermine the kind of view developed in this book. For one thing, there is at least an indirect check on our judgments in such matters: how things turn out in terms of the basic reasons. Return to underdetermination: it may not be clear which theory is preferable in terms of the data; but we are entitled to believe that if a theory we choose implies consequences we can perceptually tell are false, then the otherwise equally confirmed theory is preferable. And if one of two equally rational-seeming actions turns out to have painful consequences, this can show objectively that we were mistaken in preferring it.

It may be clarifying to widen the perspective of the moderate rationalism proposed. For all we clearly know a priori, there could be basic epistemic sources other than the classical four — perception, consciousness, memory, and reflection (including intuition). The claim here is only that at least these are essentially constitutive of justification (in a sense allowing other elements, such as coherence, to play a major role with respect to justification). Certainly we could have been such that our perceptual justification is provided by some other kind of sensations or type of sense organs; wide differences of these sorts can be accommodated by the idea that perception, in the broadest sense, is a basic source of justification.[52] Moreover, our problems of balancing competing justificatory considerations may at least be confined to the sphere in which the four basic sources I have noted supply the crucial principles.[53] The constitutive grounds of practical rationality may also be broader than hedonists, eudaemonists, or even many valuational pluralists have suggested.[54]

Similar sorts of points apply to the special case of moral reasons for action that are grounded in basic principles of ethics. To maintain the parallel with the theoretical case, I will assume that there is a plurality of such principles, as argued by Ross.[55] Each principle gives us an internal route, through applying that a priori principle, to knowledge or at least justified belief about our prima facie moral reasons for action, which Ross saw as corresponding to special and general duties: we might owe someone recompense, we might be bound by a promise, and we are prima facie obligated not to harm others. As in the theoretical case, it may be — though it certainly need not be — difficult to tell how our reasons balance when we have competing alternatives before us, but (as in that case) we can at least use the same principles to help us do the weighting and, after making our choice, to check on whether we have done right. Whether my recompense for a wrong I did was adequate may be verified by whether, for instance, it relieves pain or produces pleasure in the person wronged.

If there is an element of subjectivity in the use of practical wisdom suggested here, it is not an unbridled subjectivity; nor does it prevent our convergence toward commonly acceptable solutions insofar as we can share experiences and, as it were, equalize our starting points or at least maximize their overlap. Just as we can minimize theoretical disagreement in general by observing the same data and critically discussing our theories in the light of those data, we can maximize agreement on practical principles by trying on the shoes of our fellows.

This approach is quite consonant with realism but does not entail it. The objectivity in question is epistemic and methodological, not ontological: an objective method of judging value is defended, but the main defense does not entail that there are such properties as intrinsic goodness and moral obligation. Goodness is not, however, reduced to evidences thereof; the concept of the good, for instance, is not that of the pleasant. The view is not a simple internalist subjectivism like the position that goodness is simply desire satisfaction, nor an epistemic subjectivization of goodness, like the view that it is satisfaction of desires suitably grounded in rational belief, but a non-reductive internalist objectivism.

In part because fallibility is granted by the view, the approach is also non-dogmatic, even in its realist form. Even if I can be certain I have prima facie reasons for belief or action, I cannot plausibly proceed from there to any smug certainty that I have overall reasons. Prima facie justification, however well grounded, does not entail justification on balance. Similarly, some degree of intrinsic goodness encountered in an experience does not entail that the experience or anything else is (intrinsically or otherwise) good on the whole. On the other hand, the internalism of the approach enables it to capture part of what is appealing in subjectivism without depriving us of universal standards of judgment.

Conclusion

If the internalist, intuitionistic objectivism sketched here is correct, then the analogy between theoretical and practical reason extends both to considerations that make skepticism plausible and to arguments that enable us to avoid the strong skeptical conclusion that we lack knowledge of the world and of what kinds of things are valuable — knowledge of external truths and of objective goods. Supposing, however, that those anti-skeptical arguments fail, there are further, stronger arguments for the moderate conclusion that we can have, if not theoretical and practical knowledge, then adequate reasons for beliefs about the world, adequate reasons for believing certain things to be good, and, by virtue of the rational grounds for those evaluative beliefs, at least prima facie reasons for action.

Our grounds for justified belief and rational action are ultimately internal. In the theoretical case, they are perceptual, introspective, memorial, and rational; and in the practical case, they include at least hedonic and moral considerations. That there are such theoretical and practical grounds seems to me ascertainable by sufficiently thorough and adequately informed priori reflection. This is not to say that the relevant normative principles of theoretical and practical reason are immediately self-evident, and I grant that our justification for such principles is defeasible. For all that, it may turn out that the defeaters must come from among the factors figuring in those very principles; this would help us to determine, by appeal to a manageable number of basic considerations, where our overall justification for action lies.

We surely sometimes have practical justification, whether for desire or even for action, though even when we have it we cannot be dogmatically certain of it. We also have adequate justification for holding certain normative principles. Even if we did not have this cognitive justification, we could still have a measure of conative justification, in the form of desires that are rational in virtue of being appropriately directed toward good things, such as beneficent deeds and aesthetic enjoyments, and are a motivational ground on which we sometimes act rationally or morally or both. On the basis of either kind of practical reason — the cognitive kind constituted by justified beliefs of practical principles or of particular judgments that conform to them, or the conative kind constituted by rational desires that accord with those principles — we can, in some cases, perform actions that are rational. There is no adequate reason, moreover, not to take our justified beliefs to be quite often true and our rational actions to achieve, quite often, one or another kind of intrinsic good.

Notes

This essay has benefited from discussions after its presentation at Emory University, the University of Georgia, the University of Missouri, Columbia, and Wheaton College, where Thomas Senor provided a valuable commentary. For helpful comments on earlier versions I also thank William Alston, Randolph Clark, Muhammad Ali Khalidi, and Paul Moser.

1. See, e.g., Christine M. Korsgaard, "Skepticism about Practical Reason," *Journal of Philosophy* 83 (1986): 5–25. It is noteworthy that motivational skepticism is compatible with rejection of theoretical skepticism: a motivational skeptic could hold that one might know that one ought to A, yet lack any motivation to A.

2. For a wide-ranging critique of some of these theorists, especially W. V. Quine and Richard Rorty, see Paul K. Moser, *Philosophy after Objectivity* (Oxford and New York: Oxford University Press, 1993).

3. The *content* of the proposition might guarantee its truth, as where what I believe hap-

pens to be a necessary truth and, by that good fortune, cannot be false. The skeptic is entitled to insist on distinguishing evidence's (trivially) entailing *p* from its *guaranteeing* truth: any evidence entails (in the sense of strictly implying) any necessary truth, but if my evidence does not guarantee it (in an epistemically relevant sense that is hard to specify) I might believe it just by good luck; then I surely do not know it.

4. Some of the directions of argument here are quite familiar to students of epistemology and even of philosophy in general, but a short treatment of some of them, and various bibliographical references, are provided in my *Epistemology: A Contemporary Introduction to the Theory of Knowledge* (London and New York: Routledge, 1997).

5. This phrase is indeed the title of an article by Fred Dretske, *Australasian Journal of Philosophy* 49 (1971): 1–22, though for him 'conclusive' is not a logical term. Anyone who talks of "scientific proof" or even of "scientific knowledge" (and both phrases are common) takes it that we do sometimes have evidence, even about the external world, that "rules out" mistakes.

6. This is not uncontroversial. Richard Foley, in *Working without a Net* (Oxford and New York: Oxford University Press, 1993), argues that (as many pragmatists have held) reasons for belief can be reasons for holding a believing attitude as opposed to reasons supporting the truth of the believed proposition. See esp. ch. 1. But the relevant data are probably at least well explained on the hypothesis that these reasons are really practical reasons for causing oneself to believe, nurturing one's belief, or the like — hence reasons for action rather than belief.

7. This conception of the good is well developed as early as Plato and is elaborately treated by Aquinas.

8. This treatment of truth and goodness as respectively the "points" of the theoretical and practical attitudes is consistent with a quite different but also wide-ranging understanding of both kinds of attitudes: the virtue approach. Truth and goodness can be construed as providing the overall criteria for the relevant virtues. For a variety of approaches to understanding virtue, especially intellectual virtue, see Ernest Sosa, "Knowledge and Intellectual Virtue," *The Monist* 68, no. 2 (1985): 226–45; Jonathan Kvanvig, *The Intellectual Virtues and the Life of the Mind* (Lanham, Md.: Rowman and Littlefield, 1992); James A. Montmarquet, *Epistemic Virtue and Doxastic Responsibility* (Lanham, Md.: Rowman and Littlefield, 1993); and Linda Zagzebski, *Virtues of the Mind* (Cambridge: Cambridge University Press, 1996).

9. A similar idea is (the probably very old thesis) that belief aims at truth, argued by Bernard Williams in his widely discussed "Deciding to Believe," in his *Problems of the Self* (Cambridge: Cambridge University Press, 1973), and often echoed as if unproblematic even by careful writers. See, e.g., Roy Sorensen, "Rationality as an Absolute Concept," *Philosophy* 66 (1991), p. 476. Cf. Peter Railton's interesting use of the idea that to believe is to believe true, in "On the Hypothetical and Non-Hypothetical in Reasoning about Action," in Garrett Cullity and Berys Gaut, eds., *Ethics and Practical Reason* (forthcoming).

10. On wants as expressing — as opposed to constituting —(normative) reasons for which we act, see my "Acting for Reasons," *Philosophical Review* (1986): 511–46. This point leaves open that there *are* reasons for action not necessarily expressed in wants and that wants are (non-normative) reasons *why* we act.

11. The analogy between intending and believing is pursued in ch. 3 of my *A Theory of Rationality* (in preparation).

12. This higher-order proposition is not even an equivalent of *p* so close that we may plausibly claim that any *rational* person who believes one of them necessarily believes the other. For a partial account of belief supporting this and the previous paragraph see my "Dispositional Beliefs and Dispositions to Believe," *Nous* 28 (1994): 419–34.

13. Arguably, just as first-person expressions of belief are commonly not primarily self-

ascriptions of belief but assertions of the proposition in question, first-person expressions of wants are commonly not primarily self-ascriptions of desire but requests for the object in question. Still, there is disanalogy as well as analogy here (the cognitive case, e.g., may have no analogue of 'I want cake, but don't give it to me — I'm dieting'), but the analogy remains significant.

14. I state the analogy in a way that invites the comment that the goodness gap is just a special case of the truth gap: it is a gap between evidence of goodness and the truth of the proposition that something is good. This is fair enough for a cognitivist construal of normative predicates, but I think the analogy is significant even viewed as holding within the category of the truth gap. If, however, noncognitivism is coherent, as I am assuming, then the value gap lies between evidences as grounds for the positive attitudes appropriate to what is "correctly" called *good* and the soundness (the noncognitive counterpart of truth) of those attitudes themselves.

15. This issue is discussed in some detail in ch. 11.

16. An objection to this effect was put by Thomas Senor in his commentary on an earlier version of this essay.

17. This point holds unless the mere possession of certain beliefs guarantees the rationality of certain actions, even apart from rendering rational any desires. That is an unlikely possibility at best, but I cannot argue the point directly here.

18. In a loose and popular sense of 'skeptic' such a person might be called a *skeptic* about the good; but this is hardly skepticism proper when driven by a belief that one *knows* there is no intrinsic goodness.

19. John Dewey is the most famous proponent of the warranted assertability approach.

20. Richard B. Brandt's theory of rational desire in A *Theory of the Good and the Right* (Oxford: Oxford University Press, 1979) is a good example of such a view.

21. For a detailed account of subjectivism in the domain of theoretical reason, see Richard A. Foley, *The Theory of Epistemic Rationality* (Cambridge: Harvard University Press, 1987).

22. A striking statement of subjectivism is B. F. Skinner's idea that we should aim not "to design a world that will be liked by people as they now are but to design a world that will be liked not by people as they now are but by the people who live in it." *Beyond Freedom and Dignity* (New York: Knopf, 1971), p. 156. This is certainly a subjectivistic desire-satisfaction view of what seems a vision of the good.

23. I leave open many details that are not crucial here, e.g. whether rational action must maximize desire satisfaction and must be based on rational belief.

24. Since Hume thought of pleasure and pain as good and evil, he was not (at that point, anyway) a pure instrumentalist. But notice that reason can be the slave of the passions even if some of them are passions *for* what is good. Perhaps Hume should be read as withholding or even rejecting the idea that what is good is a basic reason for desire; for one thing it is not clear how his empiricist epistemology would allow him to account for this point, which seems neither empirical nor analytic. The reason-giving power of intrinsic goods is discussed further in chs. 10 and 11.

25. This is a psychologistic naturalist view of justification suggested in part by W. V. Quine's "Epistemology Naturalized," in his *Ontological Relativity and Other Essays* (New York: Columbia University Press, 1969).

26. Both views might be combined with what J. L. Mackie called an error theory, roughly an account of how it is that people believe there is intrinsic goodness and some kind of epistemic counterpart, such as a strong form of non-inferential justification.

27. In part because attitudes imply motivation, holding them is normally taken to imply having at least motivational reasons for action; e.g., a positive aesthetic attitude might provide its possessor with such a reason to view a beautiful painting. These reasons are not my con-

cern here. A description of them and a partial account of their relation to moral judgment is given in ch. 10.

28. For an account of some main kinds of relativity and of their connection with problems about the status of realism, see Moser, *Philosophy after Objectivity*.

29. This is connected with the idea that the moral supervenes on the non-moral, an idea that even R. M. Hare, to cite one noncognitivist, uses in grounding the kind of attitudinal consistency referred to in the text. See his *Freedom and Reason* (Oxford: Oxford University Press, 1963). The relevant kind of consistency is noted in connection with the categorical imperative in ch. 12.

30. Some of them are instructively discussed by William P. Alston in *The Reliability of Sense Perception* (Ithaca and London: Cornell University Press, 1993).

31. A good example here is Ralph Barton Perry, who argued in *General Theory of Value* (New York: Longmans, green,1926) that "[a]ny object . . . acquires value when any interest, whatever it be, is taken in it." Some of the Cornell realists also approach goodness naturalistically, though less psychologistically. See, e.g., Nicholas Sturgeon's "Moral Explanations" and some of the other papers in Geoffrey Sayre-McCord, ed., *Essays on Moral Realism* (Ithaca and London: Cornell University Press, 1988). Critical discussion of Sturgeon's strategy and the relevant kind of naturalism is given in my "Ethical Naturalism and the Explanatory Power of Moral Concepts," ch. 5 below. Still another move is to argue that goodness is at once natural and normative in the way health is, as Paul Bloomfield argues in a paper forthcoming in *Philosophical Studies*.

32. For a plausible and scholarly recent discussion, see William P. Alston, *A Realist Theory of Truth* (Ithaca and London: Cornell University Press, 1996).

33. For noncognitivism, wanting things that are "not genuinely good" might be interpreted in terms of the possibility of wanting something under conditions in which it is not reasonable to have the positive attitude toward it one would express by saying it is good.

34. Their status, which is apparently both synthetic and a priori, is discussed further later, where references are given to explications of the relevant notion of the a priori. This synthetic character of propositions of this sort was a central point stressed by G. E. Moore in *Principia Ethica* (Cambridge: Cambridge University Press, 1903); cf. his reply to William Frankena in *The Philosophy of G. E. Moore* (New York: Tudor Publishing Co., 1942), esp. pp. 571–80. Frankena's critique, "Obligation and Value in the Ethics of G. E. Moore," is in the same volume, pp. 93–110.

35. I argue for this in detail in ch. 10.

36. The failure to respond to (at least believed) practical evidence, especially in the moral case, is what motivational internalists tend to think impossible. This issue is discussed in ch. 10.

37. This is probably the view of Brandt, *A Theory of the Good and the Right*. For critical discussion see my "An Epistemic Conception of Rationality," in my *The Structure of Justification* (Cambridge and New York: Cambridge University Press, 1993). Also relevant are Foley, *Working without a Net*, and Richard A. Fumerton, *Reason and Morality: A Defense of the Egocentric Perspective* (Ithaca and London: Cornell University Press, 1990).

38. Data statements do not include more general theories — from which obviously a theory might follow — but the sort of inductive evidence normally used in confirming a theory, e.g. its predictions' bearing out, its explaining lower-level generalizations, as Newtonian gravitational theory explains the laws of free fall and the behavior of the tides, and so forth.

39. Peter Geach's point (that normative statements operate in conditional propositions as one would expect if the former are truth-valued), as applied to Simon Blackburn's and Allan Gibbard's anti-realism, is developed by Mark van Roojen in "Expressivism and Irrationality," *Philosophical Review* 105 (1996), 311–35.

40. This is plausibly argued by Nicholas Sturgeon; ch. 5 sets out his view and appraises it.

41. Both conclusions are defended in my "Justification, Truth, and Reliability," in my *The Structure of Justification*.

42. Some reasons to doubt that it can succeed are given in ch. 5.

43. For arguments in defense of these points see *Epistemology*, ch. 5, and my "Deductive Closure, Defeasibility, and Skepticism: A Reply to Professor Feldman," *Philosophical Quarterly* 45 (1995):494–99. These works, though leaving open some closure principles, attack a representative sample of the kinds important for the success of skepticism.

44. A case for this is made in my "Justification, Truth, and Reliability." The principle applies, of course, only to those having the concept of green and any others necessary for believing the proposition in question. Prima facie justification for believing something is compatible with far better justification for believing something incompatible — say that one is merely being caused to hallucinate something green. Note, however, that if principles like the one is question are not accepted, it is at best difficult to explain how one acquires enough justification for a contrary.

45. In calling it a version of rationalism I assume the relevant principles are not analytic; this may need argument but would be widely granted even by those willing to countenance the existence of analytic propositions.

46. As I have argued in "Justification, Truth, and Reliability" and "Religious Experience and the Practice Conception of Justification," in Thomas D. Senor, ed., *The Rationality of Belief and the Plurality of Faith* (Ithaca and London: Cornell University Press, 1995). Ch. 12 outlines an ethical intuitionist in which Rossian principles of duty play a similar role for moral justification.

47. This is a stronger claim than I have granted so far: that experiential evidence does not entail that anything is good *overall* (thereby having the valuational analogue of truth). For reasons detailed in ch. 11, even the experience of pleasure in administering a punishment might have an intrinsically good *element* without being good on the whole.

48. This second, more controversial assumption is defended, in part along Aristotelian lines, in ch. 11. I should add that the sense in which the objectively good provides a reason is objective — it is a reason *there is* to promote the good in question. It is not a reason I *have* to do so until it is in some way in my ken, e.g. through my believing the thing in question is intrinsically good.

49. At least normally, I would also *have* reason to get out; but here I am talking about an objective kind of reason that in principle one might not have because of, e.g., justified false beliefs, such as that one is only hallucinating cold water. It is questionable, however, whether there can be reasons for us to do something that we *could not* have, say by acquiring suitable beliefs.

50. There is one asymmetry that may show that theoretical reason is basic for practical reason in a way practical reason is not basic for theoretical reason: arguably, an action is rational only if both its underlying desire(s) *and* belief(s) are rational, whereas neither the justifiedness nor the rationality of belief depends (in general) on that of desire. I doubt, however, that this asymmetry undermines any point in this essay.

51. For an account of such difficulties and a defense of the internalist view suggested combined with the causal basing requirement that a belief is justified *by* a ground only if (causally) based at least partly *on* that ground, see my "Causalist Internalism," *American Philosophical Quarterly* 26 (1989): 309–20.

52. The case with knowledge is different and may lead those who associate justification too closely with knowledge to overstate the room the concept of justification leaves for other justifiers to displace the standard four. If, as I am inclined to think, the concept of knowledge is external, there are no a priori limits on what sorts of factors can objectively indicate truth to

us: this depends on how the world is and not on our concept of justification. Discussion of the internality of justification contrasted with the externality of knowledge is given in my "Justification, Truth, and Reliability"; cf. Fred Dretske, *Knowledge and the Flow of Information* (Cambridge: MIT Press, 1981), and William P. Alston, *Epistemic Justification* (Ithaca and London: Cornell University Press, 1989).

53. The kind of role these sources play, and the relation of coherence to them, is indicated in some detail in "The Foundationalism-Coherentism Controversy," in my *The Structure of Justification*.

54. Ch. 11 argues that this non-hedonist valuational pluralism is reasonable.

55. These are explained in detail in ch. 2. I would emphasize that (as argued there) the apriority of a principle by no means implies that it is an obvious truth or believable with indefeasible justification.

II

Ethical Concepts
and Moral Realism

4

Moral Epistemology and the Supervenience of Ethical Concepts

Can there be moral truths, as opposed to truths merely about morals, say about people's moral attitudes of approval and disapproval? If there can be moral truths, can they be known, or even justifiedly believed? And if there can be moral knowledge or justification, what sorts of evidence can ground it? Would the evidence be, for instance, the same kind that grounds scientific beliefs? Or would it be more like the evidence that grounds mathematical truths, if indeed this is different from the former kind? These questions are fundamental in moral epistemology and will be my subject.

I. Some Major Aims of Moral Epistemology

Consider the following as typical of moral principles, and hence as indicating some of the main items for which moral epistemology must account: (1) we must not kill other people; (2) slavery is wrong; (3) we ought to keep our promises; (4) we should not lie; (5) parents must not beat their children; and (6) it is unjust to give different sentences for the same crime committed by highly (or at least relevantly) similar people in the same circumstances. Many moral theorists would say that all of these principles may be justifiedly believed and are indeed widely known to be true; but this epistemological point is plausible — or most plausible — only on the assumption that the principles are *prima facie*, in at least this sense. The prohibition, obligation, or appraisal they express is defeasible, not absolute: in each case, there are possible considerations — which some philosophers would say must be other moral factors — that defeat the prohibition, obligation, or appraisal. Imagine, for instance, that a child has a life-threatening hysteria which the parents have excellent reason to believe can be assuaged only by electric shock. They may then shock the child without violating their parental obligation.[1]

If we think of a prohibition as a negative obligation, we can express the main point here by saying that the principles cited (or at least the first five) express prima facie, not absolute, that is, indefeasible, obligation. Self-defense, for instance, is a consideration that may defeat the obligation not to kill. Granted, a prima facie obligation can be *strong*; and not just any claim of self-defense can defeat the prohibition against killing. But it is doubtful that any of the specific moral principles we are guided by in day-to-day life expresses indefeasible obligation.[2]

It turns out, then, that some of the most important kinds of statement for which moral epistemology must account have at least one significant element of vagueness: the (often tacit) prima facie qualification. One might think we can eliminate this by simply listing the defeaters. Thus, there might seem to be an absolute obligation not to kill others *except* in self-defense, warranted capital punishment, or justified euthanasia. But when, if ever, is capital punishment justified? And what about the problem of morally *un*justified self-defense, for instance action sincerely but unreasonably taken in protecting oneself? If we put the concept of justified self-defense into our purportedly absolute moral principle, a defeasible moral notion — something like that of self-defense that is not "excessive" — enters into our attempt to eliminate such notions. If we try to define 'excessive', we face something like a prima facie qualification all over again, for example the idea that other things equal, force is excessive when greater than required to deter the danger. The implicit point is not just about the notion of prima facie obligation. We could also express moral obligations in terms of moral reasons. We could say that there is good moral reason not to kill, or that an action's being a breaking of a promise is a moral consideration against it. But, like obligations, such moral reasons are surely defeasible by counter-reasons.

These points might seem to make the task of moral epistemology more difficult than it would be if all the principles whose epistemic status is in question were utterly clear or indefeasible. If our target is not clear, how can we hit it? The metaphor is misleading: only the outer edges of the target are not clear — or not there. Its center is, if not perfectly clear, quite visible: we know what killing is, and what constitutes breaking a promise; and we know much about what a reason is — or at any rate, we deal with reasons or comparably difficult notions in doing epistemology at all and even in daily life. Furthermore, for the non-skeptical moral epistemologist, there is an advantage in having target principles that are prima facie. Other things equal, it takes less in the way of grounds to know, or be justified in believing, a prima facie principle than its absolute counterpart. A prima facie moral principle expresses *some* reason for a kind of action; an absolute principle expresses a *sufficient* reason. Compare the grounds for believing that killing is prima facie wrong with such grounds as there are for thinking it absolutely wrong. Few philosophers would defend the stronger claim.

It is reasonable, then, to take the task of moral epistemology to be largely (though not entirely) to clarify and account for the epistemic status of moral principles construed as defeasible. Ideally, a related aim should be pursued simultaneously: to unify moral principles in a way that indicates why they are moral and, if possible, to conceive them as grounded in the same or similar kinds of considerations about the beings to whom they apply. What follows will address both aims.

II. Cognitivism versus Noncognitivism in Moral Epistemology

There is a fundamental division in ethical theory which must be addressed immediately. It concerns the semantic status of moral judgments, by which I mean the everyday moral declarations by which we guide much of our lives. We tell our children that lying is wrong; we say that we have obligations to colleagues which prevent our doing something we might like to do; we criticize certain actions (such as cheating) as wrong when they violate our moral standards. Are these statements *cognitive*, in the sense that they express propositions, the sorts of things that are true or false? Or are we, for instance, using the relevant declarative sentences not to state truths but to express attitudes and thereby influence behavior in the desired direction, say attitudes of disapproval toward lying and approval toward veracity?

The latter, noncognitivist view is not irrationalist or even subjectivist. It is entirely consistent with noncognitivism to distinguish between rational and irrational attitudes and to allow that objective considerations, such as the suffering produced by slavery, are a justifying ground for moral attitudes. The main point for moral epistemology, then, is not that for noncognitivism, there is no moral *justification*. It is rather that there is no moral *truth*, and so moral justification applies not to beliefs of propositions but, above all, to attitudes (or other non-truth-valued elements). Noncognitivists may even talk of moral "knowledge" (and of knowing moral truth) if it is taken to be, not the grasp of moral propositions, but the possession of a suitably objective justification for the relevant moral attitudes, for example the negative attitude one expresses in saying to children that stealing is wrong.

Noncognitivists can agree with cognitivists on what acts *are* right, or wrong; the disagreement is over the kind of meaning to ascribe to (apparent) *attributions* of right and wrong. I do not accept noncognitivism, but I recognize it as an important alternative. My main point here is that even if it should be true, it would not undermine one task of moral epistemology — to account for moral justification: specifically, for the nature and function of the grounds that can warrant moral attitudes. Thus, while cognitivism will be presupposed in what follows, some of the points that emerge regarding moral justification can be preserved in a noncognitivist framework. It is possible, however, to do a great deal of ethics without presupposing *either* cognitivism or noncognitivism. One can, for instance, give pragmatic arguments for adopting a set of moral principles while leaving their semantic status open.

III. Rationalism, Empiricism, and Supervenience in Moral Epistemology

As one would expect, a major divide in moral epistemology, as in general epistemology, is between rationalism and empiricism. Rationalists in moral epistemology regard the basic moral truths — those not epistemically derivable from other moral truths[3] — as knowable (or at least justifiedly believable) a priori: roughly, through reasoning about, or reflection on, the relevant concepts and their relations (I ignore the possibility of being a rationalist and moral skeptic, since the historically important rationalists in moral epistemology were not moral skeptics). Empiricists in moral epistemology (if cognitivist and non-skeptical) regard the basic moral truths as knowable (or justifiedly believable) only empirically: roughly, through experience that provides relevant evidence, for instance evidence that lying (or maiming or killing) causes suffering.[4] Kant seems to be a paradigm of a rationalist in moral epistemology, Mill of an empiricist. For Kant, the categorical imperative is knowable a priori; for Mill, the principle of utility seems knowable only on the basis of at least one premise, namely the valuational hedonism which (just after introducing the principle of utility) he calls a "theory of life." In Kant's view, I can know what particular sorts of acts are right by reasoning in the light of the categorical imperative, which, in one form, says that we are to treat rational beings always as ends in themselves, never merely as means. For Mill, I can know what specific kinds of acts are right only on the basis of knowing how various types of acts affect human happiness. Thus, Kant would say that lying to people is wrong because — as reflection will reveal — it treats them merely as a means; Mill would say that it is wrong because — as the experience of humanity has shown — it tends to cause suffering (with no adequate compensation in happiness).[5]

A narrower contrast would have the rationalist committed, as Kant is, to the existence of basic moral principles that are *synthetic* a priori. One might reasonably build this in, but I am supposing that rationalists in moral epistemology are, *as such*, committed only to the existence of a priori basic moral knowledge; they have often argued for its syntheticity, but that is not entailed by their general rationalist commitments alone. I also leave open that an empiricist in *general* epistemology can be a rationalist in moral epistemology, say by construing some basic moral principle as analytic. But surely a moral theory's taking something as substantive as a basic moral principle (such as a version of the principle of utility) to be analytic is a good reason to consider that position rationalist.

The controversy between rationalist and empiricist epistemologies is very much alive today, and I see no hope of escaping it — or readily resolving it — in moral epistemology. We can, however, clarify the controversy by pursuing it in the moral domain. Indeed, examining it there is particularly appropriate because, in the recent literature of ethical theory, discussion has often been dominated by empiricist assumptions. This holds particularly for a number of plausible attempts to account for the reality of moral properties in terms of their explanatory power, and so in principle to ground the possibility of moral knowledge in the same way one grounds the possibility of scientific knowledge.[6] Before comparing the resources of empiricism and rationalism in moral epistemology, however, it is important to sketch some of the associated metaphysical options.

On the cognitivist assumption that there are true and false moral propositions, it is useful to speak of moral properties. Concrete acts may have the property of being wrong; persons may have the property of being unjust; and policies, say of reparation, may have the property of being obligatory. Let us also make another assumption, which is common ground between rationalism and empiricism: that the ultimate source of evidence for ascriptions of moral properties is facts about non-moral properties. For instance, an act might be wrong because it is a lie or a breaking of a promise, where the properties of being a lie or a breaking of a promise are apparently not themselves moral and can be known, on a non-moral basis, to belong to an act.[7] Using the terminology standard in the literature, we might call these non-moral properties *natural*; the idea is roughly that whether a thing has a particular natural property is a matter of (empirical) fact, not of value or rightness. Alternatively (but not quite equivalently), it is to be determined by observation and scientific procedures and is not a matter of what is morally right or of what is intrinsically good or bad.

We can now raise the question, for both empiricism and rationalism, of what ontological relation holds between moral properties and the sorts of natural ones that provide evidence for their presence. As in the case of the mind-body problem, there are at least three major possibilities: (1) reductive naturalism, which says that moral properties are identical with certain natural ones; (2) eliminativism, which rejects our question and says that there *are* no moral properties — noncognitivism is the most important version of this view;[8] and (3) what I shall call the supervenience view. In the strong form that concerns me here, (3) is the view that moral properties supervene on — or, in what may be more natural terminology, are consequential upon — natural ones. This is (roughly) to say that there is a special non-reductive relation between moral and natural properties such that (a) no two things (including actions) can have the same natural properties and differ in their moral ones, and (b) certain of the natural properties of a thing determine what moral properties it has (if any).[9] (One may also speak of supervenient concepts; simply substitute the notion of two things instantiating the same concept for the notion of their sharing a property.) Thus, the injustice of a tyrant, a moral property, might supervene on his brutality toward the people. Usually, moral supervenience is taken (as I shall take it) to preclude moral properties (or concepts) being reducible to natural ones, and so is an option incompatible with reductivism. More will be said about supervenience as we compare empiricism and rationalism. In making this comparison, I will generally take up only cognitivist options.

IV. *Empiricism and Reductive Naturalism*

It is very natural for an empiricist to be a reductivist: metaphysically, because reductivism implies that moral properties are experienceable, or are at least related to what is experienceable, in the same way as the natural properties the empiricist already countenances; and epistemologically, because reductivism apparently implies that moral knowledge can be as securely grounded as knowledge of the natural properties constituting the moral ones — such as obligation and justice — of which knowledge is sought. These points hold, at any rate, for the strongest kind of reductivism: the kind based on conceptual reduction, which takes moral concepts to be equivalent to certain natural ones. This kind of reduction, however, is widely believed to be impossible, in part for reasons brought out by G. E. Moore and later writers who refined his views.[10] If reduction is possible, it is currently felt to be most likely along the lines of scientific reduction, say that of biological properties to physico-chemical ones. Unfortunately, there is perhaps even more controversy over what is required for scientific property reduction than over the conditions for conceptual reduction.

For our purposes, the main point here is that if moral properties are only ontologically, but not conceptually, equivalent to natural ones, then the epistemology of the latter does not as easily shore up that of the former. Suppose, for example, that injustice is conceptually equivalent to a kind of factually ascertainable inequality (unequal treatment), and wrongness is conceptually equivalent to producing a net balance of suffering over happiness. We can then use facts and conceptual analysis to ground our knowledge that injustice is wrong in factual knowledge of how inequality affects suffering: we simply show that inequality causes a net balance of suffering; and since inequality is equivalent to injustice, and causing a net balance of suffering is equivalent to wrongdoing, it follows that injustice is (a kind of) wrongdoing (it is a producer of a net balance of suffering). It is quite another thing, however, to say that since injustice is ultimately, though not conceptually, the same property as a kind of inequality, and wrongness is implied by such inequality, we can show that our knowledge that injustice is wrong is grounded in knowledge of its causing a net balance of suffering. Here the justification is less elegant; its route must go through some doubtless controversial theory equating the properties of injustice and inequality; and any moral knowledge we gain will depend *both* on the truth of the theory, especially its identification of injustice with inequality, and on our knowledge of how inequality affects people. In short, the contrast is between connecting the natural and the moral by an analytic bridge and connecting them by a theoretical one; the latter may, to be sure, bear the weight of reduction, but it cannot be established either a priori or in any straightforward empirical way.

To say that reductivism is problematic, however, is not to say it is dead,[11] and given its epistemological *and* ontological appeal as a view which avoids positing non-natural properties, it should be expected to have considerable vitality. An empiricist need not, however, be a reductivist, for the weaker view that moral properties supervene on natural ones can apparently serve at once to ground — though not by itself to create — moral knowledge and to root moral properties firmly in the empirically accessible world of the natural properties that constitute their base.[12] The central idea is this: if moral properties are determined by natural ones, then *provided* we can know which natural ones are relevant to which moral properties, we can know moral truths on the basis of knowing non-moral truths. And both empiricists and rationalists are likely to hold that if we understand moral terms at all, we know what sorts of non-moral properties are relevant to their application: considerations of equality are relevant to justice; considerations of honesty in speech and of fidelity to promises are relevant to good moral character; and, more generally, facts about the consequences of a kind of act for human flourishing — about what makes us happy, unhappy, satisfied, frustrated, and so forth — are relevant to the truth of moral judgments in general. We can certainly know that if two cases are alike in the relevant natural properties, they are alike in their moral ones. This permits us to know that (as Aristotle saw but expressed in terms of justice) there is a prima facie obligation to treat like cases alike, and that a prima facie wrong has been done if like cases are treated unequally. Granted, moral knowledge is not as elegantly grounded by such supervenience relations as by reduction of moral to natural properties; but the grounding still seems sufficient to provide moral justification that can satisfy non-skeptics.

V. Rationalism, Naturalism, and A Priori Supervenience

Let us see if similar options are available to rationalists in moral epistemology. His-torically, rationalists in ethics have not been reductivists and have indeed tended to treat moral and other normative properties as non-natural.[13] It might seem that a rationalist cannot be a reductivist. Granted, rationalists cannot be thoroughgoing naturalists committed to the claim that all knowledge is natural in the sense of *empirical*, for they deny the underlying ontological view that the only *truths* are nat-ural — a view I call *substantive naturalism*. But a rationalist can hold a *conceptual naturalism* — a view on which there are no irreducibly normative concepts: the only ultimate *concepts* are natural.[14] This does not require empiricism. Even if there are no irreducibly normative concepts, moral *knowledge* need not all be empirical, any more than mathematical knowledge, which is plainly non-normative, need be. Some of the relations among moral concepts might not be empirical even if their application to the world should be an empirical question. A conceptual naturalist, for example, whether rationalist or empiricist, might maintain — against Kant's view — that it is an empirical question whether it is ever right to break a promise. But rationalists will tend to reject both forms of naturalism, as Kant certainly would. Utilitarians need not reject either form; they would take it to be a factual question whether promise breaking is ever right, and they could in principle treat as analytic or as empirical the relation between the concepts of being right and maximizing good.

One reason why it is at best unusual for rationalists to be naturalists of any sort is this: why trouble to produce a reduction of the moral to the natural if one has an epistemology that readily accounts for moral knowledge without reduction? Simi-larly, there is no incentive for rationalists to be eliminativists, for example noncogni-tivists. The chief appeal of eliminativism is to save empiricism when reduction fails and supervenience seems too weak to serve one's ontological and epistemological ends. Still, it should not be thought that a rationalist in epistemology *must* be a non-naturalist in ontology.

Supervenience is the kind of relation which a plausible rationalism is likely to posit between moral and natural properties. In outline, the view might be this. First, as I suggested earlier, the relation is likely to be conceived as one of non-reductive determination. Second, it will be construed as epistemologically a priori. Third, it will be viewed as conceptually constitutive: criterial, in one sense. And finally, so un-derstood, the relation will be taken to ground a priori knowledge of general moral truths.

Let me illustrate with an example of injustice. First, since the supervenience relation is non-reductive, the account of supervenience does not commit a moral theorist to specifying a set of base properties — "subvenient" ones — necessary *and* suf-ficient for injustice; it is enough that, say, unequal punishments for the same crime, or any punishments for an act the punishee did not commit, are sufficient for — and determine — injustice. Second, we can know a priori that, for instance, it would be unjust to punish Janet for a crime she did not commit. Third, such misbegotten punishment is partly constitutive of what injustice *is*; it is not, say, a mere cause of injustice. Far from it: in order to determine causes of injustice, one must first *identify* it in terms of such things as unequal sentencing. These natural properties of acts, then, are conceptual criteria for injustice; their connection with it, epistemologically as well as semantically, is a priori. Fourth, certain general moral truths can now be seen to be knowable a priori. Consider those to the effect that a kind of act is wrong. There are two possibilities. Either being wrong supervenes directly on such natural properties as the property of being a lie and that of being a punishment given for a crime not committed, or it indirectly supervenes on them via supervening on other moral properties, such as injustice or immorality (this does not entail that in general supervenience is a transitive relation, but there is some reason to construe it as such). In the first case, one might know a priori that, say, lying is wrong because lying is among the constitutive criteria for wrong action; in the second case, one might know a priori that punishing for a crime not committed is wrong because one knows that this is a constitutive criterion of injustice, which, in turn, is a constitutive criterion of wrong action. Parallel points hold for justified moral belief, which is grounded in much the same way as moral knowledge.

A natural source of resistance to this view is that it underestimates the role of experience in accounting for moral knowledge. Rationalists may grant, however, that experience is crucial for *acquiring* the relevant concepts; it is knowledge of their *relations* that they account for non-empirically. A rationalist may also hold any of several views on the priority of general over particular moral knowledge. When Kant said that it is an injustice to morality to derive it from examples,[15] he seemed to be implying that knowledge of moral generalizations is prior to knowledge of specific moral judgments, for example the judgment that a given sentence is unjust. One grasps, perhaps from reflecting on the concept of what is appropriate to rational beings in such a case, that sentencing for a crime not committed is unjust, and one *thereby* knows that this act is unjust. Call this a *generalist* account. A rationalist can hold, however, that one grasps the injustice of this case and others like it and only thereby acquires the general knowledge. This would be a *particularist* account.[16]

There is a third view that combines virtues of both the generalist and particularist positions: one must see something general *in* the particular in order to know that it is an injustice; and to know the truth of a generalization one must see how it might apply to particulars. Further, we can refine our general moral knowledge in the light of concrete cases and modify our understanding of concrete cases in the light of our general knowledge. This *interactionist* view seems to me most plausible; and it is consistent both with rationalism and with the view that experience is a genetic, as opposed to epistemic, requirement even of a priori knowledge.[17]

VI. *Prospects for a Rationalistic Moral Realism*

Both rationalist and empiricist views in moral epistemology have now been sketched. Rationalist views have been less prominent in many recent discussions and seem to me to need development. Even Kantians in ethics, who should presumably be sympathetic with Kant's rationalism, often seem to defend his normative ethics at as safe a distance as they can get from his — or any rationalist — epistemology. It should be worthwhile, then, to explore further the prospects of a rationalistic view, in contrast with a plausible empiricism. (I shall assume that the rationalist view in question is realist, at least in presupposing that there are moral properties; but much of what is said in the following paragraphs could be adapted to a non-realist rationalism.)

J. L. Mackie has well expressed one source of resistance to rationalism in moral epistemology. Referring to the relation between an action's being a causing of pain just for fun and its being wrong, and denying that having the former, natural property logically entails having the latter, moral one, he says, "The wrongness must be somehow 'consequential' or 'supervenient'; it is wrong because it is a piece of deliberate cruelty. But just what *in the world* is signified by this 'because'?"[18] Much recent literature defending moral realism can be fairly described as an attempt to get this 'because' into the world, to *naturalize* it, one might say; it is felt to be queer otherwise, not only ontologically but also epistemologically.[19]

Another source of resistance to the rationalist approach in question — and to any non-reductive realist approach — is the fear that unless moral properties turn out to be natural, they are merely epiphenomenal: their presence is explained by that of the natural properties they supervene on, but they themselves explain nothing.[20] Why countenance them at all, as opposed, say, to taking a noncognitivist view, if they have no explanatory power?

A third problem for rationalism is its apparent arbitrariness. Why can't one say of any plausible claim one likes that it is a priori? And why are there just the moral properties and just the eternal, a priori moral truths there are, of which those so far discovered are supposed to be representative? Are we projecting into absolutes what are at best historically conditioned commitments of our culture?

Connected with the third problem is a fourth: what unifies the various moral principles we have? Why call them all moral? And why call "wrong" behaviors as disparate as apathetically leaving a bleeding stranger on the sidewalk and brutally beating a business competitor?

There are, then, at least four problems to be addressed: the queerness problem, the epiphenomenon issue, the arbitrariness question, and the unity problem. Let us consider some rationalist resources for dealing with these.

Regarding the queerness problem, it may be salutary to begin with the commonplace that every theory or explanation presupposes something, and what goes against a presupposition fundamental to a view is likely to seem queer to its proponents. To say that a view is queer, however, is not to argue against it. Rationalists would challenge the presupposition that the relation must be "in the world." If the supervenience relation between moral and natural properties is a priori, it is not empirical. It is not, for instance, a causal relation. More positively, consider the familiar domain of arithmetic. Is not eight, for example, an even number *because* it is — or in virtue of its being — divisible by two without remainder? But does this 'because' signify anything "in the world"? The truths of arithmetic are surely not queer, yet they have not been shown to be grounded either in the world in the way Mackie's view requires or in formal logic. The same holds for such propositions as that nothing is both round and square.[21] Like arithmetic propositions, these seem to have neither the blessing of testability by scientific procedures nor the lofty protection of derivability from pure logic.

Granted, we might not be interested in numbers if objects in the world did not generally seem to add up in accordance with the rules of addition, but this does not imply that these rules are grounded in what we have observed about those objects. Similarly, we might not be interested in the notions of right and wrong if they had no bearing on human well-being; but this does not imply that they are analyzable in terms of the (causal) consequences of acts for our well-being. The upshot of these points is that if empiricists cannot show that all important *non*-moral truths conform to their epistemic standards, then synthetic a priori moral truths need not be considered queer in any sense deserving suspicion. Empiricists have simply not shown that reason is purely formal: that the only a priori truths are truths of logic (or are reducible to such truths through the use of definitions). Moral discourse is a domain in which many philosophers have thought reason to be, by contrast, highly substantive; moral epistemology, then, is an unacceptable place simply to assume that all substantive truth must be empirical.

There remains, however, a disanalogy between the moral case and that of arithmetic and other domains of self-evidence. Arithmetic can (let us assume) be axiomatized given a few self-evident propositions; and that nothing is both round and square has a similar axiomatic self-evidence. Moral principles, by contrast, seem to many reasonable people neither self-evident nor comparably simple. There is truth in this disanalogy claim. But, first, it does nothing to undermine the point that there are synthetic a priori propositions. Second, it is not clear that self-evidence, at least of the kind in question, should be expected in substantially vague generalizations. Third, there are different kinds of self-evidence, and at most one of them need be claimed by rationalists as appropriate to moral truth.

Two kinds of self-evidence are especially relevant here. Let us assume (controversially) that the basic notion of self-evidence is this: a self-evident proposition is (roughly) one such that understanding it, while (1) not entailing that one must believe it, is (2) sufficient for being justified in believing it and indeed (3) sufficient for knowing it provided one does believe it on the basis of understanding it. We may still distinguish those self-evident propositions that are readily understood by normal adults and those understood by them only through reflection on the sorts of cases they concern. Call the first *immediately self-evident*, and the second *mediately self-evident*, since their truth can be grasped only through the mediation of reflection — as opposed to inference.[22] As this distinction suggests, a rationalist may be a fallibilist and hence grant that a non-self-evident (or even false) proposition may seem to someone to be self-evident. If there are self-evident moral truths, at least the majority can be expected to lie in the mediate category. The point is not that they cannot be known inferentially but that even for non-inferential knowledge or noninferential justified belief of them, reflection, even conceptual maturity, is required in normal rational persons.

Even if a self-evident proposition could not be known inferentially, it is plausible to hold that certain a priori propositions can be, and if so then the rationalist's options in moral epistemology are widened. The crucial question is whether the required premises can be grasped in such a way that knowledge of the conclusion is not based on memory. Human capacities in this respect are a contingent matter; but it is arguable that, for instance, one can hold in mind some version of the categorical imperative together with some premise connecting it to a moral maxim and, as conclusion, that maxim itself.

A further point may help here. Particularly when a proposition is questioned, if only by a skeptic or by someone who wants a derivation of it in order to understand it better, then if the proposition is not immediately self-evident we may think that it is not self-evident at all, or not a priori. We are especially likely to think this if we cannot give an argument for it. But surely we can know a proposition even if we cannot show it, or even defend it by argument, as opposed to illustrating or explaining it.[23] None of this implies that there cannot be good arguments for at least certain self-evident propositions; but even when there can be, it does not follow that we do not know the propositions in question unless we can show them by argument.

Moreover, if a proposition is not immediately self-evident, then those who do not reflect adequately on it cannot be expected to accept it. Add to this that since moral principles are practical in implying reasons for which we should act or at least be disposed to act, there are biases that may impede accepting them. For those who accept them, moral principles are constraining, even a burden: they express reasons that make a claim on our allegiance, particularly if, as motivational internalism has it, motivation to act on them is implicit in accepting them, and the principles thus claim motivational as well as intellectual allegiance from those who hold them.[24] If I believe that lying is wrong, I must, for example, countenance 'it would be a lie' as expressing a reason not to say something, or for criticizing someone who plans to say it; and if motivational internalism is correct, I must even be disposed to act negatively toward such action. I must, then, bear at least an intellectual burden and, on many views, a behavioral burden as well.

Is it really implausible, then, to hold that we can know a priori (even if in some way inferentially) that beating children is prima facie wrong? Perhaps one thinks one does not know this until one knows what the defeaters are. That is a natural but mistaken view. If only by analogy with defeaters in another context, one can understand that there *are* possible defeaters of an obligation, without knowing what they are, and perhaps without knowing of any in particular.[25] Similarly, knowing that r is a reason to A does not require knowing whether r is defeasible, and is consistent with knowing that it is defeasible while *not* knowing what would defeat it.

One might also think that if there are a priori moral principles, then one can know a priori what one should do in certain concrete moral situations. But this is another mistake. It can be readily exposed if we disentangle the rationalist epistemology from the moral rigorism often associated with it because of, for one thing, common interpretations of Kant. To know what one should do in a concrete situation, one would need empirical knowledge of the circumstances and empirical justification for taking those circumstances to contain no defeaters. The rationalist view is not, then, either naive about the readiness with which moral truths can be grasped or rigoristic about their implications for human action.

The epiphenomenalism problem is quite different. One response is simply to argue that moral properties *are* explanatory. This is certainly open to a naturalistic rationalism; but even on the view that moral properties only supervene on natural ones, it is arguable that they can explain. Surely, it might be claimed, Juan's wrong-

ing Juanita can explain why she drops him from her circle of friends. There is, however, a serious objection to this explanationist defense of moral realism and thereby
the possibility of moral knowledge as cognitivists understand it. There is some reason
to think that it is only the natural properties on which moral ones supervene — such
as an act's being a breaking of a promise to Juanita and its thereby angering her —
that do the explanatory work, at least in any causal sense of 'explain'. I cannot argue
this point here.[26] If it is sound, it is a problem for empiricist naturalism, not for realist
rationalism. On the latter view as construed here, possession of moral properties is not
an *effect* of possession of the natural properties they supervene on; as explained earlier, the former are conceptually (but not analytically) *constituted* by the latter. They
need not be taken as part of the causal order. They function (for one thing) to provide
moral descriptions, such as 'injustice' and 'lying'. These can explain the *appropriateness* of certain behavior and attitudes (another normative property); the causal
explanatory work can be done by the properties underlying the moral descriptions.

Let us now consider the third problem: arbitrariness. First of all, it must surely
be granted that not just any claim that a proposition is a true moral principle need
be taken seriously. Perhaps it is felt that where one does not have to argue from prior
premises, one can choose what one likes. But even if one in some sense "can"
choose what one likes as one's axioms, some starting points are plausible and others
are not. If this were not so, no appeal to premises would help; to justify one's favorite
view, one could simply keep constructing properly loaded premises to serve as one's
axioms. Moreover, what is not derived from prior premises is not thereby arrived at
arbitrarily. It can even be *argued* for in at least the indirect sense that objections can
be met and the consequences of accepting it can be displayed and perhaps made
attractive.

Still, why should we maintain just the moral principles we in fact hold, concerning equality, non-injury, veracity, and so on? One relevant point is that surely
these principles have not been simply invented; and there is no reason to deny that
they are learned or discovered. For most people, they are learned in the course of
moral upbringing, and for many they are believed on authority. But presumably they
could be discovered — as the rationalist claims they can be justified — through reasoning on concepts that arise and become familiar in the course of human experience, or through inferences from principles learned in that basic way. If so, then
these (sound) moral principles are not merely projections of cultural preference, nor
ways by which the strong control the weak, or the weak protect themselves from the
strong. Far from being manipulative, the moral principles I am talking about are a
bulwark against manipulation. Ethnocentric principles may masquerade as moral;
but we must not suppose that there is no genuine article, or even that we cannot
identify it, simply because there are incentives to counterfeit.

The arbitrariness problem, then, is not crippling to a rationalist approach and
perhaps no more a challenge to it than to an empiricist moral epistemology, which
can be equally accused of bias in selecting the natural properties that determine
moral ones. The unity problem, however, may be even more troubling. This is a difficulty for any non-reductive theory of obligation, including an empiricist one. If
there is nothing that ties together the various principles we call moral, then it is at
least more difficult to be confident that none is merely a cultural projection, and it

is harder to achieve a good understanding of the range of natural properties that constitute the base for moral properties. Consider, for example, W. D. Ross's famous list of prima facie duties: fidelity, reparation, gratitude, justice, beneficence, self-improvement, and non-injury. What makes them all moral? As Ross apparently saw, there is no obviously correct answer.[27]

It may seem that here empiricism, especially if reductive, has a good answer. For instance, if there is just one fundamental obligation, and hence the property of being obligatory is equivalent to, say, that of optimizing happiness, then all moral principles can be seen to be simply specifications of behaviors that optimize — or do the opposite. But this consequentialist view is far from obviously correct and is in my judgment mistaken, for reasons brought out in the literature critical of utilitarianism. It is doubtful, for example, that the view can explain why a moral obligation to do something can apparently persist even where the consequences of the act are less conducive to happiness than those of its non-performance. Keeping a promise may be obligatory even where no one but the promisor and promisee is significantly affected and where breaking the promise produces more net happiness for the promisor than keeping it would yield for the promisee.[28]

Consider, by contrast, a Kantian unification of moral principles. Again, the intrinsic end formulation of the categorical imperative is highly suggestive. Above all, it stresses respect for persons: they are to be treated as ends and never merely as means. Is it not plausible to hold that in lying, breaking promises, subjugating, manipulatively injuring, and the like, one is using people as a means? And in keeping faith with people, acting beneficently toward them, and extending them justice, is one not treating them as ends, roughly in the sense of beings with intrinsic value (or whose experiences can have intrinsic value)? Surely as good a case can be made for such a Kantian unification as for the unifying power of a naturalistic hedonism of the kind associated with utilitarianism. Indeed, the former can be combined with the idea that moral principles are appropriate to the aim of guiding human conduct in society toward a materially and spiritually fulfilling life. Contributing to this aim is surely demanded by treating people as ends. This view has a hedonic component, but that component is subordinate to the goal of treating people with respect; it is not the basis of moral obligation (the suggested Kantian unification of Rossian intuitionism is developed in some detail in chapter 12).

To be sure, the categorical imperative is not immediately self-evident.[29] Indeed, it may not be self-evident at all, but knowable (assuming it is true) only on the basis of a derivation from non-moral principles. That is not the issue here; what unifies moral principles need not be self-evident; presumably it need not even be a set of moral principles. This suggests another possible route to unification and perhaps also to the conclusion that a suitably informed, rational person would hold certain moral principles.

What I have in mind might be called the argument from the impersonality of reason. Let me just sketch the argument and its application to practical reason.[30] Rational persons have, among other things, rational intrinsic desires as motivational foundations of their conduct, even if not the only foundations. There are things we (normal persons) rationally want for their own sake, not as means to something further, and on the basis of at least some of these desires we want other things. What rational persons want regarding these things is not in general that *they* have them, but, typically, the things themselves or something intrinsic to them. I want to read Shakespeare for the rewards of so doing; I do not want *my* reading him. I can want that; but such egoistic wants are not the primitive case. Similarly, when I have pain, I want *it* to stop. That it is my pain need not enter my mind, and I need not conceptualize the pain as mine in order to have a rational desire to be rid of it. Indeed, the experience of certain things as desirable or undesirable is prior to development of a self-concept: as tiny children we are acquainted with pain and pleasure, for instance, and, in virtue of their phenomenal qualities, rationally want elimination of the former and realization of the latter. These hedonic desires, at least, arise even before we have a self-concept. The foundations of rational desire, and thereby the basic normative reasons for action, are impersonal. Even when I develop a self-concept, my seeing the literary pleasures I want as mine does not make them seem any better.

Now in a world like this, rational, generally informed persons believe that other people are much like them in rationality, motivation, and sentience. It is thus reasonable for them to believe that others' experiences are, in similar situations, qualitatively similar to their own. This, in turn, makes it reasonable to believe that what I have found painful or pleasurable, you, in similar circumstances, will find so (or, more cautiously, any person like me, if there is one, will find so). It is a short step — though admittedly not a step that logic, as opposed to substantive reason, requires us to make — from here to the view that certain kinds of things — for instance aesthetic and social enjoyments, and physical and mental suffering — are human goods and evils. Now the circumstances to which the basic moral principles apply are often simple: they involve abstaining from causing pain, treating like cases alike, and, sometimes, contributing to pleasure. I know what I want in this regard; I may assume you want similar things. What is good in what I want is impersonally good; it is thus reasonable to take it to be as good for you as for me. Selfishness may oppose my acting accordingly. The point is that it is still reasonable to act so. I need not favor others over myself, but I have no rational ground to favor myself over others. The impersonal foundations of practical reason require scrupulous equality. The intrinsic desirability of our pleasures, like the rationality of our wanting them, supervenes on what they are, not on whose they are.

It is no accident that if we proceed from the foundations of practical reason to fundamental ethical principles, we find some of the basic ingredients of a good argument for the intrinsic end version of Kant's categorical imperative. That principle reflects the intrinsic valuation of persons implicit in taking them to have desires whose satisfaction is a good thing, or can at least be rationally considered to be good; and it accords with, even if it does not quite capture, the reasonableness of treating persons equally which is implicit in the impersonal character of rationality. If something like this principle can be shown to be the or even *a* basic moral principle, we would have a systematic rationalism, as opposed to the less unified rationalistic intuitionism of theorists like Ross.

There is also a connection with the contractarian strain in Kant on which John Rawls, among others, has drawn. If rationality is to be understood as I have suggested, then it is to be expected that rational persons would choose, as guides for life in a shared world, the sorts of moral principles I have suggested might be central. Rawls's veil-of-ignorance framework might help to show this, but I cannot argue that here. The general point might be this: surely rational persons who regard themselves as fundamentally similar to others in rationality, motivation, and sentience would want principles that, first, protect them from harm and assure them of a certain kind of equal treatment, and second, within these limits, encourage positively good treatment of others (encourage rather than require, because being made to behave beneficently is one way in which we can be treated as means).

This is of course only a sketch of a unifying approach that a rationalist may take in moral epistemology. An empiricist may take a similar approach, to be sure; but insofar as the principles of practical reason that emerge are held to be knowable, as opposed to merely reasonable objects of favorable attitudes, the (cognitivist) empiricist must try to reduce them to either analytical or empirical truths. The prospects for such reduction do not seem to me good.

Conclusion

I have reviewed some of the major options in moral epistemology, concentrating on cognitivist views. The main contrast here is between rationalist and empiricist approaches, such as those of Kant and Mill. Both kinds of position can plausibly use the notion of supervenience in providing an ontological ground for moral properties and an epistemological account of our knowledge of, and justification for believing, moral statements. One or another version of the empiricist view, especially in its naturalistic forms, has dominated much recent moral epistemology. I have presented the outline of a contrasting rationalist approach. If I am right about such a view, it can meet a number of difficulties that have dimmed its prospects. A priori knowledge of moral principles need not be mysterious, nor its proponents dogmatic or epistemologically infallibilist; moral properties can be seen to play important roles in description, explanation, and inference without being either reduced to natural ones or consigned to the status of epiphenomena; self-evident moral principles need not be either immediately obvious or, on the other hand, arbitrary or merely historically conditioned products of a culture; moral principles, even if they can be known without prior premises about rationality, can be supported by plausible principles of practical reason; and the diversity of moral obligations can be accounted for, in a variety of ways, in a unifying framework.

Notes

This essay has benefited from discussions of earlier drafts with Scott Berman, John Deigh, James Klagge, Joseph Mendola, Nelson Potter, and a number of people in the audiences at the 1990 Spindel Conference and at colloquia at the Universities of Nebraska (Lincoln) and Texas (Austin).

1. This is not to say they have not violated a prima facie obligation: defeasibility does not entail eliminability. They do in fact owe an explanation to anyone who (non-meddlesomely) asks why they are shocking the child, and that confirms the existence of some kind of obligation.

2. The wording here is meant to suggest a contrast with such overarching principles as Kant's categorical imperative and the principle of utility: they are designed to hold without exception but cannot be applied to everyday decisions without further information or added premises, e.g. facts about how an action would affect human happiness.

3. The idea of epistemic non-derivability from some other moral principle(s) is difficult to explicate. A rough approximation is this: there is no set of *moral* principles (as opposed, say, to general principles of practical reason) such that (1) on the basis of this set one could inferentially come to know (or justifiedly believe) the principle(s) in question if one knew (or justifiedly believed) each proposition in this (premise) set, and (2) the proposition(s) in this set could be known or justifiedly believed without relying on the principle(s) in question.

4. An empiricist in general epistemology can (as I note in the following text) take a version of the principle of utility to be analytic or even hold that right action *by definition* maximizes (say) happiness. In this case there would be some question whether the proposition in question is properly construed as moral, rather than as, say, a second-order principle from which, using facts about the consequences of actions, we can derive moral principles. It is more likely, however, that empiricist consequentialists will take, as their basic analytic principle — if any — that right action maximizes intrinsic *goodness*. This, however, is highly abstract and yields *moral* principles only when conjoined with substantive assumptions about what has intrinsic value and — if we are to get specific principles to guide action in concrete situations — about the consequences of action for intrinsic goodness.

5. Kant may not directly say what I attribute to him, but it seems implicit in the *Grundlegung*. See, e.g., sects. 429–30, pp. 47–48 in *Foundations of the Metaphysics of Morals*, trans. Lewis White Beck (New York: Liberal Arts Press, 1959). Mill says the sort of thing I ascribe to him in more than one place, e.g., ch. 2 of *Utilitarianism* (Indianapolis: Hackett, 1979).

6. In ch. 5 I discuss some of the relevant literature and appraise a plausible form of what I there call *explanationist naturalism*. That essay also sketches an alternative account (reflected in a few later paragraphs) of both the reality of moral properties and the possibility of moral knowledge.

7. Arguably, one could not have the concept of a promise without having moral concepts; but it does not follow that one can know that someone has made or broken one only on the (inferential) basis of some substantive moral knowledge or belief, e.g. that the agent has violated an undefeated moral obligation. Note, too, that one might take the evidence for applying a moral property to be a non-moral, (partly) normative truth, e.g. that the act in question produces a net balance of intrinsic goodness. The ultimate evidence for believing this, however, would presumably be factual.

8. It would be consistent with a kind of noncognitivism — a linguistic version — to maintain that though there are moral properties, our moral language does not express them. But we may ignore this (I suspect undefended) position.

9. Two comments. First, I leave open the kind of modality expressed by the 'can' and the sort of determination relation. Second, by 'non-reductive' I mean simply 'not entailing a reducibility relation'; I would not rule out that possibility *by definition*. For a good general discussion of supervenience see Jaegwon Kim, "Supervenience as a Philosophical Concept," *Metaphilosophy* 21 (1990). For discussions of supervenience in relation to moral epistemology see Alan H. Goldman, *Moral Knowledge* (London and New York: Routledge, 1988), Panayot Butchvarov, *Skepticism in Ethics* (Bloomington: Indiana University Press, 1989), Michael R. DePaul, "Supervenience and Moral Dependence," *Philosophical Studies* 51 (1987), and James C. Klagge, "Supervenience: Ontological and Ascriptive," *Australasian Journal of Philosophy* 66 (1988). Klagge's paper highlights the sense in which noncognitivists can appeal to supervenience.

10. This is not to suggest that Moore decisively showed conceptual reduction to be impossible; but later writers, such as C. L. Stevenson, refined his attack on the strong reductionist program I am speaking of, which would require, if not synonymy relations between moral and non-moral terms, then at least analytic equivalences.

11. Indeed, there are times when writers who appeal to supervenience sound as if they have in mind a kind of reduction one would not expect from their characterization of supervenience. See, e.g., David O. Brink, *Moral Realism and the Foundations of Ethics* (Cambridge and New York: Cambridge University Press, 1989), p. 191, which speaks of moral facts as "constituted by" and thus supervening on "natural facts." Presumably the criteria for sameness of facts are meant to be weaker than conceptual or metaphysical ones.

12. The *general* thesis that moral properties supervene on natural ones implies that moral properties are grounded in natural ones but leaves open what the grounds for any given moral property are; but an empiricist who thinks we have moral knowledge will presumably take it to be based on knowledge of relevant natural facts; e.g., knowledge that lying is wrong might be thought to be based on knowledge of its tendency to cause suffering or to disrupt human relations, etc.

13. Moore belongs in the rationalist tradition on this score, as does Ross, whose moral epistemology is quite explicitly rationalistic. See *The Right and the Good* (Oxford: Oxford University Press, 1930), esp. ch. 2.

14. I suggested these two kinds of naturalism, and associated the former with Quine, in "Foundationalism, Epistemic Dependence, and Defeasibility," *Synthese* 55 (1983): 119–39. One might add that a thoroughgoing naturalism must also deny that there are irreducible supernatural concepts, but there is no need to add that point here.

15. See the *Foundations*, 408–9.

16. The acquisition of knowledge here must not be taken to imply derivation of a priori propositions from contingent, existential ones. The particularist idea, rationalistically interpreted, is presumably that whatever the role of experience in the genesis of concepts, it is abstract particulars whose grasp is crucial for achieving knowledge of moral principles.

17. Interactionism illustrates a procedure well known in, but not peculiar to, science. The general method is what I called the *theoretical method*, in "Realism, Rationality, and Philosophical Method," *Proceedings and Addresses of the American Philosophical Association* 61 (1987): 65–74. The term 'theoretical' is appropriate because this method is neutral not only between rationalism and empiricism but also between foundationalism and coherentism. The same holds for 'reflective equilibrium'. For discussion of this neutrality issue regarding reflective equilibrium, see Margaret Holmgren, "The Wide and Narrow of Reflective Equilibrium," *Canadian Journal of Philosophy* 19 (1989), and for related considerations see Michael R. DePaul, "Reflective Equilibrium and Foundationalism," *American Philosophical Quarterly* 23 (1986).

18. J. L. Mackie, *Ethics: Inventing Right and Wrong* (London: Penguin Books, 1977), p. 41 (italics in original).

19. Nicholas Sturgeon, e.g. in "Moral Explanations," in David Copp and David Zimmerman, eds., *Morality, Reason, and Truth* (Totowa, N.J.: Rowman and Allanheld, 1984), and Brink, *Moral Realism*, can be fairly described as in part naturalizing the 'because'. Terence Horgan and Mark C. Timmons plausibly criticize their attempt by arguing that certain important parallels to the mental-physical relation are missing. See their "New Wave Moral Realism Meets Moral Twin Earth," in John Heil, ed., *Rationality, Morality, and Self-Interest* (Lanham, Md.: Rowman and Littlefield, 1993). I criticize the attempt from a rationalist point of view (to be reiterated — in part — here) in ch. 5, "Ethical Naturalism and the Explanatory Power of Moral Concepts" For further discussion of the queerness problem, see Joseph Men-

dola, "Objective Values and Subjective States," *Philosophy and Phenomenological Research* 50 (1990), and Richard T. Garner, "On the Genuine Queerness of Moral Properties and Facts," *Australasian Journal of Philosophy* 68 (1990).

20. For a statement of the case for moral epiphenomenalism see Gilbert Harman, "Moral Explanations of Natural Facts — Can Moral Claims Be Tested against Nonmoral Reality?," *Southern Journal of Philosophy* 24 (suppl.) (1985).

21. I have argued for these claims in ch. 4 of *Belief, Justification, and Knowledge* (Belmont *Epistemology* (London and New York: Routledge, 1997) but do not claim that the issue is closed. My point is that Mackie should not talk as if he could refute the view he is discrediting.

22. On the assumption that one cannot reflect in the relevant way on the concepts in question without *some* kind of understanding of them, I take it that there is a level of understanding of mediately self-evident propositions, or at least of parts of them, not by itself sufficient for justification but capable of leading to that as the understanding develops by reflection. Self-evidence of the relevant kinds is discussed in more detail in ch 2.

23. This is a broadly foundationalist assumption. It has been defended in detail and, I think, cogently by a number of philosophers. A sketch of my defense is in my *Epistemology*, chapter 7. For further defenses and relevant references see some of the papers in W. P. Alston, *Epistemic Justification* (Ithaca and London: Cornell University Press, 1989), and Paul K. Moser, *Knowledge and Evidence* (Cambridge and New York: Cambridge University Press, 1989). For a contrasting view applied to moral judgments, see David Copp, "Considered Judgments and Moral Justification: Conservatism in Moral Theory," in David Copp and David Zimmerman, eds., *Morality, Reason, and Truth* (Totowa, N.J.: Rowman and Allanheld, 1985).

24. I doubt that precisely this kind of internalism is true, but it may be true that a *rational* person who accepts a moral principle is to some degree motivated to act accordingly, and that is the relevant point here, since our concern is rational persons. Internalism is appraised in detail in ch 10.

25. The language of this point is meant to avoid the implication that knowledge here requires the specific concept of a defeater. The key point is to grasp that such beatings are to be avoided unless, say, there is an adequate reason (excuse, ground) to do otherwise. It might be granted, however, that upon adequate reflection, one must be disposed to discover what some of the defeaters are.

26. I do, however, argue for its plausibility in ch. 5.

27. For a case against there being a correct answer, see Bernard Gert, *Morality: A New Justification of the Moral Rules* (Oxford: Oxford University Press, 1988).

28. Rule utilitarianism was devised largely to meet this problem, but I doubt it fully succeeds. Whenever it is optimific to break a promise and this can be seen to depend on certain features of the case — such as the unhappiness to the promisor as a result of keeping it outweighing the unhappiness to the promisee of its being broken — a rule can be formulated to license breaking the promise when those features are present, even if, morally, breaking it would be objectionable. R. B. Brandt, "Toward a Credible Form of Utilitarianism," in Michael D. Bayles, ed., *Contemporary Utilitarianism* (New York: Anchor, 1988), deals with this by (among other things) requiring that the relevant rules be learnable and comport with "retention by individuals of already formed and decided moral convictions" (p. 184). This does not entirely solve the problem. For one thing, it is not clear that all the relevant decided moral convictions deserve this status; for another, if they do, it is not clear how, on purely utilitarian grounds (such as conducing to happiness), their deserving it can be shown. If it cannot be shown, then (as Brandt might possibly grant) rule utilitarianism would succeed extensionally because, intensionally, it incorporates deontological (or other non-utilitarian) restrictions.

29. Here and elsewhere I speak as if there were just one categorical imperative. Even if that is not so, the point here probably applies to all the formulations.

30. Here I draw on a few paragraphs in my essay "The Architecture of Reason," *Proceedings and Addresses of the American Philosophical Association* 62, no. 1 (suppl.) (1988): 227–56. In neither case is the suggested argument meant to be fully formulated; that paper contains references to related literature, a more detailed statement of the argument, and various qualifications.

5

Ethical Naturalism and the Explanatory Power of Moral Concepts

There are many kinds of naturalism, and several of them are important in ethics. The appeal of ethical naturalism, in any of its plausible forms, is strong: it promises ontological economy by construing normative phenomena as in some way natural; it provides for objectivity in ethics, at least assuming that there are objective methods for the study of natural phenomena; it sustains the hope that the rationality of scientific procedures can help in resolving moral issues; and it dispels the sense of mystery which, for many, beclouds other accounts of the ontology and epistemology of ethics. There are well-known obstacles to working out a naturalistic ethics. At least since Hume, many philosophers have been impressed with the argument that if moral judgments are factual, they cannot be practical in the motivational sense which full-blooded practicality is commonly felt to require; and at least since Moore, it has seemed to many philosophers that even if factual judgments can be full-bloodedly practical, moral judgments cannot be reduced to any kind of factual statement.

In the recent literature of ethics, the debate over the status of naturalism has taken a different turn. Most proponents of ethical naturalism are now above all concerned to show that moral properties have explanatory power and that moral statements are quite continuous with others that can explain concrete phenomena. Call this *explanationist naturalism*. Its guiding idea is, in part, that if moral properties can be shown to have such explanatory power, then naturalism need not accomplish a reduction of the kind Moore held impossible, and the way will be open to explicating the practicality of moral judgments without the burden of defending a naive reductionist account of them. This essay will assess explanationist naturalism in ethics and, in the final section, sketch a plausible alternative whose resources appear to have been underestimated.

I. The Supervenience of the Moral

It is instructive to compare ethical naturalism with materialism about the mind-body problem. Within each position, the main alternatives — each with its own variants — are reductionism and eliminativism. In ethics, the most far-reaching reductionist view would be to the effect that moral concepts, such as *rightness*, are analyzable in terms of naturalistic notions, such as those of *pleasure* and *pain*. Mill sometimes appears reductionistic,[1] though his main thrust is surely to establish a normative, not a conceptual, identification of rightness with hedonic optimality. The most important, though probably not the closest, ethical analogue of eliminativism is noncognitivism, construed as denying that there *are* any moral properties or other real moral entities: rather, the function of distinctively moral terms is not assertive but, in some way, expressive.[2] There is also a noteworthy intermediate strategy, which I shall call *substitutionism*. Unlike noncognitivism, this view, most prominently represented by Richard Brandt,[3] does not deny that moral terms have any "descriptive meaning" but proposes instead that we undertake to use them with a reconstructed sense that is elaborated within broadly naturalistic constraints.

If there is any framework currently shared by ethical naturalists outside the eliminativist camp, it is that of supervenience. It is widely held that moral properties — however they are in the end to be analyzed conceptually — supervene on natural ones. Supervenience has been characterized in many different ways,[4] and there is no need here to settle on a precise account. For my purposes it should be sufficient to conceive the notion of moral supervenience roughly as follows: first, no two things, whether acts or persons, can share all their natural properties and differ in their moral ones (if they have any); and second, any entity having moral properties possesses those properties *in virtue of* its natural properties (or certain of them), where 'in virtue of' expresses an asymmetric relation of dependence and is usually held to imply an explanatory connection as well, such that a thing's possession of a moral property is explainable, at least in part, by appeal to its possession of one or more of the natural properties on which the moral property supervenes.[5] There are differences of opinion over the modalities in question; and a similar supervenience view can be linguistically formulated for those who do not wish to countenance properties (we might, for example, speak of *terms* supervening on others and explicate this by appeal to relations among their uses). But it is commonly supposed that since the relation between the base properties and the supervening ones is in some sense explanatory, it is (for at least that reason) non-analytic, in the sense that there are no analytic propositions of the form 'X is M because it is F', where 'M' ranges over moral properties and 'F' over the natural ones on which the former supervene.

This conception of supervenience allows that moral properties might *be* natural, and hence leaves a kind of *ontological reduction* open. What it is meant to avoid is any implication of an analytic reduction of the kind Moore held to be impossible. But the supervenience relation is still *non*-reductive in the sense that it does not entail any kind of reducibility of the supervening property to some set of the base properties; indeed, it is usually understood in a way that rules out one kind of reduction — the strong kind implying property identity — since the relevant dependence relation is irreflexive and asymmetrical. Moreover, while I am thinking of supervenience as a relation between properties (or types of properties), I take this relation to be explicable (as described earlier) in terms of relations between an individual's *having* a supervening property and its *having* one or more of the relevant base properties. We might thus speak of *general supervenience* between moral and natural properties or of *particular supervenience* between an individual thing's having a moral property, say (an action's) being a violation of a moral right, and its having a natural one, say (the action's) being a seizure of someone else's land.

Since the supervenience view leaves open the ontological reducibility of moral properties to natural ones (whether to the natural properties *in* the base or, more likely, others), and because it *grounds* moral properties in natural ones, one might be inclined to call it a (weak) form of naturalism. For instance, by leaving reducibility open, it contrasts with Moore's non-naturalism, for he held that goodness and rightness are irreducibly *non*-natural properties. On the other hand, he also maintained a supervenience doctrine apparently rather like the one sketched, and so provided moral properties with a *naturalistic anchor*. But this anchoring view by itself falls short of naturalism, because it leaves open the possibility that moral properties in themselves are in no way natural. They might have their feet firmly planted in the natural world and still, as Moore seems to have thought, rise above it.[6]

One might wonder how, as the supervenience view may be taken to allow, there could be an identity of moral with natural *properties* unless it *is* based on an analytic equivalence. To see how this might be, one could model a conception of ethical supervenience on a scientific analogue: supervenience as exhibited by, say, biological properties with respect to physico-chemical properties as their base. Here one may plausibly claim that there are property identities, without positing analytic equivalence between predicates expressing them. This opens the way for a view of moral properties that is not merely naturalistic, but a *scientific* naturalism.[7]

The supervenience view of moral properties is also linked to the general issue of scientific realism. Insofar as one is inclined toward realism about scientific theories, and particularly insofar as one takes ontological questions to turn ultimately on what entities science will finally countenance, supervenience naturalism in ethics, especially the explanatory kind, will be appealing. There may indeed be some tendency for scientific realists to suppose that for concrete entities, to be is to be a term in a causal relation, and for properties, to be is to be instantiated by those terms *as* such, that is, to figure predicatively (very roughly, in cause or effect position) in some lawlike generality linking cause to effect.[8] If moral properties can have causal efficacy — or, more liberally, at least explanatory power — which they apparently can if they are *reducible* to natural ones, then their reality is beyond serious question.[9] To be sure, if there are epiphenomena — items that have no causal power but appear only as effects — then being real is consistent with being inconsequential. But the supervenience naturalism that concerns us attributes both causal and explanatory power to moral properties. Section II will outline such a view.

II. Explanationist Moral Realism

Much recent discussion of moral realism, conceived naturalistically, has centered on a controversy that has been most prominently represented in a debate between Gilbert Harman and Nicholas Sturgeon.[10] The issues have engaged many other philosophers, and there is no hope of recounting all the major moves here. I shall simply try, in this section, to formulate some central issues and to assess the prospects for explanationist naturalism.

Moral Realism versus Moral Epiphenomenalism

It is useful to start with a challenge to the moral realist. Consider a case in which Jan, who is a reliable moral judge, observes an action, such as one person's violently slapping another, and judges the action wrong. One might think that if its wrongness had no causal power, then Jan would not have judged it wrong. But as Harman points out, this causal impotence view would be held by a moral epiphenomenalist, one who "takes moral properties to be epiphenomenally supervenient on natural properties in the sense that the possession of moral properties is explained by possession of the relevant natural properties and nothing is influenced or explained by the possession of moral properties."[11] After all, the moral properties and what they *seem* to explain might be common effects of the same causes; and if so, then (other things being equal) the phenomena explained would not have occurred if the moral properties had not been instantiated. But this no more entails that the moral properties have explanatory power than the fact that (other things being equal) a car would not have moved if its shadow had not moved entails that the movement of the shadow caused the movement of the car.

The naturalistic moral realist can safely grant, however, that the truth of counterfactuals of the kind just cited is not sufficient to show that moral properties are explanatory. This concession leaves open a number of plausible arguments for the view. Three in particular are important here.[12] First, note similar cases in physics: Harry, seeing a vapor trail in a cloud chamber, may think, "There goes a proton." An instrumentalist colleague might hold that Harry's reaction is not produced (indirectly) by a proton but is simply due to his sensibility and his observation of the "track," just as a moral judgment is produced not by moral factors functioning causally but by observations in the context of a certain sensibility. However, surely we need not take such instrumentalism as a serious objection to attributing explanatory power to protons. The second consideration concerns the observable impact of the moral. A morally sensitive person may be a "reliable detector" of moral wrongness, and observing such a person can change one's mind about a moral matter, as where one revises a moral view on hearing the person's differing account of the relevant action. Hence, there is a kind of moral observation — of persons and their moral judgments — that plainly affects one's views. Third, we must take seriously attributions of *causal* efficacy to moral facts, as where we cite injustice, along with poverty, as a cause of revolution. This is significant in itself; but it also suggests that the supervenience of the moral on the natural is like that of biological facts on physical ones — "a kind of 'causal constitution' of the supervening facts out of the more basic ones, which allows them a causal efficacy inherited from that of the facts out of which they are constituted."[13]

Moral Realism and Moral Naturalism

Each of the three considerations just cited seems to me plausible, yet inconclusive. Let us consider them in turn, with an eye to what metaethical view, other than moral epiphenomenalism — which (if mainly for different reasons) I join Sturgeon in rejecting — might account for them.

Since the instrumentalist case against realism is not peculiar to ethics and will in any case be discredited if the other lines of attack on moral realism are blocked, there is no need to discuss instrumentalism here. Indeed, my main interest is in the prior issue of whether moral statements are explanatory in the *way* causal and scientific ones are; if they are not, then moral realism must be either given up or reformulated in a way that is not vulnerable to instrumentalist criticism. Let us, then, consider how moral observation may bear on the status of moral realism.

It is certainly true that some people seem to be reliable moral observers, and if there are such people then moral realism gains support. But why need a *naturalistic* version in particular be supported? It is true that observations of such persons and their judgments may influence one; but this is not only compatible with epiphenomenalism, it is also consistent with a wholly different realism, such as the kind held by Kant (on one interpretation), which implies that moral properties are not causal in any sense: they figure non-causally in a priori principles as opposed to playing a causal role in empirically explanatory propositions. This kind of realism need not deny the causal impact of moral reliability. Consider a logical analogy. If we observe Jan proving theorems, we may obtain good grounds for concluding that she is logically reliable. Then, observing her pronounce a questionable proposition to be a theorem can influence (even change) our judgment. It does not follow that theoremhood, the property she reliably judges certain things to have, is causally efficacious. But suppose that the property is in some way causally efficacious. *This* kind of causal efficacy does not seem to be the sort the naturalist has in mind; for it is a kind possible for abstract entities whose fundamental place is in necessary truths, as opposed to testable causal or testable nomic truths.[14] Such efficacy is certainly possible for goodness and rightness as Moore construed them: namely, as *non*-natural properties. This reliability line of argument, then, may be useful in defending moral realism, but it does little if anything to support moral naturalism.

The Epistemic and Explanatory Dependence of Moral Properties on Natural Ones

The next defense of ethical naturalism to be considered here begins with an undeniable datum: we do *cite* what appear to be moral facts or moral states of affairs, such as a regime's injustice to its people, in explaining why certain events, such as a widespread revolt, have occurred. We also say things like 'It was because he was unjustly punished that his friends sought revenge against the authorities'. These locutions suggest that moral properties have both causal and (if it is different here) explanatory power. But this point does not follow from their having this use. For one thing, what we *cite* in giving an explanation need not be what, in the context, really *does* the explaining. I may say that I am taking an umbrella because it is going to rain; but the apparent fact I cite, that it will rain, is not what explains my behavior: my *belief* that it will rain does this work. I would take the umbrella if I believed it would rain, whether it will or not. For pragmatic reasons (such as my wanting to avoid suggesting doubt about the weather by *saying* 'I believe'), I *express* my belief by asserting the proposition believed, rather than by self-ascribing a belief of that proposition. But it is what I express in the context, not what I cite as a causal factor, that does the explanatory work. We must distinguish, then, between cases in which a statement offered in order to explain something simply *provides an explanation* when conjoined with contextual information and cases in which, taken together with that information, it *constitutes an explanation*, in the sense that the purported explainer is what actually wields the explanatory power.

There is also a further issue. We have already noted that the supervenience of moral on natural properties reflects an *ontological dependence*: even if moral properties are not themselves natural, their possession presupposes that of certain natural properties as their basis. This is how, for any plausible moral realism, moral properties are anchored in the world. Now the moral epiphenomenalist, in effect, suggests that it is certain of the base properties which do the explaining that the moral properties seem to do. Explanationist moral realists may plausibly resist this move. For one thing, it leaves one wondering why we should *ever* attribute explanatory power to supervening properties, unless they can be plausibly claimed to be identical with sets of base properties not themselves supervenient on other properties. But is there good reason to think that any explanatory properties are *ultimately* irreducible or do not even supervene on others? And, supposing that some properties meet this condition, there are supervenient properties, such as temperature, solubility, and elasticity, which, in their own right, apparently do have explanatory, even causal, power.

This line of reply to moral epiphenomenalism has limited force, however, once we appreciate a difference between moral and scientific supervenience. Unlike, say, temperature and elasticity, moral properties are not only ontologically dependent, but also *epistemically dependent*, on their base properties: roughly, knowing a particular to have a moral property depends on knowing it to have one or more of a certain range of base properties, and justifiedly believing it to have a moral property depends on justifiedly believing it to have (or at least on being justified *in* believing it to have) one or more base properties in this range.[15] This is not to deny that one might, upon noticing a man severely beating a child, "just see" that he is wronging the child; there need be no process of inference (certainly no conscious one), and it may be that the moral belief formed here arises — given one's moral experience and cognitive ethical constitution — "directly" from what is perceived. But if the case is like ordinary perception of, say, color and shape, in exhibiting a kind of directness of belief formation — and may to that extent be called an instance of moral "observation" — it differs from such ordinary perception in requiring either an underlying belief ascribing relevant natural properties, or at least a perception of those properties sufficient to be at once a basis *for* justified ascription of them and a ground for attribution of the moral property "seen" to be present. If, for instance, I do not believe (or disbelieve), but "just see" that the man is hitting the child hard, my visual perception of his behavior justifies me in believing that and is thereby a ground for my believing (observationally) that he is wronging the child.

It might be more accurate to say that our descriptive and explanatory *uses* of moral properties exhibit this epistemic dependence, but nothing to be said here will turn on which formulation we use. My point is that if there is such a dependence, then *whenever* we explanatorily invoke a moral property, it will be in part on the basis of, or at least in the light of, some belief or presupposition to the effect that one or more natural properties is playing an explanatory role. We are thus in a position to rely — often unselfconsciously, to be sure — on those other properties to do the explanatory work, and it is arguable that they, and not any moral property, are in fact what does it. Let me illustrate.

Recall the possibility of citing governmental injustice in explaining a revolt by the people. One cannot know (and normally would not even believe) that there is such injustice except through some kind of awareness of, say, government seizure of land, arbitrary curfews, and police brutality, where these are construed behaviorally in terms of, for example, soldiers' occupying farmland, clearing streets at night, and clubbing non-protesters. But these are just the sorts of non-moral factors that, in their own right, we suppose (on the basis of our general knowledge of social forces) can perfectly well explain a revolt.[16] They also seem to have causal power in a quite intuitive sense.

Perhaps it is on the basis of pragmatic reasons — for instance, out of a desire to combine explanation with moral assessment — that we *cite* the moral factor, such as injustice, as cause. Notice also that when we invoke a moral factor in giving an explanation, we are generally willing to say *how* it explains, and we always tend to do so in terms of the relevant base properties. We are indeed expected to be able to indicate, in this way, how the factor explains, on pain of being unjustified in our explanatory claim. Imagine John's claiming that injustice explains a revolt but being unable to say, in terms of the sorts of factors I have cited, how it actually does so, or even how it might explain the revolt. If we thought his unwillingness came from inability to answer the question due to ignorance of the inferential relationships, as opposed to uncooperativeness, we would surely conclude not only that he is not entitled to accept the explanation but probably also that he does not understand what injustice *is*. Nor, I think, would we be likely to cite moral factors in explanation of events if we could *not*, at least in a sketchy and general way, *see* causal connections between the base properties and the event to be explained.

There are, to be sure, several importantly different kinds of explanation that might be called moral. One might, for example, explain a revolt by simply saying that there is underlying injustice and it is a response to that. Call this kind of moral explanation *existential*: it represents the item to be explained as due to some causal factor or other belonging to an appropriate range. By contrast, one might explain a revolt by citing *the* injustice of the regime against which the people rebel. This kind of moral explanation is *referential*. To be warranted in the first kind, one needs justification for believing that *some* element in the base for injustice is operative in producing the revolt; to be warranted in the second, one needs justification for believing some element to be operative through its realization in the behavior of *the regime*. If, in addition, a referential explanation is *specific*, as where one cites the brutality of the regime as the injustice causing the revolt, one needs a justification for believing the *particular* base element in question to be operative.

One can of course give a *true* explanation without being justified in accepting it (truth here simply does not require justification). But what is of interest in these cases is how the epistemic dependence mirrors the ontological dependence: just as there cannot *be* an (actual, correct) explanation in terms of injustice unless some element in the base for injustice plays an appropriate causal role, one cannot be *justified* in believing that injustice explains something, such as a revolt, without being justified in believing that some such element, for instance brutality, plays an appropriate causal role. One need not, of course, conceive the brutality or curfews or other crucial elements *as* part of the supervenience base of injustice; one need only grasp (in some appropriate way) how these elements figure in producing the item(s) one explanatorily attributes to injustice.[17]

Moral Explanations Naturalized

These points do not entail that moral properties *cannot* in their own right explain events; but there seems to be better reason to think that it is the base properties which do the real work when moral properties appear to provide explanations. Our understanding of how ascription of moral properties can explain (at least so far as causal explanation goes) seems wholly *derivative* from our understanding of how the relevant base properties can do so.[18] Indeed, *given* an explanation of (say) a revolt by appeal to such things as police brutality and seizure of lands, it is not clear what explanatory element one would *add* to the explanation of why the revolt occurred by pointing out that these things constituted governmental injustice. This is an appropriate moral comment but does not seem to enhance the explanation of the event — unless it is taken to imply base variables *other* than those cited in giving the original explanation. If, in explaining why the revolt occurred, *all* the factors making the case one of injustice are cited, their constituting an injustice seems explanatorily, as opposed to morally, superfluous: at best it tells us something about why the revolt occurred which we should already know.

This view of explanations adducing moral properties might be said to *naturalize moral explanations* without *naturalizing moral properties* (or, at any rate, predicates). The idea is roughly that the empirical explanatory power of those explanations is natural and not due directly to any explanatory potential of the moral properties in question: explanations of empirical phenomena (above all of events) by appeal to moral properties are construed to be successful in virtue of implicitly exhibiting those phenomena as causally grounded in (or in some way due to) one or more of the relevant base properties. The view is, however, entirely consistent with granting that one's *citing* a moral property can succeed as an explanatory *act*. After all, it can call attention to the actual causes. There are, then, moral explanations in an *illocutionary* sense: explanatorily successful speech acts with a moral constituent playing the linguistically central role. Moreover, the appeal to injustice in explaining the occurrence of the revolt can also succeed in explaining why there *should* have been a revolt, in the sense that the revolt was a reasonable (or normatively appropriate) response. But this is an explanation of the rationality, not the occurrence, of the behavior: of why it is rational in the circumstances, not of why it happened. It seems doubtful that either kind of explanatory success is to be attributed to moral properties having, in their own right, either causal power or, more generally, the capacity to explain events. And that is what explanationist realism requires.

Causal versus Conceptual Supervenience

This brings us to a further defense against moral epiphenomenalism: briefly, that moral properties inherit causal efficacy from the natural properties from which they are constituted. Here it is crucial to recall the scientific analogy. The parallel point is plausible for, say, a biological property like dark skin color and its physico-chemical base properties. There are, however, at least two cases here. First, if a subset of the latter properties can explain resistance to sunburn, and the former supervenes on that set, we would expect that dark skin color can also explain the resistance. Second, if the constitutional relation represents not supervenience as usually understood but property identity (a kind of identity some theorists posit in the case of certain scientific reductions), then, *a fortiori*, we would expect the same explanatory power in both cases. We are not, however, considering reductive naturalism; hence, only the first case — constitution without identity — is a relevant analogy here. How good is the analogy?

Notice that in the biological case the supervenience is causal, or at least nomic: it is a nomic, not a conceptual, truth that dark skin color depends on a certain biochemical constitution. In the moral case, however, the supervenience relation is surely not causal or nomic: it is some kind of conceptual truth, and not a causal or nomic truth, that governmental injustice depends on (indeed, is in a way constituted by) such things as seizure of land or other property, police brutality, arbitrary restrictions of free movement, and the like.[19] These are the things one must point to in order to say what injustice *is*; they do not cause the injustice they underlie — though they may cause *further* injustice. Thus, the plausible assumption that the intermediate effect might be a cause of the distant one, by contrast with being epiphenomenal or with both events being common effects of the same causes, cannot be invoked to show that the moral properties must have at least some of the causal powers of their base properties. Hence, except on the strong — and reductionist — premise that the injustice simply *is*, or is at least necessarily equivalent to, a set of such natural properties, it is not evident that the causal heritability condition holds here.[20] If there is a weaker relation between the base properties and the supervenient one, why must the causal powers of the former accrue to the latter? So far as I can tell, no good answer to this question has been given in the literature.

One might reply that the strong assumption is probably true: moral properties are identical with sets of their base properties; it is simply hard, owing to vagueness and inadequacies in our moral theory, to spell out the equivalences. But it is surely not clear that the moral properties are identical with any set of their base properties, certainly not with any subset to which we might attribute the explanatory power of a moral property on every occasion of its plausible explanatory use. Indeed, if the relevant supervenience relation entails an *asymmetric* dependence between the moral and natural properties that are their base, the former presumably cannot be identical with the latter. It might be replied that the dependence is only epistemic: there is just one property, but we can know it to be present under a moral description only by virtue of knowing it to be present under a natural description. This is arguable; but it certainly appears that there is, as usually supposed, an (asymmetrical) ontic dependence. One might in fact take the apparent explanatory dependence of the moral on the natural to confirm this. A particular's having a moral property always seems explainable in terms of the relevant base properties; if it were identical to their conjunction one would not expect this. One might get an explanation of what the moral property *is*, but not of why the thing in question has it. The relation is apparently one of constitution; and in general indicating what constitutes a property does not explain why something has it, and indeed can leave open various alternative explanations of that fact.

There is further reason to doubt that moral properties explain in the way many ethical naturalists tend to believe they do (and here I speculate). On the face of it, one would think that moral terms are applied to events, including acts, on the basis of naturalistic criteria, either when the effects of these events — such as painful consequences for persons — meet those criteria, or when the events themselves have a certain intrinsic character, such as being the telling of a lie. The first case is illustrated by "That was wrong; it killed people." An example of the second is "Don't say that; it's a lie." If this suggestion is correct, then moral terms are apparently more classificatory than (directly) explanatory, at least if being explanatory is a matter of explaining the occurrence of natural phenomena as opposed to explaining the constitution of such moral facts as that a regime is unjust.

Moreover, we cite facts to explain the application of moral terms even more than we use moral terms in the course of explaining non-moral phenomena. Perhaps moral terms function primarily to describe what kind of act or person or situation is in question, and only secondarily in explaining, or paving the way for explaining, some (non-moral) event or situation. In saying, then, that the injustice of a regime caused an uprising, one may, from the moral point of view, be above all *morally describing the cause* — and perhaps thereby also condemning it — as opposed to *subsumptively explaining the phenomenon under a moral concept*. One need not, of course, be taking *only* the moral point of view in so speaking; it is indeed common that we have multiple purposes in making a single statement, and here one may also be trying to provide an explanation. One does put forward a *basis* for explaining the uprising in naturalistic terms, say by subsumption under a sociological generalization whose constituent concepts are "natural" — above all, both non-moral and non-normative. One thereby at once provides an understanding of why the people rebelled, in terms of the presumed base properties that warrant the ascription of injustice, and an appraisal of the explanatory variables, in terms of the ethical implications of the moral term one implicitly applies to them, in this case 'injustice'.

III. An Alternative Moral Realism

It might seem that the difficulties which section II raises for ethical naturalism suggest that moral epiphenomenalism is correct after all. One merely softens the blow by allowing moral concepts to play a role in classifying natural phenomena, in expressing attitudes, and in contextually providing the materials for non-moral explanations. But this is a mistake.

First, I have simply been presenting an alternative to moral naturalism and do not even claim that anything said in the preceding section decisively shows that the view is wrong. Nothing said here even decisively rules out a reductive form that gives moral properties all the explanatory power of the set of natural properties to which they are reducible, and so, on which they reductively supervene — if we may speak of supervenience at all here, where we would perhaps have a kind of degenerate case.

Second, if, as I have suggested, moral properties are conceptually rather than nomically connected with their naturalistic bases, then they are not *candidates* to be epiphenomenal: roughly, since they are not causally dependent variables, there is no reason to lament if they are not causal variables at all; they are apparently not the right sort of property to be in either category. In a sense, they do not belong to the causal order, though they are anchored in it. It might seem to follow that they play no role *at all* in explanations; but that, too, would be an unwarranted conclusion, as we shall see by considering a variety of explanations in which moral notions figure.

It is important to note that even if injustice by itself cannot explain events, *beliefs* that injustice is occurring can. This point might lead one to attribute explanatory power to moral properties by the following line of reasoning. Beliefs are what they are in part by virtue of their content. It is surely not qua neural state that a moral belief explains action. Even if beliefs turned out to be (by a synthetic identity) some kind of neural state, any explanation possible by appeal to such states will be quite different from those provided by appeal to the relevant beliefs. If moral beliefs (and other propositional attitudes essentially involving moral concepts and properties) are crucial in explaining action, and if moral concepts and properties are essential to those beliefs, then those concepts and properties are themselves explanatorily indispensable. They do not have *direct explanatory power*, in the sense that the ascription of moral concepts or properties by itself suffices to explain why some particular phenomenon occurs; but they might be said to have *contributory explanatory power*, in the sense that they can make an indispensable contribution to the direct explanatory power of propositional attitudes in which they figure. Even if the sheer possession of a belief, neurally characterized, could causally explain the occurrence of an action, it is only by virtue of the content of the belief that the agent's having this belief makes the action *intelligible* in the way appropriate to intentional human behavior: say as righting an injustice, taking revenge, or expressing gratitude. If there were no moral concepts or properties, then there would be no moral beliefs, such as the belief that one's government is unjust and one ought to fight it.

This case for the contributory explanatory power of moral properties is open to two objections. First, even beliefs that, say, something contains phlogiston can explain behavior, but we do not thereby want to claim for phlogiston any significant kind of explanatory power. Second, it might be objected that there are no moral properties, but only moral sentences and moral concepts, and we can give a noncognitivist account of them and thereby do justice to moral discourse without granting any explanatory power to moral attributions.

The first objection is quite plausible, though it may be argued that the kind of explanatory power in question does have some significance, since not just any property can figure in people's action-explaining beliefs in the same way. Perhaps so, but the point is not obvious and I see no need to try to work out this line here. It would not affect my overall case if contributory explanatory power should turn out to be significant; for it is weaker than the sort required by explanationist naturalism. As for the noncognitivist line, it seems open to a similar objection: one would still have to grant that the moral attitudes (or other non-truth-valued items they express) have contributory explanatory power, and just about any attitudes could apparently have it too. The theoretically important point here (though I cannot argue it now) is that rejecting explanationist naturalism need not lead to noncognitivism. Indeed, that rejection can be combined with recognizing a kind of explanatory power considerably stronger than noncognitivism allows. Let me explain.

Again, let us start with the assumption that moral properties are not *directly explanatory*, in the sense that events can be explained by virtue of instantiating them and thereby being subsumed under some explanatory generalization, as where (to take an example from social psychology) an angry outburst is explained by calling it aggression and subsuming it under the generalization that frustration tends to produce aggression. This is quite consistent with moral properties' having a kind of explanatory power that goes beyond the contributory kind: they may be *collaterally explanatory*, in the sense that phenomena to which they apply — such as arbitrary curfews and rigging of elections — have direct explanatory power. The idea is that while a successful explanatory *use* of a moral term does not provide an explanation of the phenomenon *in terms of the causal or direct explanatory power of the moral property*, it does *contextually imply a direct explanation in terms of one or more base properties*. This is in a way to grant that there are moral explanations; what is denied is that they are causal or otherwise direct. More precisely, moral explanations are naturalized in the (indirect) sense that they point us to explanations in terms of the natural base properties whose presence is their ground; and *these* are the properties that do the direct explaining of events.

This view of the explanatory role of the moral is most naturally construed as realistic, at least regarding moral concepts and properties. For one thing, it allows them to figure predicatively in the propositional objects of beliefs to which truth and falsity apply, and it thus contrasts with noncognitivism. A noncognitivist, for instance, would tend to maintain that moral concepts and "properties" function solely in the expression of moral attitudes and have no ontological status beyond the minimal one implicit in that linguistic role. By contrast, on the most plausible realist interpretation of the collateral explanation view, concrete entities *have* moral properties and can be known to have them; and by attributing them to objects we are able both to understand those objects — in terms of certain of the base properties grounding the moral attribution — and to appraise the objects morally. Even taking the collateral explanation view as a modest version of moral realism, however, it is not naturalistic, but neutral with respect to whether moral concepts or properties are natural.

Are we now at the edge of a mysterious rationalist conception of moral truth and knowledge? How one answers this question depends heavily on one's position on what is traditionally considered a priori, for instance on the status of arithmetic truths. If one regards these as ultimately grounded in experience, and as testable in the way that the most general scientific theories are, then one is likely to find the view rather mysterious. But I doubt whether that conception of arithmetic truth is correct and am inclined to think that, whatever experience is required in order for one to *acquire* arithmetic and various other abstract concepts, *what* we grasp when we do acquire them, the object of our understanding of them, is abstract.[21] On this view, numbers are not numerals, propositions (or any other bearers of truth value) are not sentence tokens, and moral concepts and properties are not nouns or predicates.

In the case of moral concepts, doubtless experience is required for our acquisition of them — indeed, even experience of the natural base properties on which they supervene. But it does not follow that they themselves are natural properties or have a direct causal or nomic connection with such properties. Indeed, it appears *necessary* that given certain base properties, a thing has a certain moral property. Consider, for instance, two convicted offenders receiving punishments of radically different severity for the same offense under the same conditions, say one versus five years for a first-offense gas station knifepoint robbery at the age of eighteen. Is it a contingent matter that an injustice has been done? It is surely not (it also does not seem analytic, though my purposes here do not require assuming that it is not); nor does the unequal sentencing *cause* injustice: it constitutes it, in a conceptual as opposed to causal sense of 'constitute'. Yet injustice so construed could hardly be more real. We need not suppose that its reality entails its having either causal power or direct explanatory power.

The view I am suggesting is one that seems to fit a broadly Kantian ethics, though the view implies neither the specific content of Kant's normative ethics nor the categorical imperative itself. A view of this sort need not be mysterious. Perhaps it can also be naturalistic, in one sense: that moral properties are not directly explanatory is neutral regarding the question whether moral concepts can be ultimately explicated in appropriate non-evaluative terms, say in terms of what will fulfill eudaemonistic desires purified of the effects of logical and factual error, and freed from the influence of egoism. Such a view would be *conceptually naturalistic*, since it would employ no irreducibly normative concepts. But this would not imply its being *substantively naturalistic*, that is, empirical. It is the latter kind of view that is represented by a strong scientific naturalism, since this position holds out the hope of construing all truth, including all moral truth, as empirically confirmable. It thus aims at a naturalism of both sorts, since if moral notions are not reducible to naturalistically characterized ones, it is at best hard to see how all truth could be empirical. But to think that only the substantive naturalism genuinely deserves the name is to take naturalism to be the property of empiricism.

If a conceptually naturalistic analysis of moral properties can be carried through, then they have approximately the same explanatory powers as the properties to which they are conceptually equivalent. But if, as seems more likely, moral properties have only collateral rather than direct explanatory power, the rationalistic alternative I have been sketching is still as well off as the most plausible versions of empiricist ethical naturalism in accounting for moral explanation of concrete events. In both cases, these events are explained directly by nomically relevant properties. But the empiricist view, with its causal-explanatory conception of significance, must face the problem of how to show that moral properties are not epiphenomenal, whereas the rationalist view assigns them a kind of descriptive and evaluative role that makes the charge of epiphenomenalism inapplicable.

Both the rationalist and the empiricist views can account for the objectivity of moral judgments. On each account, they are ontologically objective because they attribute real properties; they are naturalistically anchored because they supervene on natural properties; and they are epistemically objective because there is an intersubjective way to know that an object possesses them: by appeal to the base properties on which they supervene. But whereas empiricist naturalism treats even general moral knowledge as empirical, the rationalist view construes it as a priori. Even if one thinks of the a priori as simply differing by degrees from what is directly testable, there is surely much plausibility in construing as a priori at least such simple moral knowledge as that it is unjust to give unequal sentences for equal crimes committed under the same circumstances.

There is much reason to think, then, that the issue of moral realism should not be cast wholly in terms of the comparison with scientific models. It simply may not be assumed that only causal or nomic properties are real, or that moral knowledge is possible only if it is causally or nomically grounded in the natural world.[22] Our moral beliefs often concern particular persons or acts; they are responsive to observations; and, together with our wants, they explain behavior. But this does not require that moral properties are natural, and it allows that general moral knowledge is a priori. It may be that, rather than naturalize moral properties and thereby take explanations by appeal to them to be in some sense causal, we should instead naturalize such moral explanations and construe their power to explain events as due to causal patterns to which we are already committed. The view sketched here is not the only plausible non-naturalist realism in ethics, but it provides as good an account of the epistemology of moral judgment as its empiricistic alternatives and a better account of our sense of the necessity of certain general moral principles.

Notes

This essay has benefited from comments by Panayot Butchvarov, Joseph Mendola, Louis Pojman, and Steven Wagner and from discussions with Jaegwon Kim, Nicholas Sturgeon, Mark van Roojen, and a seminar I gave at the University of Nebraska in 1989.

1. See, e.g., *Utilitarianism* (Indianapolis: Harlsett, 1979), where he says that "to think of an object as desirable (unless for the sake of its consequences) and to think of it as pleasant are one and the same thing; and . . . to desire anything, except in proportion as the idea of it is pleasant is a physical and metaphysical impossibility" (p. 38). To be sure, even if Mill took the good (the intrinsically desirable) to be naturalistically analyzable, he may have been suggest-

ing only a weaker equivalence between the rightness of acts and their hedonic optimality; but a case could be made that he took that equivalence, too, in a metaethical spirit.

2. If we think of an eliminativism that takes mental attributions to be cognitive but false, then noncognitivism is not as close an analogue as an "error theory," such as J. L. Mackie proposes to account for what he takes to be the falsehood of standard, purportedly objective moral claims. See his *Ethics: Inventing Right and Wrong* (New York: Penguin Books, 1980).

3. See Richard B. Brandt, *A Theory of the Good and the Right* (Oxford: Oxford University Press, 1979). For a further indication of how the overall view is naturalistic, with some detailed criticism of its central elements, see my "An Epistemic Conception of Rationality," *Social Theory and Practice* 9 (1983): 311–34.

4. For discussion of many of these and a plausible general account of the notion, see Jaegwon Kim, "Supervenience as a Philosophical Concept," *Metaphilosophy* 21 (1990).

5. It may be adequately explainable by appeal to a proper subset, but I leave this open. On some views, a "full" explanation might require appeal to all of the base properties, assuming that this is a finite set. The sort of explanatory appeal important for this essay will be illustrated later.

6. Cf. Jaegwon Kim's case for the view that non-reductive physicalism based on the supervenience of the mental on the physical is an unstable position subject to pressures toward dualism on one side and eliminativism on the other. See "The Myth of Nonreductive Materialism," *Proceedings and Addresses of the American Philosophical Association* 63, no. 1 (suppl.) (1989).

7. There are powerful considerations supporting scientific naturalism, and the influence of the success of science and technology on recent philosophy is immense. In "Realism, Rationality, and Philosophical Method," *Proceedings and Addresses of the American Philosophical Association* 61 (1987): 65–74, I describe and critically discuss this influence. I should add that while the formulation in this paragraph leaves open the possibility that moral properties are identical with their base properties or other natural properties, there is at least one difficulty with the former identification: the relevant in-virtue-of relation seems asymmetrical and hence not an identity relation. If we say that x is M in virtue of being N, it is at best unclear how these two properties can be identical and simply referred to under different descriptions.

8. A view not unlike this is criticized by Panayot Butchvarov in *Skepticism in Ethics* (Bloomington: Indiana University Press, 1989). His focus, however, is more on explanatory than causal power as a standard of ontological commitment.

9. This is not to say that there *must* be an equivalence in explanatory power between a set of properties and any other set of them to which the former is reduced; but it is plausible to suppose that a set with *no* explanatory power cannot be reduced to a set that has it. More will said later about what it is for a property to have explanatory power.

10. See, e.g., Gilbert Harman, *The Nature of Morality* (New York: Oxford University Press, 1977), and Nicholas Sturgeon, "Moral Explanations," in David Copp and David Zimmerman, eds., *Morality, Reason, and Truth* (Totowa, N.J.: Rowman and Allanheld, 1985). Selections from the former and all of the latter are reprinted in Louis P. Pojman, ed., *Ethical Theory* (Belmont, Calif.: Wadsworth Publishing Co., 1988). That collection also contains relevant papers by (among others) David Brink and Bruce Russell. Other valuable sources are the *Southern Journal of Philosophy* 24 (suppl.) (1985), which is devoted to moral realism, and David Brink, *Moral Realism and the Foundations of Ethics* (Cambridge and New York: Cambridge University Press, 1989).

11. Gilbert Harman, "Moral Explanations of Natural Facts — Can Moral Claims Be Tested against Moral Reality?," the *Southern Journal of Philosophy* 24 (suppl.) (1985).

12. See Nicholas Sturgeon, "Harman on Moral Explanations of Natural Facts," the

Southern Journal of Philosophy 24 (suppl.) (1985). Both the concession just described and the three considerations to follow are given in that paper. In the interest of brevity, I generally do not quote Sturgeon but simply try to keep fairly close to his wording.

13. See Sturgeon, "Moral Explanations." It should be noted that his speaking of facts being constituted from other facts is apparently not meant to suggest *propositional* equivalence, as one might think from the common treatment of facts as true propositions, but simply the equivalence of moral properties with the relevant natural base properties or other natural properties (though even this kind of equivalence has been thought to require a conceptually as opposed to nomically necessary equivalence). Compare Brink's apparently similar (and I think insufficiently explicated) use of 'constitute' in *Moral Realism* (e.g. pp. 191–93).

14. Two clarifications are needed here. First, I leave unexplicated the idea that the fundamental place of abstract entities (or some of them) might be necessary truths; but in part the idea is that these abstract entities do not enter into causal relations and bear necessary, rather than causal, connections to certain other abstract entities. Second, a nomic truth is a lawlike one, hence one that supports counterfactuals and is confirmed by its instances; it may be that not all such truths are plausibly taken to express causal connections. Consider, for instance, the law relating the period of a pendulum to its length: is the length clearly a causal variable, as opposed to being suitably connected (causally) with gravity as the causal factor?

15. This concerns what might be called *primary knowledge* (and justification): I do not deny that one might know a thing to have a moral property on the basis of testimony, or that one might know there is an injustice from a pattern of events plausibly considered its effects. But surely no one can know of injustice in these ways except by virtue of *someone's* knowing of it through one or more or the base properties. It should also be said that knowledge may be like justified belief here in that its ground need not be actual belief, e.g. belief to the effect that the relevant base properties are present, but an appropriate justification for believing something to this effect.

16. Bernard Williams would, to be sure, call brutality a "thick" ethical concept to contrast it with the very general, "thin" ones like 'ought' and 'right'; but he does nothing to show that it is not simply a character trait *relevant* to moral assessment, and in any case there is certainly a behaviorally (and non-morally) specifiable narrow notion of brutality that would serve the limited purpose the notion must play here. See his *Ethics and the Limits of Philosophy* (Cambridge: Harvard University Press, 1985), esp. chs. 7 and 8.

17. Perhaps Brink took Harman to miss this point when, in reply to a claim of Harman's, he said, "I don't think we need know any of the naturalistic bases of the moral facts we offer in explanation, much less do we need a full-blown naturalistic reduction of all moral claims, in order for these moral explanations to be legitimate" (*Moral Realism*, p. 191n). In any case, if 'legitimate' here is used to mean 'true' I grant the point. But I think a stronger, epistemic claim is intended — and would be needed to block the line of argument I am developing. Perhaps Brink has in mind that (as he nicely brings out) one can appeal to a moral notion like injustice in explanation without knowing what form the injustice takes, and one's explanation might remain sound even in circumstances where its form is different (see, e.g., pp. 195–96). I grant this too, but it surely does nothing to undermine the point that one's warrant for such an appeal depends on justification for believing something to the effect that one or another of the base properties obtains. One need not be able to tell *a specific* story about how some base element operates, but if one is not warranted in positing *some* such story, the explanatory appeal to injustice is not legitimate. Thus, I am warranted in giving a purported moral explanation only if I am warranted in positing one or another naturalistic explanations by virtue of which the former can be true.

18. One might go further. As Warren Quinn puts it in explicating Harman's line of argu-

ment, "The better explanations that may always replace our moral explanations can . . . be fashioned from concepts that the intelligent moral explainer must already have because his own application of moral principles depends on them. Moral theory, in presupposing a rich supply of naturalistic concepts, contains the full-blown means by which its own explanations may be put aside." "Truth in Ethics," *Ethics* 96 (1986): p. 531 (this paper as a whole is a helpful treatment of the controversy between Harman and Sturgeon). My point is that moral properties seem to be only indirectly explanatory of concrete events and that moral explanations, spelled out, depend on appeal to natural properties. But the explanations are not put aside, or even replaceable, as somehow inadequate; indeed (as Harman would perhaps not deny), pragmatically, they may be indispensable.

19. It is perhaps noteworthy that Sturgeon himself speaks of a necessary connection in such a case; see, e.g., his "Moral Explanations," p. 69.

20. It is an interesting question whether Bernard Williams is committed to a premise of this sort for "thick" ethical concepts, e.g. those of cowardice, lying, brutality, and gratitude — the kind he countenances. See *Ethics and the Limits of Philosophy*, esp. ch. 8. One might of course question whether these are moral at all, as opposed to singling out elements which figure *in* moral principles, such as the prohibition of lying; but this is an issue I cannot pursue here. For a valuable critical discussion of Williams's treatment of these and the contrasting "thin" concepts such as that of rightness and obligation, see Warren Quinn, "Reflection and the Loss of Moral Knowledge: Williams on Objectivity," *Philosophy & Public Affairs* 16 (1987): 195–209.

21. This is a large issue, and I am simply sketching one plausible alternative. For a brief discussion of this position in comparison with empiricist (including conventionalist) alternatives, see my *Epistemology: A Contemporary Introduction to the Theory of Knowledge* (London and New York: Routledge, 1997), ch. 4.

22. Bernard Williams's insistence on world-guidedness and action-guidingness seems to reflect such a view. A related, explanationist view of knowledge informs Alan H. Goldman's recent treatment of moral knowledge. See his *Moral Knowledge* (London and New York: Routledge, 1988). For a critical discussion of Williams's approach on this matter see Joseph Mendola, "Normative Realism, or Bernard Williams and Ethics at the Limit," *Australasian Journal of Philosophy* 67 (1989).

III

Character, Responsibility, and Virtue

6

Self-Deception, Rationalization, and the Ethics of Belief

An Essay in Moral Psychology

Self-deception is a philosophically challenging subject. It interests psychologists as well as philosophers,[1] and it raises important ethical questions about the scope of moral responsibility and the ethics of belief. There is, however, continuing disagreement over whether self-deception is to be explained, or explained away.[2] Construed literally, the notion suggests that self-deceivers both believe and disbelieve the same proposition: believing it as victims of deception, disbelieving it as perpetrators. *Literalists* often seek to show how believing and disbelieving the same proposition is possible; other literalists contend that this is irreducibly paradoxical and self-deception thus impossible; still others have argued that taking the term literally does not entail a complete analogy with other-person deception. Non-literalists have sometimes provided analyses of self-deception, sometimes characterized it without quite giving necessary and sufficient conditions, and sometimes argued that since there are no such conditions to be found, we do best by detailing the features of various interesting cases.

For all this diversity of approach to self-deception, there is much agreement about the territory to be charted. We must explain what sort of behavior merits the term, how self-deception is related to thought and action, how its presence affects rationality, moral responsibility, and psychological integrity, and what uses the notion may have in ethics, philosophy of mind, or psychology. This essay assumes that self-deception, understood literally — though not precisely on the model of one person's deceiving another — is common. My specific project is to clarify connections between self-deception and rationalization, to describe their bearing on reasons for action and reasons for belief, and to show how standards belonging to the ethics of belief apply to all of these elements. Rationalization is one facet of behavior in which self-deception shows its true character. Why does self-deception produce rationalization? And when it does, does it give the subject genuine reasons for acting or for believing? Moreover, if rationalization can be caused by self-deception, it can also produce it. The two are mutually supporting and mutually illuminating, and both sometimes result from or produce behavior that is morally objectionable from the point of view of the ethics of belief. Let us start with the question of what self-deception is.

I. Self-Deception and Rationalization

We might first locate self-deception in relation to some of the central points of theoretical decision that shape approaches to the topic. One issue is whether self-deceivers must believe and disbelieve the same proposition. Second, the ontology of self-deception is important. Is it wholly behavioral, a matter of one's actions, or is it, by contrast, a state? Third, if there are both acts and states of self-deception, it matters greatly which is fundamental. Should we conceive the state in terms of the acts or vice versa? In either case, there is a fourth question: whether to take cognitive concepts, such as belief and knowledge, as fundamental, or to rely primarily on volitional concepts, such as focusing one's attention and selecting one's sources of evidence. A fifth issue is whether unconscious elements play a role, say in providing different levels for the deceiver and the dupe.

Self-Deception

Speaking in terms of these theoretical divisions, my account does not construe self-deception as entailing the paradox of believing and disbelieving the same proposition; it takes the state of self-deception as primary and interprets acts of self-deception as deriving their character from their relation to the state; and it uses cognitive concepts, including that of unconscious belief, as its principal building blocks, though it connects them with both motivation and action. The core of the account is this: a person, S — Steven, let us say — is in self-deception, with respect to a proposition, p, if and only if S (1) unconsciously knows that not-p (or has reason to believe, and unconsciously and truly believes, that not-p); (2) sincerely avows, or is disposed to avow sincerely, that p; and (3) has at least one want which explains, in part, both why S's belief that not-p is unconscious and why S is disposed to avow that p, even when presented with what he sees is evidence against p.[3]

I construe unconscious belief non-technically, as simply belief which S cannot, without special self-scrutiny or outside help, come to know or believe he has; it is not buried in a realm which only extreme measures, such as psychotherapy, can reach. In every other respect, for example in directing behavior and serving as a basis for inferences, the belief can be almost entirely like any other; the often thin and delicate veil between it and unaided consciousness affects it little.

Consider an example. Jan is an adolescent girl who has had an unhappy childhood, is subject to depressive moods, and craves attention. She might "attempt" suicide by taking an overdose of aspirin, say, six tablets. The result might be that her parents show alarm and pay more attention to her. She might inform friends about the incident and perhaps tell them, when she feels low, that she is again contemplating suicide. So far, the case might be either plain insincerity or genuine contemplation of suicide. But suppose Jan knew that such doses of aspirin are unlikely to be fatal and knew that she left conspicuous evidence of her taking the pills (such as the open bottle on the sink). And suppose her talk of suicide increases as her parents and friends ignore her, yet does not lead to another apparent attempt, and decreases when she gets attention. Imagine, too, that she does not find herself thinking about killing herself when she is alone; instead, she thinks about family, friends, and school activities. At this point, we might doubt that her attempt was genuine and wonder whether she is just lying about suicide to get attention. But suppose we know that she is generally very honest and, in addition, does not in her own consciousness even have the thought that she did not really try to kill herself, nor the thought that she is not really contemplating suicide when she says she is. In line with this, we may imagine that when she does say she is contemplating it, she does not have the intention to deceive her hearer, at least not any such intention or motivation that she can discern by ordinary reflection.

We now have, on one side, evidence that Jan in some way realizes that her "attempt" was not serious and that she is not really contemplating killing herself, and, on the other side, evidence that she is not simply lying when, wrought up, she tells friends that she may kill herself. I submit that the case could be one of self-deception with respect to the proposition that she is seriously contemplating suicide. When she says this, she is deceiving herself because she knows, unconsciously, that she is not so inclined. But she is, despite this knowledge, deceived, for in saying it she is both saying something false and yet not lying, at least not to us: she is, as it were, taken in. She does not, however, quite believe what she says; she is too aware of her own behavior and feelings for that; and this is why we do not expect the full range of behavior one would expect from genuine belief, including planning which presupposes that she will die (though in a well-developed case, even planning might be self-deceptively done). Yet her sincere avowal of the proposition is like an expression of belief; normally, in fact, sincerely avowing that p implies believing it. We have, then, both knowledge that not-p and the satisfaction of a major criterion for believing p. The criterion is not a logically sufficient condition, but it is strong enough to render its satisfaction in avowing a false proposition a kind of deception. In a weak sense of 'accept', she accepts what she avows and is in that sense deceived *in* her avowal. Not believing p, however, she is not deceived *by* that avowal.

The case also exhibits appropriate motivation. It is completely understandable that Jan should want and need attention, and should believe that appearing suicidal will get it. These elements need not even be unconscious; in fact, it is in part because Jan consciously knows of their presence that she can scarcely help grasping, though without being conscious of it, that she is not suicidal. But as a decent and honest person, she would not want to lie and would recoil from the thought of herself as lying to others.[5] Thus, to fulfill her desire for attention in the way she believes will succeed, while maintaining her self-image, she must avoid being conscious that she is not suicidal. This is one respect in which being moral, far from preventing self-deception, can, in certain conditions of psychic need, help to produce it. If, for instance, she were not moral, she might simply scheme for more attention. Morality can help to drive some beliefs and desires underground.

Self-Deceptive Conduct

So far, my main concern has been to sketch an account of the state of self-deception. It is also important to see, however, that the account enables us to understand other aspects of self-deception and to distinguish it from similar notions.

First, consider *acts of self-deception*. These may be conceived (roughly) as those manifesting, or in a certain purposive way conducive to, a self-deception state. An example of the first sort would be Jan's declining a weekend invitation from a friend on the ground that she may not be alive then; an instance of the second would be her putting out of mind what she knows about the effects of aspirin as she initially "plans" to commit suicide by taking six tablets. One might think that since there are acts of deceiving others by a mere utterance, there are also acts of deceiving oneself at a stroke. I suspect that there are few if any such acts. Moreover, we should not expect the analogy to other-person deception to extend to this; for there is only one person, and the dynamics of self-deception requires, at least normally, a gradual onset. Nor should it be thought that self-deception is ever identical with an act; the term may be used to refer to patterns of behavior, but neither those patterns nor the existence of acts of self-deception entails that self-deception is ever constituted by an act, any more than the existence of acts of compassion entails that compassion itself is sometimes an act.

The account of self-deception also enables us to understand *being deceiving toward oneself*. This is the sort of behavior by which one gets into self-deception: putting evidence out of mind, concentrating on an exaggeratedly favorable view of oneself, selectively exposing oneself to admirers, and so on. But it does not entail self-deception. For one thing, it may simply produce *delusion*: one may, for instance, really come to believe that one's motives are noble, without the veiled realization that this is false. Granted, one might first have been in self-deception, but it need not be this way: as a result of being deceiving with himself, Joe might simply come to be deceived in believing that *p*, yet not enter self-deception, because he is too whole-hearted in holding this belief and there is nothing about him in virtue of which he could be conceived as perpetrating the deception. This is not self-deception; it is *self-caused deception*.

Much of the behavior just described is morally criticizable. Avoiding that kind of behavior is a main responsibility we have under the heading of the *ethics of belief*: roughly, the part of ethics concerned primarily with regulating what we believe and how strongly we believe it. There is no need for a full-scale discussion of the ethics of belief. Three basic points should serve here. First, such cognitive regulation is normally not possible by mere acts of will; normally we do it by such things as properly attending to relevant evidence, to which we then respond in the ways appropriate to rational persons considering grounds for or against various propositions of concern to them in the context.[6] Second, normally, a sound ethics of beliefs requires that we try to develop dispositions that lead us to seek (evidential) grounds in certain matters (say, questions on which people's welfare turns), to form beliefs when and only when the grounds are adequate to this, and to avoid having a degree of conviction at variance with the strength of our grounds. Third, for many of our beliefs we do not need to seek grounds. Some are, for instance, obviously true, and some not obviously true are plainly unimportant.

Now suppose that the ethics of belief applies to cases in which one does not come to believe the unwarrantedly favored proposition but only to "accept" it in the mode of self-deception. I suggest that it does so apply, though (for reasons that emerge later) where other things are equal it is less reprehensible to accept a proposition in this mode when one has preponderant reasons to reject it (or at least suspend judgment on it) than where, under the same conditions, one believes it. I think, then, that one implication of the account of self-deception as positing the category of non-belief-entailing acceptance is that the scope of the ethics of belief is wider than simply the regulation of *belief*. It extends at least to what one accepts, in the way one accepts what one sincerely but self-deceptively avows.

Self-Deception as Fertile Ground for Rationalization

If self-deception is conceived as I have proposed, rationalization should be expected to be among its effects. I have suggested that, far from being simply irrational, a self-deceiver not only knows something but also exhibits a complex ability, often using considerable skill, in concealing it. I have also suggested that a desire to preserve one's self-image may be important in causing self-deception. If it is, and if, as seems likely, most people do not like to appear unreasonable, we might expect that rationalization often provides self-deceivers with a way to make otherwise unreasonable behavior seem appropriate. Thus, if Jan is asked, by a friend who thinks she is faking, why she has not tried to kill herself for many months since the last incident, Jan may reply that her parents have been depressed themselves and she cannot kill herself when they are too weak to stand the blow.

The same example illustrates another point: rationalization can help to support self-deception by providing a plausible account of behavior that might otherwise reveal the falsity of what one sincerely avows. Jan herself, being of normal intelligence, needs an explanation of her not even attempting to carry out any of her numerous threats, else she may question her own sincerity, as she would anyone else's under the same circumstances. Her rationalization helps to keep intact the veil between her consciousness and her knowledge that she is not really suicidal. And in rationalizing, she would normally be expressing two things she wholeheartedly believes: that her parents were depressed and that this was a reason for not killing herself at the time. She may even believe that this was the reason *why* she actually did not do so. But suppose that she unconsciously knows that it was not why. Still, in suggesting that it was, as she rationalizes her not having made any attempt for months, she is not lying, except possibly to herself (and lying to oneself is a kind of act of self-deception). She lacks the specific intentions (or other motivation) required for ordinary lying, such as the intention to get the hearer to believe something false. For she knows, though unconsciously, that the statement in question is true; this is why she lacks the intention to get the hearer to believe something false, and if she is lying to herself, it is roughly in the sense that she is deceiving herself.

Rationalization

In speaking about rationalization, I have assumed — what I think is implied in the non-technical use of the term — that a rationalization of something one has done does not explain why one actually did it. Rationalization, at least of particular actions, contrasts with explanation of them (in the success as opposed to attempt sense of 'explanation'). It is, however, nearly as hard to explicate rationalization as to explicate self-deception. Perhaps Freud's view can be fairly readily formulated (though I doubt that); but the notion has an active life of its own in standard parlance, and it is this range of uses that I try to capture.

With the example of Jan's appeal to her parents' well-being as background, let me suggest the following account of rationalizing an action (A): a rationalization, by S (Steven, we may imagine) of his A-ing, is a purported account of his A-ing, given by him, which (1) offers one or more reasons for his A-ing, (2) represents the deed as at least prima facie rational given the reason(s), and (3) does not explain why he did it.[8] Jan takes the fact that her parents are too depressed to deal with her suicide to be a good reason for delaying it; she offers it as explaining her delay and as rendering her delay reasonable (or something of the sort); yet it does not explain the delay.

Several comments on this account are needed. First, the notion of a purported account is intended broadly, but the commonest cases are attempted explanations and attempted justifications. Second, one may satisfy (2) without saying anything to the effect that given the reason(s), A is at least prima facie rational. Typically, the context will indicate that the factor(s) cited are supposed to show this about the action. Third, 'rationalization' need not be disapprobative, as it usually is in the Freudian sense; for we are including cases in which, for example, one quite properly rationalizes an intuitive decision by citing good reasons there were for it which one could have sought had one needed them. Finally, the formulation is meant to suggest that rationalizations are normally — and often self-defensively — motivated; yet the conditions can be satisfied by a purported account which one does not give in order to represent the action as rational, and even by a purported account that fails to explain the action owing merely to error with no psychological significance, as where I have simply forgotten my real reason for doing something and cite another perfectly ordinary one I had for it. Under various circumstances, one can produce an unintentional rationalization.[9]

In describing our example, I am assuming that Jan appeals to a reason she has for delaying; for the fact that her parents are too depressed to deal with her suicide is a reason to delay it, and she *has* it as a reason because she believes this and sees that it favors her delaying. I also assume that this is not a reason for which she in fact delays. For if it is, clearly it explains, at least in part, *why* she delays; we would then have an explanation, not a rationalization. Suppose, however, that Jan did not believe, at the time she acted (e.g. abstained from proceeding toward suicide), that her killing herself would be unbearable to her parents. This fact is still a reason for her delaying, since it weighs significantly in favor of that. Thus, our account of rationalization would take her appeal to it to be rationalization.

There are writers who hold that an appeal to a reason should not be counted as rationalizing unless S at least does not disbelieve that it was a reason for which he acted. One ground for saying this is that we would otherwise assimilate self-deception to lying.[10] But surely such deceitfulness need only affect the kind of rationalization we have. I propose to distinguish *rationalizations by appeal to alleged reasons* from *rationalizations by appeal to reasons one had*. The latter are more typical, but the former have the intuitively crucial properties. The former are often, in addition, deceitful rationalizations, though a rationalization may also be deceitful because one falsely implies, of a reason one had but did not act on, that it *was* a reason for which one acted.

Deceitful rationalizations, in turn, are sometimes self-deceptive, sometimes not, as where I am well aware that I did not have the reason I offer as accounting for (say) my not inviting someone to a meeting. Deceit, then, like self-deception, may occur either with respect to whether one had a reason or with respect to whether one acted for that reason. If a number of reasons are cited in rationalizing, the result may be a mixture of reasons one had and did not have. Call these cases *heterogeneous rationalizations*. They may at the same time be partially or wholly deceitful, depending on what beliefs one has concerning whether one in fact had, or acted for, the reasons in question.

We often act for many reasons, just as we sometimes rationalize an action by appeal to many. Suppose I offer an account of my A-ing by appeal to several reasons, where some are reasons for which I have acted and some are merely reasons I had for acting. Surely I am to some extent rationalizing; I am, after all, committing myself to at least a partial account of my action by my appeal to the reason(s) I merely had. Let us call such mixed accounts *partial rationalizations*, since they are in part rationalizations and in part (successful) explanations.

II. The Self-Deceptive Rationalization of Actions and Attitudes

All of the differences so far noted among kinds of rationalization may affect how self-deception is connected with rationalization. Let us explore some important aspects of this connection.

The Circumstances of Self-Deceptive Rationalization

There are at least three variables here: the kinds of occasions favorable to the process by which self-deception leads to rationalization; the self-deceiver's threshold for rationalization; and the degree of success of the process once it begins. I want to address these in that order.

First, consider those common occasions on which circumstances threaten to penetrate the veil between one's consciousness and one's unconscious knowledge. If I am self-deceived about my competence, there will likely be frequent evidences that go against my sincere avowal that I am good at my job; these will threaten to make me conscious of what I already realize deep down. Suppose that I hire the wrong person for a task, say because I think her bright. Later, asked why I hired someone with so little experience, I might say I was impressed by a letter from Donald. If I do not want to conclude that I decided incompetently, I will be biased in favor of believing that this was why I hired her, even if it was not. Suppose I do falsely believe this; we would then have a non-deceptive rationalization, though the false belief that prevents its being deceptive may be one that would not have been formed by someone abiding by an adequate ethics of belief. If I did not hold this belief and was quite aware I did not, we would have a deceptive rationalization. Both rationalizations are generated by self-deception, because of the way they are ultimately attributable to my desire to view myself as competent (or desires to this effect), and they each function both to nurture this desire and to help in keeping out of consciousness my realization that I am not good at my job. Both are produced by self-deception; but neither is a self-deceptive rationalization, since neither appropriately embodies self-deception. Suppose, however, that my saying I hired her because I was impressed by Donald's letter was a self-deceptive avowal, since I unconsciously knew this was not why I did it. Then the very giving of the rationalization is an act of self-deception. This feature seems sufficient for its being a self-deceptive rationalization.

Second, on some occasions, although nothing particularly threatens the veil that preserves one's self-deception, one's behavior or thoughts simply do not seem rational or appropriate, so that a desire to preserve one's general self-image motivates one to find reasons for them. If Joe discovers that he often recalls experiences with Jane, whom he self-deceptively tells himself he is happy to be through with, he may simply feel this is strange, and rationalize that he is recalling the experiences because he likes to recall pleasant times. Granted, some people might feel such recollections to be threatening, for instance as belying their claim to be happy to be through with the romance. But they need only be felt to be, say, awkward or puzzling in order to generate rationalization. If the recollections are not voiced to anyone else, there may be no need to offer the rationalization to anyone else. But one's own standards of rationality, or one's need to maintain a certain view of oneself, may be as demanding as the incredulity or suspicion of others. Rationalization, like self-deception, need not be just for the benefit of others.

A third case is a kind in which one is, so to speak, forced to put one's money where one's mouth is. This need not involve external circumstances. For instance, Jan may simply get to a point where she feels hopelessly depressed, and in such a way that if she fails, without a suitable explanation, to form a plan to kill herself, she may become conscious that she has never intended to do so. This is a likely time to seek reasons for delaying. She may already have some, for instance her having promised to meet a friend the next week. Or she may find some, say by discovering how hurtful to her parents it would be to do the deed now. It is possible, of course, that she may actually form a plan to commit suicide later. She might, however, form a self-deceptive plan, that is, roughly, one which she sincerely avows while unconsciously knowing that she is not resolute about following it. One might argue that this is not a plan, but only self-deception with respect to the proposition that one *has* a plan; but I am supposing that, for most of the elements in the plan, she does have intentions to carry them out, and has considerable motivation, though not firm intention, to take the last step.

Regarding the self-deceiver's threshold for rationalization, we should note a number of factors. Self-deception always creates a tendency to rationalize in the sorts of cases just described, but people differ in the strength of this tendency. One factor is simply the degree of desire, or perhaps felt need, to seem rational. Some people also like, more than others, to explain themselves. This applies particularly to the audibly pious: not only those who are religiously pious, but many who regularly express their sense of righteousness, or criticize others for missing the mark. Another factor is S's ability to marshal the reasons he has, to fabricate reasons he does not have, and to avoid the kind of scrutiny, of his consciousness or his behavior, which would expose a rationalization as such, and thus perhaps threaten to lift the veil of self-deception. There are other variables, such as the ability to compartmentalize one's behavior; one's capacity to avoid systematically interpreting one's thought and action; and one's ability to avoid or shorten interactions with people who, like critical older siblings, are likely to expose embarrassing truths about oneself. But we need not discuss the determinants of the threshold for rationalization further; enough has been said to suggest that although self-deception tends to lower this threshold, self-deceivers differ considerably in their thresholds for rationalization.

Self-Deception as a Route to Rationalization

There are several ways in which self-deception can produce rationalization. A rationalization based on self-deception will arise in some sense in the service of that deception, for example as obliquely aimed by S at keeping out of consciousness a crucial proposition he unconsciously knows, for instance that he is not good at his work. It is not that he says to himself something like 'If I don't find an account of my mistaken decision which supports my avowal that I am competent, then I may have to face my incompetence'. It is more nearly that his wanting to believe he is competent leads him both to do the things that prevent his realization of deficiency from becoming conscious (e.g. his selectively exposing himself to evidence for his competence) and to rationalize away actions of his which point toward the deficiency. The self-deception and rationalization are similarly motivated, one might say; and at least typically the relevant motivation reflects some "ego need." Even when we restrict success in producing rationalizations to those based on self-deception, however, there are still many degrees and kinds of success. Let us consider some.

One factor important to evaluating the success of self-deception in producing rationalization is of course the number of instances in which the agent gives, or is prepared to give, the rationalization. Another is the number of different rationalizations the self-deception produces. Success is also greater in proportion to the plausibility of the rationalizations. This has an objective side: the more plausible, the less likely to be rejected by others or, ultimately, by the agent. But the subjective side is even more important in the preservation of the self-deception: how convincing S himself finds the rationalization(s). A foolish attempt may backfire and lead one to become conscious of one's real reason. (Why am I inventing ridiculous reasons to explain my hiring her?) But if a rationalization is really convincing, it may nicely protect one's self-deception (Donald's letter was really cogent and I even had it at the top of my list of reasons to hire when I made the decision). From this point of view, a self-deceptive rationalization may be less supportive of the underlying self-deception than one appealing to reasons one genuinely (but falsely) believes explain one's (otherwise telltale) action. Here self-caused deception may serve ego needs better than self-deception.

By contrast, if self-deception creates only partial rationalization, it is less successful, other things equal — though it may be that an admixture of truth helps to raise the accompanying falsehoods above suspicion. Similarly, the more readily disconfirmable a rationalization is, the less its production by self-deception is a success (other things equal). For others, or the subject himself, may discover either that he did not act for the indicated reason(s) or, in the case of fabricated reasons, that he did not have the reasons. This may lead him to see that he has been deceiving himself.

Many kinds of rationalization, then, can arise from self-deception; and from the point of view of preserving the agent's self-deception and, thereby, his self-image, self-deception may be more or less successful in generating rationalizations. Not all rationalizations, of course, arise from self-deception. Sometimes rationalization produces self-deception. Exploring how it may do so will help us understand both notions.

Rationalization as a Route to Self-Deception

We should again consider at least the following three kinds of variables: occasions favorable to rationalization's producing self-deception, the agent's threshold for passing from rationalization to self-deception, and the success with which rationalization produces self-deception when it does so. Not just any instance of rationalization is favorable to self-deception. I may be quite consciously and clearheadedly rationalizing to deceive people about my real reasons and may approve of those reasons and feel no need whatever to protect my ego by accounting for anything I have done. It may be, however, that I rationalize precisely because I want to represent myself favorably, and this may in turn be because of, say, fears or insecurity. If, broadly speaking, such ego needs underlie my rationalization, the occasion is favorable for self-deception.

Imagine, for instance, that Joe rationalizes his not taking a stand on an important issue by claiming that doing so would be needlessly divisive, but is aware that he really did it to avoid a fight. Suppose, moreover, that it is important to him to feel that he is courageous, so that he is publicly ashamed of his evasion and privately ashamed of his rationalization. As time passes, he may put out of mind his recollection of the reason for which he acted and focus often on the point that taking a stand would have been divisive. He may also expose himself to others who both accept that point and take it to justify avoiding the issue. In time, his knowledge of why he avoided it may become veiled from his consciousness, and he may be sincere in saying that he acted to avoid divisiveness. One kind of occasion favorable to rationalization's leading to self-deception, then, is the sort in which the former is itself produced in the service of an ego need that can be allayed by the subject's becoming self-deceived with respect to the rationalizing reasons.

A second kind of favorable occasion arises when, again assuming the presence of a suitable ego need, rationalizing reasons abound in one's environment or one's thinking, in a way that makes it relatively easy to find mutually supporting accounts of one's behavior, in the shadow of which one can veil one's disturbing grasp of the truth. Recall our case of avoiding the issue. Suppose that at the time when Joe declined to take a position, the hour was late, the majority disposition was clear, someone neutral would be needed to patch things up afterward, and so on. Other things equal, rationalization here, whether by appeal to one or to all of these reasons for avoiding the issue, is more likely to produce self-deception.

The third kind of occasion we should note may, but need not, occur together with one or both of the previous two. I refer to cases in which one is thinking about oneself and, dissatisfied with what one finds, rationalizes as a way to put one's disturbing actions in a more favorable light. Some such rationalizations might themselves be self-deceptive. But suppose that they are not and, in failing to relieve one's dissatisfaction, they are less successful than some self-deceptive rationalizations. Sometimes one's realization that one is rationalizing heightens disapproval of oneself and, like a line of residual glue on the crack of a repaired vase, calls attention to what was meant to be hidden. Feeling disappointed with myself, I might now be inclined — especially if I lack a strong ethics of belief — to do the sorts of things which conduce to self-deception: selectively expose myself to information on the matter; stress to myself the welcome evidence and avoid contemplating the unwelcome; and, in doing this, use the reasons figuring in rationalizations that led me to begin the process toward self-deception.

People differ in the frequency with which they encounter occasions that are favorable to rationalizing or to their becoming self-deceived if they do rationalize. They differ markedly in their threshold for proceeding from these occasions to self-deception. Other things equal, this threshold is lower in proportion to one's (1) ability to rationalize convincingly; (2) capacity to evade systematic exploration of one's own thoughts and behavior — a morally significant aspect of character; (3) ability to assemble what one takes to be information confirming either the elements in one's rationalization or the sincere avowals crucial for the self-deception, or both; and (4) ability (and willingness) to bias, say, by selective attention, the relative weights of evidence for, versus evidence against, those elements and avowals — another ethically significant aspect of character. Still another factor is the strength of his relevant desires or needs; those important to one's self-image (roughly, to one's ego) are the typical motivating elements. Consider a need to feel that one is masculine — or feminine, compassionate, brilliant, creative, well liked, and so forth.

In addition to the success with which rationalization produces self-deception, there is the "success" of the resulting self-deception. At least two indications of success deserve mention. First, consider degree of satisfaction of the relevant desire or need. If Joe rationalizes his avoiding the issue because he desperately wants to see himself as courageous, then one indication of the success of self-deception produced by that rationalization is the extent to which it fulfills that desire, say, by contributing to the strength and conscious visibility of his beliefs to the effect that he is courageous. A second indication of success is the extent to which the self-deception supports a rationalization producing it. The degree of support depends largely on the kind of rationalization. Imagine that in giving it Joe falsely believes not only that he had the reason cited but also that he acted *for* that reason. Self-deception that helped him maintain both beliefs would support the rationalization better than self-deception that helped him maintain only one of them.

A third measure of success might be called *underpinning*: the degree to which the self-deception equips one to withstand forces that would expose the rationalization, for example comments by others to the effect that Joe he is whitewashing himself. Underpinning tends to vary with the first two measures of success I have cited, but it is affected by others. Even if some of the information surrounding a rationalization does not support it directly, it may be relevant to rebutting or simply stopping attacks on it. Being able to show, for instance, that others were biased in favor of someone not hired does nothing to support the merits of one's own choice, but it may silence their criticism of it. Self-deception and rationalization about one's own conduct, particularly on an important matter, such as a decision not to revive a relative who suffers heart failure, can be embedded in information about oneself and others that can be used in fending off all manner of criticism of one's motives or self-image.

The success of rationalizations in producing self-deception is also related to the character of the self-deception produced. There are many important variables in terms of which cases of self-deception may be distinguished; here I indicate only some quite general dimensions. One is that of *accessibility*: the more readily S can become consciously aware that p, for instance by unflinchingly facing the evidence for it, the more accessible is his self-deception with respect to p. This is connected with *entrenchment*. The more it would take, say in self-study, to undo the self-deception, the more entrenched it is. High accessibility implies shallow entrenchment; but the notions are not equivalent, since shallow entrenchment may combine with low accessibility where, although S's self-deception would be very difficult for him to discover, there are forces that would dissipate the self-deception without exposing it. For instance, my needs might change radically and I might simply forget my self-deceptive avowals and cease to be even disposed to repeat them.

Accessibility and entrenchment concern roughly the depth and strength of single cases of self-deception. Self-deception is also connected with other psychological elements in the agent. It may, for instance, exhibit more or less *stratification*, depending on the number and kind of second-order elements. One can have second-order self-deception, being self-deceived about whether — as friends say — one is self-deceived. There are also differences in *systematization*, depending on whether one piece of self-deception is connected with one or more others or with rationalization and other elements, such as desires and beliefs. Self-deception about one's courage could be supported both by rationalizations about faint-hearted deeds and by self-deception about whether one's ideals and competence really express courage. Systematization tends to contribute to, but is not necessary for, *integration*: the degree to which the self-deception fits the agent's personality, especially long-term motivation and cognition. Even an isolated case could be well integrated, as where my only self-deception concerns my motives for not reviving a aging heart attack victim.

The Scope of Self-Deception and Rationalization

We have seen how self-deception tends to produce rationalization and how rationalizations may generate self-deception. In both cases the agent acts in ways that are intelligible in terms of desires and needs, either because the actions are straightforwardly motivated, as where one quite consciously seeks a reason one had for an action in order to present the action in a favorable light, or where, in some oblique way, one's desires or needs produce the relevant phenomenon, for example when self-deception arises gradually: not as something intended, but as a result of diverse actions individually aimed at such things as putting unpleasant thoughts out of mind, getting others to accept one's story about oneself, and constructing good arguments to support that story. Now if desires and needs produce self-deception and rationalization in the ways we have suggested, and if the latter play the role they seem to in the psychic economy, we should expect both self-deception and rationalization to concern not only actions, which have been our main focus so far, but any aspect of a person or his life for which there can be comparable desires and needs. This is just what we do find.

Take self-deception first. As characterized in section I, its subject matter is unrestricted. One can be self-deceived about one's beliefs or actions, about others or oneself, about one's property or one's character, and so on. Although self-deception is always grounded in one's desires or needs, it need not be about oneself. Jack could be self-deceived about whether Jill loves her country as well as about whether she loves him. Now if self-deception is unrestricted as to subject matter and is a common route to rationalization, there is some reason to think that rationalization need not be only of actions but may target other things for which having reasons can serve one's desires and needs.[11] Let me illustrate this.

If one can rationalize one's action of avoiding taking a stand, it would be strange if one could not also rationalize a belief that doing so was right. Indeed, if we substitute belief for action in the account of rationalization given in the preceding paragraphs, we get a plausible characterization of *belief rationalization*. Taking off from the action case, we may distinguish between reasons one merely has for believing and reasons for which one believes, and we find a similar contrast between explaining and non-explaining reasons. The same holds for desires and all the other propositional attitudes, including even emotions so far as they are propositional, as with fear that somebody intends one harm.

There are, then, rationalizations of beliefs, desires, emotions, and many other elements. Moreover, self-deception can produce such rationalizations, and they in turn can lead to self-deception. If I am self-deceived with respect to my fear of philosophers, this may lead to my rationalizing. I will almost certainly not rationalize my fear, since, being self-deceived about it, I sincerely avow that I do not have it. But I may rationalize actions, such as my avowals to the effect that I merely dislike philosophers; beliefs, such as my belief that philosophers are argumentative; and emotions, such as my hatred of a philosopher who has shown me up. Rationalizations of elements besides actions may, in turn, produce self-deception.

Given what has been said about how self-deception and rationalization interact, we should be able to achieve a comparable understanding of the interaction where the relevant rationalization is directed toward something other than an action. The individual cases have distinctive features, but we need not discuss examples in detail. Instead, I want to conclude this section with general remarks applying both to self-deception and, by implication, to self-deceptive rationalizations.

As conceived here, self-deception tends to be unstable. This is in part because self-deceivers avow, or are disposed to avow, sincerely, something they (unconsciously) know is not true. There are at least two important points here. First, by and large it takes special conditions, and often special efforts — such as selective exposure to relevant information — to make us capable of being simultaneously sincere (at least in the sense that we are lying at most to ourselves) and mistaken in avowing a belief. Second, we are generally rational enough to make our becoming aware of evidence for a proposition cause us to tend to believe it (as self-deceivers unconsciously do believe the truths they find somehow unpleasant) and even to acknowledge it.

Take a case in which Joe is self-deceived in avowing that he is courageous (p). There is a certain tension that is characteristic of self-deception and partly explains its typical instability: the sense of evidence against p pulls him away from the deception and threatens to lift the veil concealing from his consciousness his knowledge that he is not courageous; the desires or needs grounding the self-deception pull against one's grasp of the evidence and threaten to block one's perception of the truth. If the first force prevails, one sees the truth plainly and is no longer deceived; if the second prevails, one passes from self-deception into single-minded delusion and does not see the truth at all. Self-deception exists, I think, only where there is a balance between these two forces. Rationalization helps to keep that balance. It can also create such a balance when it occurs where the appropriate elements are waiting to be so arranged.

My account of self-deception in relation to rationalization has at least two implications for the ethics of belief. First, if we think of the ethics of belief as extending to keeping one's avowals — "stated beliefs," one might say — in conformity with what one actually believes, then on that count self-deception is, from the point of view of the ethics of belief, prima facie criticizable. This point holds even if (as will be argued in chapter 7) it is chiefly one's acts — such as putting evidence out of mind — which are the *direct* bearers of responsibility, though that point would help to explain why, other things equal, where one has grounds clearly favoring not-p over p, accepting p in the mode of self-deception is less reprehensible than believing it: one's failure to control cognition is more extensive in the latter case, both in the degree of one's cognitive "commitment" and in the likelihood of acting on the basis of that commitment. Second, insofar as rationalization operates in the service of producing or maintaining self-deception, it too is prima facie criticizable from the point of view of the ethics of belief. Both of these points will be developed later.

The account also implies that self-deception is a phenomenon that manifests a measure of rationality. It is an *evidence-sensitive* state. Indeed, since its subjects (unconsciously) know the relevant truths and do not quite believe what they self-deceivingly avow, the evidence has, in an important way, prevailed. Moreover, viewed as I suggest, self-deception powerfully exhibits the extent to which our beliefs are not under the direct control of our wills. Otherwise one could simply refuse to countenance the evidence and could bring oneself to believe what one self-deceivingly avows. If we were not minimally rational, as well as complex enough for a kind of dissociation, self-deception would not be possible; and if we did not both care about, and have a minimal grasp of, reasons, we could not rationalize.[13] This explains in part both why self-deception and rationalization come within the scope of the ethics of belief and why not every case is one in which there is anything inexcusable.

III. Self-Deception and Reasons for Acting

Rationalizations of action do not deserve the name unless they produce at least one thing that qualifies as a reason for action. This is one difference between them and excuses. An excuse may cite a cause of action that is not a reason for it. A bee sting may cause a driver to swerve but is not a reason to do so. If rationalizations must produce at least one reason, and if they often manifest our rational capacities, can suitable rationalizations of an action show that it is rational? And can this be so even when the rationalization is produced by, or embodies, self-deception? To see our way more clearly, let us first consider how self-deception provides reasons for action, both through rationalization and otherwise.

Self-Deception as a Source of Reasons for Acting

We have already distinguished reasons one merely has for acting from reasons for which one acts. Both kinds are supplied by self-deception. If I am deceiving myself out of a desire to see myself as courageous, that desire may provide me with a reason for volunteering for a dangerous job. Suppose I do volunteer. Is this acting out of self-deception? It is not natural to call it that, in part because too little of what constitutes the self-deception figures in producing the action: only the motivating desire, which, in addition, is of a common and normal kind. And while the unconscious knowledge embodied in self-deception certainly can provide a reason for acting — say, for not taking on a job so dangerous that only the courageous can succeed — we certainly do not think of acting on this sort of reason as acting out of self-deception. By contrast, if I do something which either manifests the self-deception as a whole or seems in some sense designed to preserve it, the case is different. An instance of the first sort might be selectively attending to evidence for my courage. Here his desire to see himself as courageous and my need to support my self-deceptive avowals (perhaps among other things I need to support) are responsible for the action. An example of the second sort would be my vehemently arguing against plausible evidence to the effect that I lack courage.

If self-deception can provide not only reasons for action but also reasons *on* which one acts, do self-deceivers have any control over whether, when they act in line with one or more of these reasons, they do so out of self-deception? In answering this I shall not assume that one ever has direct control over which of two or more reasons one has for acting will be a reason for which one acts. But one may have indirect control over this, and self-deception may provide motivation to exercise it. Imagine that by virtue of his desire to seem reasonable, together with his self-deceptive avowals that he avoided the issue because taking a stand would be divisive, Joe has a reason to mediate between two colleagues who are at odds: he is, after all, on record as strongly opposing division among colleagues, and here is a chance to confirm that he really acts out of this concern. But suppose that he also has reason to mediate because he would benefit if the colleague who shared his view were joined by the other. It might help him maintain his self-image if he could see himself as acting to oppose division; this would help to keep out of his consciousness his knowledge that he avoided the original issue from cowardice. What he might do, then, is emphasize to himself how his mediating might reduce division; and in deciding to mediate he might explicitly say to himself that he is going to try to make peace, and might keep out of mind (as much as possible) his selfish reason for mediating. When he does mediate, could he then be doing it out of concern to oppose division, or would that claim be self-deceptive rationalization? And how can we tell?

To begin with, although the sort of self-manipulative strategy just sketched might succeed, one could not be confident that it would. From Joe's concentrating, when he A's, on one reason he has to A, and putting another reason out of mind, it does not follow that he does not A in part, or even wholly, on the banished reason. One way he might know that the latter is influential is by noticing that as the going gets hard, the thought of that reason, or of something connected with it, such as his getting what he selfishly wants, seems required to keep him going. But even this is not conclusive, and an ingenious self-deceiver might tell himself that he was merely tempted to act for the wrong reason, and managed to resist. What we would need to know to settle this is nothing less than what he would have done, other things equal, if he had not had the banished reason. This would be difficult to know, though we may in some cases know it.

Self-Deception and Our Responsiveness to Reasons

There is a strong presumption we may make here about reasons for action. Where we are aware of a reason for A-ing that represents it as realizing some want of ours, then (1) we have some tendency to A; (2) if we A intentionally while aware of the connection we take A-ing to have to the relevant want(s), then we tend to A at least in part *for* that reason, even if we also do so for another reason; and (3) the more rational we are, the stronger these two tendencies are. (1) indicates a principle of instrumentalist moral psychology; (2) says roughly that reasons one is aware of tend to play in certain of one's actions an explanatory role corresponding to their instrumental import; and (3) says roughly that the more rational one is, the more likely is a coherence in one's conduct between the rational and explanatory roles of reasons one takes as instrumentally supporting that conduct. It is not clear whether this threefold presumption is a conceptual truth; I suspect that it is, but it is in any case plausible, particularly for rational persons. For rationality surely is, in part, a matter of appropriately responding to the reasons one has when one is suitably aware of them and of some broadly instrumental relation they bear to something one wants. Thus, in the example just drawn, we would expect the action to be performed for both reasons.

Much the same applies to reasons for believing: where I have a reason for believing p, then if I become aware of its supporting p (say rendering p highly probable), (1) I will tend to believe p; (2) if I come to believe it while aware of this supporting reason, I will tend to believe p on the *basis* of the reason, even if I also believe it on the basis of some other reason; and (3) the more rational I am, the stronger these tendencies are. Call this and its counterpart for action (and for the other propositional attitudes) the *responsiveness presumption*: it says in effect that (under certain common conditions) rational agents tend, in proportion to their rationality, to respond both in action and in attitude (and again in a roughly proportional fashion) to reasons they have for these actions or attitudes.

As applied to belief, this presumption seems to be one of the truths underlying the highly overstated idea (expressed by W. K. Clifford and other proponents of the ethics of belief) that one should proportion one's conviction to the evidence.[14] Unlike that view, this one does not imply either that one has direct voluntary control of one's beliefs in this regard or that one has even roughly quantitative indirect control of them or that the cogency of evidence is quantifiable in the relevant way. It does imply, however, that if one fails to believe p for a reason one offers in support of p, there should be (in the sense that it is reasonable to expect) an explanation for this. A conscientious person aware of this anomaly should be disposed to ask why this is so, for instance whether it is because one is self-deceived in offering the reason as such or is merely offering it as a rationalization or both.

Suppose, by contrast, that Joe rationalizes his action deceitfully, by making an explanatory appeal to reasons there were for his having mediated, which are not reasons he *had* at the time. Imagine that, when he mediated, he had the thought that his role as family friend carried a responsibility, to the colleagues' spouses, to mediate, but he had no desire to fulfill this responsibility (or to do anything else to which he believes fulfilling it would contribute). He thus had no instrumental reason to mediate, and there would be much less ground for expecting him to act on to the normative reason constituted by the responsibility. He has no desire that would motivate his acting to fulfill that responsibility. This is not to imply that motivation can come only from desire (an issue discussed in some detail in chapter 10); the point is that when a reason lacks the relevant connection with desire, then even if one acts with an awareness of that reason, there is a lesser presumption that one acts *for* the reason. Joe could have acted on this admirable (normative) reason he recognizes, but we lack compelling reason to expect him to, even if he thinks of it as he acts: that might indeed be an excellent self-deceptive strategy — camouflaging one's real reason for acting by focusing, as one does the deed, on a good reason there is to do it. Indeed, factors he believes were, objectively, reasons to perform the action are a convenient source of rationalizing elements: citing them does a good job of making the action seem reasonable, and his citing them suggests, to him anyway, admirable motivation.

Self-deception, then, is not only a fairly direct source both of reasons for acting and of reasons for which one acts, but, by producing rationalizations, an indirect source of further reasons that may turn out to be of either sort. The reasons for acting which, in either of these ways, it provides, may or may not be conscious; and in part because they are sometimes not conscious it is very difficult to determine which of our reasons for A-ing is one for which we in fact A's. Our own beliefs on the matter are not to be ignored, yet they can be mistaken. These considerations may help to explain why Kant apparently thought it impossible to determine whether, when one has a motive of inclination aligned with one of duty and then do the deed in question, we has acted *from* the motive of duty.[15]

It is very hard to generalize about the conditions under which S will act on a particular reason provided by his self-deception. For one thing, if indeed he does act out of his self-deception, it may be for several reasons together. There is also the possibility raised by partial rationalization: that there are reasons which only partially explain his action. It might then be difficult to decide how much influence each one has on the action. Clearly, self-deception can influence action in complicated ways, and rationalization can compound the difficulties of sorting out and weighing the different influences. Our efforts here are largely conceptual. But if we can see the distinctions clearly, we at least know where to look empirically in trying to understand the agent.

Self-Deception, Rationality, and the Ethical Regulation of Belief

Self-deception, we saw, requires a certain minimum of rationality and sometimes plays a very significant part in the agent's psychic economy. If, in addition, it provides reasons for action, may it thereby produce rational actions should the agent act in accordance with those reasons? Take, for instance, the case in which the unconscious knowledge embodied in self-deception provides a reason on which one acts, as where our cowardly subject declines a highly dangerous assignment because deep down he sees that he cannot manage it. To be sure, he may self-deceptively rationalize this, for instance by pointing to conflicting obligations. But the rationality of his declining surely does not depend on the cogency of his rationalizing reasons. If they are not good, he fails to *show* that his action was rational, yet the reason for which he did it may still be sufficient to render it rational. This kind of reason, however, is not the usual sort provided by self-deception, the kind such that acting on it is considered acting out of self-deception. The other cases are more difficult to resolve, and I want to consider some of them briefly.[16]

Perhaps the most general point to be made here is that although the rationality of actions arising out of self-deception is typically more difficult to assess than that of ordinary intentional actions, different *criteria* of rationality apparently are not required. One might think that if unconscious beliefs or other unconscious explanatory elements operate, we need different criteria. But if, as I hold, even unconscious beliefs may be appropriate responses to evidence — which is typically how (when true) they count as the unconscious knowledge in virtue of which the self-deceiver deceives — then perhaps other unconscious propositional attitudes may also be rational. I also assume that unconscious conative elements can render an action rational if they motivate it in the right way, as a rational belief does an action based on it. There may be a sense in which action arising from self-deception is a test case for criteria of rationality — it certainly poses a challenge to them — but it does not require special criteria.

Another important general point is that there is a profound difference between particular actions and action-types, and what renders one rational may be different from what renders the other rational. Let me first develop this point with respect to rationalization and then apply it to action arising from self-deception.[17] When Joe rationalizes his avoiding the issue, may we conclude that the avoidance was rational, assuming his cited reason is a good one? The question is ambiguous: is the reference to the type "avoiding the issue," which might be instantiated by him (or others) on different occasions, or is it to his particular action of avoidance? It makes perfect sense to say that his rationalization shows that the type "avoiding the issue" was rational yet deny that *his* doing this was rational. This is precisely what I claim (and have defended elsewhere).[18] I hold that a reason one has for an action renders that action rational only if one performs the action at least in part for that reason. Unless we say this, we must allow that a rational action can be performed for very bad reasons, for example wholly on the basis of irrational beliefs and foolish desires, so long as S has a good enough reason for it. I would call this irrationally doing something which, in the circumstances, is a rational kind of thing to do. This point is parallel to Kant's view that a deed is moral only if done out of a sense of duty, not merely in accordance with it: in both cases the (causally) grounding reason, as opposed to the merely available evidence or reasons, is what is crucial for the rationality of the particular action the agent performs.

Similar points hold for beliefs, whose rationality is also determined by the overall quality of the grounds *on* which they are held rather than those the person can offer, which may be mere rationalizations. If one believes for a bad reason, such as a prejudiced appraisal, one may irrationally believe something that is a rational *kind* of thing to believe — a well-evidenced proposition. This view allows that some genuine justificatory grounds can be unconscious; but where there are unconscious grounds, especially beliefs, there may be a tendency to form false beliefs, if only about what one's real reasons for belief are, since one cannot readily access the actuating ones. This last point raises the question whether a sound ethics of belief requires that one seek to avoid repression or any other process by which one may form unconscious beliefs that may adversely influence one's belief system as a whole. I do not know that there is any such general prima facie duty on the part of responsible believers; but we can easily incur such a duty *if* we become aware of having a significant tendency to form unconscious beliefs that might adversely affect us, for instance getting us into self-deception or causing us to do things not otherwise rational.

In the light of the points that have so far emerged, we can discern three dimensions of moral responsibility for self-deception, each connected to some degree with the ethics of belief (each also has a causal counterpart with which it may be usefully compared, but there is no need to make such comparisons here). First, there is *genetic responsibility*, responsibility for getting into self-deception, as where one selectively exposes oneself to slanted information and biased people until one becomes self-deceived. Second, there is *retentional responsibility*, responsibility for remaining in self-deception when one should get out of it, as where one continues such tactics to offset the effects of encounters with evidence against the proposition one self-deceptively "accepts." Third, if one can have a duty to avoid becoming self-deceived or indeed to become self-deceived, there may be *prospective responsibility*, either negative responsibility to avoid entering self-deception or indeed positive responsibility to enter it. The latter may seem out of the question, but suppose one can see that unless one becomes self-deceived about one's spouse's fidelity the marriage will crumble, with disastrous effects on the children. This might yield strong prima facie responsibility to become self-deceived.

Failing to live up to any of these three kinds of responsibilities might be a case of unethical regulation of belief. Just how far must one go, however, in being sure one does not get into self-deception or remain in it if one has become self-deceived? Much depends on what is at stake if one is self-deceived and on how burdensome the relevant cognitive activities are. Practical wisdom is needed here as in many other cases in ethics.

With rationalization, which is an action or activity, the ethics of *belief* might seem to have little or no relevance. But there is an analogy to self-deception: the suitably strong disposition to give a rationalization, something like being in a rationalizing frame of mind that needs only to be activated by, for example, a question why one did or believes something. With this focus, we can discern the same kinds of variables — genetic, retentional, and prospective — and *some* failures in the relevant responsibilities are deficiencies in belief regulation. The most obvious occur where one can rationalize a given action or attitude (or be disposed to do so) only through first becoming self-deceived. But rationalization can also occur where one has a false belief to the effect that one has given a cogent reason or has acted (or believes) on the basis of a set of reasons, whether it is cogent or not. In many cases, one could not rationalize — and would have to face one's real reason for belief or action — if one were more attentive to available evidence.

Regarding both self-deception and rationalization, what we might call cognitively conscientious agents — roughly those who adhere to a sound ethics of belief — will so regulate their conduct that they will have at least the following tendencies: to withhold belief or abstain from action in situations where something significant is at stake and there is insufficient ground for one of the alternatives; to seek evidence on a wide range of important matters; to develop dispositions to believe *on* their grounds rather than merely in conformity with them, as by scrutinizing what seems to influence them and trying to habituate themselves to respond to adequate grounds rather than to other kinds of attractiveness in their options; and to review a suitable proportion of their conduct and cognitions with the adequacy of grounds, as contrasted with the influence of prejudice, in mind. These are only tendencies, and they are described in guarded terms. The kinds of examples and elements discussed in this essay can help to elaborate each of them, but each reflects a complexity far beyond what can be further explored here.

Self-Deception and Rational Action

If I have been roughly correct so far, self-deception must not be stereotyped as intrinsically irrational or as vitiating the rationality of every action it generates. Since action produced by self-deception can be ingeniously self-serving, it can be at least minimally rational; this may be in much the way some deeds we consider morally wrong are, and in either case the rationality of the action may not prevent the agent's deserving criticism. Whether an action produced by self-deception is in fact rational and does or does not warrant criticism of the agent will depend not on what reasons for it are provided by the self-deception (or by any other source), but (chiefly) on the reasons for which it is performed. Consider some typical cases of actions produced by self-deception. In one, we are in effect putting our money where our mouths are: doing something in order to conform our behavior with our self-deceptive avowals, say, to the effect that we are not frightened by philosophers. Another is self-deceptive rationalization, as where Joe self-deceptively says that he avoided the issue because taking a stand would have been divisive. There is also the artificial focusing of attention on considerations favorable to sustaining the self-deceptive avowals, such as concentrating on why a stand would have been divisive and on how, on other occasions, one acted to avoid division. Some of these cases may be regarded as reducing cognitive dissonance, in that one acts to achieve greater harmony among one's beliefs and attitudes. Let us consider other cases in which actions arising from self-deception are prima facie rational.

Consider first putting one's money where one's mouth is. Is it irrational to act in support of a self-deceptive avowal? It may be: certainly it is in general reasonable to act in order to live up to the image of oneself one has projected, at least if the image is admirable, as it often is with self-deceivers. Granted, it would not normally be rational to act specifically to live up to a self-deceptive avowal; it is not even clear how this is possible, since it seems to entail a kind of awareness of one's being self-deceived that is inconsistent with one's being so. But this is not what Joe does; such is not the content of his intention (at least not of any conscious motivation). The reason for which he acts may be a perfectly good one. That he would not have that reason if not self-deceived neither vitiates the reason nor prevents it from conferring rationality on the action it explains. To be sure, there could be sufficient counter-reasons to prevent it from conferring rationality; my claim is that an action is rational in virtue of a reason only if performed *for* that reason, but not that every action performed for at least one good reason is rational. Thus, while living up to one's avowal of courage might render taking a stand on a controversial issue rational, it would not warrant doing a daredevil trick for which one knows one is unprepared. Even where self-deception provides good reasons, then, they are at best defeasible.

With this much said, the other cases may be dealt with more briefly. Self-deception may provide one with a reason to rationalize because, say, one's deeds are incongruous with one's words, as in the case of the adolescent repeatedly threatening, but never seriously attempting, suicide. Again, if one rationalizes in order to explain one's behavior, doing so may be rational. The way one does so, for example citing the kinds of reasons one does, may be foolish, but that is another matter. But should rational persons be rationalizing at all, instead of seriously inquiring into their own motivation? And if self-deception is at the heart of an attempt to rationalize, should we call the attempt rational? It is true that the inquiry might be a better thing for one to do and that self-deception may lead to irrational action. But if I have been right, self-deception buries and manipulates, yet does not wholly overthrow, reason. It is self-protective, and in some cases, like that of the husband who would fall apart if he had to face his wife's infidelity, it may be one's best protection against a blow one cannot withstand.

From the point of view of self-interest, then, which is at least one fundamental basis for determining rationality, being in self-deception may be on balance desirable, and some of the ultimately self-protective actions arising from it may also be rational when they are good means to a reasonable end like preserving an admirable self-image. But if rationalizing, even self-deceptively, is sometimes a rational thing to do, it is risky for self-deceivers; for even without others' help, they may see through their own rationalizations, discover that they are largely speaking for their own benefit, and perhaps grasp what their real reasons are.

Parallel points may be made about selectively focusing one's attention on relevant evidence, about evading things one perceives as threatening, and about other actions arising from self-deception. And counterparts of many of the points made in the preceding paragraphs hold for non-behavioral elements that may be produced by self-deception: particularly propositional attitudes, for which I would also argue that they are rational in the light of a reason one *has* for them only if it is a reason *for* which one holds (or has) them. For them, too, we should distinguish particular instances, such as Joe's belief that preventing division is a reason for avoiding a stand, from types, such as the belief that it is such a reason. And again, that a type of action is rational in the light of a reason does not entail that an instance of that type is rational, even where the agent has the reason. If Joe's real reason for avoiding the issue is that he wants to be spared unpleasant consequences of doing so, and this want is itself based on irrational fear and operates through an irrational assessment of what the consequences will be, then his simply having a reason for this type of action does not make his doing something of that type rational. A rationalizable action need not be rational. It is the same with beliefs and other propositional attitudes: rationalizability does not entail rationality.

If self-deception is not an intrinsically irrational state, nor even always an undesirable state for a normal person to be in, and if many kinds of actions arising from it can be rational, then it should not be surprising that an action's stemming from self-deception does not imply that the agent is not morally responsible for it in one or another of the ways indicated earlier.[19] Indeed, it does not even imply that the agent has less than normal control in doing it. Partly for these reasons, an action's genesis in self-deception does not necessarily provide moral extenuation.

We do sometimes talk of "victims" of self-deception, but being a victim in this sense need not be extenuating, and there is such a thing as highly culpable credulity, which can make the ill-fated dupe a subject more fitting for reproach than for extenuation. Self-deception adds the burden of being responsible for both deceiver and dupe. Why does one, qua deceiver, put evidences against p out of mind? And having done so, one may still be criticizable, qua dupe, for accepting p even at the level of avowal. Attributions of moral responsibility for actions arising from self-deception, then, may be largely or wholly unaffected by the self-deception. In any event, they are similar to attributions of rationality in being governed by multiple criteria.

Conclusion

Self-deception is primarily a state in which a kind of psychological dissociation gives rise to a disparity between what self-deceivers know, albeit unconsciously, and what they avow or are disposed to avow. It tends to be an unstable condition and to exist only so long as there is a balance between the pressure of the evidence, to which the self-deceiver's knowledge is typically a rational response, and the strength of the defenses maintaining the veil that camouflages that knowledge from consciousness. Self-deception is rarely if ever a static phenomenon. Like a craving for reassurance, it usually gives rise to efforts to satisfy the underlying desires or needs. It produces many kinds of behavior. Rationalizations are among the most important. They often support the self-deception which produces them, and they often reveal much about self-deceivers: what they value, believe, and want; even what ego need is responsible for their self-deception.

Rationalizations are not simply products of self-deception; they may produce it themselves, even if they are not self-deceptive to begin with. Self-deception *is* fertile ground for rationalization. This is because rationalization can so well supply reasons for action — or belief, desire, emotion, and other elements — which protect the subject. They protect in at least two ways. They cloak both the motivation and needs actually underlying the actions or other elements; and they help to keep buried whatever unconscious knowledge the subject has concerning those reasons. But rationalizations are also fertile ground for self-deception: they provide, for instance, considerations on which one can focus in putting out of mind, and gradually pushing beyond conscious access, knowledge, beliefs, desires, and emotions which are painful to acknowledge as one's own.

Plainly self-deception, so conceived, can have a role in maintaining not only its subjects' comfort but even their sanity, or at least their ability to function without drastic interference from guilt-ridden thoughts or distracting preoccupations. Moreover, if self-deception both embodies knowledge and leads one to want to see oneself as, for instance, reasonable, it should not be a surprise that it provides one with reasons for acting or for believing and, at times, leads one to act rationally or form rational beliefs. Some rational acts and rational beliefs of this sort are guided by the unconscious knowledge; others are directed toward living up to the self-deceptive but often high-minded avowal; and still others are aimed at finding or interpreting relevant evidence: an activity that can be admirably rational even if the evidence gathered is not impartially assessed. Here the fulfillment of one standard belonging to the ethics of belief serves to undermine another. It is an irony of self-deception that it seems possible only for those capable of meeting these rational standards to some degree, yet it typically flies in the face of the set as a whole.

In some cases in which self-deception leads one to seek rationalizations, one undertakes a search for evidence quite rationally; the rationalization one produces may then be plausible or foolish, and it may support one's self-deception or, occasionally, expose it by virtue of somehow pointing to what it was meant to hide. In either case, the ethics of belief may require of one actions that would prevent one's ever becoming self-deceived or, if one is in self-deception, either dismantle the deception altogether or limit the beliefs one can acceptably form as a result of it. The application of this branch of morality is subtle and complex; there are both duties of self-observation and self-regulation and excuses for certain failures to live up to them.[20]

Self-deception and rationalization are, in an important way, manifestations of, though also typically defects in, our rational makeup. But it would be a mistake to think that when they provide reasons for action, and one acts in accordance with those reasons, one thereby acts rationally. Just as we must distinguish (in ways illustrated in chapter 9) between actions merely in conformity with duty (or virtue) and actions from duty (or virtue), it is vital to distinguish between reasons one simply has for doing something and reasons for which one does it. A rationalizing reason, and many of the reasons for acting provided by self-deception, are only of the former kind. One may act in accordance with them while acting for very poor reasons. We then have an irrational action which the agent can rationalize; at best he has irrationally done what is a rational kind of thing to do. Similar points hold for the propositional attitudes, which bear counterpart relations to self-deception and rationalization. Both self-deception and rationalization can provide one with an account of oneself that can be used in meeting criticism; but if the defensive reasons they yield are only reasons one has, then they do not support the rationality of the actions they rationalize, and they cannot absolve one of moral responsibility for them. They can veil, from others and even oneself, what one is really like; but whether one's action is rational and how, in general, one's overall rationality and morality are to be assessed depend on how one's behavior is attributable to one and not on the portrait one can paint of it.

Notes

For helpful comments on an earlier version of parts of this essay I am grateful to Mike W. Martin, Brian McLaughlin, Alfred Mele, and Allison Lea Nespor.

1. For a wide range of recent papers on self-deception, by psychologists as well as philosophers, see Mike W. Martin, ed., *Self-Deception and Self-Understanding* (Lawrence and London: University Press of Kansas, 1986), and Brian McLaughlin and Amelie O. Rorty, eds., *Perspectives on Self-Deception* (Berkeley and Los Angeles: University of California Press, 1988). My view on the topic is further developed and systematically connected with a theory of practical reasoning in "Self-Deception and Practical Reasoning," *Canadian Journal of Philosophy* 19 (1989): 246–66.

2. See, e.g., M. R. Haight, *A Study of Self-Deception* (Sussex and Atlantic Highlands: Harvester Press, 1980); some authors in Martin, *Self-Deception and Self-Understanding*, take a similar view, though most of them, philosophers and psychologists alike, think self-deception possible.

3. I have developed this account in "Self-Deception, Action, and Will," *Erkenntnis* 18 (1982): 133–58, and "Self-Deception and Rationality," in Martin, *Self-Deception and Self-Understanding*. Martin takes acts of self-deception, rather than the state, as fundamental, and develops a different view. See, e.g., his "Demystifying Doublethink: Self-Deception, Truth, and Freedom in 1984," *Social Theory and Practice* 10 (1984), in which he characterizes self-deception as "any refusal to acknowledge the truth to ourselves," where this may involve persuading ourselves into false beliefs holding inconsistent beliefs, or being willfully ignorant. For a detailed account that makes motivated false belief central in self-deception and is intended to contrast with mine on several points, see Alfred Mele, "Self-Deception," *Philosophical Quarterly* 33 (1983): 365–77. For Mele, the self-deceiver has a desire that p (which is actually false) be true; he thus manipulates apparently relevant data in a way that causes him to believe p (p. 370).

4. The 'cannot' is only empirical, and I leave open how strong it is. I have discussed unconscious belief in some detail in "Self-Deception, Action, and Will." For an account of believing which makes clear sense of this notion and indicates how our multiple criteria for it permit both discovering unconscious beliefs and conceiving them as beliefs in essentially the same sense as conscious ones, see my "The Concept of Believing," *The Personalist* 57 (1972): 43–62.

5. Her reaction to the thought of lying (or manipulating others) would depend on many factors, including her ability to rationalize it away (as we shall see later); and normally self-deception would prevent its occurring to her. Kent Bach argues that a person self-deceived with respect to *p* avoids "the sustained or recurrent thought that *p*" (e.g., that she will kill herself). "An Analysis of Self-Deception," *Philosophy and Phenomenological Research* 41 (1981), esp. pp. 362–65. It is important to recognize a tendency toward such avoidance; still, *S* may even focus on the thought in a sustained way provided he has adequate defenses.

6. For instructive discussion of difficulties with construing belief as under voluntary control see William P. Alston, "The Deontological Conception of Epistemic Justification," in his *Epistemic Justification* (Ithaca and London: Cornell University Press, 1989). For a partial reply and contrasting view see Matthias Steup, "Epistemic Obligation and the Voluntariness of Belief" (forthcoming).

7. For an indication of relevant complexities in Freud's view, as well as other discussion pertinent to this essay, see John Deigh, *The Sources of Moral Agency: Essays in Moral Psychology and Freudian Theory* (Cambridge: Cambridge University Press, 1997 esp. ch. 4.

8. This formulation is developed and defended in my "Rationalization and Rationality," *Synthese* 65 (1985): 159–84.

9. For a narrower conception of rationalization which does make motivation necessary (and may in other ways be closer to Freud's than mine), see Béla Szabados, "The Self, Its Passions and Self-Deception," in Martin, *Self-Deception and Self-Understanding*. Szabados says, e.g., that a rationalization "is a form of justification prompted by a mixture of desire and fear such that the rationalizer tries to put his action or conviction or emotion into better light" (p. 155).

10. See, e.g., Andrew Oldenquist, *Normative Behavior* (Washington, D.C.: University Press of America, 1983), esp. pp. 155–60, in which he contrasts rationalization with insincerity and requires that a rationalizer be "mistaken" (not deceitful) if we are to call the reason he offers a rationalization (p. 156).

11. In "Rationalization and Rationality," I argue that the notion of rationalization applies to propositional attitudes other than belief.

12. There is a kind of privileged access here, but the privilege is highly limited, as I have argued in *Epistemology: A Contemporary Introduction to the Theory of Knowledge* (London and New York: Routledge, 1997), ch. 3.

13. For contrasting perspectives on the rationality of both self-deception and rationalization, see Bach, "An Analysis of Self-Deception," who speaks at one point of "the irrationality of the rationalizing self-deceiver" (p. 359), and Jon Elster, *Sour Grapes: Studies in the Subversion of Rationality* (Cambridge: Cambridge University Press, 1983), esp. pp. 148–57. For related discussion, including defense of the view that self-deception is not necessarily evil or irrational, see John King-Farlow and Richard Bosley, "Self-Formation and the Mean," in Martin, *Self-Deception and Self-Understanding*. Also relevant to the relation of self-deception and rationality is Amélie Oksenberg Rorty's "Self-Deception, Akrasia, and Irrationality," *Social Science Information* 19 (1980): 905–22.

14. W. K. Clifford's view is set forth in his famous essay on the ethics of belief in his *Lectures and Essays* (1879), reprinted in Louis P. Pojman, ed., *The Theory of Knowledge* (Belmont, Calif.: Wadsworth Publishing Co., 1993).

15. Kant's view, and the options his overall position allows, on this matter are treated in detail in ch. 3 of my *Practical Reasoning* (London and New York: Routledge, 1989).

16. Here I draw on my "Self-Deception and Rationality."

17. Here I draw on my "Rationalization and Rationality."

18. Ibid.

19. Self-deception in relation to moral responsibility is discussed at length in my "Self-Deception, Action, and Will."

20. I provide a further indication of how one may tell for what reasons one believes (or does) something in my paper "The State, the Church, and the Citizen," in Paul J. Weithman, ed., *Religion and Contemporary Liberalism* (Notre Dame: University of Notre Dame Press, 1997). The question is important for distinguishing acting from civic virtue as opposed to acting merely in conformity with it.

7

Responsible Action and Virtuous Character

Much of the literature on moral responsibility is dominated by the question whether moral responsibility is compatible with determinism. Indeed, sometimes philosophers assume that actions for which we bear moral responsibility are equivalent to free actions, and they often say little about moral responsibility beyond illustrating the equivalence claim and discussing the relation between free action and determinism. There is, however, much about moral responsibility that needs clarification; and even when we understand what moral responsibility is, questions about its scope persist. My aim is to clarify both its nature and its scope. I particularly want to explore responsibility for character. In doing this I shall partially assess the Aristotelian idea that our character traits are under our voluntary control.[1]

I. The Conceptual Territory

There are various kinds of responsibility. One is *causal responsibility*. The pressure of a tree can be responsible for the crookedness of a trellis. Similarly, an agent can be responsible for a fire simply by virtue of causing it, though to be sure we do not usually attribute even causal responsibility to agents unless we think they might bear some other kind of responsibility. In sharp contrast is *role responsibility*, as illustrated by a teacher's responsibility to present course materials competently. Whereas causal responsibility for something presupposes its having occurred, role responsibility for it does not: the latter need not be fulfilled. The former is usually attributed retrospectively, the latter usually prospectively, though it makes sense to say that by being careless someone *will* be responsible for a forest fire, or that a teacher was responsible (say, under the agreed rules) for grading one hundred papers by Monday and did it.

Philosophical discussions of responsibility have focused mainly on a third kind, illustrated by the notion of an agent's moral responsibilty for giving up a military secret or — as a result of being kidnapped —*not* morally responsible for failing to

157

keep a promise. Our widest term for this might be *normative responsibility*, which is above all a kind of eligibility for normative assessment regarding an action.[2] The most common kind of assessment appropriate to normative responsibility is moral; but one can be normatively responsible in other ways, say aesthetically or prudentially. Perhaps the central idea is that responsible action, that is, action for which one is normatively responsible, is an appropriate partial basis for assessment of one's character and indeed of an agent overall, insofar as such global assessment is different from assessment of character. For instance, responsible action that fulfills a duty counts positively in the appraisal of character; responsible action that wrongs someone counts negatively; and so forth.

Normative responsibility should not be assumed to apply only to action. One may be responsible for one's students' failing to know a certain technique, and that failure is not an action. Arguably, this responsibility must be owing to, say, one's *deciding* not to teach the technique; but even if that is so, the responsibility is still truly predicable of something other than action. Is responsibility for non-actions derivative, then, from responsibility for actions? This is among the questions to be addressed shortly.

One of the most important distinctions we must observe in discussing responsibility (of any sort) is between direct and indirect kinds. Consider Jack, who is responsible for a forest fire. He threw a lighted cigarette into dry leaves and walked on. He is indirectly responsible for the fire by virtue of doing something that caused it. He is, on the other hand, directly responsible for the causative act — discarding the lighted cigarette in dry leaves, or at least for some basic act by which he did this, such as throwing his hand out and releasing his fingers (presumably knowing that the cigarette would remain lighted). Plainly, if we are responsible for anything, we are directly responsible for something. It is not reasonable to posit either an infinite regress or a circle here.[3]

Must all normative responsibility ultimately rest on responsibility for basic acts, understood roughly as those we do not perform *by* performing any other act(s)? The answer is apparently yes, at least if we are talking about responsibility for acts. Call this view, that all normative responsibility rests on responsibility for basic acts, the *traceability thesis*. To be sure, we commonly attribute responsibility for non-basic acts without either having a sense of inaccurate ascription or making any specific assumptions about the underlying basic act(s). But even here we take it that there *is* some basic act to which the responsibility can be traced. Suppose, however, that the issue is responsibility for an *omission*. Not all omissions are acts. Some, to be sure, are *abstensions*. These are acts. But others are mere *failures*, mere non-performances. These are not acts. The teacher who abstains from introducing a technique may thereby be responsible for the students' ignorance of it, whereas mere failure to introduce it need not trace to responsible conduct. I am not now taking a cruise, but I have not considered or had occasion to consider doing so, and my non-action is neither an abstension nor traceable to any responsible conduct.

What should be said, however, about a happy-go-lucky couple who unthinkingly fail to provide for their children's future? They do not squander their earnings in gambling or abstain from saving for the children or even reject a suggestion that they save. It is possible that there is simply a series of non-performances which, together with the couple's pattern of normal expenditures, accounts for the absence of savings for the children's future. Must there be actions on which one might hang their responsibility for this deficiency in savings?

Such a case presents two main options. The theoretically most appealing is to say that *by* spending money as they do, say on many non-necessities, they culpably preclude saving for the children and so irresponsibly use their resources. The other main option is to say that although they should do something to save, the lack of savings is only preventable by what they might have done and not indirectly attributable to deeds they actually have done. The former solution seems preferable. For one thing, if they really are responsible for the state of affairs in question — the absence of savings for their children — by virtue of what they can be expected to have done, surely we may describe what they in fact have done as a case of culpably, or at least responsibly, precluding or supplanting what they ought to have done. If they could have saved and did not, and if they are responsible for not saving, presumably they must have done something instead, such as lavishly entertain friends, that resulted in the absence of savings and for which they bear responsibility.

Where the agent is responsible and praiseworthy (a case in which responsibility for the action is not commonly ascribed, at least in those terms), there is less reason to doubt the traceability thesis. Perhaps this is because we tend not to attribute such positive responsibility unless it seems clear to us that the agent did something causally responsible for the good outcome in question. If Maria is responsible for the discovery of the missing manuscript, it seems clear that (ultimately) she must have found it because she decided to search for it, or, perhaps, simply began searching for it, as a basic action in response to the author's perceptible distress.

Considerations like those cited provide some reason to conclude, then, that all (normative) responsibility traces to acts and ultimately to basic acts. If one is responsible for a non-act, such as a fire or the children's lack of future resources, it is by virtue of some act or omission; and for that, in turn, there will be some basic act for which one is responsible — say a careless movement of the hand, or the purchase of an expensive car. Such responsibility seems ultimately traceable to the making of certain bodily movements or to uttering certain words or to some other basic act.

Supposing, however, that the traceability thesis is false and that there is responsibility not traceable to acts, it will be understandable *in terms of acts*. For instance, if I am (criticizably) responsible for a state of affairs' having occurred which I did not bring about by something I did, there must have been some option that I should have taken and did not.[4] The concept of responsible action, then, seems central to responsibility in general even if not all normative responsibility rests on some actual deed. Even if traceability to a basic act is not necessary to normative responsibility for some state of affairs, intelligibility in terms of such acts is necessary.

II. Responsibility for Character

With this framework in mind, we can explore the extent of our responsibility for our character. Sometimes 'character' is used broadly, to encompass personality. But my main concern is moral character, which must be distinguished from personality.[5]

Two people can be radically different in personality yet very much alike in moral character. Strong personality, moreover, is compatible with weak character, and charming personality can go hand in hand with execrable character. Moral character is largely an interconnected set of traits, such as honesty, fairness, and fidelity, which, in turn, are largely deep-seated dispositions to do certain things for an appropriate range of reasons. (I cannot now give an account of moral character, but much can still be determined about the extent of our responsibility for our character.)

A trait of character, unlike an action, is not an event; it is, like a state of being, something that both persists over time and does not entail change, at least not in the way the occurrence of events does. A trait need not be unchanging or static, however; one can, for instance, become more fair, or more judiciously fair. Because a trait is not an action, responsibility for a trait cannot be direct (assuming the traceability thesis is correct). Instead, it will be a matter of something one does which appropriately affects one's character. One might, for example, practice polite acts in an effort to become a polite person.

Three Kinds of Responsibility

It is essential to distinguish among three kinds of responsibility for traits, none of which implies the others. As applied to traits, there is *generative responsibility*, which is responsibility for having produced the trait in question (a kind of genetic responsibility); *retentional responsibility*, which is responsibility for retaining the trait; and *prospective responsibility*, which is responsibility for taking on the trait — as where one promises to develop patience — and normally also for retaining it thenceforth. There are other cases as well, for instance responsibility for altering the trait and responsibility for making it more influential in one's conduct, say by reducing the strength of competing traits. But if we can adequately understand just two major cases — generative and retentional responsibility — that will serve our purposes well. Let us consider these in that order.

It might seem that we cannot be wholly responsible for producing our traits of moral character, since one must *have* a character in order to do the things necessary to affect character. But this reasoning will not do, particularly if we distinguish character and personality. For one might have a *personality* antecedently to having a moral character, and might then, as a result of sheer personal preferences, produce a character by, say, arranging for appropriate brain manipulation to instill it in oneself. Even apart from this, one might choose a new character, whether by psychosurgery or by adopting a regimen that gradually yields the result; then one might be generatively responsible for one's present character, though not one's *initial* character. In everyday life, however, few if any agents set out to produce a wholly new moral character.

A normal goal of such moral self-reconstruction as there is, is to retain some trait, say benevolence, and seek to strengthen it and to subordinate certain new traits to it. This subordination is largely a matter of becoming such that one does not tend to act from the subordinate traits unless the actions in question are consonant with maintaining the governing trait. Such subordination would be required for successful, morally motivated moral self-reconstruction (at least first-order self-reconstruction, whose aim is to acquire or alter a trait, as opposed to becoming a different kind of person overall); it would be expected as a factor in any successful self-reconstruction. Second-order moral self-reconstruction, the kind aimed at becoming a moral person overall, is also possible. A non-moral person might simply want, for reasons of self-interest, to become a moral one (and moral agents who falsely believe they are not moral persons could also seek to become such). But this second-order reconstruction is a very different case, and since it implies no antecedent moral commitments, unqualifiedly calling it moral reconstruction would be misleading: its target is moral, but its grounds and at least its initial execution are not.

Ascriptions of generative responsibility imply that by appeal to the agent's own deeds, there is an answer to 'How did you get like that?' But this historical question is by and large of less moral importance than 'Why are you like that?' If I am responsible for becoming a certain way but can now do nothing to alter it, my retaining the trait is not a blameworthy condition, nor can I be expected to reform.[6] I am thus not eligible for the kind of assessment pertinent to moral responsibility for retaining the trait now. And if I can reform now, but became as I am unavoidably and through no deeds of my own, then I can now be eligible for assessment on the basis of retaining the trait and can be both blamed for staying in my present condition *and* expected to reform. From the point of view of ethics, then, the central question here is the extent of our retentional responsibility for our character.

Consider Jean, who is dishonest but has the decency to feel guilty about it. Some of her values go against dishonesty, and she has some desire to reform. Perhaps she became dishonest because honesty was not stressed to her as a child and in her childhood environment she found lying a defense against certain frightening prospects. It is consistent with such a story that she not bear generative responsibility for her dishonesty. This does *not* imply that she is not responsible for dishonest *acts* or that she cannot, at least gradually, change her character so as to become solidly honest. Thus, the crucial question of what one should do now and in the future can remain open even if one could not help getting to where one now morally is. Virtue is not a precondition for its own development, any more than it is necessarily self-sustaining; it can arise from the ashes of vice as well as from sound moral education.

It is an interesting question whether responsibility for an act that expresses a trait of character depends on one's ability to change that trait: certainly if Jean can become honest, then, other things being equal, she is responsible for dishonest acts. But could she be incapable of becoming an honest person, yet still be responsible for an individual act of dishonesty? I think so. For even when an action manifests an inextirpable trait, it need not be such that one could not have done otherwise, nor need it be in any lesser way compelled. We can expect people to do better on individual occasions even if we cannot expect them to change their initial dispositions. The ineradicability of a trait does not imply the inevitability of actions that manifest it. A major point that emerges here, then, is this: even if responsibility for traits of character always traces to acts for which one bears responsibility, the converse does not hold. Responsibility for an act — even one that expresses a vicious trait — need not trace to or imply responsibility (of any relevant kind) for that trait. The agent need not be generatively or retentionally responsible for the trait and may be quite unable to uproot it.[7] Similar points hold for emotions in relation to action. Acts done from passion, for instance, need not be excusable even if the causative emotion is both strong and unavoidable.

In pursuing the extent of our responsibility for our moral character, it is useful to think of the relevant traits as constituted by fairly stable and normally long-standing wants and beliefs — or at least by beliefs, provided they carry sufficient motivation.[8] Consider fairness. If it is a trait, it must have a measure of stability. If Jean's fairness can be slept off, or she can be dissuaded from it by a mere suggestion, then it is at best a disposition of hers, not part of her character.[9] Moreover, normally a trait must be long-standing. One can imagine a massive (e.g. surgical) change making someone immediately fair, in the deep-seated way characteristic of a person with the *trait* of fairness, but then being reversed shortly afterward by similar changes in the opposite direction. But if this is the only kind of trait one has, it is unclear that one has a character at all. Regarding the makeup of fairness, it requires appropriate wants, such as to treat people equally, and certain beliefs, say the belief that providing the same opportunities and rewards for people in the same circumstances is morally required. The more self-consciously fair an agent is, the greater the moral content of the appropriate wants and beliefs, or at least the greater the tendency for the agent to entertain the relevant content; but even being spontaneously fair is more than a matter of simply doing the relevant kinds of deeds. They must be appropriately aimed, in terms of what the agent wants and believes, or they are not moral but merely consistent with morality. If I give my seminar students the same grade only because I like them equally well, then even if they all deserve that grade I am not exhibiting fairness in my grading; the fairness of my results is quite coincidental.

Cognitive and Motivational Dimensions of Responsibility

Once we conceive traits as cognitively and motivationally constituted, we can explore responsibility for them through our knowledge of our responsibility for our wants and beliefs. Again, we should consider generative and retentional responsibility separately.

Normal agents are not directly responsible for producing either their beliefs or their wants. We can produce them *by* doing certain things, but normally we cannot produce them except through indirect and often tedious means. This does not imply, however, that we are not indirectly responsible, generatively, for having produced certain of our traits. A selfish person may, as a result of the selfishness, become unfair through strategies that are undertaken with clear awareness that they cheat others. This pattern might imply responsibility for becoming unfair and even retentional responsibility for remaining unfair. Moreover, such a person who wants to reform sometimes can, through repeated self-discipline, become unselfish and fair. In this way, one could fulfill a prospective responsibility and become, to a large extent, morally self-made.

In categorizing the techniques by which one can produce a trait, it is useful to note the dynamics of a related, trait-like phenomenon: self-deception.[10] One way I may get into self-deception, say about the seriousness of my cancer, is to seek appropriate *social support*, for instance to associate with people who express the desired view (say, that recovery is in the offing). I can put out of mind evidence against that view; this is *evidential denial.* I might dwell on any evidence I can find for the view —*evidential magnification.* I can do things that support the view, for instance play sports whose practice suggests one is in good health; call this *consonant behavior.* And I can reward and punish myself at strategic times, say when I do something, such as play good tennis, consonant with the view, or succumb to the temptation to do something that tends to undermine it, say acting sickly; this is a strategy of *selective reinforcement.*

Similar points hold for altering one's moral character (though there are also important differences). Suppose Jean wants to reform by developing fairness. She can associate with people who behave fairly and support fair conduct; here again is a strategy of seeking *social support.* She can put out of mind considerations that lead to cheating people; call this *banishing temptation.* She can dwell on the extrinsic rewards of acting fairly — a kind of *instrumental goading* — or simply focus on any intrinsically pleasant or attractive features she can think of that belong to so acting — a kind of *self-encouragement by association.* She can make it a point to rehearse reasons for being fair —*magnification of incentive* — and to behave fairly where it will bring appreciation —*practicing in the limelight.* And she can reward herself with desired purchases upon finding that she has been fair despite temptation, while denying herself pleasures if she slides into the old ways; here again is *selective reinforcement.*

The same kinds of techniques that can induce a trait can generally be used to uproot it, especially where doing so is in part a matter of developing a competing trait, say fairness in place of injustice. Many of these techniques involve sheer self-discipline, for example reminding oneself what is right and exercising will power to do it. Certainly, enough is known about how one can improve one's character to make it reasonable for us to expect people to engage in a certain amount of moral self-monitoring and, when they find themselves deficient, to take appropriate action (chapter 6 applies similar points to the less global phenomena of self-deception and rationalization). If Jean is a psychologically normal person with no special excuse for being dishonest, she should disapprove of her own dishonest behavior and take appropriate action to change both that behavior and the immoral trait underlying it.

Notice that the responsibility in question is largely fulfilled when Jean becomes a person who, in virtue of sufficiently deep wants and beliefs with the right content, can be counted on in respect of honesty. She need not become a person who is never or scarcely ever tempted to lie or deceive. Moreover, the distinction between obligation and supererogation applies to traits, as it does to actions (or at least to appropriate actions affecting traits, such as maintaining a trait by self-discipline). We are responsible for being honest, where this implies meeting a certain standard of conduct for the right reasons. To rise above that standard, say by maintaining a highly scrupulous honesty, is to go beyond fulfilling our responsibility. The applicability of supererogation to traits confirms the point that responsibility for them is traceable to responsibility for the (responsible) actions of ours that produced them, sustain them, or might alter them.

While my focus has been on responsibility for traits of character, I have not meant to imply that one cannot be responsible for other traits. Much depends on the extent of our (indirect) control of our constitution. We can construe aspects of personality involving prudence as somewhat parallel to the moral aspects. Suppose that Gary has an unpleasant but not morally criticizable personality trait, say loquacity: he can be responsible for the trait, especially retentionally. But imagine that he has become anxious through growing up in a war zone and under abusive parents. In practice, it might not be possible to alter his anxiety, and in that case he is not appropriately criticized for retaining it. It should be emphasized again, however, that even an inextirpable trait is not an excuse for doing any given thing among those it might incline one to do. For incurable anxiety, Gary may not be responsible; but this would not excuse his making others miserable to console himself.

III. *Responsibility and Control*

Our discussion has presupposed that one is not (normatively) responsible for something over which one has no control. Whereof one has no control, thereof one is not responsible — at least not directly. If at present I have no control over the extent of my honesty, then I am not (retentionally) responsible for the degree to which I possess that trait; nor can I be prospectively responsible for acquiring a trait if I do not have (at least indirect) control of variables that might instill it. On the other hand, if I did something over which I had control, in order to prevent my now having control over the degree of my honesty, then I may be indirectly responsible for the extent to which I now have the trait. In fact, I do have a measure of control over the traits constituting my moral character: even if I have not contributed much to creating this character, I can affect it, and I may be expected to monitor it in ways that will lead to my trying to reform it if the need becomes evident or to buttress it under conditions of impending erosion. The control I have over my traits derives from my control over my actions, which in turn affect my acquisition or retention of traits. This raises the question whether, in order to control, or be able to control, my actions, I must control, or be able to control, the variables underlying those actions, notably my wants and beliefs.[11]

The answer is surely that I can have or even exercise control over my actions even if I do not have or exercise control over their underlying wants and beliefs. Indeed, if I had to satisfy this condition, would it not be through other actions? And then I would need to have or exercise control over the variables underlying *them*, which would be further wants and beliefs. We would have a vicious regress or a vicious circle.

Why, however, should we want in general to control our wants and beliefs? Our wants are often natural and such that we approve of them and enjoy fulfilling them;[12] and our beliefs, we suppose, generally reflect reality and often show us how to satisfy our wants. We should certainly not seek unrestricted control of our beliefs; if we had it, it would undermine the presumption that they are under the control of the facts external to them which we like to think they capture.[13] So even if we do not control the cognitive-motivational basis of every action, we need not feel that *alien* forces produce our conduct. Moreover, we have a reflective capacity whereby we can single out any particular want or belief for scrutiny and potential elimination so long as we have some want and belief as a basis for the reflective process. This applies even to our foundational wants and beliefs, those not based on others, such as wants to be liked by peers and beliefs grounded in memory. I think, then, that no paradox underlies the notion of control with which I have been working in setting out an account of our responsibility for our traits. Our normal wants and beliefs are not alien determinants of action which we must control in order to control it; they are that by virtue of which our actions express our reasons and, in some sense, our nature. Hence, they are essential to our control of the actions they underlie.

It must be granted, however, that we should want to have control of our desires at least to this extent: we should, as rational beings, want our desires to conform with our values in roughly the following sense. We should want that if we rationally believe that a state of affairs is on balance desirable, this will tend to bring about, or enable us to bring about, our wanting on balance to realize it, that is, wanting to realize it more than to realize anything we believe incompatible with our doing so. After all, it is rational to want that, within certain limits, our faculty of reason, of which valuational beliefs should presumably be a manifestation, control our desires and thereby our conduct. This is largely what our control comes to, and the idea indeed expresses one concept of *autonomy*.[14] Reason indicates what is good for one and how to get it; desire conforms by motivating the appropriate action.

If we pursue this picture of autonomy in relation to responsibility, it takes us in an unexpected direction. The picture makes it natural to hold motivational internalism: roughly, the view that beliefs — and, especially, judgings — to the effect that one ought on balance to A imply motivation to A. After all, how can reason exercise control over conduct without having its own motivating power? The question for us, then, is whether responsibility requires internalism. In particular, does my having control over an action, in the sense required by (normative) responsibility, depend on certain of my beliefs or judgments about the action themselves implying motivation to act accordingly? Suppose I judge that I must become more fair. If this judgment does not produce any motivation to change my character, then unless I am fortunate enough to have the appropriate motivation from another source, how can I have any control over the trait, or be responsible for remaining unfair? On the face of it, responsibility implies motivational internalism.

This reasoning is plausible but not conclusive. Notice that even if the relevant practical judgments — those to the effect that on balance one should A— do not imply motivation, there is no reason to think that their purely cognitive status would interfere with the existence of such motivation. That motivation might come from an independent source such as a general desire to do what on balance one ought to do, or from desire for the sort of thing to be obtained by the action — whether it is moral, say achieving justice, or not, say restoration of health. Responsibility requires that one *can* do the crucial thing, for example act to change one's character; it does not require that one must do it, or must be motivated to.

Granted, in a *fully* rational person the implication in question presumably holds, since in fully rational people there is a good integration between cognition and motivation. But we need an account of responsibility for persons in general, who are seldom if ever fully rational. The only internalism implied by responsibility, then, is at most a weak form asserting that (1) practical judgments (and perhaps certain beliefs with similar content) tend to produce motivation to act accordingly — call this *inclinational internalism* — and (2) by virtue of the principle that *ought* implies *can* their truth entails a capacity to act accordingly and so implies the possibility of any motivation such action requires — call this *capacity internalism*.[15]

If an account of responsibility leads us to see how natural a view motivational internalism is, we must also remember that motivational internalism — in a form strong enough to guarantee that agents *will* act on their practical judgments if they can — has its own liabilities. One is the difficulty of accounting for weakness of will, construed as implying (uncompelled) action one takes to be against one's better judgment. Another is the problem — at least for cognitivism about normative judgments — of accounting for how a cognitive faculty is intrinsically motivational. As already stressed, however, it may well be that in a fully rational person, a strong motivational internalism holds; and certainly most of us have desires that concern our own good and can supply the motivation needed to move us to act on most of our practical judgments. For most of these judgments are such that we see acting on them as conducing in some way to our good, broadly conceived, and so, often, as involving realization of moral ideals.[16]

The control required by responsibility, even prospective responsibility, does not, then, entail motivational internalism. Having such control does require that certain options be open. It is natural to want to guarantee that we will take them if we judge we should, so that responsibility depends only on reason, but it is more realistic to suppose that responsibility depends in part on our motivational makeup. If we *could* not have the wants needed to produce responsible action, for instance because having them is causally or psychologically impossible, we would not be responsible agents. But there is surely no reason for any such pessimism, and rejecting motivational internalism would do nothing to support it.

IV. The Internality of Responsibility

Motivational internalism is not the only kind. There is also what I shall call *normative internalism*, of which internalism in epistemology is a special case. For normative internalism, normative judgments of a person, such as an attribution of justified belief or of responsibility for an action, are true (or false) largely in virtue of the presence (or the absence) of certain facts, states, or events whose obtaining or occurring is either *accessible* to that person by reflection, including introspective reflection, or *producible* by the person at will.[17] Epistemic internalism as applied to justification is quite plausible. What justifies my belief that there is paper before me, for instance, is largely my visual experience of white, which is accessible to me in the strong sense that it is actually present in my awareness.[18] Similarly, what makes me responsible for having started a fire is, ultimately, something like this: my deciding not to put out the coals of my campfire (an internally accessible act) or at least my having been able (1) to abstain, at will, from the crucial careless deed, and (2) to realize, by reflection on what I already know, that if I did not abstain I might start such a fire (this would imply producibility at will of a suitable alternative to the perhaps unintentional causative act). The ultimate *bearer* of responsibility here is some act, whether internal or not; the ultimate *grounds* of responsibility are internal. In this section I want to explore the possibility that responsibility for both actions and traits is internal in this sense.

Normative Internalism about Responsibility

To begin with, let us continue to assume that the fundamental bearers of (normative) responsibility are acts, in the sense that it traces to them. On the assumption that this traceability thesis is true, normative internalism as applied to action would be roughly the view that one is eligible for the relevant assessment, say as responsible for remaining dishonest, in virtue of types of acts that are (or were) internally available to one (roughly, producible at will) and such that by reflection, say reflection on one's moral obligations, one can (or could) see that one should perform them. There are thus three main cases in relation to responsibility for traits: those of genetic, retentional, and prospective responsibility. On the internalist view in question, genetic responsiblity for, say, being aggressive might trace to, and rest on, a decision to undergo assertiveness training and to various deliberative acts of reinforcing the decision. Responsibility for retaining it might also trace to, and rest on, similar reinforcing acts, together with such things as an awareness of resentment and hurt feelings in others and, in the teeth of that awareness, abstention from efforts to change. Prospective responsibility is different in that there need be no antecedent act to which it traces — except insofar as all our moral responsibilities are *behaviorally incurred*, for example by promises or other actions of ours that morally bind us to others.[19] Here the internalist view would be something like this: because of my awareness of others' responses to me, or at least because I can by reflection become aware of those responses, I should (given my obligations, which are also accessible to my reflection) seek to reform.

Perhaps the clearest form of the internalist position on responsibility would embody both a volitionalist view on which our basic acts are willings or tryings, and a Kantian moral view on which reflection can tell us our general obligations.[20] Ultimately, it is by *trying* to change my character — or by trying to do something constituting a special case of this — that I do so; and if I do try, say by undertaking to improve my relations with others, yet circumstances prevent me from succeeding, I am still behaving properly and am fulfilling my responsibility to change myself as well as I can.

The central point here is that we assess people by their most fundamental deeds, not — except contingently — by those which, like delivering a book across the country, they do only through the cooperation of circumstances that they cannot, by their fundamental deeds, control. One reason for the plausibility of this idea is that what we do basically, and especially internally, we tend to see most clearly. A related point is that we tend to have better control over such deeds than over what we can accomplish only with the help of external circumstances. A third is that these deeds best indicate the deepest projects we harbor or pursue. We are judged not by how well nature cooperates with our projects but by our volitional nature.

It is important to see that while volitionalism perhaps enables us to give the clearest expression of normative internalism about responsibility, it is not the only theory of the foundations of action available to internalism. One might deny that all basic action is volitional or even internal, while still holding that agents are responsible only when, *in* their purview, and so accessible to them, are considerations in the light of which they act, can act, or could have acted, in a relevant way. Thus, Jack might be responsible for the physical act of flipping his hand, but only because he could have reflected on what he was doing and thereby at least tried to do otherwise, say by stepping on the discarded cigarette, and so prevent fire. He is responsible *because* of what is internally accessible and producible; but the responsibility need not trace, causally, *to* an internal act. On the other hand, we need not deny that there are tryings or that they can be bearers of responsibility; if, for example, his brain had been so wired that when he tried to put out the cigarette he still threw it away lighted, we might then say that he nevertheless behaved responsibly by virtue of trying to do otherwise.

Responsibility depends on what is internally accessible to us and on what we can do internally; but it need not require that we actually do something internal which serves as its ultimate bearer. My responsibility can depend on what act-types are internally accessible to me — roughly on those I am aware of as (directly) producible options or those which by reflection I could become aware of and at least try to perform — without tracing to what, if anything, I actually do internally. The culpable basic action need not be an act of will, even if my responsibility for it depends on my internal access to a countervailing act of will. Neither internalism nor the traceability thesis entails volitionalism.

The internalist account of responsibility may sound plausible enough to leave one wondering what would count as an externalist view of normative responsibility. That there should be a contrasting view might be expected from the Kantian character of the internalist view suggested, at least if the difference between the Kantian and consequentialist perspectives is as pervasive as I think it is. To see how the contrast applies to responsibility, suppose that, as a hedonistic utilitarian might hold, agents are — normatively as opposed to causally — responsible for an action provided that so construing the action is, say, optimific. One cannot tell whether an action has this property by reflection (since inductive grounds are needed to determine the hedonic consequences of an action), whereas, on the internalist view, one can tell by reflection (at least given certain factual assumptions) whether an action is one's obligation. Thus, whether I am responsible for changing my character depends on whether people's taking me to be responsible for it, and perhaps acting accordingly, has the appropriate consequences. Now I might have no way of grasping, by reflection, that my character needs changing; thus, by internalist lights, I might not be responsible for retaining it. But if my changing would have better consequences, externalists might, by their principles, properly regard me as responsible and goad me accordingly. And suppose that by accident I do make an optimific change. It might then be appropriate to consider me responsible and praise me, since one might want to reinforce the behavior that produced the change.

This externalist view seems unsound. It is too weak, since I might only think I freely and responsibly A-ed, when I was in fact compelled to A. Taking me to be responsible and praising me might still have optimific consequences, but surely I would not have been responsible. This view apparently confuses being praiseworthy with being, by the relevant consequentialist standard, worth praising (a distinction developed in chapter 1). The view is also too strong. If I am an unregenerate malefactor, it might be fruitless to consider me responsible; yet I surely might be responsible, having intentionally and freely done evil. Responsibility is more a matter of what I deserve in virtue of my acts than of what I might produce by being considered responsible.[21]

This issue over whether responsibility is ultimately an internal or external notion cannot be settled here. I simply want to bring it to the fore. Some of the materials for resolving it are developed earlier, but others require ethical and metaphysical arguments not appropriate to this chapter. That responsibility ultimately traces to acts, and that we are nonetheless (indirectly) responsible for aspects of our moral character, are points which can stand on either an internalist or an externalist view.

Normative Responsibility, Determinism, and Causation

If action is central to responsibility in the way I have indicated, there is one further question we must ask. Is (normative) responsibility ultimately an incompatibilist notion, that is, does its existence presuppose that determinism is false? I cannot see that it does and have elsewhere offered a compatibilist account of freedom and responsibility and of the possibility of alternative action — an account meant to be free of the difficulties besetting conditional accounts of 'could have done otherwise'.[22]

It is true, however, that incompatibilism is natural from the deliberative perspective, that in which we are considering what to do.[23] To decide meaningfully what to do, we must see ourselves as having options, in the sense of alternatives each of which, in some appropriate sense, we *can* perform. Similarly, to consider ourselves responsible we must take it that we had or have options. This allows us to think of ourselves as causes of our action but sits ill with thinking of those actions as caused by anything else. The reason for the latter point may be twofold. First, we may not realize that *we* cause our actions by virtue of their being produced in a suitable way by certain elements in us with which we do or can identify; and second, we tend to think of what is caused as *necessitated*, when actually it is necessary only relative to its cause: generalizations are the bearers of causal necessity, not singular events.[24] Still, this is only a tendency; we sometimes think of others as causing us to take action, as where they ask a favor we cheerfully do, and do not see ourselves as necessitated or unfree in choosing our response.

Whatever we conclude about compatibilism, we may say that (normative) responsibility for an actual deed or other event entails whatever causal connection with it is implied by an explainability relation. For surely if an act is in no way explainable owing to how it is rooted in my character, or due to elements in me, or if an event is in no way explainable in terms of my doings, I am not responsible for it. I am not responsible for others' (past) actions unless I had an appropriate role in producing (or at least enabling) them, nor even for my non-intentional actions if they are not, say, negligent and hence in some way reflective of my character. Even if I merely should have abstained from a deed, or prevented an action, there must be some act of mine because of which (at least in part) the deed or action occurred. This suggests that whether determinism is true or not, a measure of causal power must issue from something in the agent — presumably from wants and beliefs or something essentially connected with them — as a condition of responsibility. An action or event that is accidental so far as my wants and beliefs are concerned may be rationalizable by me so long as I had appropriate reasons for it, though I did not act *from* those reasons; and I may even take responsibility for it, say in claiming credit or agreeing to make amends. But if it does not trace to me by an appropriate causal line, I am not responsible for it.

Conclusion

We have explored the nature and scope of moral responsibility. It may be direct or indirect, applicable to events or states of being or character, and generative, retentional, or prospective. But responsibility for actual deeds seems always to trace to at least one act, and it presupposes the agent's having a certain kind of control over the relevant behavior. By virtue of our capacity to affect our traits, our responsibility extends to our character. Such responsibility may be generative or, more often, retentional. It is sometimes fulfilled in part through the influence which our practical judgments or normative beliefs exercise upon our actions, but responsibility for character does not presuppose any strong version of motivational internalism. The basis of responsibility seems to be internal, though that basis need not always lie in inner acts, such as volitions; but even if the basis of responsibility is not internal, its scope extends to the future and reaches beyond the category of action. Agency, and thereby moral responsibility, indirectly extends to how we are constituted and not just to what we do.

Notes

This essay has benefited from discussion at the University of North Carolina — Greensboro symposium at which it was given in 1990, and particularly from remarks by my commentator, Gerald Dworkin, and by Jeffrey Poland, Ferdinand Schoeman, Robert Schopp, and Michael Zimmerman.

    1. See, e.g., *Nicomachean Ethics*, bk. 1, in which Aristotle says that moral virtue is formed by habit (1103a) and that we are praised and blamed for virtues and vices (1106a). Cf. his remarks, in bk. 3, that our character is determined by our choosing good or evil (1112a) and that the virtues "are in our power and voluntary" (1114b).
    2. This is at least roughly equivalent to what Michael Zimmerman calls appraisability. See *An Essay on Moral Responsibility* (Totowa, N.J.: Rowman and Littlefield, 1988), esp. ch. 1.
    3. On some views basic action is equivalent to volition. I leave that possibility open; the point here is that there apparently must be a behavioral locus of responsibility for action. The kind of behavior in question is a largely independent matter.
    4. This needs qualification to take account of the kinds of cases Harry Frankfurt has introduced in which, though I act (or do not act) without interference, were things to be different so that I *would* do otherwise, a demon would then compel the very action (or non-action) in question. Can we say that I should have picked up a lighted match, even where, had I so much as gone into a motivational state inclining me to do so, a demon would have

compelled my abstention? Need we not say that I "could not have done otherwise" than leave the match where it lay? It is not clear to me that the sense of 'could not have done otherwise' here is the one crucial for moral responsibility (as perhaps Frankfurt might grant). I have explicated that sense, and briefly discussed cases of this sort, in "Moral Responsibility, Freedom, and Compulsion," *American Philosophical Quarterly* 11 (1974): 1–14. We might, of course, say that what Frankfurt's cases show is that there is a sense of 'could' in which 'ought' does not imply 'could' (or 'can').

5. For valuable discussions of personality and character see William P. Alston, "Toward a Logical Geography of Personality," in Howard Kiefer and Milton Munitz, eds., *Mind, Science, and History* (Albany: State University of New York Press, 1970); Richard B. Brandt, "Traits of Character: A Conceptual Analysis," *American Philosophical Quarterly* 7 (1970); and Laurence Thomas, *Living Morally: A Psychology of Moral Character* (Philadelphia: Temple University Press, 1989).

6. The qualifications expressed in note 4 are also needed here.

7. To be sure, it is always logically possible for an agent to change a trait (unless it is essential to the agent's identity); for it is possible that some machine are devised such that the agent's pressing a certain button, even unintentionally, produces the change in question. But the text concerns people's actual capacities.

8. Two points are in order here. First, this formulation is intentionally vague, but it should serve our purposes adequately. Second, I do not think beliefs can carry all the motivation required; but for this chapter, as opposed to a full-scale analysis of traits, what is essential to the point is only that traits require both a cognitive and a motivational dimension. It is at least more perspicuous to separate these as I do in the text.

9. That a trait must be stable is plausible independently of the idea that traits are constituted by fairly stable wants and beliefs. Indeed, if one's wants or beliefs changed often but within a suitably restricted range, a changing set of them might still constitute a trait. Moreover, in distinguishing traits from mere dispositions of a person I am not implying that the former are not dispositional, as opposed to occurrent, properties.

10. Some of these are discussed in essays (by me among others) in Mike W. Martin, ed., *Self-Deception and Self-Understanding* (Lawrence and London: University Press of Kansas, 1985), and Brian McLaughlin and Amélie O. Rorty, eds., *Perspectives on Self-Deception* (Berkeley and Los Angeles: University of California Press, 1988).

11. That wants and beliefs do underlie actions was apparently held by Aristotle and probably Plato, among many later great philosophers, and is at this point scarcely controversial. I have given an account of how they do, with a partial explication of the relevant notion of our control of our actions, in "Acting for Reasons," *Philosophical Review* 95 (1986): 75–105.

12. Approval of, and other propositional attitudes toward, our wants, especially those we act on, are important for understanding both our freedom and our autonomy. For detailed discussion of the relation between second-order attitudes, including wants, and, on the other hand, freedom and autonomy, see Gerald Dworkin, "Acting Freely," *Nous* 4 (1970) and *The Theory and Practice of Autonomy* (Cambridge and New York: Cambridge University Press, 1988), esp. pt. 1.

13. This is in part why skepticism is not plausible: intuitively, that our beliefs tend to reflect reality correctly is a better explanation of our having the ones we do have — given that they are not produced by our will — than any skeptical explanation.

14. In ch. 9 this conception is developed and compared with an instrumentalist conception of autonomy.

15. For something like this weak version see Christine M. Korsgaard, "Skepticism about Practical Reason," *Journal of Philosophy* 83 (1986): 5–25. It should be added that the principle that *ought* implies *can* is problematic and is plausible only in carefully qualified forms.

16. Motivational internalism is discussed in detail in ch. 10, and ch. 9 reinforces the points made here about its connection with autonomy.

17. Four comments are in order here. First, this is not an analysis of responsibility and leaves much unspecified, for example just what aspects of the facts, states, or events is relevant, and how. Second, as before I leave open whether volition is required to account for the relevant notion. Third, while it is odd to speak of facts as producible where this does not mean just 'citable', the point is simply that one can bring about, at will, states of affairs, such as the extinguishing of a cigarette, in virtue of which the corresponding fact holds, for example that the cigarette is out. Fourth, if judgments of excusability are (plausibly) taken to be normative, then some normative judgments seem exceptions to internalism. Consider a judgment that I am excusable for not A-ing. This could be true because, owing to a manipulation of my brain that I had no inkling of (and internal access to), I was made to forget to A.

18. For discussion of internalism in epistemology and references to relevant literature see Paul K. Moser, *Knowledge and Evidence* (Cambridge and New York: Cambridge University Press, 1989), and my "Causalist Internalism," *American Philosophical Quarterly* 26 (1989): 309–20.

19. Suppose, however, I simply see someone fall and get hurt, where it is obvious that I am the only one who can help. I here acquire responsibility simply through what I become aware of. The behavioral incursion view would require arguing that the general obligation of beneficence which underlies my special obligation here is acquired by acts of mine. This view is consistent with both internalism and the traceability thesis but cannot be assessed here.

20. For accounts of trying and volition see Hugh J. McCann, "Volition and Basic Action," *Philosophical Review* 83 (1974), Raimo Tuomela, *Human Action and Its Explanation* (Dordrecht and Boston: D. Reidel, 1975), Brian O'Shaughnessy, *The Will* (Cambridge: Cambridge University Press, 1980), and David Armstrong, *The Nature of Mind* (Ithaca and London: Cornell University Press, 1984).

21. Michael Zimmerman has pointed out (in correspondence) that there is no incompatibility between an internalist theory of responsibility and an externalist theory of obligation. True; but at least on the assumption that the consequences to be sought by moral agents are not in general intrinsic to the actions at which they should aim, as on a hedonistic view the crucial consequences are often not, then actions' having the normative status of responsibility will not in general be a matter of internally accessible factors — or at least our attributions of responsibility will be justifiable only on the basis of their total consequences. If the truth conditions of these attributions of responsibility are explicated along internalist lines, that would yield a theory with what seems an objectionable disparity between the (internal) truth conditions and the (external) justification conditions for one of its key notions.

22. See my "Moral Responsibility, Freedom, and Compulsion," *American Philosophical Quarterly* 11 (1974). The difficulties I refer to concern accounts of 'could have done otherwise' that take it to be equivalent to propositions of the form of 'if S had . . . then S would have ___'. Peter van Inwagen skillfully brings out difficulties for such accounts in *An Essay on Free Will* (Oxford: Oxford University Press, 1983).

23. Tomis Kapitan, in a number of papers, has given detailed expression to a view rather like this; he holds that deliberating agents view prospective actions they are considering as contingent relative to the world as they see it, but they need not take what they will do as undetermined relative to the entire past. See, for example, "Doxastic Freedom: A Compatibilist Alternative," *American Philosophical Quarterly* 26 (1989).

24. Suppose it is causally necessary that all Fs are Gs. Even if it is true that a is F, it does not follow that it is *necessary* that a is G; that would follow if it were causally necessary that a is F, but there is no reason to think, nor does determinism entail, that the occurrence of any singular event is causally necessary. Incompatibilists who, like Carl Ginet, seem well aware of

this nevertheless speak of events, under determinism, as *"nomically necessitated* by the antecedent state of the world and the laws of nature." Ch. 6 of his *On Action* (Cambridge: Cambridge University Press, 1990). Cf. William L. Rowe's reference to causally necessitated action, in "Causing and Being Responsible for What Is Inevitable," *American Philosophical Quarterly* 26 (1989). Compatibilists, too, sometimes speak as if what is nomically (causally) determined is necessary. Daniel Dennett, for example, says at one point: "Suppose . . . he could *not* have done otherwise. That is, given Jones' microstate at *t* and the complete microstate of Jones' environment . . . no other Jones trajectory was possible. . . . If Jones were put back into exactly that state again, in exactly that circumstance, he would pull the trigger again." *Elbow Room* (Cambridge: MIT Press, 1985), p. 137. A compatibilist should be unwilling to accept the equivalence claim; as the second sentence implies, Jones *would* pull the trigger again, but this act is not categorically necessary and, even if determined, need not be considered such that he "could not do otherwise."

8

Acting from Virtue

Virtue ethics should tell us not only what virtue is but also what constitutes acting from it. Merely to do the right thing, say from self-interest, is not to live up to a standard of virtue. But despite the extensive recent discussion of virtue ethics, the notion of acting from virtue still needs clarification. The problem is especially challenging because it straddles ethics and action theory. It cannot be solved without an adequate understanding of virtue, but the relation of actions from virtue to the virtues they express is — I shall argue — mainly a question of how such actions are to be explained. Aristotle is highly instructive on this problem and is my point of departure. It is also rewarding to consider Kant's conception of acting from duty, construed as a case of acting from moral virtue, for instance from rectitude, and viewed as a foil for Aristotle's notion of such action. Even if Kantian action from duty ought not to be so viewed, Kantian ethics, like any rule ethics, needs an account of something closely analogous to acting from virtue: acting from whatever rule-guided elements of character render the actions that express them morally praiseworthy. My first task will be to sketch — of necessity without doing detailed textual analysis — Aristotelian and Kantian conceptions of acting from virtue. I shall then construct a general account of acting from virtue. The final section will show how the account helps in answering an important question of general ethics: whether regularly acting from virtue — and thereby achieving the chief normative goal of virtue ethics — is sufficient for a morally good life.

I. Aristotelian and Kantian Conceptions of Action from Virtue

Aristotle distinguishes between acting from virtue and acting merely in accordance with it.[1] This wording, though true to Aristotle, recalls Kant's distinction between acting from duty and merely acting in conformity with it.[2] On the plausible assumption that acting from duty is, often, acting from moral virtue, Kantian actions from duty are often similar in important ways to Aristotelian actions from virtue. Aristotle's concern with virtue and with acting from it went far beyond the moral domain, but there is much to be learned about morality from studying his general conception of acting from virtue.

By way of preliminary explication, note that although for many virtues, such as fidelity, generosity, and kindness, we speak simply of acting "from" the trait, for others the notion is usually expressed less directly, for instance by locutions like 'acting from a sense of justice' and 'paying the debt out of an honorable nature'. Our task has two main parts: to capture the explanatory force of 'acting from', where the source of the action is virtue, and to clarify how such action is from *virtue*, especially with respect to the normative and character elements this entails. The first task is complicated because, as a disposition, a virtue does not produce action in the "direct" way typical of, say, decisions or volitions, but only through cognitive and motivational processes connected with the virtue. The second task is complicated because of how many kinds of normative and dynamic elements can figure in connecting the trait with the action. Both tasks are complicated because some virtue names, for instance 'beneficence' and 'fidelity', also name passing desires with the appropriate content. Aristotle was aware of this range of problems, but he left much to be worked out.

In explaining how virtue differs from craft, Aristotle notes that while the products of craft determine by themselves whether they are well produced, this does not apply to the products of virtue, since "for actions expressing virtue to be done justly or temperately [and hence well] it does not suffice that they are in themselves in the right state. Rather, the agent must also be in the right state when he does them. First, he must know [that he is doing virtuous actions]; second, he must decide on them, and decide on them for themselves; and, third, he must do them from a firm and unchanging character" (1105a29ff). Consider this from the point of view of justice, which is adequately representative of a moral virtue (at least in the current sense of 'justice', which, though narrower than Aristotle's, will serve adequately). Aristotle's first point is negative. Whereas a statue, for instance, can be beautiful when it is in the aesthetically right state, regardless of how the sculptor produced it, it would be a mistake to say that regardless of how an action is produced, that action can be performed from justice. It is not sufficient that an action simply be of the right *type*, for example a meting out of equal shares to equally deserving claimants. In short, action from virtue is not a behavioral concept, in the sense of one defined in terms of *what* is accomplished, as opposed to *how*. One way to see this is to note that the adverbial forms of virtue terms — such as 'courageously', 'honestly', and 'justly'— can apply to actions not performed from the relevant virtues and even to actions aimed at pretending to manifest those virtues. Given this thin use of virtue terms, the distinction between action merely in conformity with virtue and action from it may be regarded as a special case of a distinction between conduct of a behaviorally specified type, say meting out equal shares, and conduct described mainly in terms of how it is to be explained, say as done from a sense of justice.

Three further points in the passage help to explain its central contrast. Suppose I am the agent. First, I must know that I am, say, meting out equal shares; it will not do if, in signing an order by which I do this, I mistakenly take it to be a check. Call this the *recognition requirement*. Second, I must decide on this equal distribution and decide on it for its own sake. This implies two conditions: that my action must be (1) decided upon — call this the *selection requirement* — and (2) in a special way motivated by the relevant virtue — call this the *intrinsic motivation requirement*. Not just any intrinsic motivation will do, however; it would not suffice to make the distribution for its own sake in the *way* I do things for their own sake when I do them simply for pleasure, as where I swim simply because I like doing it. Aristotle seems to require that I decide on the action on the basis of a conception of it as, say, just, or as rendering each a deserved share, or as something else that connects my deed with justice as an element in my character. This intrinsic motivation requirement is confirmed (though not entailed) by his third condition: that one must act from a firm and unchanging character. If Jack is usually motivated by greed but, after a moving moral exhortation from a colleague, passes into a temporary just disposition, then even if Jack's resulting just behavior toward a hated rival meets the other conditions, it does not express the *virtue* of justice. Call this the *character requirement*: virtues are elements of character; those elements are "firm and unchanging"; hence, an action from virtue must be from an element with the appropriate entrenchment and stability.

Some of the deontological counterparts of these requirements seem implicit in Kant's conception of acting from duty.[3] Acting from duty, for him, seems necessary for acting from *moral* virtue. If we may conceive good will as roughly the master virtue, this point is easily explained, at least insofar as acting from duty is a case of acting from good will. A stronger requirement for Kantian action from duty is suggested by Kant's second principle of morality: "An action performed from duty does not have its moral worth in the purpose which is to be achieved through it but in the maxim by which it is determined" (400). Taken in the context of his examples, this requirement suggests that Kant conceives action from duty as motivated solely by a commitment to a suitable principle of duty. Even promoting one's happiness from duty must be grounded in a commitment to the duty of so doing, not in the happiness to be achieved (399). This position parallels Aristotle's intrinsic motivation requirement. And if we suppose that action on a maxim requires a decision favoring that action over one or more alternatives, then Kant, like Aristotle, would have a selection requirement on acting from duty and thereby on acting from moral virtue.

One thesis of Kant's, however, has no exact counterpart in the *Nicomachean Ethics*: "[A]s an act from duty wholly excludes the influence of inclination . . . nothing remains which can determine the will objectively except the law, and nothing subjectively except pure respect for this practical law" (401). This *exclusiveness requirement* rules out any motive other than duty as actually motivating an action truly performed from duty. Aristotle does not say that an action cannot express virtue unless *nothing else* (i.e., nothing besides elements in the virtue) plays a part in motivating it, though he might perhaps have said, what Kant's overall position seemed to allow Kant to say, that an action *purely* from virtue must meet the exclusiveness requirement. I shall return to this question.[4]

Aristotle's selection requirement may sound psychologically unrealistic, but I do not think he should be read as holding that a virtuous action must arise from a piece of deliberation. For one thing, he stresses that habit is required to develop virtue, and he allows that acting from virtue can be an expression of habit; it can even be a habitual action. And note his description of the grammarian as an analogue of the virtuous agent: the "way" the former produces a grammatical sequence is to produce something "expressing the grammatical knowledge that is in us" (1105a25); presumably, Aristotle conceived such knowledge as capable of yielding action quickly and without our considering alternatives. Similarly, Kant's notion of maxims from which we act does not seem to require their conscious rehearsal before action. Granted, in *reconstructing* the genesis of an action with a view to judging that action, Kant imagines agents carefully formulating maxims (as with his famous four examples); but his view does not require this kind of reflection for acting from duty in general. It may sometimes be needed to *determine* one's duty, but not for simply acting from a grasp of what that duty *is*, as where it is obvious that one is to tell the truth.[5]

II. The Motivation and Range of Action from Virtue

My own account of acting from virtue presupposes some of what Aristotle and Kant say, extends other points they make, and sets forth requirements not contained in their treatments of the topic. I begin with the questions of intentionality, deliberateness, and voluntariness.

An action that, under a given description, is performed from virtue, must at least normally also be intentional under that description.[6] To be sure, if I do something knowingly but not intentionally, as where, on a weekend visit, I benefit one child as a foreseen but not intended consequence of giving its sibling a Ping-Pong set, I am not acting *merely* in accordance with a relevant virtue, say generosity. My benefiting the second child is not merely fortuitous; and more important, this predictable result of my generosity might be both an incentive toward my acting from that virtue again and an indication that I have done something from virtue. A deed not done from virtue may still be at once a result of virtue, a natural sign of it, and identical with an action that, under another description, is performed from virtue.

An action from virtue may, however, be intentional without being premeditated or even deliberate in the strong sense that implies underlying deliberation. Perhaps in some places Kant conceived action from virtue as emerging from pieces of practical reasoning and, on that ground, considered such action deliberate in the strong sense.[7] Depending on the conditions for acting on the basis of practical reasoning, such deliberateness might be entailed by Kantian action from virtue. I prefer to conceive practical reasoning as possible without such deliberation, for instance where one seeks a means, reasons instrumentally to the conclusion that it will achieve one's end, and concludes in favor of it, but never weighs any alternative.[8]

The matter of voluntariness is more difficult. If "having to do" something, say reprimand a friend, because it is a duty, is a case of not doing it voluntarily, then obviously acting from virtue need not be voluntary. Let us call this *discretional involuntariness*: you act not at your pleasure but because you "must"; yet you do something that is "up to you." By contrast, *volitional involuntariness*, the kind that reflex "actions" exemplify, bypasses the motivational system, "the will." Discretional voluntariness may be set aside as clearly not necessary for acting from virtue, whereas volitional voluntariness is necessary: actions from an inescapable duty may express virtue, in that special way implied by acting *from* duty; involuntary "actions" do not go through one's will and cannot express virtue.

The more difficult issue is lack of voluntariness owing to (non-moral) compulsion — *coercive involuntariness*. If, under threat, I am compelled to keep a promise, can my keeping it be done from virtue, say from fidelity? One would think not, but there is at least one hard case. Suppose that although I would keep the promise owing to the threat, I would also do so from duty, and *each* reason figures in me as an actual, causally sufficient motive for the deed. Might we say that the action is performed *partly* from virtue? Arguably, it can express virtue in the right way; it simply expresses fear as well. This is a permissive view, allowing both that actions from virtue can be heterogeneously motivated and that motives of virtue are not necessary conditions for the agent's performing the act in question. One might instead hold the strong view that the motive of virtue must be at least a necessary condition for the action. (There the elements of compulsion would not be sufficient: if the compulsive pressure would not succeed without the cooperation of the virtuous motive, then the action is not compelled.) Kant would probably require still more: that a motive of duty operate as both necessary and sufficient in the actual grounding of the action.

Both the permissive and the strong view have some plausibility, though the strong view is less plausible when separated from compulsion, since compulsion may be felt to be a *pre-emptive* rather than merely cooperating motive, eliminating rather than enhancing the effect of any virtuous motive that is also necessary for the same action. I doubt that compulsion must be pre-emptive;[9] in any case, the wisest course is to allow different degrees to which actions may be performed from virtue, and hence progressively stronger conceptions of acting from virtue. Actions may be performed wholly from virtue when no other kind of motive cooperates; partly from virtue when another kind does; and, in this mixed case, from virtue to various degrees depending on the relative weights of the aretaic and non-aretaic motives in producing or sustaining the action.

The notion of sustenance is crucial, especially for actions and activities — which I am not here distinguishing from actions — that take a significant amount of time, such as giving a lesson as a fulfillment of the duty to instruct. Self-interest and duty could alternate as sustainers, and an action I am performing from duty at one moment might be performed from self-interest at the next. This possibility is perhaps not ruled out by Aristotle's character requirement; for even a firmly entrenched virtue need not pre-empt a quite different, independent motive that is aligned with it. Entrenchment of a trait in one's character is one thing; exclusivity of its motivational influence on a given action is quite another.

Perhaps even more than Kant, Aristotle expresses what seems a strong requirement on the content of the motivation underlying an action from virtue. When Aristotle says of an action from virtue that one must "decide on it for its own sake," he may appear to be implying that if an action is virtuous under a description, the agent must decide on it under that description (or under the corresponding concept, the one expressed by the relevant description — the requirement would not be linguistic). But surely his examples and overall discussion allow a wider reading: there must be some description of the action relevant to the virtue such that (roughly speaking) the agent decides on the action on account of its fitting that description. This thesis needs both qualification and explication.[10]

If deciding on an action implies selecting it from among options, then the view that an action from virtue must be decided upon — the selection requirement — seems mistaken. There need be no question in the agent's mind of options, for example of alternatives to giving each needy person an equal amount of rice. If Aristotle's point is that the action is in some sense "chosen," it is probably true, at least if choosing simply to do something is distinguished from choosing it from among alternatives. But if deciding on an action implies either its prior consideration or, especially, its selection from one or more alternatives, then deciding is not necessary for action from virtue.

The larger question here is not how the elements underlying the action interact in the mind to produce or sustain that action, but what those elements are. What is it that makes a description relevant to the virtue in the right way, that is, what reason-indicating description of a would-be action from virtue is such that if one performs the action for a reason the description indicates, then it is an action *from* the virtue in question? No *name* of the virtue need occur in the description; my equal treatment of those in my care can be intentional and done from justice even if I do not, internally or aloud, describe or conceive it specifically as just. Must the description entail that the action is of the kind that "by definition" may be said to instantiate the virtue, for instance justice (as that virtue applies to action)? I think not. For one thing, it is enough if there is a strong presumption, say a strong probability that justice is served by proportioning the pay one gives to several hourly coworkers to their time on the job; the description of this act would not be, by definition, a case of justice (not an easy condition to satisfy non-trivially, in any event). For another, an action can be done from virtue when there is only good reason for the agent to believe it meets an appropriate condition. Virtue allows for fallibility, and although there are limits to how far off the mark one can be, action from virtue is consistent with some degree of "unavoidable" error.

Just what is required in the virtuous agent's conception of the action, if that action is to be performed from virtue? The problem is to capture what I shall call *aretaic connectedness*, the connection between the action and the agent's beliefs and desires, that we must clarify in order to understand action from virtue. Perhaps it is in part the difficulty of explicating this special connection, as distinct from the commonly discussed difficulty of formulating rules for virtuous action, that led Aristotle, and leads other virtue theorists, to try to understand virtuous action, in the sense of the kind of action appropriate to a virtuous agent, in terms of what is consonant with virtuous character, as opposed to understanding such agents in terms of dispositions to perform a kind of action specifiable independently of the virtue, say in terms of the categorical imperative, the principle of utility, or Ross's prima facie duties. Doing the right kind of deed in the wrong way is not virtuous, even if the deed is just the one required by sound principles.

We might begin, in the spirit of Aristotle, with the idea that the relevant range of descriptions is of a kind by which a person of practical wisdom would, in exercising virtue, be motivated, and that these will fall on some dimension from excess to deficiency. This is vague, but note that if we try to achieve specificity in some of the

standard ways, we encounter falsehood; for example, not just any description implying that the action maximizes human happiness will serve: one could still want to do
the deed for the wrong kind of reason and thereby fail to qualify, at the time, as a
(morally) virtuous agent. For instance, being motivated by considerations of aggre-
gate happiness might lead one to make an optimific but inequitable distribution of
rewards to employees. Moreover, virtue theorists, at least, seem committed to denying that aretaic connectedness can be captured by descriptions which, in the light of
rules (such as the principle of utility), determine the appropriate action.

One might think that a Kantian approach to acting from virtue could lead us to
a solution of the aretaic connectedness problem. But if that approach is to be more
than schematic, it must take us from an account of action from a morally acceptable
maxim to an account of acting from some appropriately related virtue. It might be
argued that all Kantianism needs here is a notion of acting from moral virtue conceived as dutifulness, and it matters little how we distinguish, say, the virtue of justice from that of fidelity, since, independently of these terms, our overall ethical theory (based on the categorical imperative) will require the same actions in any given
circumstance calling for moral decision. But this high-handed approach would
leave us with too thin a theory of how to describe, credit, criticize, and even educate
people morally. Even if all we cared about were getting people to do the right thing
from some appropriate moral reason, we must surely teach morality in terms of more
specific categories — and quite possibly in terms of the "departments" of morality
that the virtues can be taken to represent. I believe, then, that for both normative
and analytical purposes even a well-developed Kantian ethics needs a better way of
clarifying the notions of virtue and of action from it.

III. The Cognitive and Motivational Grounding of Action from Virtue

I want now to propose an account of acting from virtue built around six notions, corresponding to situational, conceptual, cognitive, motivational, behavioral, and teleological dimensions of such action. These dimensions are, first, the *field* of a virtue,
roughly the kind of situation in which it characteristically operates; second, the characteristic *targets* it aims at, such as the well-being of others in the case of beneficence and the control of fear in the case of courage; third, the agent's *understanding*
of that field; fourth, the agent's *motivation* to act in that field in a certain way, where
that way is appropriate to the virtue; fifth, the agent's acting on the *basis* of that
understanding and motivation; and sixth, the *beneficiaries* of the virtue, above all
(and perhaps solely) the person(s) who properly benefit from our realizing it: for
beneficence, other people in general; for charitableness, the needy; for fidelity, family and friends; and so forth. These six notions are specially appropriate to explicating action from virtue (and, to a lesser extent, action from emotions and vices), as
opposed to actions from very different sorts of dispositions, for example boredom,
fatigue, and misapprehension. None of those actions has, for instance, a distinct
field or target, though emotions, such as love (of one kind) may also have beneficiaries or, like vices, characteristic sufferers, such as the victims of passionate anger; and
with fatigue, at least, while the 'from' is (as in combination with action-locutions in

general) explanatory, it does not imply what it most often does with those locutions: a *motivational* explanation.[11] Let us first consider the field of a virtue.

The field of justice might be roughly retribution and the distribution of goods and evils; that of fidelity might be conduct required by explicit or implicit promises; and so forth. Such fields may overlap other aretaic fields, but each has some distinctive feature(s). How does a virtuous person understand the field of, for example, fidelity? It would be natural for the appropriate understanding to manifest itself in believing that promises create a duty to keep them, that working with others generates obligations to them, and so on. But suppose someone did not use the concepts of duty or obligation (at least here) and thought simply that it is *good* to keep promises and good to criticize people who do not. A virtuous person could be skeptical about moral concepts or think them indistinguishable from aretaic concepts in general. We can imagine someone who, upon making a promise, wants to keep it because that is appropriate to human relationships, and tends to feel disapproval of anyone who does not keep promises, on the ground that the behavior is inappropriate to such relationships. And of course, a person might want to keep a promise because promise-keeping is commanded by God.

A moral field cannot be understood without a sense of its (moral) normativity, but that sense is not restricted to either virtue concepts (as Aristotle may seem to imply) or hedonic ones (as some utilitarians perhaps tend to think) or deontological principles (as Kantians may tend to think). It *does* appear that there are some general requirements for understanding any moral field, for instance that a kind of impartiality must be recognized as necessary, that the well-being of people must be given some weight, and that the relevant norms must be, if not "designed" to overrule self-interest, then capable of conflicting with it.[12] It may be that action from virtue requires an exercise of some normative concept, if only that of what is in some appropriate way good or bad; and certainly the possession of a virtue entails a *recognitional capacity*. A loyal person, for example, must have a sense of when to act in support of friends: this is part of what it is to understand the field of a virtue, and without it one would not act from virtue. But neither this special requirement for understanding the field of a virtue nor the general requirements for comprehension of a moral field entail that action from a virtue must have any particular motive among those appropriate to its field.

With all this in mind, we can see that aretaic connectedness need not proceed through any direct application of a moral or even a virtue concept (though this apparently does not hold for all normative concepts). This point bears especially on the motivational dimension of acting from virtue. Most important, action from a given virtue need not be *internally motivated*, that is (roughly), performed from a desire to realize that virtue. Let me clarify this by example first, then in general terms. Suppose I see two children dividing apples they have just picked, and I notice that their pickings are about equal. I see one child take far more than half, and I want to intervene. I do so in order to persuade the greedy one to share equally. I may see this persuasion as just; but I may also see it as appropriate to their similar investments of time and energy; as imposing on them the way civilized people should treat each other; as affirming the equality of the two as persons; as promoting harmony between them; or in other normative ways appropriately connected with justice. If I am motivated to intervene on the basis of any of these conceptions, my action seems suitably connected with justice to enable me to act from it: in the first case the concept of justice applies directly, in the others (on plausible assumptions) indirectly. If I act from any of these motives, I act from justice and, if they are properly grounded in my character, from virtue.[13]

We can discern, then, two ways in which, on the basis of an understanding of the field of a virtue, an agent can act from it: directly and indirectly. Both notions — which we might pair with direct and indirect aretaic grounding — need explication. I act directly from, say, justice provided that, first, an adequate concept of justice (whether I would use the word or not) figures centrally in my motivation; second, the content of my motivation is appropriate to justice, as where I want to compensate a victim of wrongdoing; and third, the motivation itself, for instance a desire to treat people equally in distributive matters, is properly grounded in my character. I act indirectly from justice when an adequate subsidiary concept, such as fairness, is motivationally central in that way, or where (a) my motivation is appropriately subsumable under the relevant virtue concept or a subsidiary one, say where I act in order to divide the children's takings in accordance with their efforts, and (b) again the relevant motivation has a specific content appropriate to justice and is sufficiently connected with the relevant aretaic elements to ground the action in them. (The motivation of an action from virtue need not, however, be a standing element in the agent, e.g. a long-term commitment to the moral education of children, as opposed to a desire responding to a unique situation.) The second, indirect case is the more complicated. Suppose that need, in addition to effort, is crucial for the justice of the division in question; then my (exclusive) concern with equality of effort will not suffice to subsume, under the concept of justice, my attempt to distribute in accord with effort: I am too far off the mark. I might qualify as *trying* to act from justice, and even as coming close; but there is a limit to how much one can misunderstand the features of a situation relevant to a virtue and still count as acting from that virtue as opposed to unsuccessfully trying to do the relevant kind of action.

One way to give a theoretical account of acting indirectly from virtue is to assume that an action's being performed from virtue supervenes on natural properties of the action, or at least on some set of properties underlying its virtuousness. The idea would be that an action from virtue is such because of its more basic properties, such as being motivated by a belief that the children should have shares of apples proportionate to their efforts in picking them. The suggestion is meant to be minimally controversial, and for anyone who finds the notion of supervenience unhelpful we could also put the point in terms of a dependence of the virtuousness of an action on other properties of it. Thus, even an intuitionist who thinks that the obligation of beneficence is normatively basic could allow that an action could be performed *from* beneficence when motivated by properties of the action that are, for the agent, psychologically more basic than its beneficence. The agent might, for example, conceive the action that in fact is performed from beneficence not in terms of beneficence but simply as relieving suffering.

It is difficult to specify in a general way what properties are basic to an action from virtue, but suppose for the sake of argument that, say, generosity in an action supervenes on its character as a giving of something voluntarily and in the (reasonable) belief that it will benefit the recipient (as opposed to giving it from a sense that it is owed). We can now say that an action is indirectly grounded in a virtue provided it is not directly grounded in it but is based on the agent's believing the action to have a suitable subset of the base properties of action from that virtue (though not necessarily under this or any other technical description). Roughly, the difference is between aiming at the target of the virtue under the relevant aretaic concept and aiming at it under some appropriate description framed in terms of the base properties of action from that virtue. This need not be all of those properties: if Carol gives more time to students than she thinks they deserve, in order to teach them more, this may be enough to qualify her pedagogical actions as performed from generosity. But one can act *from* a virtue by acting from its grounds without having that very virtue in mind. This is a pattern characteristic of indirect aretaic grounding.

The case of generosity raises the question whether, for some virtues, indirect aretaic grounding is the only kind possible. Suppose I give a Ping-Pong set to a child not in order to benefit the child but simply because, after years of preferring the sibling, I want to behave generously toward this child. Can this act be performed from generosity (and thereby directly grounded in it)? Acting from generosity is surely not entailed by acting from a desire to be generous. Even if one has this virtue, one might instead be acting for the wrong kind of reason, though in accord with the virtue. Surely my action here, unlike a just deed performed from a desire to be just toward those concerned, would not be an action from virtue at all and so would not exhibit direct aretaic grounding.[14]

Suppose, however, that I give the Ping-Pong set *both* because I want to benefit the child for its own sake and because I want to behave generously. Perhaps I may now be acting from virtue — though not purely so. This would be a case of partial direct aretaic grounding. The action would also be performed in the *service* of virtue, since I act partly from a second-order pro attitude toward generosity. Such higher-order attitudes are, however, not necessary for having virtue; nor does acting from them entail acting from virtue. Acting from a virtue requires promoting or otherwise properly dealing with certain elements in its field — its beneficiaries, say children or the needy or the oppressed, where the beneficiaries figure in the scope of the target of the virtue. Acting in the service of a virtue, by contrast, requires promoting the *virtue*. Doing that may affect the beneficiaries little or not at all. There is no need to explicate here all the categories these points bring out. It is enough to have provided a framework for doing that and to have shown that an action's being explicitly directed toward promoting a virtue is neither necessary nor sufficient for its constituting acting from virtue.

The distinction between direct and indirect grounding in virtue is neutral between Kantian and Aristotelian conceptions of virtue and acting therefrom: it applies whether virtues are internalizations of independently knowable moral (or other) principles or, on the contrary, moral (or other) principles are knowable only as generalizations from the behavior of people with virtues of character. The distinction is also neutral with respect to the cooperating motives problem in ethical theory. My conception of acting from virtue does not require that one be motivated *solely* by the relevant aretaic ground(s), the ground(s) appropriate to action from that virtue. This exclusivity of motivation is required only for acting *purely* from virtue. If one acts from both love and a sense of justice, one does not act purely from moral virtue; but love is not a companion that must prevent, as opposed to outshining, one's acting from the virtue of justice.

Imagine, however, that by contrast with a cooperating non-moral motive, I have a *further* reason; for example, I am persuading the greedy child to share equally, not for its own sake but in order to promote human happiness, or in order to abide by the will of God. There are at least two relevant possibilities (both also applicable to non-moral virtues): first, that I *take* the further end to be morally relevant, for instance to be an appropriate moral ground of the action, and second, that I take the further end to be an adequate ground but have no moral conception of how this is so. In the first case, we could say that the ultimate end of my action is moral; and in part in the light of such cases we might adopt what I shall call the *moral motivation thesis*: that an action from (moral) virtue must be morally motivated, though not always intrinsically so motivated, for example performed for the sake of justice. Here my action serves a moral end, but not directly, "in itself"; if it is from, for instance, justice, it need not be internally motivated, although it would be motivated by some consideration *consonant with* an aretaically internal motive, such as to rectify an unequal distribution.

The second case suggests a *moral connection thesis*: that given a suitable immediate motive connected in the right way with the moral field of the virtue, the action can be performed from that virtue even if the action's ultimate motivation is not moral.[15] Acting ultimately from love, for example, seems consonant with acting (partly) from justice, provided the immediate motivation of the action is of the right kind, say a determination to treat people equally. This would be a beneficent, perhaps a natural, kind of justice.[16] If natural justice exists, it shows that action from virtue need not be from a *single* virtue — a point that is in any case implicit in the possibility of acting at once from, say, courage and justice, as where one justly and courageously denies an unfair request made by an intimidating employee.

The moral motivation thesis seems plausible: it appears characteristic of acting from moral virtue that the agent act at least indirectly from a suitable moral motive. The moral connection thesis, which denies that even ultimate moral motivation is necessary for action from virtue, also seems plausible but is harder to assess (there are of course counterpart aretaic connection and motivation theses, and we should not presuppose a sharp distinction between moral and other virtues). What if moral obligation is rooted in (non-moral) considerations of happiness, or in God's will, conceived non-morally? If this is possible, then it should be possible for considerations of human happiness or of divine will to ground moral actions, and hence to be ultimate, independent motives for actions from virtue. Perhaps we must allow that possibility if we are to have an account of acting from virtue neutral with respect to all of the major moral theories. For suppose that a hedonistic or divine command view of the grounds of morality is correct. Why, then, could I not be acting from moral virtue if I am motivated by hedonic considerations, or by divine command, even if I see no connection between those motives and morality as such (perhaps because I simply do not operate, directly at least, with moral categories)? I am, after all, acting from the grounds of such virtue, and to this extent one might regard my action as (indirectly) aretaically grounded. There would thus *be* a connection, which I could come to see, between my conception of the action and moral virtue; still, my acting from moral virtue would not require my being, in any direct way if in any way at all, morally motivated.

The right conclusion to draw here may be that it is simply not clear how narrowly we should construe acting from moral virtue (or acting from virtue simpliciter). It is best to distinguish a narrower and broader notion. One might hold that in the case of acting ultimately for a non-moral purpose, say from a desire to treat someone lovingly, the agent, if acting *from* a moral virtue, is nonetheless not doing so in a moral *way*. Perhaps so; but must we require of all actions from a moral virtue that they must be performed in a moral way? If acting from virtue were equivalent to acting *for the sake of it* (in some senses of this phrase), that might be so; but acting for the sake of virtue is not necessary for acting from it. This applies both to acting for the sake of the virtue *promotionally*, as where one tries to enhance the amount of honesty in the world, and to acting for the sake of it *acquisitionally*, as where one acts to try to produce the virtue in oneself. The latter case shows that acting for the sake of a virtue is also not sufficient for acting from it.

We should add, then, to the distinction among degrees of acting from virtue which emerge when we consider the cooperation of virtuous with non-virtuous motives, a distinction between (1) acting, to any degree, from a virtue, in the way(s) (conceptually speaking) most closely tied to it as to the grounds of the action, particularly in regard to the action's being conceived in terms of the relevant concept, for instance justice or fidelity, and (2) simply acting from it in some other way that manifests that virtue. The former cases are most often found among actions that exhibit direct aretaic grounding; one acts both from the virtue and in a certain way under the concept of it. The latter are most often found among actions that exhibit indirect aretaic grounding; one acts from the virtue but not under the concept of it, only under some suitably connected concept. Aristotle sometimes had in mind the former, stronger notion — acting from virtue in the way most closely tied to it as to the grounds of the action; but his overall moral theory, like the most plausible virtue and rule theories in ethics generally, leaves room for the weaker notion. It is clear that in either case the action is rooted in the agent in a way that makes it plausible both to say, with Aristotle, that the action expresses virtue as a feature of character and, with Kant, that it manifests good will. These points, in turn, make clearer an important point suggested earlier: action from virtue, as opposed to action merely in conformity with virtue, is so important in appraising people: the former, unlike the latter, is commonly a reliable indication of their aretaic character.[17]

IV. The Moral Scope of Acting from Virtue

In the light of the connections now apparent between virtue concepts and more general ones, both moral and non-moral, we can explore the moral scope of action from virtue and, in particular, whether action from moral virtue is sufficiently comprehensive for a morally adequate life. Suppose (artificially) that one acted only from moral virtue, and always from some moral virtue appropriate in the circumstances. Would this suffice for living a morally adequate life?

An affirmative answer is certainly plausible, at least for those views that take the possession of the moral virtues to be the internalization of some comprehensive set of sound moral standards. If, however, we try to frame a list of moral virtues in terms of which to focus the question, there is greater difficulty. One problem is getting a sufficiently comprehensive list of virtues from the moral domain alone: would justice, fidelity, honesty, and beneficence be sufficient, if broadly construed, or must we add to the agent's repertoire, say, courage and even intellectual virtues, since these seem required for realizing the moral virtues where danger produces fear, or where insufficient information threatens to make reasonable choice impossible?

A more difficult problem is how to cover *aretaic conflicts*: just as obligations of beneficence and fidelity can conflict when beneficently helping someone in distress requires breaking a promise, a virtuous agent can be pulled in two directions by different virtuous tendencies. Here practical wisdom is required in the same way that, for Ross, it seems required to deal with conflicts among the prima facie duties he thought morally fundamental.[18] Practical wisdom is not a specifically moral virtue but a higher-order one applicable to reflections and decisions concerning moral and other kinds of virtues. If, as is likely, it is required for a morally adequate life on the part of an otherwise virtuous agent, then the exercise of moral virtue alone is not sufficient for such a life, even if the exercise of *virtue*, overall, is.

To say, however, that acting from moral virtue is not sufficient by itself for a morally adequate life does not entail that virtue ethics is not sufficient for the action-guiding task of normative ethics. By virtue ethics I mean roughly the kind of ethical position according to which the following two ideas are central: first, the fundamental moral concepts are virtue concepts, as opposed, above all, to rule concepts; and second, the basic normative aims of moral agents are aretaically determined, in the ways we have seen, by the requirements of acting from virtue, as opposed, say, to being dictated by a commitment to following certain deontic rules. Aristotle can be read as holding such a view in some places, for instance in saying that "actions are called just or temperate when they are the sort that a just or temperate person would do. But the just and temperate person is not one who [merely] does these actions, but the one who does them in the way in which just or temperate people do them" (1105b6–9).[19] Taken as a statement of virtue theory as applied to these traits, this passage implies that what makes an act, for example, just, is its being the kind a just person as such would perform (in a certain way); we do not explicate what a just person is by first identifying certain types of acts and then characterizing that kind of person in terms of a suitable disposition to perform acts of that kind.[20] This metaphysical conception of virtue ethics is consistent with taking practical wisdom or other higher-order virtues as crucial for directing the virtuous agent in everyday life. Thus, a virtue ethics is at least not prevented on that score from providing a basis for the morally adequate life.

There remains, however, a significant problem. Even if the notion of a virtuous person is metaphysically more basic than that of a virtuous action, there is the epistemological difficulty of determining *what*, or even who, a morally virtuous person *is* without already knowing what sorts of things such an agent would *do*. Can we reasonably take someone as a model of justice or fidelity without relying on some idea of what deeds are appropriate to such a person? If not, how can a virtue theory ever tell us what we should do, even in the matter of building character, if we do not already know? One Aristotelian answer is that if we know our proper function and see how it is properly exercised, that is, so exercised as to produce a life of flourishing, we can see how the agent in question — the virtuous agent — chooses in matters involving pleasure and pain, which constitute the larger field of moral virtue.

In rough terms, the virtuous agent aims at targets appropriate to human flourishing and acts so as to hit a mean between excess and deficiency. Suppose this is correct. There is still a normative notion built into flourishing, and this would seem at best difficult to discern without a sense of what behavioral *outcomes* are to be sought. Some such outcomes seem essential for hitting the right targets. Are we happy when merely content, or must we perform certain intellectual, aesthetic, and physical tasks with a certain kind of result? Are there not intellectual standards, such as those of logic and mathematics, at least, that must be brought to our activities as guides within which virtue develops? (Aristotle himself must have thought so, for he considered philosophical contemplation the highest happiness and surely saw it as governed by logical and epistemic standards.[21])

It is true that once we have role models, virtue can be taught by their example and without antecedent (propositional) standards. Historically, then, virtue ethics might operate independently of rule or other non-virtue accounts, such as intuitionism. But conceptually, virtue notions seem dependent on other normative concepts.

This negative conclusion must not be overstressed. It remains quite possible that the *moral worth* of actions depends on their being actions from virtue: even if virtue concepts cannot by themselves tell us what conduct befits us as moral agents, it may be that the only (or the most) morally creditable way to *do* the things in question is from virtue. A second major moral thesis is also left open: that even the moral worth — in the sense of goodness — of persons lies in their virtuous character (or lack of it).[22] Together these theses constitute a *virtue theory of moral worth*, and they may be regarded as partially explicating what it is for character to be morally fundamental. This kind of virtue ethics is consistent both with Kantianism and with other views commonly contrasted with virtue ethics when the latter is construed as embodying a theory of moral obligation.[23]

If there is a conceptual dependence of virtue concepts on other normative concepts, it does not indicate a one-way street. Any moral rules with enough specificity to guide day-to-day behavior need interpretation and refinement to be useful in making moral decisions. It could turn out that practical wisdom is indispensable in using these rules, and that a basic element in such wisdom is a tendency to seek a reflective equilibrium between plausible rules and virtuous inclinations. Even thoroughgoing virtue theorists can grant rules a place. Such rules as they countenance are generalizations from virtuous conduct, for instance from the choices of the *phronimos*, rather than, say, formulae for optimizing non-moral good (as for utilitarianism), or specifications of obligatory act-types (as for the Kantian tradition). But these rules still have a degree of authority and can override virtuous inclinations in some cases. At worst, the rules are a generalization from many such inclinations, and these rules may thus imply that inclinations conflicting with them are aretaically deviant. Even making virtues conceptually fundamental need not make them indefeasible sources of moral authority. Similarly, if one could specify the types of actions a virtuous agent should in general perform, practical wisdom and a virtuous disposition would be required for applying the relevant rules in particular cases.

Conclusion

On the broad conception of acting from virtue developed here, it is aretaically grounded intentional action: it is action grounded in virtue either directly, as where the agent acts explicitly in the light of the concept of the virtue in question, or indirectly, as where one acts on the basis of a different kind of consideration that is suitably relevant to the virtue in terms of its field and target. Such action is, then, *from* virtue in being explained by beliefs and desires properly connected with the appropriate aretaic elements in character, and it is *virtuous* both because of its connection with those elements and because of what kind of action it is. This conception of action from virtue provides a model for a broad understanding of moral action in general, conceived as action having moral worth: just as action from moral virtue does not require acting for the sake of moral virtue, and can instead be grounded in it indirectly through beliefs and motivation appropriate to the moral virtue in question, moral action, even conceived non-aretaically, need not be performed for the sake of a moral principle, or even as an application thereof, and can be grounded only indirectly in such a principle. Moreover, in addition to direct and indirect ways of acting from virtue, there are *degrees* to which one may act from virtue, depending especially on the extent to which non-virtuous motives contribute to the action in question. The moral worth of an action can also depend on the balance among moral and non-moral influences on its performance, and this point applies to non-virtue theories as well as to virtue theories.

   One of the largest questions raised by the account of acting from virtue presented here is what values, if any, constrain the development of virtue. If the notion of virtue is not merely historical, not just a notion rooted in the established practices of one or another society, if instead it belongs to a universally valid ethic, then it is apparently not entirely autonomous with respect to moral and other values. Moral virtue seems best construed as a kind of internalization of moral values or perhaps moral principles or other standards of moral conduct. It is not their ground, though it may influence their content through the effort we regularly make to achieve reflective equilibrium between virtuous inclinations and general principles. Moral virtue may ground moral conduct genetically, but not conceptually; and this is confirmed by the way in which we must understand acting from moral virtue: not simply in relation to people with certain traits, but in relation to the reasons for which they act, above all the kinds of reasons pertaining to what is of moral value or to what is morally required by general rules or standards.

   In the theory of moral worth, however, virtue is absolutely central. This point is easily obscured by the common attempt to construe virtue ethics as providing by itself an adequate theory of moral obligation. Virtue can be the ground of the moral worth of agents even without being the ground of moral rightness or obligatory conduct. Granted, agents cannot truly act morally if, as moral nihilism has it, there are no sound moral standards; but according to both virtue theories and other plausible ethical views, actions gain no moral worth by mere conformity with sound standards of conduct: the right actions performed in the wrong way, and especially from the wrong motives, have no moral worth. The mere existence of objectively true moral standards, even together with our regular conformity to them, would not guarantee moral action — action from virtue or from duty or from any other morally appropriate ground — and might for that very reason bring no moral goodness into the world.

Virtue need not be acquired, moreover, from studying moral values as such; it is normally acquired by imitation and socialization, and it probably cannot be taught without models. These two truths do much to account for the appearance of conceptual autonomy the notion of virtue seems to have. In normal human lives, virtue may be genetically prior to moral principles. It also has a kind of operational autonomy, both in the sense that one can act from virtue without being motivated by any aretaically external standards and even in the sense that one's immediate motivation need not be moral at all. Whether the fundamental moral standards are rules or intuitions or non-moral goods or something else again, virtue is required to realize those standards, and acting from virtue is the main basis of the moral worth of agents.

Notes

An earlier version of this essay was given at Santa Clara University's Conference on Virtue Ethics in March 1994, and I benefited from discussion with the other speakers, especially Philippa Foot. I also want to thank Norman Dahl, Julia Driver, Philip Kain, Christopher Kulp, Michael Meyer, William Prior, Elizabeth Radcliffe, and Mark Sainsbury for helpful comments.

1. This is not exactly his wording, but the distinction seems clearly implied in his contrast between merely doing just and temperate deeds and doing them in the "way in which just and temperate people do them" (*Nicomachean Ethics*, (trans. Terence Irwin (Indianapolis: Hadsett, 1985], 1105a25–1105b15.

2. See esp. Kant's *Foundations of the Metaphysics of Morals*, trans. Lewis White Beck (New York: Liberal Arts Press,1959), 397–400, 406. (Lewis White Beck's translation will be used throughout, and the Akademie numbers will be given in the text.)

3. Kant says, e.g., "Virtue signifies a moral strength of will . . . the moral strength of a *man's* will [as opposed to that of a "superhuman" being] in fulfilling his *duty*, a moral *necessitation* by his own legislative reason in so far as reason itself constitutes a power of *executing* the law." "Introduction to the Doctrine of Virtue," trans. Mary McGregor (New York: Harper and Row, 1964), p. 66 (A. 404).

4. Discussion of some of the possible kinds of mixed motivation and some of Kant's theoretical options concerning them is provided in ch. 3 of my *Practical Reasoning* (London and New York: Routledge, 1989). I would add, on the bearing of the categorical imperative, that (1) we surely need not be treating people merely as a means, or failing to treat them as ends, if we act justly toward them both from a just character and from love; (2) *perhaps* in such a case one might still regard the relevant maxim of the action as one formulable in terms of the just motive alone. The motive of justice might have to be not only sufficient but *primary* relative to that of love; but even then the motive of love could play a significant motivational role.

5. This is defended in ch. 3 of *Practical Reasoning*. Aristotle's term *prohairesis* is usually

translated as meaning 'decision', when Aristotle himself describes it as "deliberative desire" (1113a10). Susan Sauvé Meyer calls it "the desire most important to virtue and vice of character" (*Aristotle on Moral Responsibility* [Oxford: Basil Blackwell, 1993], p. 24). Cf. Sarah Broadie, *Ethics with Aristotle* (New York and Oxford: Oxford University Press, 1991), pp. 78–79. If it is any kind of desire, 'decision' is not quite the right word, since, unlike desires, decisions are made and are events in the ordinary sense entailing change.

6. Even qualified by 'normally' this point may be too strong. If a humble person characteristically and "automatically" does not intervene in an argument between parties who, though competent, know less about the topic, might this be both an action from humility and non-intentional? Supposing the answer is affirmative, it still appears that an action from virtue must have some description under which it is performed from virtue *and* intentional, e.g. avoiding the appearance of instructing people.

7. Kant's famous four examples in sect. 2 Two of the *Foundations*, especially in their first occurrence intended to illustrate universalization of maxims, would be a case in point.

8. A possibility argued for in my *Practical Reasoning*, ch. 5. Cf. Broadie, *Ethics with Aristotle*, pp. 85–89.

9. What chiefly makes it seem so is that for typical compulsions the agent will be *preoccupied* with, e.g., avoiding the threatened consequence; but preoccupation with one motivating scenario need not be proportionate to its impact on action: people can do things mainly for prestige or money while stressing to themselves and others that they are acting from charity or friendship.

10. Cf. the view, commonly attributed to Aristotle, that "[o]ur rational actions [including actions from virtue] are the actions we perform because we think they will contribute to our happiness" (Meyer, *Aristotle on Moral Responsibility*, p. 25). Rational action is *subordinate* to our desire for happiness, but I doubt Aristotle implies that all such action is *directly aimed* at it. I defend these points in *Practical Reasoning*, ch. 1.

11. I thank Mark Sainsbury for drawing my attention to this contrast (which deserves independent elaboration on another occasion). I must also forgo addressing contrasts between actions from virtue and (certain) actions from vice (e.g. slovenliness) and from emotion (e.g. anxiety). Still, some of what is said in the following paragraphs about action from virtue should help in clarifying action from vices and emotions, especially where the latter is intentional and to the extent that vices or emotions are constituted by desires or beliefs or combinations thereof.

12. One problem is how to characterize the moral point of view. For discussion of this see Kurt Baier, *The Moral Point of View* (Ithaca: Cornell University Press, 1958); William K. Frankena, *Ethics*, 2nd ed. (Englewood Cliffs, N.J.: Prentice-Hall, 1973); and Bernard Gert, *Morality: A New Defense of the Moral Rules* (Oxford and New York: Oxford University Press, 1988). I assume that just as one can take the moral point of view even if one regards it as derivative from that of rationality, people can take the moral point of view even if they consider moral standards theologically grounded, and that there is thus a way to conceive divine commands so that obedience to them can be morally, not just religiously, motivated. A similar problem is how to square the possibility of conflicts between morality and self-interest with the kind of egoism apparently implicit in Aristotle and others who offer a plausible ethical theory from egoistic starting points. The beginning of an answer is that for Aristotle, while moral virtue is essential to our flourishing and hence moral conduct tends to serve self-interest, long-run self-interest has social dimensions and can thereby conflict with moral demands.

13. Acting from justice would be acting for the relevant reason. Acting for a reason is a complicated notion which I presuppose here; an account of it, and appraisal of other accounts, is given in my "Acting for Reasons," *Philosophical Review* 95 (1986): 511–46.

14. This sort of problem is insightfully discussed by Bernard Williams, e.g. in *Ethics and*

the Limits of Philosophy (Cambridge: Harvard University Press, 1985), pp. 10–11. He has suggested (in conversation) that justice is the one virtue such that action from it must be internally motivated. Justice does seem the best candidate for a virtue meeting this condition, but I doubt that it does — unless, perhaps, we restrict it to a specific kind, e.g. the "trait" of being retributively just (cf. Broadie, *Ethics with Aristotle*, p. 88). If we construe any trait narrowly enough, actions from it will be correspondingly restricted as to appropriate motivation.

15. An immediate motive is one that the action is performed (directly) in order to satisfy, as where one drinks simply to slake thirst; but one could drink to rehydrate the body, which one does in turn to avoid suffering. If one does not avoid suffering in order to satisfy a still further motive, this (self-protective) motive is ultimate. Motivational chains can be long, so that the connection between an action and a virtue ultimately grounding it may be extended; and since the (direct) in-order-to relation is non-transitive (in the sense that one can A in order that B and B in order that C, yet not A in order that C), an action's ultimate motives need not underlie it in the way its immediate motives do.

16. This contrasts with the austere principled kind of justice Kant would have us cultivate and act from. He is not, however, committed to treating acting from virtue as something we can do "at will," nor is there a direct duty to satisfy this description.

17. Hume goes so far as to say it is the motive, not the action, that (directly?) deserves praise or blame. See *A Treatise of Human Nature*, ed. L. A. Selby-Bigge (Oxford: Oxford University Press, 1888), p. 477; cf. p. 464.

18. See esp. W. D. Ross, *The Right and the Good* (Oxford: Oxford University Press, 1939), ch. 2. The sorts of problems emerging in the text may indicate one reason why Aristotle might have thought the virtues *unified*; reflection on the problems certainly suggest that in a virtuous person at least many virtues are interconnected, but that by no means requires a strong kind of unity.

19. Cf. *Nicomachean Ethics* 1129a7–9, which seems at least to reverse the emphasis: "the state everyone means in speaking of justice is the state that makes us doers of just actions."

20. A contemporary defender of virtue theory especially sensitive to some of the conceptual problems arising here is Jorge L. A. Garcia; see, e.g., "The Problem of Comparative Value," *Mind* 98 (1989): 277–83.

21. Some of the large literature on Aristotle's conception of happiness supports my points here. See, e.g., John Cooper, *Reason and Human Good in Aristotle* (Cambridge: Harvard University Press, 1975); Richard Kraut, "Two Conceptions of Happiness," *Philosophical Review* 88 (1979): 169–97; Alasdair MacIntyre, *After Virtue* (Notre Dame: University of Notre Dame Press, 1981); Broadie, *Ethics with Aristotle*; and William J. Prior, *Virtue and Knowledge* (London and New York: Routledge, 1991).

22. Moral worth in the sense of dignity is a different, capacity notion, but it is related — it is largely the capacity for good character.

23. Regarding Kant, we would have to assume that actions from duty, which have moral worth, are also performed from virtue. Some passages in Hume suggest he might be committed to the virtue theory of moral worth, e.g., " 'Tis evident, that when we praise any actions, we regard only the motives that produced them. . . . The external performance has no merit. . . . [A]ll virtuous actions derive their merit only from virtuous motives, and are consider'd merely as signs of those motives" (*Treatise*, pp. 477–78). Even a utilitarian can hold the virtue theory of moral worth — though only as a contingent truth — since virtuous character, or its producing actions, need not contribute to intrinsic value. Frankena suggests that "a man and his actions are morally good if it is at least true that, whatever his actual motives in acting are, his sense of duty or desire to do the right is so strong in him that it would keep him trying to do his duty anyway" (*Ethics*, p. 70). This differs from the virtue theory of moral worth in at least

two ways: the relevant actions need not be performed *from* virtue (since the actual motives are not crucial); and the content of the relevant motivation is both specifically moral and indeed restricted to the deontic concepts of *right* and *duty*. (However, I see nothing in Frankena's overall position that requires his holding either the first, permissive thesis or the second, restrictive one.)

IV

Practical Reason and the
Foundations of Ethics

—
—
—

9

Autonomy, Reason, and Desire

The notion of autonomy is often pivotal in recent ethical literature. One common theme is *rights* of autonomy, such as the right to direct one's medical treatment; another focus is *ideals* of autonomy, for instance those determining how much freedom is allowed by legitimate government; and still another theme is the *value* of autonomy, for example as the basis of human dignity, a moral notion often stressed by Kantians. One easily gets a general sense of what autonomy is thought to be, but it is quite difficult to characterize philosophically, if indeed there is any single conception that can be plausibly taken as basic. This chapter has two aims: to sketch an account of autonomy useful in understanding its place in descriptive and normative contexts, and to explore its relation to what seem the two dominant lines in the theory of value: instrumentalism as expressed in the Humean tradition, and axiological realism — or at least objectivism — as expressed in the Kantian tradition.[1] For instrumentalism, there is no intrinsic value; whatever is good is so only as a means. For realism, there is intrinsic value, and realists often take moral goodness to be one kind. Approaching autonomy in relation to these two traditions will yield a better understanding of the notion than is otherwise possible; it will also help us to appraise the traditions themselves and to see the implications of autonomy for the general theory of practical reason. As often as these traditions have been compared, the debate about their relative merits has not as yet extended to their resources for providing an account of autonomy and articulating plausible ideals of autonomy for rational agents. This chapter may begin to accomplish that task.

I. Autonomy as Self-Government

There are many views about what constitutes autonomy.[2] There are, moreover, many sorts of things of which it can be predicated, for instance persons, actions, faculties — most notably, the will — and, more broadly, disciplines, institutions, and nations. I propose to take the notion of an autonomous agent as primary and to view other cases, such as autonomous action, in relation to it. Thus, autonomous actions may be conceived roughly as those that, by virtue of the way they are grounded in certain of the agent's reasons, express the autonomy of the agent. If we can adequately understand the autonomy of agents, the other notions of autonomy can be explicated far more readily. I start, then, with general points about the notion as applied to agents.

So far as etymology is a reliable guide, one might expect autonomy to be above all self-legislation: setting down laws or rules for oneself. It — or its exercise — is at least this, given a liberal understanding of laws and rules; or at any rate, this notion seems implicit both in everyday contexts in which questions of autonomy arise and in much philosophical literature in which it figures.[3] But autonomy must surely be more than self-legislation conceived simply as laying out rules of conduct. One can set forth rules to which nobody pays any attention; and just as a government does not truly govern if its laws are ignored, agents who prescribe rules for themselves by which their own conduct is not guided are not autonomous. As I understand autonomy in the contexts that matter most — above all those in which autonomy is put forward as an ideal in ethical and political discussions — the notion implies not mere self-legislation, but self-government. It may indeed be roughly equivalent to the latter concept. We may certainly say this much: other things equal, the more self-governing an agent is, the more autonomous.[4]

A kind of self-government is, then, at least a major constituent in autonomy. Governing oneself is an exercise of autonomy, and probably its major exercise. The primary notion of autonomy is (I take it) that of a complex characteristic of the agent which manifests itself both in behavior (including decisions) and in certain attitudes, beliefs, and desires. Perhaps autonomy is a virtuous state of character; but being autonomous does not imply being virtuous overall, though autonomy tends to support virtues one already has. Granted, we do not think of persons as autonomous if they have never exercised autonomy; but I leave open that autonomy can exist in such a case, as where someone is created in an adult state with all the required dispositions. In much of what follows, the references to autonomy will be to the state and not its exercise, but we must also consider examples of its exercise. It cannot be understood apart from a grasp of how it is expressed.

Autonomy, Freedom, and Independence

It might seem that autonomy is equivalent to freedom.[5] But while the two are closely related, freedom is not sufficient for autonomy. A creature of pure whim, utterly lacking the self-direction required for autonomy, can still be free and can regularly act freely. Indeed, perhaps children achieve autonomy only by using their freedom in more and more disciplined ways until they develop the motivational integration that autonomy produces when desires are subordinated to principles. A free action, then, need not express autonomy, as opposed to mere desire; and a free being need not *have* autonomy as a standing trait.

Is freedom, however, a necessary condition for autonomy? Certainly a person who, being in prison, is not free can be autonomous. The *scope* of autonomy would be limited, but not (in one sense, at least) its *degree*. For individual actions the relation may be even more complex. Most unfree action is not autonomous to any significant degree, and neither an unfree agent nor a compelled action is fully autonomous. But a significant degree of autonomy can exist even where compulsion undermines freedom. Imagine that I am compelled, by threats against the lives of loved ones, to speak for a candidate I do not support. I do not speak freely, but may still be able to assess what I am doing, govern the manner of my doing it — for instance, by withholding my best efforts — and bring my critical capacities and opposing motivation to bear in a way that leaves me ready to take countermeasures at the first opportunity. I control myself, then, even in acting under this kind of compulsion, though my control is not normal and not determined by the ideals that I think should govern the behavior in question. More precisely, speaking for the candidate is not determined by my political ideals, though protecting loved ones — which is something I do *by* so speaking — is determined by values I hold dear. Thus, the overall governing standards — standards of the protection of others — are mine; if they were not, I would lack even the impaired autonomy the case exhibits. But they are standards I consider inappropriate to my conduct, which I think should be governed by my political beliefs. Still, in contrast to someone whose behavior is not a response to reasons at all — for instance because of brain manipulation that produces irresistibly strong and wholehearted motivation to give the speech — I retain a measure of self-government. I have been forced to pay a price to save people I love; but unlike the thoroughly manipulated agent, I both know what I am doing and am so disposed that if the price were unacceptably high, I would not pay it.[6]

Autonomy has been associated at least as strongly with independence as with freedom. But independence is not sufficient either. The thoughtlessly self-indulgent person, like one who acts entirely on whims, may be quite independent without being autonomous. Such people are not under the control of others; autonomy requires more than the absence of *external* control. That notion is even more negative than the concept of independence. It is true, however, that independence is necessary for (full) autonomy; and other things equal, the more independence one has, the greater one's autonomy.

Internal and External Threats to Autonomy

We can achieve further understanding of autonomy by exploring the sorts of things that tend to undermine it, and how they do so. I shall briefly consider three: compulsion, dissociation, and weakness of will (incontinence). Each can reduce autonomy as a general capacity of the agent; but their most direct application is to individual acts, and I focus on those.

Since autonomy normally implies freedom and independence, it should be no surprise that it is undermined by compulsion. This can be external, as where one acts on severe threats, or internal, as where paranoiac fears drive one to desperate behavior in which one is "out of control." Some external compulsions are coercions, others not; some benevolent, as with parentalistic prevention of folly, others malicious. In any of these cases, one can retain a measure of autonomy, especially in the manner in which one acts; but clearly, the higher the degree of compulsion, the lower the degree of autonomy, other things equal.

Dissociation is a subtler threat to autonomy. So far as there is one person in cases of, for instance, a split personality, such a dissociated condition tends to reduce autonomy, either because one element is in control, or because none is, or because there is an unsatisfactory division of control, as where the agent acts on whatever impulse is stronger at the time, without due regard for the cost to any other constituency in the divided self. Self-deception is a special case of dissociation; a self-deceived agent can be significantly autonomous, but self-deception tends to impair autonomy. Particularly where behavior is determined by the need to maintain self-deception, for instance when a cancer patient self-deceived about the prognosis has to behave "normally," the actions in question are imperfectly autonomous. There is much complexity in the way dissociation affects autonomy; and there are doubtless times when the effect is minor, or for the good. Still, other things equal, dissociation reduces autonomy.

Similar points hold for incontinence. For instance, acting against one's better judgment is typically a paradigm of a failure of autonomy.[7] Typically, such judgment represents the agent's self-legislative directive, and going against it, as where passion takes over, indicates a deficiency in autonomous control. The agent is commonly regretful about the action; and people acting incontinently may even *feel* that they cannot control themselves. The impulses or motives that determine action may or may not be felt to be alien, but they are not normally those the agent takes as properly directing action. A good account of autonomy, then, should make it clear why incontinence, like compulsion and dissociation, tends to undermine autonomy.

Neutrality with Respect to Normative Theories

If autonomy is important in ethical and political discussions, that is not because it is a notion crucial for any one normative position, such as Kantianism. Far from it: the notion seems to express an ideal for which every serious moral or social-political theory should have a place, in at least two ways. First, it should be *satisfiable* by autonomous agents: its demands should be realizable by an autonomous agent, as opposed, say, to requiring such extreme self-control that they can be met only by agents rigidly programmed to perform the required actions. Second, the theory should (potentially) guide autonomous agents: a serious moral or social-political theory should be one by which autonomous agents can direct their lives. Like Kantians, utilitarians and other theorists should articulate both a theory that can effectively guide autonomous agents and a notion of autonomy that provides an ideal for moral agents. As this suggests, autonomy is plausibly conceived as, if not a virtuous trait, then at least a generally desirable capacity for agents to have. This chapter does not argue that it is a kind of virtue, in part because of difficulties about what constitutes a virtue, but the points that emerge should bring out why autonomy is at least naturally considered a virtue.

Neutrality among different moral theories does not, however, imply value neutrality, in the sense of non-normative status. Nothing I have said implies that autonomy lacks intrinsic value, or even, as the Kantian tradition tends to hold, moral value.[8] It can be an ideal for agents as well as a constraint on theories. On the other hand, the notion seems analyzable without presupposing that it has intrinsic value.

For instance, whether an agent is autonomous is to be decided on the basis of what we think of as facts: about beliefs, desires, behavioral capacities, and so forth. Suppose, however, that autonomy does have value, whether moral or non-moral. This would not imply that only a narrow range of moral theories can account for its value. Autonomy can represent an ideal morally worth achieving, or a condition of character worth valuing, even though neither an account of the concept nor someone's actual possession of the trait implies any specific normative claims.

Autonomy and the Internalism-Externalism Controversy

There is another important respect in which the notion of autonomy is neutral with respect to moral theories. While it implies a measure of self-government, it is intelligible apart from a commitment to either motivational internalism or motivational externalism. In the sense that concerns me here, the former is the view that some degree of motivation is intrinsic (and in that sense internal) to a (first-person) practical judgment — one favoring a particular action, whether (say) on a moral, prudential, or merely conative basis — and the latter denies this, usually on the ground that some desire independent of the judgment is needed as a ground of motivation to act in accord with that judgment.[9] Granted, the notion of governing oneself has clearest application where one's practical judgments not only show the direction conduct is to take but also have the power to lead one in that direction: to close the gap between *ought* and *is*. A legislature is most clearly in control if it has its own executive powers. I believe Kant saw this; certainly he took reason to have both the normative power to determine what we ought to do and the motivational power to produce that conduct. It may be that part of what led him to hold an internalist view was the naturalness with which it fits the notion of autonomy as self-government.

Still, just as a legislature may need an executive, an autonomous agent can be one in whom motivation to act on the relevant judgments is not internal to those judgments but requires a cooperating desire. It is true that the autonomous agent must be *capable* of wanting what reason directs, but this weak requirement is scarcely controversial. Moreover, even those who insist that desire need not listen to reason rarely hold that it may be utterly deaf to reason, or even persistently uninfluenced by reason where this implies one's lacking so much as an inclination to act in accord with one's own reasoned judgments. It *is* implicit in the notion of autonomous action that motivation for it does not come predominantly from certain external forces, such as threats to one's life or, less dramatically, an upbringing that makes one a mere follower of society. This negative requirement is a matter of independence. But if, for instance, an agent will actually keep a promise only if a desire to do what is right cooperates with the judgment that keeping it is the only option right in the circumstances, keeping the promise may still express autonomy. The required desire, after all, is not only on the side of a principle underlying the agent's autonomy but is also capable of being reasonable; this desire is not an unrelated passion that just happens to push in the same direction as the judgment. Moral ideals can figure in the content of desire, and it is arguable that in a fully rational agent they are also pursued by the agent for good reasons and not as a result of mere social conditioning. Thus, if practical judgment should motivate only with the cooperation of desire, the motivation thereby received need not represent an alien force whose influence threatens autonomy.

There is, to be sure, a kind of internalism implicit in autonomy. If we cast the issue broadly, in terms of the motivating power of reason, and we then speak of certain judgments or principles being endorsed by *practical* reason, we might plausibly argue that on the basis of this endorsement, the holding — or at least the thinking — of these judgments or principles *is* intrinsically motivating. For how could the endorsement by reason be practical if it does not imply motivation? Perhaps it is not in every autonomous agent that there is such a strong endorsement of judgments or principles by practical reason; but there are kinds of autonomy (including, on some views, the paradigm cases) that imply such endorsement and hence imply the limited internalism just sketched.

This line is plausible; it may indeed be unassailable, given some conceptions of practical reason, perhaps including Kant's. But confusion may easily arise if we also take practical reason, as we normally do, to be, qua reason, concerned with discovering truth. For even from the discovery of a normative truth about what one should do, it does not follow that one is motivated to do it: grasp of a proposition is one thing; motivation to act accordingly is another. I prefer to conceive reason as, in the most basic cases, directed toward propositions, to grant that reason is *normatively practical* when it endorses practical propositions, such as judgments expressing moral obligations, and to deny that it must be *motivationally practical*, in the sense that practical judgments representing it *entail* motivation to act accordingly. There is a trade-off here: if practical reason is taken to be necessarily motivating, its practicality is made prominent, but the capacity in question is easily assimilated to will, in which case its connection with the grasp of truth is attenuated; and if practical reason is taken to be wholly concerned with truth rather than action, its connection with reason is made prominent but its practicality can be lost. My view attempts to integrate both elements. It locates the practicality of reason mainly in the normative content and guiding role of practical judgments, yet takes these to be justifiable by rational cognitive procedures.[10] Consistently with this view, one might distinguish full from partial endorsement by practical reason: full endorsement of an action implies both practical judgment favoring it and adequate motivation to produce it; partial endorsement implies only the former. Practical judgment unsupported by adequate motivation often bespeaks weakness of will; adequate motivation to produce the action, without the judgment or at least a disposition to hold it, may bespeak unbridled desire. Reason without motivation is powerless; motivation unguided by reason is blind.

We might go a step further in accommodating what is plausible in motivational internalism. There are two points here, one bearing on autonomy in relation to rational agents, the other concerning behavioral coincidence between what one would expect given motivational internalism and what would be expected from a normal autonomous agent externalistically conceived. First, it may be that rational agents are so constructed that they necessarily *tend* to act in accordance with their practical and moral judgments. This qualified internalism may derive from the plausible view that rational agents must have desires in line with certain of their normative beliefs, above all those about what they should do. Suppose the thesis is correct and hence that in rational agents, and thus autonomous agents so far as they are rational, there is such an integration between practical judgment and behavior. If autonomous agents as such must be rational, we may conclude that a kind of motivational internalism is *true of them*, even if not true simpliciter.[11] The second (and related) point is this: even on an externalist view, the agents who are most autonomous tend to act as if their practical judgments had motivational power; for regardless of what *grounds* their motivation, say judgment alone or desire, these agents will count as autonomous only insofar as their behavior properly conforms with the directives of their practical reason. Whatever else it is, autonomy requires an integration between conduct and practical reason.

My stance is qualifiedly externalist: motivation is not intrinsic to practical judgment, yet the latter *tends* to produce it, and in a fully rational agent either the judgment or some cooperating (or common) cause will produce it. One may wonder what practical power this view of practical judgment allows reason to have that is, so to speak, all its own and distinct from the theoretical power to grasp practical truth. It may still guide action: even if I keep a promise from a desire to meet my obligation, my keeping it is guided by — and would not occur without — my (practical) belief or judgment that keeping my promises is obligatory. Belief is required to put the action in the *path* of desire, even if belief does not motivate the action apart from so directing it; and it may play this guiding role whether or not it is embodied in a conscious judging, as it is where it emerges from moral reasoning. Similarly, where a legislature governs only with the help of an executive, the executive may still be responsive to the legislature and indeed unwilling to take certain actions without it.

The guiding role of practical judgment just described is strong enough to explain in part how an action can *express* autonomy and not merely *conform* with it: autonomous actions are done in part from an appropriate judgment or belief, not merely in accordance with its content. But not just any action grounded in a practical judgment is an expression of autonomy. Even if an agent is highly autonomous and, on the basis of appropriate principles of action, makes a judgment in favor of A-ing, the action must be non-waywardly produced by the judgment, as opposed to a merely accidental result of the judgment together with fortuitous circumstances. This is in part to say that the action is not a mere effect of, but also a response to, that judgment; and the action must be under the agent's *control*. That, in turn, is partly a matter of the agent's openness to reasons for or against the deed, and hence such that counter-reasons could deter or at least retard the agent in performing it.[12]

Second-Order Attitudes

Does autonomy require, as some philosophers have thought, that the agent have second-order desires, for instance a want to act on moral motives, or other second-order propositional attitudes, such as a conviction that it is important to form true beliefs as a basis of action?[13] Plainly, autonomous agents must have the *capacity* to reflect on their desires, for example to ask why they want to influence people; and they should be able to form beliefs about a goodly range of their first-order desires and other first-order propositional attitudes, say a belief that they must acquire both correct views about what morality requires and motivation to act accordingly. Thus, mere agency does not imply autonomy, just as mere state action toward a population, or even a state's de facto controlling it, does not imply governing it. Nonetheless, as important as second-order attitudes can be for autonomy, it seems possible without them. Suppose that an agent does not in fact have any such second-order elements. The agent may still have certain appropriate action-guiding principles, sufficient motivation to act on them, and a grasp of their basis and mutual coherence. This capacity may be at best rare in the absence of such second-order elements; but in a sufficiently unselfconscious life, it is possible without them. Think of a simple person who is taught how one should live and uncritically accepts the relevant standards (some of Tolstoy's peasants might be like this). Think of a wholeheartedly religious person guided by unquestioning devotion to the principles of a simple faith.

If the agent has the capacity to reflect on the desires that are to be governed by the relevant principles, it is not necessary to have actually formed beliefs or desires concerning them. One might be such that if certain questions arose, say because one discovered a weak-willed failure to abide by a commandment, one would reflect on oneself in second-order language. One might then "identify" with the basic desires one articulates, though this is not inevitable; the point is that the identification needed to feel the desires are "one's own" does not require prior second-order reflection. In any case, not everyone suffers these failures, and not all weakness of will produces second-order reflection. The kind of behavior crucial for a minimal degree of autonomy is action (at least internal action) governed in the right way; that government readily leads to second-order reflection, but need not.

One might argue that just as a legislature must deliberate, an autonomous agent must reflect on goals or ideals. Perhaps this is so. But one can reflect on *what* one wants without thinking about one's *wanting* of it: one might instead consider, in first-order terms, what is good, what one should do, and how we should live together. A goal *is* indeed something wanted; but it need not be — and in the phenomenologically simplest cases is not — considered by the agent *as* wanted. For a self-consciously autonomous agent it is otherwise, but it is a contingent matter whether autonomy implies being self-conscious in this way; and thinking about one's wants, even when critical, does not entail forming second-order desires regarding them. Perhaps autonomy does require some measure of self-conscious reflection on one's desires, but this cannot be inferred from the plausible but weaker point that autonomy (or at least its expression) requires a measure of reflection on ends of one's action.

To take an epistemological analogy, suppose it were said that epistemically rational persons must have beliefs to the effect that their first order-beliefs are justified, or are suitably often reliably produced. We might expect such beliefs in a philosopher. But imagine that I simply *hold* beliefs formed in response to experience and am in fact guided by reasonable evidential standards. Must I also have second-order beliefs of the kind imagined? Surely not, though I would have a readiness to form them in the face of, for example, skeptical queries. No doubt I would often think about whether certain claims are really true or certain evidence is cogent, but one can think about these objects of belief without forming beliefs about one's beliefs. Similarly, I can surely think about the objects of my wants and the standards that guide my desires and conduct without thinking about the wants themselves or my attitudes toward the standards. It is similar with autonomy: the condition itself, as opposed to its self-conscious possession or the philosophical defense of it, is not necessarily a second-order phenomenon.

The Scope of Autonomy

Autonomy is most commonly thought to manifest itself in the control of action, and action is indeed the primary domain in which it must operate. But its scope is wider — or so I shall argue. Let us consider three cases: the propositional attitudes, emotions, and traits of character.

That autonomy must extend to at least one propositional attitude — intention — should be apparent from the close connection between intention and action. Suppose I incontinently form the intention to do something of which I disapprove, but I do not get to do it because I am deterred by a benevolent friend. The formation of this intention would normally show that I lacked adequate control of myself, even if fortuitous circumstances saved me from the incontinent deed. The case of belief is similar in at least one respect. Imagine that I dispassionately judge the evidence to favor overwhelmingly a view I find distasteful, yet I go on believing the view to be false. Here, arguably, I exhibit a failure of *intellectual autonomy* similar to the kind exhibited by weakness of will: I do not appropriately govern myself but am instead dominated by influences I might hope to control.

One might think that since autonomy apparently requires governing one's desires in the sense of control over what one does as a result of them, it should limit what desires one *has*, rather in the way it should limit the intentions one has. But this is not so. While one might hope to prevent oneself from having irrational desires and, especially, shameful ones, the mere having of suitably weak desires does not imply impaired autonomy. It is perhaps uncharacteristic of the most autonomous agents, as it certainly is of the most rational persons, to have significant numbers of even weak irrational desires to do things that are against their better judgment; but that is nevertheless consistent with a high degree of autonomy. Perhaps this is because, unlike intention, mere desire does not express the overall disposition of the will, and is thus less likely to yield action.

We can now see how autonomy might be expected to apply to emotion and traits of character. For virtually any emotion, there is some degree of its possession and some set of circumstances such that one's having it to that degree, in those circumstances, does not interfere with one's self-government. On the other hand, virtually any emotion can impair one's self-government, and autonomy apparently implies a capacity to prevent emotional interferences of certain kinds. With traits of character (which may be an even more heterogeneous group than emotions), similar points apply. Think of cowardice, a trait that must be controlled by an autonomous agent somewhat as the associated emotion of fear must be. Loyalty, on the other hand, is a more complex case: while cowardice can impair autonomy no matter *what* one's goals (assuming they may require taking risks), some agents might set little store by loyalty. For normal people, however, it is quite relevant to autonomy: too little, for example, and one cannot meet one's standards of interpersonal conduct. Far more could be said about all these cases, but there is no need to discuss the details. My aim here is simply to suggest that the scope of autonomy is not just over actions, and that an adequate account, even if it takes action as the central domain of autonomy, must range much wider.

Principled Self-Control

I have stressed the extent to which autonomous agents control their behavior (and, at least indirectly, a suitable proportion of their dispositions relevant to it). But mere control is not enough: autonomy requires a kind of *principled control*. The agent must act, or at least be disposed to act, sufficiently often, by policy and not mere whim, or at least on the basis of certain (perhaps implicit) principles, ideals, or standards.[14] Does this imply that the concept of autonomy is not normatively neutral after all? It is not normative in the usual sense in which the instantiation of the concept in question implies some normative truth, say that the agent is morally upright. But the concept does seem *indirectly normative*, in the sense that someone to whom it applies must be committed to a normative standard (even if only in the way a non-cognitivist is — the point here leaves the agent metaethically free). In the former case, the normativity is built directly into the concept; in the latter, it is filtered through the intentionality of the agent to whom the concept applies.

The positive idea is partly this. Autonomous agents must be able to feel that they have made a certain kind of *mistake*, or have done something in *violation* of some principle or ideal or standard of theirs, where the mistake is more than one of failing to get something they wanted and can extend to self-criticism *for* wanting or seeking the wrong thing. No particular standard of right or wrong is presupposed, but autonomous agents must be capable of a sense of living up to, or failing to live up to, a principle, ideal, or standard that they take as a basis of self-appraisal. It should make sense for them to say, for example, 'I don't like the way my life is going; I've got to reorder it'. Imagine a capricious and self-indulgent agent with both desires and beliefs about how to satisfy them, but otherwise no principles. This could be more automatism than autonomy; the agent can make adjustments in the feedback loop but does not really set the agenda. Reason gives eyes to otherwise blind desire, but it plays no role in determining what is ultimately worthy of pursuit. It is not that in an autonomous agent reason must dictate what particular ends are worthwhile; but it must play a part in laying out a coherent pattern that guides one's conduct and makes sense of it as the "project" (or a suitable range of projects) of a person with identity over time.

Part of the point here may be put in terms of another contrast. Autonomous agents must have a sense of what kind of persons they want to be, and not just of what they want among the experiences, possessions, and consumables that the world offers. No specific category of persons must occur in their thinking about themselves, but the principles, ideals, or standards autonomy requires must have a kind of generality that goes with a sense of one's identity. This applies to overall autonomy, of course. There is also *domain-specific autonomy*: autonomy in intellectual matters, politics, religion, social relations, and so on. There the point is similar: autonomous agents will have a sense of what kind of citizens (for example) they want to be. A highly autonomous person exhibits autonomy in many domains; and other things equal, the more numerous the domains of one's autonomy, the greater it is.

Autonomy exists in degrees. Its extent depends on many factors, some of which have been suggested: the rootedness of the agent's self-governing principles, ideals, or standards; the extent to which the agent reflectively identifies with them (or tends to); the degree of the agent's independence; the number of domains in which the autonomy is exhibited; and the proportion of important conduct which the principles, ideals, or standards control. (If there is no absolute notion of important conduct appropriate here, we can relativize and speak of, say, what is important for moral or intellectual autonomy.) I cannot now go into detail; but the guiding idea is that one cannot govern oneself by arbitrary commands. There must be principles, ideals, or standards that in some sense define a regime and provide a coherent pattern in which one can locate and evaluate oneself. Arbitrary power over oneself, however successful in conforming behavior to the judgment of the moment, is not autonomy.

II. An Instrumentalist Conception of Autonomy

With the results of section I in mind, let us consider how autonomy is to be conceived on a pure instrumentalist view of practical reason. It is useful, I think, to regard this view as a kind of functionalism about practical rationality.[15] The job of reason is to serve desire, not to lay down constraints on what should be (intrinsically) wanted. Nothing is intrinsically desirable in the normative sense, that is, intrinsically worthy of desire. What is desirable is so only relative to specific persons and only insofar as it will satisfy one or more intrinsic desires they already have. It may be desirable objectively, because it will in *fact* satisfy an intrinsic desire; or subjectively, because, on the person's *beliefs*, it will do so; or in some qualified way — for instance because, on the person's justified beliefs, it will do so. Intrinsic desires are the subjective foundations of action. If one feels that this notion of subjectivity does not subtract enough from the usual, less relativistic implications of 'foundations', one might say that (1) intrinsic desires are foundational only psychologically — only in not being instrumentally subordinate to any other desires — and (2), it is not being grounded in them that makes an action rational, but simply its coherence with them.

In the instrumentalist framework, autonomy is above all a matter of keeping one's behavior suitably subordinate to the task of desire satisfaction. Subordination to (intrinsic) desire is the only principle of government. If one subscribes to moral principles *and* is motivated to act accordingly, then, by virtue of that motivation, moral conduct may be required to realize one's autonomy. It may be required, but it need not be; for if one wants self-satisfaction far more than to act morally, and sees a conflict between the two, then one's rational self-control should direct one's behavior toward the first goal, not the second: more, in the sense of satisfying a stronger desire, is always better; there are no quality constraints. Because the control is rational, one's autonomy is presumably served by it. If it seems otherwise, that may be because, as noncognitivists often point out, we tend to think of moral judgments as producing or accompanied by desires strong enough to override their normal competitors. We thus suspect, say, weakness of will when a moral person acts immorally. If moral judgments produce intrinsic motivation, then they should figure in the foundations of conduct in much the way intrinsic desires do: not by virtue of their *content*— for there are no intrinsic goods or items of intrinsic moral value — but as basic elements whose service is the only proper business of practical reason.

The instrumentalist idea I am sketching, then, is that since autonomy is roughly self-government in accordance with reason, and since reason functions solely to direct us toward the satisfaction of intrinsic desires, paradigmatically autonomous agents are those who are instrumentally efficient in finding means to their basic ends, that is, to satisfaction of their intrinsic desires. Endorsement of principles is possible, but it is inductively based on experience of what satisfies desire, not normatively grounded in judgments of what is desirable. I may adopt the principle that one should help one's neighbors because I have discovered that my acting on it satisfies my desires, but not because I think such conduct is good or obligatory. My upbringing may give me attachments to all manner of ideals, but none has any rational *claim* on me save through an instrumental connection with my intrinsic desires. This is, of course, a description of pure instrumentalism. Particularly for anyone who is not committed to pure instrumentalism and considers intrinsic desire satisfaction a good, it is natural to refine the view. Let me explain this and then proceed to a more sophisticated instrumentalist view of autonomy.

Suppose that my intrinsic wants are very modest, both in scope — since I have few and their objects are modest — and in strength, since there is nothing I want ardently. Then, while it may be easy to satisfy them, I may be missing satisfactions of desires I would have if I simply looked clearly at what the world offers and thereby came to want things I do not now want. In the light of this possibility, it is natural to modify the pure theory: actions are rational, and thus of the kind the autonomous agent should aim at, insofar as they satisfy intrinsic wants one does have *or would have* given a proper response to awareness of (or perhaps reflection on) available options.[16] Thus, if I take an apple when I would have preferred a peach had I only seen it in the refrigerator, I have not acted rationally (or fully rationally). In short, autonomous agents should seek as much desire satisfaction as they can, even if this implies pursuing things not yet desired or producing readily satisfiable desires.

Another possibility is this: first, assume that we would all, on reflection, intrinsically want to maximize our desire satisfaction, including the satisfaction of certain hypothetical wants we would believe, on reflection, we would (or might) acquire; and second, give, to the *disposition* to have this maximization want, the authority to serve as a basis of rational criticism in anyone in whom the want is not present to provide this maximization of desire standard directly, as a subjective foundation of action. Then, only actions that maximize want satisfaction will be fully rational (or rational at all, if rationality is not construed comparatively). That will be so, at least, if the maximization want is, or would be if we appropriately reflected on it, our strongest desire.[17] In short, autonomous agents should satisfy a particular hypothetical desire, the maximization want; it is indeed their *standard* of rationality. This view may be extensionally equivalent to the former, multiple hypothetical desire view, at least in that both might lead to the same actions. On the former, successful autonomous agents act in a way that in fact produces maximal desire satisfaction; on the latter, they so act in the service of a *desire* to produce that. Since the single-basic-desire view indicates the fundamental goal of action directly, it provides, if not a different standard, at least a simpler unifying picture.

On either of these strengthened instrumentalist positions, autonomous agents are not merely efficient with respect to *present* desires. They are attentive to hypothetical desires they would have under appropriate conditions, or — in the case of a posited desire, or posited disposition to desire, maximum intrinsic want satisfaction — attentive to opportunities to act in a way that maximizes desire satisfaction. To efficiency, then, we now add *prudence* and a measure of enlightened self-interest. At least in matters felt to be important, the agent considers the future and surveys options before acting, to see if some are better than those attractive on the basis of present desires and beliefs. Such agents are likely to have more in the way of principles for getting what they want than those who simply act efficiently in the service of desires actually possessed, at least if these desires do not include such second-order wants as the desire to maximize want satisfaction, or functionally similar, sweeping first-order desires, say wanting to maximize pleasure.

III. An Objectivist Conception of Autonomy

If instrumentalism denies that there are intrinsic goods, and certainly that, if there are, reason can identify them in such a way that it is rational to want them for their own sake, axiological objectivism affirms that it is rational both to believe that some things are intrinsically good and to want them for their own sake. Aristotle's eudaemonism and Kant's doctrine of the unqualified goodness of a good will come to mind as cases in point. For our purposes, it is possible to abstract from the metaphysics of the issue and concentrate on its epistemology. For just as there can be rational beliefs apparently about the external world even if there is no external world, so, even if there is nothing intrinsically good, there can be rational intrinsic desires. Thus, objectivists — at least those who are epistemologically internalist — would disagree with the instrumentalist about rational desire even if forced to admit that our rational desires might be, as it were, hallucinatory: subjectively well grounded but lacking an external good to render them objectively correct.

The point that an internalist objectivist would press is that the rationality of certain desires, like the justifiedness of certain beliefs, is grounded in what is accessible to the agent's (introspective and a priori) reflection even if, in the end, nothing external underlies those grounds.[18] This view can go with coherentism or foundationalism and with empiricism or rationalism; neither internalism nor objectivism presupposes any one of these. In constructing an objectivist notion of autonomy, then, I assume on the objectivist's behalf only that there are rational intrinsic desires; I leave open whether their objects are in fact intrinsically good. This allows for the possibility that a non-instrumentalist view is most plausible when severed from the realist ontological commitments often associated with it.[19]

There is much disagreement about whether it can be shown that rational intrinsic desires are possible. For the sake of argument I assume that they are and that (a priori) we can know or at least have good reason to believe this,[20] and proceed to the implications of the view for autonomy. The central point is that reason, on this view, is normatively practical, roughly in the sense that (a priori) reflection can deliver at least rational judgments (even if not knowledge) of intrinsic value, say judgments to the effect that pleasure is good and pain is bad. Whether reason is also motivationally practical, in the sense that an overall judgment favoring an action entails motivation to perform it, is left open, though it may be granted that in a fully rational person it does.[21]

If reason can deliver rational judgments of intrinsic value, then, through reflection, we can reasonably arrive at ideals of conduct, at least on the plausible assumption that we should act so as to realize intrinsic values of which we are aware (or rationally take ourselves to be aware). If, in addition, reflection can produce justified beliefs of moral principles, agents can also endorse these principles as standards of self-government. If, beyond this, there really are things of intrinsic value and really are moral truths, then (if they are discoverable by reason) agents can not only govern their behavior accordingly but also, in so doing, conform their conduct to features of reality, just as instrumentalists see us as doing when we take a successful means to a desired end. In the one case, our conduct is an attempt to realize an objective intrinsic value; in the other, it is an effort to satisfy a subjective value — to realize the objects of whatever intrinsic desires we have.

On the objectivist view, autonomy is roughly self-government under principles, ideals, or standards that are endorsed, even if without self-conscious reflection on them, by reason. The endorsement may come from simply abiding by the principles, ideals, or standards with a sense of approval, but it will often arise from, or at least be confirmed by, reflection. Other things being equal, the more rational and psychologically stable the agent's endorsement of the principles, ideals, or standards, and the greater the extent to which the agent's conduct is under their control, the more autonomous the agent is. The paradigmatically autonomous agent is ruled by reason. We are fallible, however, and we can adopt a principle — sound or unsound — in an unreasonable way, or reasonably adopt a mistaken one. Reflection may indeed reveal impersonal truths; but on what seems the most plausible construal of the objectivist view, the epistemologically internalist version, these truths are grasped, directly or indirectly, on grounds accessible to reflection. In the well-integrated person, they can, through such reflection, be internalized and thus become part of the agent who is in control. Desires are inputs one is to consider, but reason functions both to direct conduct to their satisfaction *and* to guide the "passions" themselves (roughly, intrinsic desires) toward what seems to one to be truly desirable. This guiding, directive role implies causal, even if not motivational, power. Particularly through our actively thinking about goals and obligations, reason regulates conduct. This truth may partly underlie motivational internalism.

There is one further point to be made in this section. While the objectivist view takes autonomy to imply principled self-control, it does not dictate any particular principles. Part of the force of calling the notion of autonomy only indirectly normative is to emphasize that while autonomous agents must be committed to some standard, principle, or ideal, *we*, in calling them autonomous, are not committed to it. Someone scrupulously self-governed under standards we think wrong can with perfect sense be called autonomous. It is not that the objectivist doubts that any standards of conduct are sound, or at least objectively preferable to alternative standards. The point is that autonomy does not presuppose any highly specific standards of conduct. Objectivists think there *are* sound (or at least justifiable) principles; but they may be both fallibilists about knowledge of them and pluralists about the range and variety of fundamental ones.[22]

IV. Autonomy and the Role of Reason

The instrumentalist and objectivist views of autonomy differ markedly. Above all, instrumentalism sees reason as subject to desire; objectivism sees desire as subject to reason.[23] I mean 'normatively subject': these are differences over the proper role of reason, not about its causal powers. Regarding the actual effects of reason and desire on each other, there need be no disagreement. Both views can be motivationally internalist or externalist. Both would also grant that we are biased in favor of taking as intrinsically good what we intrinsically desire, and that we at least tend to want things that we reflectively judge to be intrinsically desirable. But whereas the instrumentalist sees this bias as the normative ontologizing of mere desire — that is, we call things intrinsically good because we want them for their own sake and so cannot instrumentally explain their appeal to us — the objectivist sees it as a natural result of the often good integration between intrinsic desire and the cognitive grasp of its normatively proper objects — that is, we want things for their own sake because we in some way grasp their intrinsic goodness, or at least are justified in thinking we do.

Is there any reason to prefer one of these conceptions of autonomy over the other? If we take seriously the contrast between government and mere control, and certainly if we suppose that government should be guided by the ideal of achieving stability, peace, well-being, justice, or the like for the subjects it rules, then there is some reason to prefer the objectivist view. For on the instrumentalist conception, good government is simply efficiency in getting the subjects what they want. They cannot want the wrong thing: they have no constitution to guide them; and if they do not care about their education or culture or morality, this does not matter unless it interferes with the sum total of their satisfactions. There is no substantive principle of government; the specific aim of the governor varies with the content of the desires that are to be satisfied. The only general principle, apart from consistency constraints, is that one must serve one's desires *whatever they are*. If today the people want only sports and tomorrow they want only libraries, one must quickly retool.

It is not even clear how instrumentalism can discount, as a basis for autonomy, desires artificially induced by manipulators, so long as the desires are intrinsic and of sufficient strength not to be overriden by competitors.[24] For the objectivist, on the other hand, there are at least two contrasting points, one substantive, one procedural. First, not just any intrinsic desire need be rational, or for any other reason a good basis of action. Second, desires produced by manipulation are suspect, in part because there is no reason to expect them to meet the substantive constraints on rationality, whatever they are. For the instrumentalist, by contrast, why should the origin of my desires, or their compelled alignment with someone else's, matter? If they are mine, they define what is rational for me and hence what, as an autonomous agent, I should seek. But surely agents with externally implanted controlling desires are not autonomous; they are under the control of the manipulator.

The problem is not solved by noting that autonomous agents, conceived on instrumentalist lines, are likely to have standards of behavior that would demand resisting desires imposed upon them by others; for the (pure) theory provides no ground for making such standards necessary constituents in autonomy. These standards themselves must come from desires the individual already has; and if one finds oneself intrinsically and irresistibly attracted to domination by others, one's autonomy must be subordinated to this desire. From experience in satisfying one's actual desires, one can inductively generalize to principles of action, say to rules about how best to satisfy one's deepest desires; but there is no permissible appeal to standards supplied by reason or any source other than desire. Successful generalization rests not on formulation or extension of normative standards but on stable conative patterns, such as repeated satisfaction of basic desires through sports or music or travel, and these patterns may or may not yield dissatisfaction with external domination.[25]

One might object that this contrast is exaggerated. Granted, for instrumentalism one's autonomy is a capacity to subordinate one's conduct to one's strongest desire(s), and these can change. Still, objectivists must admit that one's overall judgment(s) can also change. The foundations of autonomy, then, can shift in either case. Furthermore, both frameworks are fallibilist: an instrumentalist can want unwisely in terms of actual satisfaction of desires, and an objectivist can make foolish practical judgments, say by ignoring available evidence about what one should do. These points of comparison are important, but a crucial difference remains. The objectivist framework can offer non-instrumental criteria for sound practical judgments and for rational intrinsic desire, but apart from mere consistency constraints, a genuine instrumentalism can provide neither: it has no standard of rational (intrinsic) desire. Instead, the desires one *has* determine what constitutes correct action. The objectivist theory derives the rationality and correctness of action from that of judgment and desire; the instrumentalist theory derives the rationality and correctness of action from that of instrumental judgment applied to basic desires which (apart from their internal, and — perhaps — mutual consistency) are not subject to assessment as rational or irrational. Instrumentalism can partially account for one element in autonomy: independence from others and from certain other outside influences. But it cannot account for what seems the required independence from one's own desires, for it is they that provide the standards for their own governance.

It is also useful to ask how well instrumentalism can explain why autonomy is impaired or eliminated by the kinds of undermining elements considered in section I. We have already noted its difficulty in explaining why certain externally imposed (intrinsic) desires pose a threat. The problem is not in principle different if they are so strong that they exercise a compelling force. Intrinsic desires are no less masters of conduct when they have the power to enforce it. As to dissociation, so long as I am efficiently satisfying my strongest desires, why should it matter if part of me is alienated from the gratification I achieve, or if, in close succession, I pursue incompatible projects to the detriment of them all? Yet even if I get a great quantity of desire satisfaction, my autonomy would still be impaired; it would be as if, far from any stable standards governing me, one regime after another takes over, depending on contingent circumstances.

Weakness of will may pose an even greater problem for the instrumentalist view. For it is usually intrinsic desires, for instance appetitive and emotional ones, that overcome one's best judgment when incontinence occurs. Why isn't this a legitimate overthrow of attempted tyranny, rather than an unwarranted insurrection? To be sure, as I think Hume saw, the calm passions underlying judgment may represent a greater quantity of *unaroused* (or perhaps temporarily ignored or forgotten) intrinsic desire than the agitated passion that overcomes judgment. But even if we ignore the issue of whether this move implies that desire satisfaction itself has intrinsic value, this is not the only case of incontinence that seems to undermine autonomy.

It may seem that with slight modification instrumentalism would allow substantive constraints if only by virtue of positing certain second-order wants or other second-order attitudes. There are at least two major cases here.

First, one might require that autonomous agents have a second-order want to have the *sorts* of first-order intrinsic wants they do have. But — leaving aside that such second-order wants do not seem necessary for autonomy — what grounds the authority of *this* want? For instrumentalism, it is at best just one more intrinsic want. The *order* of a want gives it no privilege; the metaphor of a higher perspective carries no normative authority. Nor will it help to substitute an attitude like approval, or even a considered evaluative belief. For attitudes and beliefs about what sorts of desires we should have can acquire authority only from our basic desires: there is no intrinsic good by which to judge the suitability of those desires; satisfying them is, functionally, the only good we have to guide us. Take an epistemological analogy again: if there is nothing to make my non-inferential (basic) first-order beliefs justified, my possessing second-order beliefs endorsing them cannot by itself confer justification upon them.

Second, an instrumentalist may posit a higher-order want for maximum want satisfaction. But — as I think has not been generally appreciated by instrumentalists — even this is not a want that rational persons *must* have; it is just one they are perhaps disposed to have on reflection. If we were to say that a rational person must have it, the question would then arise whether we are not positing some kind of intrinsic value. Granted, a normal person must have intrinsic wants;[26] but none need be about *other* wants, and the instrumentalist is not entitled to claim that every rational agent will value, or even want to maximize, want-satisfaction.

Despite the plausibility of the second, maximizing strategy, it is surely unsuccessful even if the posited want is universal among rational persons. If I believe that nothing is of intrinsic value, why should I want the satisfaction, or especially a maximal quantity of satisfaction, of my actual or potential first-order wants? Why need I want any more than the objects of the first-order intrinsic wants I find in myself? And why should I, as an instrumentalist, believe that rational agents in general ought to want more than that? If there is a case for my wanting more, such as my enjoying the satisfaction of those wants I have, we must at least ask why one should not equally require rational persons to want, say, pleasure and the avoidance of pain, which are surely at least as intuitively worthy of desire as the sheer satisfaction of intrinsic desires irrespective of their objects or origins. Indeed, if maximum want satisfaction itself is what rational persons should above all intrinsically want, presumably they should try to cause themselves to have as many as possible of the most readily satisfiable strong wants they can get, regardless of their objects, and not excluding objects to which they *now* have aversions. But neither instrumentalism nor any other serious account of practical reason endorses this.

If instrumentalism cannot explain why rational persons should have any wants with positive content, perhaps there are at least certain negative constraints it may impose, say that a rational person does not suffer from envy, construed as involving an intrinsic want that others *not* have more (in one or another respect) than oneself of what one considers good.[27] The envious person will tend to take at least somewhat less provided that is the only way to prevent others from having more. Whatever one may want, it does seem irrational to be willing to take less of it if only others will also have less. Suppose this is so. That *may* be because we think it is not *rational* to want intrinsically that others not have more. If, however, someone does intrinsically want this, it is not clear how instrumentalism can disallow the want as a foundation for action. Why should we find anything wrong with being envious unless we *presuppose* something substantive, for instance that it is rational to want to maximize one's pleasures, stimulations, or satisfactions of one's "normal" wants? I suspect we do presuppose some such thing. This may be why it is easy to miss or underestimate the difference between instrumentalism taken entirely on its own terms and objectivism, whether we are considering autonomy in particular or practical reason in general. We also presuppose a certain *historical constitution* of the self: we see people as products of their culture, education, and social relations, and we presume basic wants appropriate to such a background. But instrumentalism pulls up even such historical anchors; they may have de facto psychological weight, but they have no normative authority.

It appears, then, that unless it treats want satisfaction as intrinsically worthwhile, instrumentalism leaves us without a way to conceive desire as subject to reason, or the autonomous agent as any more than an efficient pilot steering conduct toward the satisfaction of desire. It may be that a rational person will, on reflection, tend to want maximum desire satisfaction. But surely this would be a reasonable requirement on rationality only to the extent that it is *antecedently* plausible to regard a rational agent as having to want, on their own account, that is, for their intrinsic properties, some of the *objects* of the desires whose satisfaction that agent wants to maximize: for instance, desires to avoid pain, to eat good food, experience pleasant sights and sounds, have zesty conversations, and so forth. Surely desire satisfaction in the abstract is not what seems intrinsically worthwhile; it is rational to want it, I think, only because it is rational to want certain objects of desire. And to say that is to grant a major point the objectivist is at pains to make.

It would be going too far to say that instrumentalism cannot provide any plausible account of autonomy, or that there is no interesting sense in which an agent who is autonomous can be both committed to instrumentalism and thoroughly consistent with it in behavior, desire, and attitudes. But I believe that even when it is qualified in ways that strengthen it, instrumentalism does not provide a fully adequate account; and it yields a less plausible and much thinner account than the objectivist view that autonomy is achieved only when one can criticize one's desires from a point of view that is not wholly derivative from them and, from that point of view, can exercise sufficient control over them. It is they, after all, that must be governed if one is to govern one's conduct. If all that autonomy does is direct conduct toward the satisfaction of one or another desire taken as a brute given that is beyond rational criticism, it may be an excellent achievement of efficiency but falls short of a capacity of self-government.

Notes

Earlier versions of this essay were given at Purdue University, the University of Nebraska, and Wake Forest University, and discussions with those audiences were very helpful. I benefited much from comments by Stephen Darwall, John Deigh, James Hudson, Christine Korsgaard, Win-chiat Lee, Heidi Malm, Allison Nespor, Jeffrey Poland, and Robert Schopp.

1. This is not a historical essay, and no attempt is made to deal in detail with Hume or Kant. The two positions to be discussed are, however, in major respects Humean and Kantian. Hume's dubbing reason the slave of the passions is well-known; speaking less metaphorically, he said, "Reason is the discovery of truth or falsehood. Truth or falsehood consists in an agreement or disagreement either to the *real* relations of ideas, or to *real* existence and matter of fact. Whatever, therefore, is not susceptible of this agreement or disagreement, is incapable of being true or false, and can never be an object of our reason." A *Treatise of Human Nature*, ed. L. A. Selby-Bigge (Oxford: Oxford University Press, 1888), p. 458. Kant's views are even more complicated, but the contrast with Hume appears repeatedly. Kant says, e.g., "Reason must regard itself as the author of its principles, independently of foreign influences," where the principles are normative (a kind Hume did not think reason could supply, in part because he considered them motivating), and the foreign influences include the sorts of passions Hume thought reason ought to serve. *Foundations of the Metaphysics of Morals* trans. Lewis White Beck (New York: Liberal Arts Press, 1959), p. 67 (449). The contrast with Hume is again evident where Kant speaks of "the moral law, i.e., the principle of the autonomy of the will" (ibid., p. 68 [450]). For discussion of Hume's instrumentalism see Adrian M. S. Piper, "Hume on Rational Final Ends," *Philosophy Research Archives* 14 (1989); and for a treatment of Kant's views of practical reason, see Thomas E. Hill Jr., "The Kantian Conception of Autonomy," in John Christman, ed., *The Inner Citidel: Essays on Individual Autonomy* (New York: Oxford University Press, 1989).

2. For an indication of this diversity, as well as a detailed and plausible account of autonomy and its importance in ethics, see Gerald Dworkin, *The Theory and Practice of Autonomy* (Cambridge and New York: Cambridge University Press, 1988), esp. ch. 1; Christman, *The Inner Citidel*; Stephen L. Darwall, "Autonomist Internalism and the Justification of Morals," *Nous* 24 (1990); and Harry Frankfurt, "On the Usefulness of Final Ends" (in progress).

3. This is supported by a number of the varied citations given in ch. 1 of Dworkin's *The Theory and Practice of Autonomy*. For other indications of the centrality of self-government to the notion of autonomy, see Joel Feinberg, "Autonomy," in Christman, *The Inner Citidel*, and Rodger Beehler, "Autonomy and the Democratic Principle," *Canadian Journal of Philosophy* 19 (1989).

4. In sec. 435–36 of the *Groundwork* Kant stresses both self-legislation and self-government as essential to autonomy, in addition to its foundational role in endowing persons with dignity.

5. This appears to be Thomas Nagel's position at one point in *The View from Nowhere* (Oxford and New York: Oxford University Press, 1986), esp. pp. 113–20. For criticism of this sort of view — as allegedly expressed in Joshua Cohen and Joel Rogers, *On Democracy* (New York: Penguin Books, 1983) — see Beehler, "Autonomy and the Democratic Principle" (Cohen and Rogers reply in the succeeding pages.)

6. The contrast between freedom and autonomy is developed further in my "Acting for Reasons," *Philosophical Review* 45 (1986), esp. pp. 533–34. It might be thought that there are some things so terrible that no price can render them acceptable. The claim in the text is consistent with this; the point is simply that even when one is forced to pay a price one would not freely pay, and so is acting under a kind of compulsion, the act can still be autonomous by virtue of the way one controls it in the light of one's values.

7. Norman Dahl has developed this point in "Weakness of Will as a Moral Defect," read at the Central Division meetings of the American Philosophical Association in 1987. That an incontinent action *can* be autonomous, if imperfectly, is argued in my "Weakness of Will and Rational Action," *Australasian Journal of Philosophy* 68 (1990): 270–81.

8. If autonomy is conceived in part as what we *exercise* in acting from duty and as paradigmatically expressed in our endorsement of moral laws, then for Kant autonomy may be better described not as *having* moral value but as the (or at least a) *foundation* of it.

9. For some discussions of internalism and externalism, particularly in relation to Kant, and for various references to the literature on the topic, see Stephen L. Darwall, *Impartial Reason* (Ithaca: Cornell University Press, 1983), esp. ch. 5; Christine M. Korsgaard, "Skepticism about Practical Reason," *Journal of Philosophy* 83 (1986): 5–25; Mark C. Timmons, "Kant and the Possibility of Moral Motivation," *Southern Journal of Philosophy* 23 (1985): 377–98; and my *Practical Reasoning* (London and New York: Routledge, 1989), esp. chs. 2 and 3.

10. The guiding role is discussed in some detail in *Practical Reasoning*, esp. ch. 4, and a few relevant points are also made in the following paragraphs. Much of the overall view is consistent with noncognitivism, but it is intended as a cognitivist position.

11. Note that if, as seems more likely, autonomous agents need not be rational overall, internalism may still be true of them so far as they are rational *in relation to* the domain of relevant judgment, say politics. Thus, we can take a kind of internalism to hold for rational agents, or for autonomous ones so far as they are rational, without taking it to hold for rational agents simpliciter. Moreover, even if rational agents are always motivated to some degree in the *direction* of their practical judgments, it need not be *by* the judgments. It might be by independent motivation to act in the required ways. Thus, even if a kind of internalism seems confirmed by the behavior of rational agents, we may not conclude that simply believing, or even judging, that one ought to do something implies motivation to do it.

12. In "Acting for Reasons," I have sketched an account of non-wayward connections between reasons and actions; these are the sort being briefly indicated here as necessary for autonomous action.

13. This view has been closely associated with Gerald Dworkin and Stanley Benn, though Dworkin has qualified it in recent writings, notably *The Theory and Practice of Autonomy*, e.g., on pp. 15–18. One might hold that "it is crucial for autonomy that one hold one's commitments up for inspection — even one's ground projects. Our ground projects are often formed in our youth, in a particular family, class, or cultural background. . . . Of course, autonomy could not sensibly require that we question all of our values and commitments at once." Peter Railton, "Alienation, Consequentialism, and Morality," *Philosophy & Public Affairs* 13 (1984): 147. A related thesis is that "autonomy is achieved in virtue of a two-way . . . integration within a person's hierarchy of motivations, intermediate standards and values, and highest principles. Only if a person's highest principles have been subjected to assessment in accord with her intermediate standards and her motivations, would it be appropriate to

consider them her 'own' principles." Marilyn A. Friedman, "Autonomy and the Split-Level Self," *Southern Journal of Philosophy* 24 (1986): 34.

14. The disposition clause is needed for at least two reasons. First, an autonomous agent may, for an indefinite time, lack appropriate opportunities to act in the required way. Second, in principle it is possible to be *structurally autonomous* simply at a time, as where a being with all the relevant properties is created for just a moment.

15. Here I draw on a few paragraphs of my essay "The Architecture of Reason," *Proceedings and Addresses of the American Philosophical Association* 62 (1988): 227–56.

16. We need to specify a proper response to rule out wayward chains; the agent must respond for the right sort of reason.

17. As this paragraph suggests, it is difficult to know how to sophisticate instrumentalism. One problem, I think, is that the most natural qualifications seem to grant too much to the objectivist competition. An argument illustrating this point is made in the final section. For what may be the best-developed modification of instrumentalism, see Richard B. Brandt, *A Theory of the Good and the Right* (Oxford and New York: Oxford University Press, 1979). This book has been widely discussed, and criticisms of it relevant to this chapter are made in my "An Epistemic Conception of Rationality," *Social Theory and Practice* 9 (1983): 311–34.

18. The objectivist internalism in question is sketched in "The Architecture of Reason." For discussion of the relevant notion of accessibility and many references to recent literature, see Paul K. Moser, *Knowledge and Evidence* (Cambridge and New York: Cambridge University Press, 1989). My views on accessibility are developed in "Causalist Internalism," *American Philosophical Quarterly* 26 (1989): 309–20.

19. A noncognitivist account of rational desire, and indeed of rationality in general, could be objectivist in something like the suggested sense. Surely we could have rational, non-instrumental attitudes toward objects of intrinsic desire even on a non-realist account of goodness and normativity in general.

20. I have argued for this in "The Architecture of Reason." Other, supporting considerations are advanced (among many others) by Nagel, *The View from Nowhere*, and the account of intrinsic value in ch. 11 provides further support for the view.

21. I take the terms 'normatively practical' and 'motivationally practical' from my *Practical Reasoning*, esp. ch. 3. There are of course degrees of both justificatory and motivational power, but that need not concern us here.

22. Is autonomy, then, a formal concept, implying no particular standard of conduct whatever? Instrumentalism seems committed to this, but I leave it open. Objectivism may also be committed to it; it does not follow, however, that it must leave open that there *are* reasonable standards, and Kant did not. Cf. Thomas E. Hill Jr., "The Kantian Conception of Autonomy," in Christman, *The Inner Citidel*, who appears to think that Kant's view of autonomy does leave the latter open: "[S]ubstantive values, such as desire [satisfaction?] and pleasure, do not *necessarily* provide even prima facie reasons for action. Their status as reasons depends on their endorsement by the individual agent" (p. 100). Applied to *motivating* reasons, this is plausible; but I do not see that Kant must take autonomy to imply our always *creating*, as opposed to at least sometimes discovering, normative reasons. Indeed, Kant sometimes speaks as if there are things actually having intrinsic value; it would be strange indeed if they could not provide (normative) reasons for action without prior endorsement.

23. This way of putting the point applies especially to theorists like E. J. Bond. See, e.g., his "Desire, Action, and the Good," *American Philosophical Quarterly* 16 (1979): 53–59.

24. Here one may be reminded of B. F. Skinner's striking remark that the point is "to design a world that will be liked not by people as they now are, but by those who live in it." *Beyond Freedom and Dignity* (New York: Knopf, 1971), p. 156.

25. In the special case of someone's *creating* an agent with certain preponderant desires,

there is no antecedent person to manipulate. If such an agent is then unimpeded, autonomy is possible. This suggests that even when my basic desires are changed dramatically, I can still be autonomous *relative* to the induced desires provided I am then unimpeded and I otherwise meet the relevant standards. But I am not autonomous simpliciter, since the major change in my governing structure has violated my autonomy. We can, to be sure, relativize autonomy to time; then my autonomy might be undermined at t but restored at $t + n$. Still, for the pure instrumentalist even manipulation at t does not undermine my autonomy at that very time provided it does not thwart any desire I *then* have, as it may well not.

26. Surely if we have any wants at all, we have some intrinsic wants. I make a case for such motivational foundationalism in "The Structure of Motivation," *Pacific Philosophical Quarterly* 61 (1980): 258–75.

27. John Rawls introduces this as a special assumption, apparently not treating it as highly substantive. See A *Theory of Justice* (Cambridge: Harvard University Press, 1971), p. 143 and secs. 80–81. It is an interesting question to what extent Rawls's concept of autonomy can be squared with a pure instrumentalism. He says, e.g., that "[f]ollowing the Kantian interpretation of justice as fairness, we can say that by acting from these principles persons are acting autonomously: they are acting from principles that they would acknowledge under conditions that best express their nature as free and equal rational beings" (p. 515). Even apart from the question whether rational persons would choose Rawls's principles from behind the veil of ignorance, would the crucial conditions of acknowledgment presuppose any particular intrinsic desires, if only second-order ones?

10

Moral Judgment and
Reasons for Action

The relation between intellect and will is a major concern of the theory of practical reason. In moral philosophy the central focus of this concern is the relation between reason and morality. Here the perennial question is often taken to be whether a rational person has reason to be moral. But there is really more than one question here, because there are at least two quite different though overlapping kinds of reasons: motivational reasons, roughly the kind that explain why an agent does a particular thing, and normative reasons, roughly the kind that indicate what an agent ought to do. The former are the kind an agent in some way responds to (else they could not explain); the latter are the kind that *rational* agents respond to and that can at least partially justify the action in question. There are also two directions of entailment to consider if we are to understand the relation between reason and morality: whether being rational entails being moral and whether being moral entails being rational.

Moral philosophers very commonly argue that there are overriding normative reasons to be moral, and hence that being (adequately) rational implies being moral; but as regards the converse implication, the preoccupying issue has been not the normative question whether a moral person is (qua moral) rational, or whether a moral person has normative reasons to act, but the motivational question whether the moral judgments such a person makes are by their very nature motivating — a question that on the face of it addresses the relation between intellect and will. It is here that I begin. Indeed, the question whether a rational person must be moral (or must at least intellectually accept moral standards) is not a direct concern of this essay. My main concern in the first three parts is whether an agent who makes a self-addressed moral judgment, such as 'I must resign'— an agent whose intellect is already in that sense moral at that place and time — must be motivated to act accordingly. Broadly stated, the issue is how, if at all, the behavioral will must respond to the moral intellect.

This last question concerns the relation between moral judgment and motivational reasons for action, a topic that has quite deservedly preoccupied philosophers, particularly in the past thirty years. The question is of interest both because it is closely connected with the relation between reason and morality and because it is pivotal for understanding the sense in which morality is "practical," that is, bears on action. On some views, inspired by widely known arguments in Hume's *Treatise*, if morality is practical enough for its self-addressed judgments to be necessarily motivating, then it is not cognitive; and if it is cognitive enough for those judgments to be true (or false), then it is at best unclear how it can be practical.

The question of how moral judgment is related to motivation is complicated because motivational and normative reasons not only overlap but are also discussed together (and sometimes conflated) in the literature; and it will soon be clear that the relation between moral judgment and motivating reasons cannot be adequately understood apart from some consideration of how each is related to normative reasons and how those in turn are connected with moral judgment.

My aim is to sharpen the issues and to offer the outline of an account of some major connections between moral judgment and reasons for action and of the varieties and grounds of such reasons. A subsidiary aim is to provide a taxonomy of some of the major positions concerning reason and morality and to introduce some terminology sufficiently intuitive and well defined to be of help to others examining or defending such positions. Section I will introduce the pivotal issues, lay out some essential distinctions between kinds of reason and types of judgment, and connect the former with specifically moral judgments. Sections II to V will appraise a form of what is often called *motivational internalism*. The main question here is the relation of moral judgment to motivation and hence of morality — as internally represented in judgment — to action. Moral judgments are supposed to be practical in providing motivational reasons for action. But do they necessarily do so, and can they do so apart from desire or some other independent motivational attitude?

Exploring the sense in which moral judgments may provide reasons for action brings us, in section VI, to a related but quite different internalism, often called *reasons internalism*, a view concerning the basis of normative reasons for action. Different though they are, each of these internalisms is hard to understand adequately apart from a contrast with the other, and any systematic treatment of motivational internalism should distinguish it from the reasons variety liable to be confused with it. Both views, moreover, are found (if sometimes only implicitly) in Hume, and sections VI and VII will bring the results of the examination of both internalisms to bear on the instrumentalist conception of rationality, of which Hume is often considered the historically most important source. The concluding section will sketch the wider implications of the essay for the general theory of reasons for action.

I. The Issues: Judgments, Motives, and Reasons

To see how motivation may be plausibly thought to be in some way internal to moral judgment, consider an example. Suppose that I judge, in response to a student's grade appeal sent to me after a course is over, that it would be (morally) unfair to raise the grade. Suppose further that my judgment is warranted relative to my evidence concerning the student's work and that of the rest of the class. Must I, by virtue of holding this judgment, have some degree of motivation to act accordingly, say to decline to raise the grade?[1] Many have thought so. In exploring this view I shall consider mainly moral judgments of this first-person sort, the self-addressed kind directly applicable to one's own future conduct. What we discover about these can be extended to other kinds of moral judgments.

Let us first focus on the judgment side of the issue: on what is implicit in moral judgments construed as held or sincerely made (I am taking a judgment one *holds*, as opposed to a judgment one simply entertains or makes merely for the sake of argument, to imply accepting the content judged, say that one must keep a promise). There are two questions here: whether, in *making* the judgment, I must *express* motivation, and whether, in *holding* the judgment, I must *have* motivation. Let us take these in turn.

It is natural to answer the first question, concerning the expressive content of moral judgment, affirmatively insofar as one takes 'expression' to have the sense it does when we say, for example, that a certain way of putting a complaint expresses anger: this is a linguistic, illocutionary, sense of 'express', not a causal sense, like that illustrated by 'His grief found expression in the intonation of his poems'. Expression in the linguistic sense does not entail having what one expresses. Since the main issue here is what actual motivation is essential to moral judgment, I leave this kind of expression aside and simply grant for the sake of argument that making a moral judgment expresses motivation in a sense implying that hearers are normally entitled to take it that one has some degree of motivation to act in accordance with the judgment.

The more important question for ethical theory is whether, in holding a judgment, one must *have* motivation to act accordingly, where holding such a judgment includes holding moral beliefs with the appropriate content even if they have not been formed through, or expressed in, *making* a judgment. If the answer is affirmative, then our moral judgments, whether we express them or not, are, by virtue of being intrinsically motivating, potentially predictive of our conduct, as, after all, we should like them to be.

The main issue here can be put in terms of internality (a multifaceted notion shortly to be explicated). Is motivation in some way internal to moral judgment, as opposed to coming from something else, such as the fear of punishment? The view that it is internal — call it *generic motivational internalism* — is the position that holding a moral judgment (roughly, accepting its content) is necessarily motivating. Thus, if I hold a moral judgment, I must have some degree of motivation to act in accord with it. (Some of the several ways motivation may be conceived will be clarified shortly.)

The question whether some degree of motivation is internal to (holding) a moral judgment becomes even more complex when we try to understand motivation and reasons. Whatever we think it is that constitutes motivation, and whatever we take a reason to be, surely being motivated to do something implies having at least one kind of reason to do it. This is why locutions like 'He has no reason to oppose you' can be used to rebut the attribution of a motive. Thus, if motivation is internal to holding a moral judgment, then holding such a judgment, as I do in the grade appeals matter, entails having at least this kind of reason to act accordingly. It is often called a *motivational reason*[2] for the relevant actions, the kind of reason normally appealed to when a desire is invoked as a reason I have to do something or, if I do it, as a reason for which I did it.[3] This is not to say that desire exhausts motivation (it surely does not); desire is cited here because it is a paradigm case of motivation.[4]

A motivational reason may or may not lead to action. Having a motivational reason of the kind in question does not entail my performing an action my judgment motivates — for the motivational force of the reason may be outweighed by that of conflicting desires. But my holding the judgment does entail that, to some degree, and in some sense, I *want*, and thereby am disposed, to perform an action of the kind in question, and that I can adduce my judgment as a reason for an action of this kind, either retrospectively — say in explaining it — or prospectively, say in deliberating about whether to perform the action. The judgment is, then, at least a weak reason *for* performing it, since it expresses a consideration in favor of it, and is potentially a reason *why* I perform the action, since I could act for that reason.

The kind of wanting in question need not be desire, especially in a passional sense; wanting of the kind in question is the attitude whose content is expressed by the infinitive clause in explanations of the form of 'She did it in order to . . .'[5] If one hesitates to take any notion of wanting to be broad enough for this role, the crucial point is that motivational attitudes, such as intentions and goals, are like wants and unlike beliefs both in not being true or false and in having a different "direction of fit" to the world, roughly in the sense that whereas it is appropriate to beliefs to reflect the world, and in a sense they "succeed" when they are true, it is appropriate to motivational attitudes, such as intentions and goals, to change the world, and they "succeed" when one changes it (or at least it changes) in the wanted way.[6] The points made here about motivation do not, then, presuppose a Humean theory of motivation, which I shall here take to be in outline the view that wanting (as roughly equivalent to desiring) as well as believing figures in the explanation of every intentional action and that beliefs as truth-valued attitudes do not entail wants.

Now consider normative reasons. Some who hold the non-skeptical view that there are such things — as opposed to motivational reasons conceived as mere tendencies to pursue what one wants — are nonetheless willing to disassociate them from motivation in various ways. Suppose, in contrast to the picture of moral judgment as entailing motivation, that no motivation is entailed by my holding the moral judgment that it would be unfair to raise the grade. Do I then still have a kind of reason for an action, for instance a reason to decline (a reason why I should decline) to raise the grade? If so, it would surely be a kind of *normative* reason; for it would be the sort that can (to some extent) justify the relevant type of action. This is not to suggest that a normative reason cannot also be a motivational one. The point is that it seems intelligible to hold that a judgment could entail the former without entailing the latter, as it could entail the latter without entailing the former.

I want to consider mainly two positions on the relation between moral judgments and normative reasons for action. To keep the issue from becoming unmanageably broad I will focus only on normative reasons that are also moral.

First, on some views, simply in virtue of holding a moral judgment (at least assuming it is plausible) one has a (prima facie) normative reason to act accordingly.[7] In favor of this view — taken as roughly equivalent to the thesis that holding such judgments constitutes (one case of) having reasons for acting — note that one can quite appropriately cite one's moral judgment, for instance that a deed is unfair, as a reason one has not to do it. This *judgments-as-reasons view*, as we might call it, does not entail motivational internalism. It is normative reason, not motivational reason, that it takes to be internal to moral judgment.

There are two modifications of the judgments-as-reasons view that we should note, mainly to sharpen the issue and keep the modified versions distinct from the basic view. On the first, by virtue of holding a moral judgment, I would have not only a normative reason for acting but also a motivational reason for acting.[8] One rationale for asserting this further consequence of holding a moral judgment is that only when a judgment is motivating would the reason it gives one be "practical," and a genuine normative reason must be practical. The resulting position, which takes moral judgments as embodying *both* motivational and normative reasons, is simply the motivational internalist version of the judgments-as-reasons view. Call this the *motivational internalist judgments-as-reasons view*. On the second modification of the judgments-as-reasons view, a judgment provides a normative reason for action if and only if it entails motivation (as on the first modification), and beyond this, the motivation comes from some internal non-cognitive (hence non-truth-valued) practical state, such as desire. Call it the *non-cognitive-motivation-entailing judgments-as-reasons view*. If it is sound, then a moral judgment cannot provide a reason for action apart from embodying or implying some such state.

In short, the judgment-as-reasons view takes moral judgments to provide normative reasons; the internalist version of this view adds that those judgments also provide motivational reasons; and the non-cognitive version adds in turn that the motivation must come from a non-cognitive element — as one would hold if one maintained both motivational internalism and a Humean theory of motivation. The non-cognitive version does not, however, entail *noncognitivism*: the point is that non-cognitive elements are crucial underpinnings of normative reasons, but it is not implied that a moral judgment cannot be cognitive, in the sense that their content is true or false ("cognizable" as opposed to, say, attitudinal). In terms of the widest issue that concerns us, the thrust of the non-cognitive version is not that the intellect cannot grasp morality but that its doing so provides normative reasons for action only with the cooperation of some non-cognitive element — broadly, something in the will or having potential to move the will.

Suppose we now combine the twofold idea that moral judgments are necessarily motivating (motivational internalism) and that motivation is rooted in non-cognitive elements (as on the Humean theory of motivation) with another powerful idea prominent in the Humean tradition — the naturalistic position that reasons for action must be grounded in our psychology rather than in, say, a priori truths about the good. We can then see how the second major position we must examine comes in. This is *reasons internalism*. In a generic form, it is roughly the view that normative reasons for action must be grounded in some internal conative or at least non-cognitive motivational state, such as a want, desire, passion, or emotion: paradigmatically, the kind of attitude that can be in some way satisfied by actions in its service but is not properly said to be true or false.[9] Perhaps the underlying idea is that normative reasons for doing something must represent it as fulfilling some kind of psychologically real goal, commonly the kind that produces a sense of need. Wanting food, for instance, yields a reason to get it.

For reasons internalism, to have a reason to do something is, in a simple and common kind of case, for that deed to be such that one can clearly see that it would best satisfy one's basic desires, say to relieve pain. As the view is usually developed, seeing that there are such reasons does not require either resorting to a priori truths or positing anything irreducibly normative. If we think moral judgments provide reasons for action, we must hold that they "tap into" basic desires. But if, like Hume, we see humanity as having a suitable range of socially directed, sometimes even altruistic, desires, then we can explain both why there are (for normal people) reasons to be moral and how moral judgments imply both motivational and normative reasons to act accordingly.[10]

Reasons internalism is highly controversial. Many philosophers deny that reasons for action must be grounded in that way and maintain that the *truth* of moral judgment for or against one's possible future conduct, whether one holds the judgment or not, implies a normative reason for action, say a reason not to raise a grade, and can imply a normative reason for one to do something whether or not the action would satisfy any of one's non-cognitive motivational states. This position is a form of *reasons externalism*, which, generically, is simply the denial of reasons internalism. Positively conceived, it is roughly the view that one can have a normative reason for acting simply in virtue of the externally grounded truth of a judgment for or against some item of one's possible future conduct, where this kind of external grounding implies that one's normative reasons for action — the kind that would justify it — are not grounded in any of one's non-cognitive motivational states. Thus, if it would be plainly wrong to cheat someone, that fact could provide a reason not to do so, even if one had no non-cognitive motivational attitude also disfavoring the deed, such as a desire to have the person as a friend.

As this examples indicates, there is an external sense of 'judgment' in which a judgment can be applicable to action without being *made*. Consider a case in which, after a mistake, one speaks of the judgment one should have made. A reason-giving judgment itself may thus be external at least in the sense that it may be a normative proposition that no one actually holds, hence is not internal to anyone's mind.[11] A stronger reasons externalism would maintain that some normative reasons for action *are* externally grounded in normative truths supporting the actions in question; a still stronger one would maintain that all of them are. A wide range of normative externalisms can be constructed not only by varying the kinds of normative reasons that must be externally grounded but also by changing such variables as the strength of the reasons provided by a judgment (conceived externally or otherwise), the kind or degree of their externality, and the kind of access the agent has to the grounds of the judgment.

One rationale for a fairly strong reasons externalism is apparent in our critical practices. Suppose I do not arrive at a morally sound conclusion in relation to the grade appeal and I mistakenly judge that I should change the grade. It now seems that *there is reason* for me not to change it, and to bring out that I am missing certain considerations, someone might say precisely this.[12] It appears that there is a sense in which this reason would have "been there" even if no one had noticed it. On a strong externalism, normative reasons — reasons there *are* for an action — sometimes exist apart from what anyone actually believes or wants regarding the rightness or justifiability of that action.

This strong reasons externalist view concerning moral judgment should be associated with the external, non-psychological sense of 'judgment', taken to designate the content of a judgment someone does or might *hold* (this content is what one does or would judge to be the case). For instance, after being convinced that I was wrong in judging I should raise the grade, I might say that the right judgment was that I should leave it unchanged. This judgment (in the external sense) was not made by anyone, though it was, we might say, implicit in the facts, in that any proper assessment of them would yield it. Call it *judgment in the propositional sense*, or for short propositional judgment. It is of course not the kind of judgment plausibly thought to entail motivation. Propositional judgments are abstract elements that can be external even to the intellect; they may surely fail to be internal to the will. By contrast, judgments in the psychological sense are the holding or making of judgments in the propositional sense. The holding of a judgment is a dispositional state; the making of one is an occurrence, such as an assertion; the content of either is a judgment in the propositional sense.

A good understanding of the notions of judgment and, in particular, of holding a judgment is crucial for exploring motivational internalism as well as for understanding the reasons variety. If (generic) motivational internalism is true, then holding a moral judgment implies having a motivational reason to act accordingly. Holding a moral judgment also implies having a normative reason for such action, given certain assumptions, chiefly that moral considerations *can* provide normative reasons — which seems plainly true — and that the moral judgment in question is not so ill-grounded that the agent is foolish to hold it. If these assumptions are as plausible as they seem, then appraising motivational internalism leads us directly to the question of whether holding moral judgments is also essentially connected with normative reason — the notion for which reasons internalism provides a pivotal condition.

If the kind of motivation that goes with holding a moral judgment implies (at least in common circumstances) a normative reason for action, one may wonder about the converse relation, which is equally important in ethical theory. Motivational internalism does not claim, and at least some proponents of it would deny, that having a normative reason implies being motivated to act accordingly. Some version of this thesis is, however, central in any *reasons* internalism that roots one's normative reasons for action in one's desires: desires are paradigms of motivators. Both positions are crucial for understanding moral judgment and reasons for action. It will be best, I think, to take up motivational internalism first and then proceed to reasons internalism. But, as is perhaps apparent already, these two kinds of internalism are, though logically independent, so closely related and so integral to the theory of practical reason that it is difficult to discuss either one in any depth apart from the other.

II. Motivational Reasons and Motivational Internalism

Motivational internalism is of special interest not just because, at least in its generic form, it represents important common ground between Humeans and Kantians but also because it is central to understanding the sense in which moral judgment is practical and, to that extent, the relation between reason and morality. To be sure, the Humean version in its main contemporary forms takes the internality of motivation to moral judgment to imply that such judgment is not cognitive (or at least does not "come from reason"), whereas the Kantian version implies or at least permits the cognitivity of moral judgment and takes the internality of motivation to it to imply that morality is practical. But on both views moral judgment is motivating in a sense implying an action tendency. There is no adequate generally accepted definition of motivational internalism. Rather than argue for a single definition, I will indicate the crucial variables that any detailed account should reflect, then propose a conception that can serve a number of purposes in moral theory.

It is important to characterize motivational internalism so that it is evident why it is so called and clear what is supposed to be internal to what, and in what way. Several aspects of the issue should be distinguished, and when they are we have the basis for identifying an entire family of motivational internalisms. There are at least five main dimensions of motivational internalism: (1) the *locus* of the motivation — what the motivation is internal *to*, for example obligation, duty, or the sense of obligation or of duty, or a belief or judgment attributing an obligation or duty; (2) the kind of *internality* in question, for instance conceptual containment as opposed to mere necessary implication (a distinction shortly to be explained); (3) the *degree* of motivation implied, for example only some degree vs. enough to explain why an action was performed (but on most views not so much as to make weakness of will, conceived as implying uncompelled action against one's better judgment — say one's overall moral judgment — impossible);[13] (4) the *normative domain* of the obligation to which the motivation is supposed to be internal, for example moral or also prudential (or perhaps religious or even aesthetic); and (5) the *modality* of the thesis asserting the connection, for instance its contingency or necessity (or analyticity).

Motivational internalisms representing nearly all of the combinations indicated here (and others) have been held or at least characterized as possible positions,[14] though to be sure the modality of the philosophical theses connecting judgment and motivation is most often taken to be necessity, since motivational internalists tend to regard their thesis as a kind of conceptual truth (one could, however, construe it as something weaker, say as a truth of "human nature"). It should be clear that on the view I have been working with, it is to moral judgments, as held, that motivation is internal or external. The mere truth (or even the justifiability) of moral judgments in the propositional sense cannot be plausibly taken to imply that the relevant people are motivated accordingly. When we discover what we ought to have done, we commonly discover the truth of a moral judgment that was *not* accompanied by motivation on our part.[15]

I take *motivational internalism proper* to be the view that some degree of motivation is intrinsic (and in that sense internal) to the holding of a (self-addressed) moral judgment — especially the kind that is for or against some particular action or type of action clearly representing one's future possible conduct. This goes beyond generic motivational internalism in one way, whose significance will soon be evident: it requires that motivation be not only entailed by, but (conceptually) intrinsic to, holding a moral judgment. We should probably add, what is often intended by motivational internalists though not essential to the position, that the *degree* of motivation is sufficient to explain an action of the relevant kind: one that accords with the judgment. If any other variant of the view is needed, it can likely be constructed by specifying the position further on one of the five indicated dimensions.

What are the prospects for motivational internalism proper? The view seems most plausible when we imagine someone (sincerely) making a self-addressed moral judgment. We believe, for one thing, that actions speak louder than words, and we question the sincerity of people who express moral judgments but do not act accordingly when the occasion calls for it. Moreover, it is arguably deviant or even impermissible to say such things as 'It would be unfair for me to raise his grade, but I have no motivation whatever to resist doing it'.

These points in favor of motivational internalism are far from conclusive. For one thing, we could, on the basis of a strong statistical connection between moral judgment and motivation, doubt the sincerity of someone who exhibits a disparity between expressed moral judgments and the conduct they enjoin. Moreover, the oddity just noted could be merely pragmatic, like that of saying 'It is true that p, but I don't believe p'.

It must be remembered, however, that the most plausible internalisms will take only *some* degree of motivation to be implicit in holding a moral judgment. Critics thus have to imagine someone who genuinely holds such a judgment and has no motivation at all to act accordingly. Could one really judge that, for example, raising a grade would be unfair and, in a situation of forced choice, be content to flip a coin to decide whether to raise it? It may appear that one could not. But insofar as we take this appearance to signify the internality of motivation to moral judgment, it may be because we are imagining a rational agent or a judgment made in "normal" circumstances. One question we must therefore ask is how much apparent support for motivational internalism proper may come from assumptions about the kind of agent in question, or the circumstances of judgment, or both.

Suppose, then, that we restrict motivational internalism to rational agents. Moral persons, after all, are (most of the time, at least) rational agents. There is some reason to doubt that a *rational* person could judge that it would be unfair to raise a grade yet be content to flip a coin to decide whether to raise it, at least in a rational moment. For it seems implicit in the notion of such persons that they do not make moral judgments without taking them seriously at least to the extent of *tending* to act on them when nothing else is at stake. Arguably, then, rational agents are so constructed that they necessarily tend to act in accordance with their moral judgments.

The plausibility of this qualified internalism may, however, derive not from the internality of motivation to moral judgment but from whatever plausibility attaches to the view that *rational* agents must have desires that are in line with certain of their normative beliefs, above all their moral beliefs about what they should do (I am assuming that a judgment one *holds*, say that p, as opposed to a judgment that p which one merely states or supposes for argument's sake, implies the corresponding belief, here, that p). This view applies particularly to agents who are both rational and moral — the kind of agent most people writing on this issue in the literature have had in mind.

If, in rational agents, there is such an integration between moral judgment and motivation, then a kind of motivational internalism — call it *rational agent motivational internalism* — is true of them: they must have desires (or at least wants) that are in line with their moral beliefs about what they should do. This restricted internalism would not entail generic motivational internalism, but it would establish relationships whose obtaining is a good part of what motivational internalists want to affirm.[16]

If rational agent motivational internalism is true, it can, on one special assumption, explain even the thesis that it is *necessary* for anyone who holds a moral judgment to have some degree of motivation to act accordingly. The assumption, which is admittedly quite controversial, is that the kind and degree of rationality required to hold a moral judgment at all implies an integration between judgment and motivation adequate to produce the relevant degree of motivation to act in accord with the moral judgment. On this assumption, rational moral judges are, on pain of a kind of incoherence, always motivated to *some* degree in the direction of their moral judgments. Not only do actions speak louder than words; words unaccompanied by at least appropriate action tendencies are not fully intelligible.

III. Practical Judgment and the Diversity of Internal Motivation

The line of reasoning we have been exploring — connecting rational persons' moral judgments with their motivation — does not in the end support motivational internalism proper. From the indirect connection that the reasoning aims to establish between moral judgments and the actions they favor, it does not follow that these actions are motivated *by* the judgments, in the sense that this motivation is intrinsic to (holding) those judgments. The actions might be motivated by independent elements, for instance by moral experience or by a desire to do what is right. Thus, moral motivation might be entailed by the holding of a moral judgment — because of what holding it implies about the agent overall — yet not be internal to moral judgment. That, however, is what motivational internalism, as usually understood, requires.

We might put the point like this. Moral motivation may be entailed by, and so be *consequentially internal* to, moral judgment, even if it is not *constitutively internal*, and thereby an intrinsic element in, moral judgment. On one reading of Hume, he holds a consequential internalism; and on one reading of Kant, he holds a constitutive internalism. Both apparently hold generic motivational internalism. But for Hume, on this reading, a moral judgment that, say, an act one is considering is virtuous arises from a sense of pleasure felt upon the appropriate contemplation of the act, and this associated pleasure by its very nature provides positive motivation toward the act;[17] whereas for Kant, on one reading, the will *is* practical reason, and therefore a genuine moral judgment, which represents a deliverance of practical reason — an imperative, in one sense — must be motivating.[18] In the first case, the judgment and motivation are more nearly common effects of the same causes than cause and effect; in the second case, the motivational and causal powers are intrinsic to holding (or at least to sincerely making) the judgment.

The motivational internalist wants to show a connection between moral judgment and motivation, not just one between a general — and doubtless controversial — notion of a rational person holding a moral judgment, that is, a rational moral judge, and motivation. Even a motivational externalist can grant rational agent motivational internalism, by arguing that the relevant motivation comes from the kinds of desires that rational persons, or at least rational moral judges, have (or from other non-judgmental motivational elements implied by the minimal rationality in question).[19]

Insofar as rational agent motivational internalism is plausible, it provides an explanation of some of the data supporting generic motivational internalism. This explanation is potentially externalist, in the sense that in at least some cases it attributes an agent's motivation toward actions in accord with a moral judgment to factors not entailed just by the holding of that judgment. The availability of such an explanation is, of course, not a direct argument against generic motivational internalism, or even against motivational internalism proper; but it heightens the sense that the latter, in particular, needs further support if it is to survive as part of our account of the relation between reason and morality. A major segment of such support may come from a source quite different from the rationality of a moral judgment, namely, from one or another concept of moral judgment, a notion I now want to explore further.

I have already stressed the distinction between making and holding a moral judgment. There is a further distinction that bears on motivational internalism. It is between, on the one hand, making *or* holding a judgment as a matter of simple *propositional endorsement* and, on the other hand, making or holding it as a matter of *moral appraisal*. If there are moral propositions, then it may be possible to see their truth, even as applied to one's own conduct, in a purely intellectual way. Indeed, even on the noncognitivist view that there are no moral propositions and that moral utterances are in some way expressive (perhaps of a prescription), there could probably be a corresponding distinction between (1) expressing a mere classificatory moral assessment of an action — which bears on one's inferential tendencies but need not entail motivation regarding the action[20] — and (2) expressing an attitude of action-guiding moral appraisal, which is the usual case. There is a vast difference between judgmentally agreeing with someone on the proposition that publishing pornography is an immoral activity, where one cares little about the matter — this is simply expressing propositional endorsement — and morally judging (say as a concerned citizen advising the prosecuting attorney) that one should seek a life sentence for the ruthless kidnapper of a five-year-old — this is making a moral appraisal. Perhaps, then, motivational internalism should be taken to concern only moral judgments held *as* moral appraisals.

This line is at least initially promising: if there is such a thing as simply making a cold judgment that it would be unfair to raise a grade, where one is just endorsing the proposition in question, this merely propositional judgment need not be motivational; but the normal appraising ("hot") judgment that a moral agent would make in such a case would typically be motivational. One might even go so far as to say that if there is no such motivation, then at least one of the following points holds: the agent (1) is not taking the moral point of view at all, (2) is not judging morally (in a moral *way*), or, in the case where the judgment is made as well as held, (3) is not making a move in moral discourse (in the moral game, if you like).

These distinctions seem important: there is a difference between, on the one hand, *holding* a moral proposition as a manifestation of arriving at it by taking the moral point of view on the matter and, on the other hand, simply *believing* that proposition; between judging a matter *morally* — in the engaged way characteristic of morality as applied to guiding daily conduct — and simply holding a detached judgment with *moral content*; and between *stating* a moral judgment simply as a truth and *making a move in moral discourse*, which has an entrenched action-guiding role in human life. But suppose we grant motivational internalism for the three rich cases. What we get is another restricted form of motivational internalism: the thesis that some degree of motivation is internal to moral judgments held *from the moral point of view*, roughly, to making or holding a judgment from the moral perspective as opposed to merely believing a moral proposition (a propositional judgment) with the same content. Call this thesis (moral) *perspectival motivational internalism*.

Perspectival motivational internalism is certainly significant and is quite plausible. The moral judgments of the relevant kind, which we may call *morally anchored*, apparently are motivational. For it is surely plausible to maintain that a central element in taking, or judging within, the moral point of view implies having some degree of motivation to act on the directives that emerge from one's moral reasoning and from one's assessments therein. Otherwise we have something like assuming the moral point of view for the sake of argument, simulating it, or merely mouthing it.

However plausible perspectival motivational internalism is, it still falls short of the unrestricted view, motivational internalism proper. If motivation to act on one's moral judgments, say in the form of a desire to live up to one's moral obligations, is what explains why holding those judgments implies motivation to act accordingly, there is no need, and probably no good reason, to take this motivation to be internal to holding them.[21] Motivation to act on one's moral judgments can be internal to taking the moral point of view without being internal to holding those judgments. Perhaps taking the moral point of view entails or at least causes the adoption of moral standards, or even leads to one's internalizing them in the will, so that one's moral judgments now operate on a foundation of awaiting volition. It does not follow that any such volition or any other motivational elements are intrinsic to moral judgments themselves.[22]

None of these considerations shows that motivational internalism proper cannot be sustained. But they do suggest that, at least from a cognitivist point of view, what gives it plausibility may be very largely considerations better explained on the basis of related views that locate the crucial motivation elsewhere than in the moral judgment that was supposed to be its basis. Moreover, these views provide an important thing, perhaps the most important single thing, that motivational internalists (as such) want: a connection between reason and motivation, and, insofar as the moral judgments in question represent morality as a domain of practical reason and the motivation in question is directed toward moral conduct, between reason and morality.

What perspectival motivational internalism and similar views fail to provide that some motivational internalists have wanted is a strong connection between intellect and will. The desired connection is one whereby the will must respond to moral judgment — paradigmatically, by producing action or at least generating an intention or some other motivation to act in accord with the judgment — independently of any other source of motivation, even rational desire. I want to stress, however, that this goal is more ambitious than motivational internalism in any of its plausible forms. Failure to achieve it should be kept in perspective: the executive power that would be required of moral judgment to *guarantee* action is more than any plausible internalism can claim (and more than is claimed by the best theorists in this tradition, including Kant and leading Kantians). This is in part because such executive power would make it at best difficult to countenance the possibility of weakness of will. But quite apart from this point, even if generic motivational internalism is true, there is a gap between the potentially outweighed motivation that moral judgment entails and the actions it should produce. It would be one thing to show that holding a moral judgment entails motivation strong enough to explain action that accords with such judgment; it would be quite another to show that moral judgments imply motivation strong enough to put the will firmly under the power of moral reason wherever that is invoked by moral judgment.

IV. Rational Agency and the Evidential Role of Moral Motivation

So far, I have spoken as if some form of rational agent motivational internalism may be provisionally taken as sound, so that at least the internalist idea that *in* rational persons, or at least in rational persons holding a prima facie *rational* moral judgment, some degree of motivation is internal to moral judgment. I believe, however, that even this broadened internalist idea may be too strong.

To see the problem, consider a case in which a deontologically oriented father judges that he (morally) must punish his sixteen-year-old daughter for taking the car out without permission, something she had agreed not to do. The judgment may come from a sense of good policy, a knowledge of his previous past practice with his older child, and consistency with his past pattern of discipline. We may think of the judgment as largely an inferential upshot of cool reflection based on these elements. Suppose now that his daughter gives an excuse in terms of a sudden need for some books, but he rejects the excuse as inadequate. The punishment he judges he should give her is to deny her a visit to a friend's home on the weekend. There is little reason to doubt that if he is *perfectly* rational he will have not only some degree of motivation to act on the judgment, but a degree appropriate to the context: sufficient, in the absence of obstacles or new evidence, to produce the punitive deed. But the issue is what holds for rational moral agents like you and me. If he is simply like most of us, and especially if he is even-tempered and unemotional about the matter, it is far from self-evident that he must, on pain of irrationality, be motivated to deny her the outing.

An important possibility is that despite his moral judgment's being both in character and at least minimally rational, it represents only a small segment of his overall structure of relevant beliefs and goals. Perhaps, deep down, he recognizes a young woman approaching adulthood, striving for autonomy, presuming on parental understanding, and duly penitent about breaking her word in so acting. He might, after careful reflection, recognize this and might, working from the largest perspective he is capable of, withdraw his moral judgment; but the fact that he *would* do this does not imply that either he or his moral judgment is irrational while he in fact holds it. Particularly in matters that are not earth-shaking for us, we quite normally make judgments rooted in the nearest region of the larger evidential field we could canvass if necessary. We usually succeed reasonably well and often arrive at rational judgments, though we sometimes revise our judgments in the light of a wider search.

My suggestion, then, is that the father may be motivationally influenced by the grounds for forgiveness that he senses but does not draw together into a counter-judgment. Their influence may in fact be one that he — and we — might rationally welcome as countermanding or even obliterating any motivation that would otherwise be carried by his punitive moral judgment. The case does not appeal to irrational influences: indeed, it recognizes some of the same kinds of connections between rational and motivational elements that motivational internalism seems to exaggerate or to posit with insufficient qualification. What we have, then, is not forces of reason overcoming irrational forces; his original judgment is not shown to be irrational by the more weighty considerations but only to be *less* rationally adequate than one he might form from a wider perspective.

In this special case, there seems to be no conceptual necessity, and probably no psychological necessity, that he be motivated at all to administer the punishment. Surely he may, when the moment of decision comes, have no motivation to deny his daughter the outing and may instead find himself seeking a compromise such as a rebuke.[23] Granted, his contrary motivation may lead him to reconsider and eventually abandon his judgment. The point is that even while he holds it, contrary motivation can be both rational and — possibly working together with other factors — strong enough to prevent his judgment from having its typical motivational effect.

If this is a possible case, it shows that even rational agent motivational internalism is too strong. The case suggests, however, something a proponent of that view would welcome: it is only where the *overall* weight of reason goes against a rational moral judgment that the judgment fails to motivate. This suggestion gains support from the breadth of relevant rational considerations: these are not only judgments and facts; the rational counterweight can apparently also come from either moral emotion, such as revulsion at punishing one's daughter, or from what is sometimes described as moral experience, say a sense that the deed would be wrong. This sense need not derive from a conflicting moral judgment and, in part because it is not true (or false), is not itself a judgment; it may instead be both a force that deprives the standing judgment of motivating power and a ground — both motivational and evidential — for forming a new judgment to replace the standing one.

It may well be, however, that even this restricted rational agent motivational internalism is too strong and that there are counter-instances to rational agent motivational internalism that do not depend on either the overall weight of reasons or on moral emotion or moral experience. The same father could be lacking motivation to act on his judgment even if love, or pity, or perhaps depression, rather than such things as a sense of why his daughter did what she did, is what blocks any motivational energy his moral judgment may have had or produced. It is at least not clear that this kind of motivational blockage implies any dramatic deficiency in rationality. In any case, once we can understand why motivational internalism is not a conceptual truth, the possibilities for explaining its empirical falsehood can be seen to be diverse.[24]

Granted, perspectival motivational internalism might still hold: we could say that in making the punitive judgment in question the father has not full-bloodedly taken the moral point of view. There is, however, an air of stipulation about this. Granted, too, that this man is perhaps not normal, or at any rate not highly rational, if his moral judgment has *no* motivational force. Still, that he is not highly rational is a weak thesis, and that he is not normal might follow from his violating a strong but merely contingent pattern.

The issue of normality is relevant in another way. Largely because, for our self-addressed moral judgments, we normally do have significantly strong motivation to act accordingly, citing such a judgment normally suffices to explain action of ours that we may be taken to have thought the judgment required of us.[25] This easily creates the impression that the judgment is itself automatically motivational. But that should not be inferred without further premises. Citing a lighted cigarette dropped in the leaves can explain how a fire started, but this does not in the least imply that the explanation does not depend on the additional factor of dryness, which is quite "external" to the noted cause. Citing the contact of an open wound with poison ivy can explain a rash even if in a few cases such a rash does not occur after that kind of contact or can have another source. If we conclude, from the general success (in the relevant sense of rational acceptability) of explanations of actions by appeal to moral judgments, that such judgments are intrinsically motivational, we may be doing similarly defective reasoning.

The particular way in which I have argued that rational agent motivational internalism is too strong indicates something important both for the general issue of the relation between reason and morality and for understanding motivational internalism. Often our desires, moral emotions, moral experiences, and other non-truth-valued (and in that sense non-cognitive) states have evidential value. They may provide quite good grounds for a judgment, and indeed they are so commonly both the psychological and the normative basis for our moral judgments that it can be easy to think that moral judgments imply them. A common cause of something can look like an effect of it, or even a constituent in it, particularly when the causal relation can and often does run the other way. We do not need to be motivational internalists to see that one source of moral judgment is moral experience, say of revulsion or felt obligation, and that a common source of motivation to do a certain deed is a judgment — in some cases even one arrived at by intellectual intuition or cool reasoning — that one ought to do that deed.[26] But a close association need not derive from an entailment and may mislead us about which way the causal power runs.

A special feature of the association I am stressing between motivation and moral judgment is its non-causal aspect: the normative support that certain motivational states can provide to moral judgment. The suggested view — that certain motivational states can be evidence for normative judgments concerning their objects — might be called *motivational evidentialism*. The specifically moral version of it, on which such states as wants, attitudes, and emotions are evidence for moral judgments, would be moral motivational evidentialism. This view is interesting in its own right; but particularly since the evidential value of the relevant motivational states is greatest in rational agents, the view helps to explain why rational agent motivational internalism is plausible, even if the latter holds only for ideally rational agents. In rational agents, moral judgment may *derive* from motivational elements; it is then easily seen to be accompanied by them and can mistakenly be taken to be their source.

There are, then, many truths lying in the vicinity of rational agent motivational internalism; but it turns out, I believe, that one may have to choose between giving up even this quite plausible motivational internalism and maintaining it at the price of adopting a quite idealized notion of a rational agent. Much work must be done to show how far the relevant degree of idealization would take us beyond the usual capacities of ordinary moral agents.[27] Whatever that degree, one further conclusion seems warranted here: it seems doubtful that any motivational internalism, whether restricted to rational agents or not, is both defensible in the light of the distinctions and points suggested here and strong enough to provide a good premise for noncognitivism. If it is defensible in the light of those points, then it does not force a non-cognitive construal of moral judgment. Moral judgment, cognitively construed, can be allied with motivational factors that account for its apparently having the motivational power that is arguably incompatible with its being true or false and in that sense simply an intellectual attitude. An alliance of moral judgment with non-cognitive powers, rather than a lack of cognitivity in itself, can account for the appearance it sometimes has of intrinsic motivational power.

V. Normative Reasons and Motivational Internalism

Supposing that motivational internalism proper is mistaken, there may still be strong connections we have yet to discern between holding a moral judgment and having reasons for action. For one thing, the judgments-as-reasons view may still be true: holding a moral judgment may imply having a *normative* reason for action. This view is independent of motivational internalism, but the two have been closely associated, perhaps in part because each takes holding a moral judgment to entail having a kind of reason. The judgments-as-reasons view might be rationalized as follows. First, if a (self-addressed) moral judgment is true, the agent would arguably have a sound reason to act accordingly, since the agent holds a *correct judgment* of obligation; second, if the judgment is justified but not true — a *judgment correctly held*, we might say — the agent would also have a genuine though differently grounded normative (and so in a sense objective) reason for such action; and third, if it is neither justified nor true, the agent would presumably still have a kind of subjective reason for such action, one supporting the action from the agent's point of view. (I say 'presumably' because there may be judgments qualifying as moral that are so obviously false or unjustified that one cannot be said, in virtue of holding them, to have a reason for action at all, and in that case the judgments-as-reasons view would need qualification.)[28]

If, as the judgments-as-reasons view has it, moral judgments provide normative reasons for action, one might seek a route from this normative cousin of motivational internalism to a more moderate version of that view. Such an excursion is especially likely to seem promising on the plausible assumption that at least many of our most important normative and motivational reasons for action derive from common sources in "human nature." Some theorists attracted to motivational internalism might note that, between holding a moral judgment (or at least a justified one) and having motivation to act accordingly, there is a connection that can survive the rejection of motivational internalism in all the forms I have specified. For surely, it might be argued, one can have a normative reason to do something only if one *can* do it (intentionally); and if one cannot be motivated to do it, one cannot do it (intentionally). Hence, if holding a moral judgment entails having a moral reason to act accordingly, then holding a moral judgment also entails the capacity to act in accordance with it and thereby the capacity to be motivated to do it. Call this second entailment claim *capacity internalism* (simpliciter): it takes the capacity for motivation to be internal to holding a moral judgment.

Despite its modest appearance, capacity internalism of this sort is too strong. One could hold a moral judgment in ignorance of relevant incapacities to be motivated accordingly; these incapacities might be artificially induced (say, by brain manipulation) even if they never naturally occur. Moreover, unless just any moral judgment, however ill-considered, generates a normative reason, even the basis for this internalism is unsound.

Suppose, however, that we consider only moral judgments that are true or at least justified. It is quite plausible to hold that these judgments do entail a capacity to act accordingly and to be motivated to do so, since (for instance) the judgment that I should A would presumably not be justified if I could not A, which I apparently could not do (intentionally) if I could not be motivated to do it. More cautiously, it might be held that such a motivational capacity is entailed by one's holding such a judgment, at least where holding it provides a normative reason for action — a view we might call *qualified capacity internalism*.[29]

Qualified capacity internalism is plausible, but it is quite weak. What sorts of things could one not even be capable of being motivated to do? Apart from the possibility that motivation is blocked by artificial manipulation of the brain, we might mention things one believes to be absolutely impossible. But are these candidates for things one could have reason to do? Perhaps they would be candidates if two conditions held: one had good reason to believe they are possible, and they in fact are. In any case, it is desirable to strengthen capacity internalism. In working toward a more plausible version it is natural to include a capacity for the moral judgment's playing a role *in* the motivation it implies one can have, since the point of the view is in part to connect moral judgment with the actions it should lead us to perform. But that also leaves us with a weak thesis; it would require only the capacity to want to act in accord with the moral judgment.[30] If, then, capacity for moral motivation can be derived from the notion of holding a justified moral judgment via such a judgment's implying that the judge has a normative reason, this does not come even close to deriving *actual* motivation from such judgments.

Suppose for the sake of argument that holding a true or justified moral judgment favoring an action is sufficient to give one a (moral) normative reason for that action. Is a moral judgment or something like it, such as a moral belief favoring the action in question, also *necessary* for one's having such a normative reason? It may seem so, since it may seem that the only way we can "have" moral reasons for action is through some relevant consideration's entering our cognitive system, and this may be taken to require our holding an appropriate judgment or belief (perhaps on the assumption that moral reasons arise from practical reasoning whose concluding element is or implies such a judgment or belief). Call this cognitive representation requirement the *judgmental theory of moral reasons.* It is important in part because if even generic motivational internalism is true, this view implies that having a (moral) normative reason for action entails motivation to act accordingly. That entailment, in turn, specifies an even stronger respect in which morality is practical than does motivational internalism itself: the mere having of a moral reason to do something would imply some degree of motivation to do it, since the only way to have it would require holding a moral judgment, and holding such a judgment is motivating.

The judgmental theory of moral reasons is surely too strong. For it plainly makes sense to ask whether an agent has a reason to do something even where the agent has made no judgment, and formed no belief, favoring it.[31] A colleague who knows me and my class might say that I have a good reason not to change the grade, even before I myself consider the matter and arrive at a moral judgment that explicitly states this reason not to do so. There are various ways to "have" reasons — in moral as in other matters. The notion resists analysis, but part of the idea is this: where there are considerations, of a kind accessible to one by reflection, that favor an action sufficiently to count as reasons for it, one may be said to have those reasons.[32] The more readily accessible they are, for instance in terms of how much one would need to reflect to form the relevant beliefs — those expressing the reasons — the less implicitly the reasons are had.

This way of speaking may strike some philosophers as question-beggingly objectivist; for the suggestion is that there can *be* reasons for action which no one in any ordinary sense has, and that indeed one can discover reasons which, despite their relevance to one's conduct, one did not previously have. There can, for example, be reasons not to allow donors to a university to dictate the use of their gifts, whether we are aware of these reasons or not; and as this suggests, whether or not we have any motivation to act accordingly. Perhaps there cannot be reasons for any action of ours if we *could not* become aware of them, but that may be true not because there are no objective reasons at all but because any such reasons would not be reasons *for us* to do something unless we could become aware of them. These questions about the conditions for having reasons to act bring us to the second main kind of internalism to be considered in this chapter: reasons internalism.

VI. Reasons Internalism and Moral Motivation

There is perhaps less diversity concerning what constitutes reasons internalism than regarding what constitutes motivational internalism, but again I think the wisest course is to indicate what seems central and proceed to a working characterization. The basic thesis, in broad terms, is that a (normative) reason for action must be grounded in some internal conative or at least non-cognitive motivational state of the agent, for instance a desire, as opposed to deriving from an external requirement such as a categorical imperative or the intrinsic value of pleasure in the world.

Two philosophical motivations for reasons internalism are, first, a Humean conviction that moral and other normative considerations yielding reasons for action do not "come from reason" (in a sense implying that these considerations are not true or false) and, second, a conviction that since morality is practical and can be so only if it supplies reasons for action that have the motivating power of conative states, it does supply such reasons. Commonly it is normative reasons, or at least subjective justificatory reasons — roughly the kind the agent would accept as justificatory — that are the primary concern of the view. Thus, if holding a moral judgment provides a normative reason for action, it provides an internal normative reason, just as, if holding such a judgment is intrinsically motivating, it provides an internal (motivational) reason for action.

There is a third philosophical motivation for reasons internalism, this time deriving from a positive Humean position. Reasons internalism seems most commonly to be inspired largely by the instrumentalist view of reasons for action, historically represented most powerfully by Hume and attractive even to non-Humeans for its apparent naturalism.[33] On this instrumentalist view (practical) reason functions to serve desire: it does not independently motivate desire, and the rationality of an action — roughly, its being adequately supported by one or more appropriate kinds of reasons — is determined by how well it contributes to satisfying the agent's non-instrumental ("basic") desires — above all, desires for things as ends in themselves; and these desires are held not to admit of (substantive) appraisal as rational or irrational.[34] All reasons for action, then, are rooted in desire, broadly conceived.

It might be held that this version of Humean instrumentalism entails that there *is* no practical reason. This is a plausible interpretation because reason is neither normatively nor motivationally practical: it grounds neither judgments of what we should do nor motivation to do anything. Reason still has, however, a major directive role, above all in pointing the way to desire satisfaction. It may thus be considered *instrumentally practical*. It provides our map of the world; without that map no amount of desire would lead us to satisfaction, except by good fortune.[35] We may assume for the sake of argument that this role is sufficient to make such instrumentalism a candidate to account for (normative) reasons for action.

Where instrumentalism is the chief source of reasons internalism, we get a narrower reasons internalism than the version rooting normative reasons for action only in non-cognitive states: reasons for action must be grounded not only internally, as they might be in a sense of moral obligation, but in non-instrumental desire. Call this view *conative reasons internalism*. It allows a causal role for judgments as producers of desires and for desires or other conative states as producers of judgment; but judgments themselves, at least if construed as cognitive attitudes, do not ground reasons for action. One would not have a reason in virtue of holding a judgment, but at best in virtue of something produced by, or producing, that judgment, such as a desire to help a friend or pleasure at the thought of doing this.

Although reasons internalism is independent of motivational internalism, it helps us both to understand the appeal of that view and to see the implications of instrumentalist conceptions of normative reasons for action. I think it likely that one reason why motivational internalism is attractive to some philosophers is that they hold an instrumentalist version of reasons internalism and want to accommodate our sense that (holding) moral judgment is full-bloodedly practical in providing both motivational and normative reason for action. If moral judgments do not motivate, at least in the broad sense of entailing that one has some want (suitably connected with the content of the judgment), then they obviously do not provide motivational reasons, and, by instrumentalist lights, they do not provide normative reasons either, since neither in themselves nor by what they entail do they appropriately serve desire (which implies wanting); hence, they are not practical in either of the main senses, the normative and the motivational. But notice two interconnected points that are easily overlooked or insufficiently emphasized. One concerns normative reasons, the other motivational reasons; and both indicate difficulties in the initially attractive project of combining an instrumentalist view of practical reason with motivational internalism, especially where the latter is conjoined with the usual and plausible view that moral judgments (at least when justified) provide normative reasons for action. Here are two major and closely related difficulties.

First, if, as motivational internalism proper implies, moral judgments by themselves provide normative reasons for action — independently of embodying or at least serving the agent's non-instrumental desires, for instance by indicating means to what one wants — then instrumentalism about practical rationality must be abandoned. For those judgments would provide normative reasons for action that are not necessarily rooted in the agent's desires (or in anything "passional"). Judging that I ought to keep a promise, for example, may derive from beliefs about moral standards and may indicate nothing about how my doing so serves my basic desires. Instrumentalists might reply that their view can allow moral judgments to *cause* intrinsic desires to act accordingly, and they may still claim that only intrinsic desires ultimately are, or ground, reasons for action. Granted. Still, this way of saving motivational internalism — moving to a (contingent) consequential version — has a price: it greatly attenuates the sense in which moral judgments are in themselves practical. They imply motivation only conditionally, even if the relevant conditions are commonly satisfied in normal people. Thus, if it is a Humean instrumentalism about the status of (normative) reasons for action that leads one to a commitment to motivational internalism, it may in the end be at best difficult to reconcile the two positions.[36]

Second, supposing that instrumentalism is taken to hold that our basic desires are the ground not only of normative reasons but also of motivational reasons (and so of practical reasons in general), motivational internalism must be abandoned, at least given two assumptions: that it implies, as it does in the constitutive version, that holding a moral judgment provides in itself a motivating reason for action, and that moral judgment is cognitively construed, as it must be on the natural (if resistible) assumption that it is true or false. For a moral judgment, cognitively construed, does not by itself entail possession of any relevant desire, as opposed to some other kind of motivation. These points may help to explain why, for instrumentalists committed to motivational internalism, noncognitivism is so attractive.

More generally, a common and important view — motivational internalism proper, which takes motivation to be internal to moral judgments as such — turns out to be (in its cognitive versions) incompatible with instrumentalism, and instrumentalists committed to motivational internalism must retreat to its weaker, consequential version, which is both consistent with reasons externalism — in part because lack of motivation to act on a moral judgment is perfectly consistent with having a normative reason to act on it — and too weak to be a good premise for noncognitivism. One response would be to argue that noncognitivism can be shown independently of motivational internalism and then to adopt a noncognitivist instrumentalism. But demonstrating that is no easy task; and if establishing noncognitivism can be shown to rely on arguments independent of motivational internalism, that would be a significant step.

VII. Reasons Externalism and Moral Motivation

By contrast with instrumentalists in the theory of practical reason, Kantians and other objectivists about practical reason should not be construed as reasons internalists, and Kant, on one plausible reading, cannot be one. Much depends on what is required for a reason to count as internally grounded. If reasons depend on desires or on any non-cognitive elements that motivate action independently of practical judgment, then Kantians cannot be construed as reasons internalists.

There is, however, at least one kind of internalism — an epistemic version — that is consistent with objectivism about ethics and practical reason. It must be distinguished from other kinds of reasons internalism both for clarity about the grounds and accessibility of reasons for action and lest its plausibility be mistakenly taken to support those other views. This internalist position might be called *accessibility reasons internalism*: it says simply that a reason for action, normative or motivational, must be such that the agent can, in a suitable psychological sense, *have* it, for instance be appropriately aware of it. Thus, if I can see, by reflection, that a deed would advance my ideals, I have a reason to do it, whereas an esoteric argument for doing it that I cannot understand is not accessible to me and does not provide a reason for my doing it. Advancing my ideals, moreover, need not be just a matter of desire satisfaction. Hence this epistemic internalist requirement does not entail reasons internalism. Internalism about theoretical reason is compatible with the objectivity of reasons affirmed by externalism about practical reason.

In contrast with Kantians, a reasons internalist attracted to the epistemic internality requirement might, in the theory of practical reason, hold a stronger view than such a theorist typically affirms, one we might call *actual state reasons internalism*. It says that a reason for action must be or reside in an actual non-cognitive motivational state of the agent, such as a desire, and in that sense be a reason one *has*. Neither reasons internalist view rules out *non-occurrent* desires as sources of reasons, but the actual state view does exclude hypothetical desires and other hypothetical attitudes.[37] *Pure instrumentalist reasons internalism* would be a special case of the actual state variety; for such an instrumentalism, hypothetical desires do not count as sources of reasons for action, and only non-instrumental actual desires count as reason-providing internal states. And whereas the conative version merely restricts the sources to conative states, actual or hypothetical, the pure instrumentalist version requires both a desire as the relevant kind of conative state and its actuality. Roughly, the idea is that our current reasons for action reside wholly in our current desires; these are taken to express our motivational nature conceived as the source of those reasons.[38]

It is essential to see that accessibility internalism — which represents an important and plausible range of positions in moral epistemology — lends no support to reasons internalism of any kind. It requires only that reasons for action be internally accessible, not that they must be expressed in an actual state of the agent such as a desire or belief, much less that their source be desire or only some non-cognitive state. Hence, there can be what are commonly considered *external*, objective reasons for action: such considerations as the unfairness of a certain assessment, the disrespectfulness of a certain editorial, and the beneficence of a certain policy. These can, at a given time, be reasons why we *should* do something, and can become reasons why we in fact *do* it, even if, at that time, we have no desires, and hold no judgments, that favor the action. We need only be such that by suitable reflection, say by thinking, in the light of moral standards we accept or would accept on reflection, about the factual propositions we believe, we would hold the appropriate judgment and could have the motivation appropriate to it.[39]

Judgment and motivation emerge as important, then, but not as preconditions for the existence of reasons for action: instead, they are possibilities whose realization may constitute a necessary condition for reasons' playing a practical role. I might, for instance, have to judge that raising the grade would be unfair before I actually do anything in response to the request for reconsideration. This could be either because the judgment produces or enhances motivation I already have or because the judgment triggers action by behaviorally focusing my already sufficiently strong moral desires regarding my grading.

At this point an instrumentalist might maintain that the reasons externalist has simply replaced actual desire with hypothetical desire as the ground of so-called external reasons for action. The objection might be that the accessibility requirement on reasons is really intended to guarantee — or is in any case plausible only so far as it is seen as guaranteeing — that if we have a (normative) reason for action, then we would form a desire appropriate to ground that reason. Rational action, then, is still subservient to desire, but the desire may be hypothetical. There are at least two difficulties with this line of reply.

One difficulty is that it is only moral judgment that the relevant reasons externalism (the kind compatible with accessibility internalism) says we *would* hold under appropriate conditions of information and reflection; by contrast, the relevant desires are, for such externalism, only such that we *could* have them — a very weak requirement, as already explained. The requirement is certainly too weak to guarantee a conative basis for holding the relevant moral judgment (the kind of basis one must have, by pure instrumentalist lights, in order for the judgment to express a reason for action). It could be, for instance, that on reflection I would judge that I ought to prepare a makeup exam, yet owing to how unpleasant doing it would seem to me to be, I would lack the desires necessary to get me to do it and would suffer weakness of will if brought to the test. Apart from an implausible motivational internalism so strong as to preclude weakness of will in such cases, this possibility cannot be ruled out.

Second, suppose the accessibility requirement, as embedded in a reasons externalism, did imply that we would have desires that motivate actions appropriate to our moral judgments. It would not follow that these hypothetical desires are the *ground* of the normative reasons in question. *Both* those reasons and the desires might be grounded in the judgments or in some other potentially rational source, as surely a plausible reasons externalism would require. Perhaps I would want to keep my promise because I would judge that I must keep it, as opposed to judging I must because of an antecedent empathic desire. Moreover, the normative grounds of my judgment could be external. Again, accessibility reasons internalism can be seen to be compatible with reasons externalism.

I conclude here that the most plausible reasons internalism is the (epistemic) accessibility kind compatible with what is commonly called reasons externalism and that the most plausible versions of this epistemic variety of reasons internalism are incompatible with the instrumentalist conception of reasons for action. It appears that there can *be* reasons for us to act, whether they reside in judgments or desires of ours or not, and that we can *have* reasons for action residing in moral judgments we hold, whether those judgments motivate us or not. These plausible theses are among the qualified forms of reasons externalism and motivational externalism that seem to be true.

Conclusion

Given the points that have emerged in this chapter, we may draw a number of broad conclusions about the four relationships that have been our central concern: those between intellect and will, reason and morality, judgment and motivation, and normative and motivational reasons. Let us start with the status of normative reasons, which is probably the most important preoccupation of the theory of practical reason.

If the qualified externalist — and internalist — positions I have proposed as plausible views are true, then the instrumentalist conception of (normative) reasons for action is mistaken. This is a powerful conception which I cannot directly criticize here.[40] It is important to see, however, that the most significant opposition in the theory of practical reason is probably not between motivational internalists and motivational externalists but between instrumentalists, who are a kind of reasons internalist, and objectivists, who are a kind of reasons externalist. Important as the motivational issue is, those who, like Kantians and Rossian intuitionists, disagree about what motivation, if any, is intrinsic to moral judgment can still agree that there are external reasons for action, and that accordingly reason *should* govern desire, whether, causally speaking, it does or not.

Motivational internalists and motivational externalists can also largely agree on what, overall, constitutes a rational person, for instance on what sort of motivation a rational person who holds certain moral judgments should have. They will differ on the sources of that motivation. Instrumentalists, by contrast, conceive both (norma-tive) reasons for action and the rational agent quite differently than not only all rea-sons externalists but also Kantian and many other motivational internalists. Even apart from a direct assessment of instrumentalism, we should ask how the instru-mentalist can account for moral reasons.

Above all, for instrumentalism, moral reasons are at the mercy of what one's non-instrumental desires happen to be. If I have no non-instrumental desires to meet moral standards, and — perhaps because there is, in Hume's phrase, too little of the dove kneaded into my frame — I have no such desires to whose realization I do or would believe my meeting those standards contributes, then I have no reasons to be moral, and this is so even if I happen to make moral judgments. If motivational inter-nalism (proper) were true, I *could* not make such judgments without thereby having some motivation. But if, for reasons suggested in the preceding sections, it is mis-taken, then instrumentalists cannot appeal to moral judgment as automatically moti-vational and in that sense reason-giving, nor can noncognitivists appeal to such a motivational constituent in moral judgment as a premise undermining its cognitivity.

This is an important point. In addition to undermining an initially plausible and rather elegant Humean argument for noncognitivism, it deprives instrumentalism of one of its major resources for accounting for moral reasons: all normal adults make moral judgments; these in turn normally imply motivation — typically non-instru-mental motivation capable of grounding reasons for action; hence, morality is, if only because of the desires it arouses in us, a source of reasons for action. Hume would not have put it like this, because he wanted to dissociate "morals" from rea-son; but that was above all to prevent moral judgment from being grounded *in rea-son*, which cannot by itself motivate and so cannot produce moral judgment con-ceived as motivating. He need not have denied (if he did) that holding moral judgments may, in a causal sense, provide one with reasons for action in the only sense in which, for Humeans, one can have such reasons: in virtue of one's having the appropriate non-instrumental desires, for moral judgments can certainly cause such desires.[41] To be sure, this makes the moral judgments we hold only causes of our having reasons and in themselves not expressions of actual reasons, but at least moral judgments have a practical role. They are not an autonomous voice of practi-cal reason, but they can ultimately produce the same practical effects.

If this assessment of the relation between instrumentalism and motivational internalism is sound, then for pure instrumentalism, the only motivational or moral reasons there are either are constituted by or depend on desires with appropriate content. If I do not have these desires, I not only *have* no moral reasons, there also *are* none affecting me. It might be, then, that there is no moral reason why I should not raise a grade even if doing this is unfair. That seems paradoxical. How could its being unfair not provide a moral reason to abstain? The question to ask here is what there is for 'unfair' to mean that, for instrumentalism, allows for the existence of such a reason. The word can have a conventional meaning, in terms of how society normally views such matters. But morality is not merely convention. Morality can have a moral grip on others through their desires; but whether it does is a contingent matter, and the main point here is in any case to account not for others' having rea-son to prevent my being unfair, but for my self-addressed judgment of unfairness to provide me with a reason for action. Indeed, on some views it is a hallmark of moral reasons for action that they can be normative reasons to act *against* one's non-instrumental desires and need not themselves be rooted in desires.

These and similar considerations should lead one to wonder whether instrumentalism can adequately account for what appears to be the autonomy — or at least the autonomy relative to *actual* desire — of moral reasons. I leave open that moral reasons may depend on non-moral ones, as hedonists and others have maintained. This dependence would still leave *practical* reasons autonomous from actual non-instrumental *desires*. I have not tried to show that instrumentalism cannot in some way deal with this autonomy problem. Elements in Hume and his successors are certainly suggestive.[42] But the job will be more difficult without the aid of motivational internalism and in the light of some of the distinctions I have stressed.

If we give up motivational internalism in any of its forms strong enough to undermine the existence of objective, external reasons for action, we must grant that reason, as exercised in moral judgment, need not always be *motivationally practical*, since these judgments do not entail motivational reasons. This concession in turn implies that reason — simply as reflected in moral judgment — has limited sovereignty over the will. But it does not entail that reason, as exercised in moral judgment, is not always *normatively practical*, thereby providing normative reasons: this is precisely what moral judgment must be if, even apart from entailing motivational reasons for action, it can provide normative reasons for action. Nor need we give up motivational internalism in its perspectival form: the idea that for those really judging *from the moral point of view*, holding a moral judgment implies motivation to act accordingly. More generally, we might retain *some* version of rational agent motivational internalism, perhaps the idea that, in those having a *sufficiently* good integration between intellect and will, holding a moral judgment implies motivation to act accordingly. We might even plausibly hold that in these restricted — but surely not uncommon — cases the motivation is adequate to permit explaining actions based on the judgment as performed in the service of that judgment.

It would be good if the sheer grasp of moral truth produced an appropriately strong inclination to act accordingly. We could educate the intellect and thereby properly direct the will. But although desire is commonly influenced by moral and other practical judgments — and must be substantially so influenced in truly rational persons — the influence is far from automatic. A benefit of this position is that it frees us from commitment to the idea that weak or perverse will can automatically block the perception of truths relevant to one's conduct. Reason can light our way even if the will does not or even cannot follow.

A further implication, then, of rejecting the versions of motivational internalism I have criticized is that if we expect people to be moral, we must educate their desires, emotions, and sensibilities, not just their intellects. Once we do, however — and especially if we build on the empathy in human nature — then desires, emotions, and experiences, like judgments, can provide normative reasons for action as well as motivation to perform them. To speak of genuine normative reasons for action is in one way to give a biased account of practical reason, since it tends to presuppose that there are some things, including moral ends, that it is reasonable to want for their own sake. That, in turn, implies that there are external reasons, a thesis that it is very difficult to show in the theory of practical reason. I believe, however, that its truth may well be a presupposition of morality.

Notes

This paper benefited much from discussion and comments at the St. Andrews Conference on Ethics and Practical Reason in 1995. For helpful written comments on earlier versions I thank John Deigh, Hugh McCann, Alfred Mele, Joseph Mendola, Elizabeth Radcliffe, Sophia Reibetanz, John Robertson, Michael Stocker, Mark Timmons, Mark van Roojen, Nick Zangwill, an anonymous reader, and especially Garrett Cullity and Berys Gaut.

1. This is not the only way to act accordingly; I could, e.g., also reassess the work of all the students and raise all the grades. For more complicated judgments there is an even greater variety of ways to act accordingly; that notion deserves analysis, but nothing I say will turn on the absence of one.

2. This term seems preferable to 'motivating reason' on at least one count: it does not suggest that any action motivated by the reason actually occurs.

3. Two or more motivational reasons can jointly produce or jointly explain the same action. Such reasons are not merely potential causes of action but factors that can at least partially explain action as performed *for* them. An account of reasons distinguishing five main kinds of reasons for action is given in my "Acting for Reasons," *Philosophical Review* 95 (1986): 511–46.

4. Arguably a desire is a case of motivation (to act), as opposed to a directionless energy source, only when the agent believes, or is at least disposed to believe, something to the effect that the agent's doing the deed in question would realize (or would contribute to realizing) the desired object.

5. Granted, such explanations also indicate intending, but I have argued in "Intending," *Journal of Philosophy* 70 (1973): 387–403 that intending entails wanting in the relevant sense, and in "The Concept of Wanting," *Philosophical Studies* 21 (1973): 1–21 I have explicated the relevant kind of wanting. Both papers and supporting ones are in my *Action, Intention, and Reason* (Ithaca and London: Cornell University Press, 1993).

6. It has been held (e.g. by Donald Davidson) that intending *is* a kind of belief, but I cannot see that there is a compelling argument for this or even one with appropriate content or sufficient force to explain why (literal) talk of true and false intentions is simply not English.

7. Throughout, in speaking of normative reasons I shall mean prima facie reasons, as opposed to all-things-considered reasons. Nothing of importance in the essay turns on this restriction.

8. At one point Thomas Nagel maintains this sort of view, at least in regard to the connection between a kind of judgment and being motivated to act accordingly: "[T]he first-person acknowledgment of a sufficient reason for doing something . . . is sufficient to explain one's doing it. . . . There is no need to hold that 'X acknowledges a reason to A' entails 'X does A, or X wants to do A.' " *The Possibility of Altruism* (Oxford: Clarendon Press, 1970), pp. 110–11. This is roughly equivalent to the view that holding the kind of practical judgment we are speaking of is in itself motivationally sufficient for one's A-ing, thus an adequate *reason why* one A's if one does. Nagel clarifies the claim (in a way that brings it close to another I shall later distinguish) by adding, "All I wish to claim is that such an acknowledgement is by itself *capable* of providing a motivation in the appropriate direction — that there is no need to seek an alternative or supplementary explanation of action when that one is available." Ibid.,

p. 111. (The clause following the dash strengthens the preceding one, on the assumption that the reason why we need not seek more information is that sufficient motivation *is* present; but it is not clear how much weakening of the original claim, if any, is intended in the clarifying sentence.)

9. Reasons internalism as thus characterized is close (but probably not equivalent) to the view Bernard Williams identifies as taking only internal reasons to be genuine reasons for action, in "Internal and External Reasons," in his *Moral Luck* (Cambridge: Cambridge University Press, 1981), ch. 8. The judgments-as-reasons view could also be called a form of reasons internalism, for although it does not require that a reason be automatically motivating, it does allow an internal element, like a moral judgment one holds, to constitute a reason; but this would be a weak internalism, since it neither makes internality a necessary condition for being a reason nor requires that a normative reason be (motivationally) practical. I mention the view simply to locate it in the spectrum and set it aside.

10. For reasons to doubt that this approach to normative reasons is adequate even to account for the force of hypothetical imperatives see Christine Korsgaard, "The Normativity of Instrumental Reason," in Garrett Cullity and Berys Gaut, eds., *Ethics and Practical Reason*, Oxford University Press, forthcoming. Related difficulties are brought out by Jean Hampton in "On Instrumental Rationality," in J. B. Schneewind, ed., *Reasons, Ethics, and Society* (Peru, Ill.: Open Court Publishing Co., 1966).

11. The relevant internality and externality are not easy to define and have not to my knowledge been sharply defined in the literature. In good part, the idea is that an external reason is in a certain way interpersonally and cross-culturally valid and does not depend for its normative force on what anyone believes or desires (except where the proposition is about beliefs or desires, as where a reason for doing something is that a person one loves wants more than anything else that one do it). As this suggests, some non-instrumental, non-cognitive grounding is allowable under externalism. For one thing, moral experience might be a ground; for another, where satisfying desire is taken as a prima facie intrinsic good (as perhaps, arguably, in the case of loved ones), a desire might be at least part of the ground of an external reason. Neither of these elements would be considered a ground of a reason for action by paradigmatic reasons internalists; either of them could be so regarded by certain noncognitivists, which shows that given a noncognitivist reading of "truth" for moral judgments, externalism can be held by a noncognitivist.

12. There is also *a* reason, which seems a slightly weaker point. Normally, saying there is reason (to A) implies a significant degree of justification and a greater degree than is implied in saying there is a reason. Arguably, if there is a moral ground to A, there is always reason to A.

13. R. M. Hare may be an exception to this in apparently disallowing the kind of weakness of will here described. See, e.g., ch. 5 of *The Language of Morals* (Oxford: Oxford University Press, 1961).

14. For a number of them, including many references to the literature on the topic, see W. D. Falk, " 'Ought' and Motivation," *Proceedings of the Aristotelian Society* 48 (1947–48): 111–38; William K. Frankena, "Obligation and Motivation in Recent Moral Philosophy," in A. I. Melden, ed., Essays in Moral Philosophy (Seattle: University of Washington Press, 1958) Nagel, *The Possibility of Altruism*; John McDowell, "Are Moral Requirements Hypothetical Imperatives?," *Proceedings of the Aristotelian Society* 13 (1978): 13–29; E. J. Bond, *Reason and Value* (Cambridge and New York: Cambridge University Press, 1983); Stephen L. Darwall, *Impartial Reason* (Ithaca: Cornell University Press, 1983), esp. ch. 5; Christine M. Korsgaard, "Skepticism about Practical Reason," *Journal of Philosophy* 83 (1986): 5–25; Mark C. Timmons, "Kant and the Possibility of Moral Motivation," *Southern Journal of Philosophy* 23 (1985): 377–98, David Brink, *Moral Realism and the Foundations of Ethics* (Cambridge and

New York: Cambridge University Press, 1989); Onora O'Neill, *Constructions of Reason* (Cambridge and New York: Cambridge University Press, 1989):; my *Practical Reasoning* (London and New York: Routledge, 1989), esp. chs. 2 and 3; John Robertson, "Hume on Practical Reason," *Proceedings of the Aristotelian Society* 24 (1989); Alfred R. Mele, "Motivational Internalism: The Powers and Limits of Practical Reasoning," *Philosophia* 19 (1989): 427–36; Michael Stocker, *Plural and Conflicting Values* (Oxford: Clarendon Press, 1990); Jamie Dreier, "Internalism and Speaker Relativism," *Ethics* 101 (1990): 6–26; Jonathan Dancy, *Moral Reasons* (Oxford: Basil Blackwell, 1993); Rachel Cohon, "Internalism about Reasons for Action," *Pacific Philosophical Quarterly* 74 (1993): 265–88; Michael Smith, *The Moral Problem* (Oxford: Basil Blackwell, 1994); Kurt Baier, *The Rational and the Moral Order* (Chicago and LaSalle: Open Court, 1995); John Deigh, "Empathy and Universalizability," *Ethics* 105 (1995): 743–63; and Connie S. Rosati, "Internalism and the Good for a Person," *Ethics* 106 (1966):247–73.

15. This needs various qualifications; e.g. there is a non-cognitivist version, there is the possibility that one happened to be non-morally motivated to A before one discovered one ought to A, and there is of course the contention that general moral judgments (principles) could not be true unless there were some degree of motivation appropriate to them.

16. Views that are at least similar receive sympathetic treatment in Korsgaard, "Skepticism about Practical Reason," and in Smith, *The Moral Problem*, e.g. in ch. 3, where he considers the idea behind (motivational) internalism to be roughly that "[i]f an agent judges that it is right for her to *o* in circumstances C, then either she is motivated to *o* in C or she is practically irrational" (p. 61).

17. See, e.g., the *Treatise*, bk. III, pt. I, sec. I, in which he says that "when you pronounce any character or action to be vicious, you mean nothing, but that from the constitution of your nature you have a feeling or sentiment of blame from the contemplation of it" (p. 469 in the Selby-Bigge, ed., Oxford: Oxford University Press, 1888), where such a feeling can be taken to be at once motivational and non-cognitive (at least in not being true or false), quite apart from whether it entails desire properly so called. This reading is neutral with respect to non-cognitivism; a judgment can arise from a sentiment of blame, e.g., whether it is propositional or, in a non-cognitive sense, expressive. Note, however, that in making a moral judgment one could express such a feeling only in the illocutionary sense and so not have it. Thus, if Hume holds a "consequential internalism," it should be because there is something motivating he takes moral judgment itself to imply, as there is if it *must* arise from a feeling or sentiment construed as passional or otherwise motivational. Perhaps his considered view (and certainly another broadly Humean view) is that moral judgments are consequentially but contingently motivating.

18. See, e.g., the *Grundlegung*, sect. 413, where he says that "the will is a faculty of choosing only that which reason, independently of inclination, recognizes as practically necessary, i.e., as good." See *Foundations of the Metaphysics of Morals*, trans. Lewis White Becks (New York: Liberal Arts Press, 1959). I discuss this kind of Kantian position, and explain how it may allow for weakness of will, in ch. 2 of *Practical Reasoning*. Korsgaard's "The Normativity of Instrumental Reason" is highly pertinent to this matter. Cf. John Deigh's discussion of Kant: "[I]f one holds, as Kant did, that an aversion to inconsistency is inherent in reason, then the motive would be internal to the cognitive operation and the account would therefore support taking the internalism of the categorical imperative to be true of our deeper knowledge of right and wrong" ("Empathy and Universalizability," p. 751).

19. This paragraph and the preceding one derive in part from a section of my "Autonomy, Reason, and Desire," *Pacific Philosophical Quarterly* 72 (1992): 247–71.

20. Here one might raise the question why we should not abandon the plausible view one might call *cognitive internalism*— roughly the thesis that beliefs motivate other beliefs

when one judges the propositional object of the former to entail or strongly support that of the latter, independently of separate motivation, such as a desire to believe the consequences of what one believes. There is a great deal to say here. Two important points are, first, that we are here remaining in the cognitive domain as opposed to crossing from the cognitive realm to that of motivation, with a different direction of fit to the world; and second, a tendency to infer (though not necessarily to believe) consequences of what one believes is plainly in part constitutive of the notion of a rational person in a way instantiating motivational internalism is not plainly constitutive of that notion — a point to be argued in the next section.

21. This position does not entail positing second-order desires or desires regarding one's judgments or moral standards, e.g. a desire to want to be moral or to act on one's moral judgments. There are many kinds of contents the appropriate desires could have, e.g. to be a certain kind of person, where that is understood in terms of doing the kinds of things in question, say grading students on their merits.

22. It might be objected that there are moral judgments or moral beliefs, say that people are beings with dignity, that a person cannot hold *without* taking, or in some way partially internalizing, the moral point of view. If such taking and internalizing are distinguished from capacities and dispositions thereto, this claim would seem at best difficult to show. But even if it is true, motivational elements essential to taking or internalizing that point of view may still be the source of the motivational reasons for action that go with the belief or judgment that require such a taking or internalization; these reasons need not be internal to it.

23. This case bears important similarities to one I have offered to show that weak-willed action is not necessarily irrational on balance. For a description of that case and a theory of how it is possible that case bears on the motivational counterpart presented here, see "Weakness of Will and Rational Action," *Australasian Journal of Philosophy* 68 (1990): 270–81, reprinted in my *Action, Intention, and Reason.*

24. For supporting data of the kind this paragraph notes, see Michael Stocker, "Desiring the Bad," *Journal of Philosophy* 79 (1979): 738–53. See also Alfred R. Mele, "Motivation: Essentially Motivation-Constituting Attitudes," *Philosophical Review* 105 (1966): 387–423, and "Internalist Moral Cognitivism and Listlessness," *Ethics* (forthcoming) (1996): 727–53. The former is also instructive concerning what constitutes motivation as opposed to cognition. One way to resist treating the connection between moral judgment and motivation as contingent is to argue that it is a conceptual and necessary truth that holding such a judgment *tends* to produce motivation. If this comes to saying that a full understanding of (holding a) moral judgment implies seeing its possible influence on motivation, there may be truth in it; but that (and I suspect the other plausible interpretations of the claim) is a quite weak thesis far short of motivational internalism.

25. Nagel, among others, emphasizes this. See, e.g., the quotation from *The Possibility of Altruism* cited in note 8.

26. For valuable discussions of how moral experience may evidence moral judgments see Michael William Tolhurst, "On the Epistemic Value of Moral Experience," *Southern Journal of Philosophy* 29 (suppl.) (1990): 67–87; and Michael DePaul, *Balance and Refinement: Beyond Coherentism in Moral Inquiry* (London and New York: Routledge, 1993).

27. It may be that much of the time, Kant does work with an idealization. If so, I would stress that much of his overall position could be preserved even apart from the rational agent motivational internalism.

28. We must, however, account for the notion of a bad reason, one that is relevant but utterly lacking in cogency. This favors the liberal notion of a reason I use here.

29. This kind of internalism is quite similar to a kind considered by Korsgaard in "Skepticism above Practical Reason." I bypass the point that what is entailed by holding the judgment is not necessarily *internal to it*, in which case the view under discussion is only a

generic, as opposed to a constitutive, motivational internalism, since it is simply a thesis about what is implied by a person's holding a moral judgment. For discussion of a thesis related to capacity internalism see Cohon, "Internalism about Reasons for Action."

30. This requirement is even weaker than it may look, for the reference is not to a desire whose *content* is: to act in accord with *J* (where *J* is the relevant judgment); the reference is to any of a range of action desires whose contents are appropriate to that judgment.

31. This claim is much less plausible if one assimilates dispositions to believe, e.g. tendencies to form beliefs upon reflecting on relevant data, to actual, dispositional beliefs. A case for rejecting the assimilation is given in my "Dispositional Beliefs and Dispositions to Believe," *Noûs* 28 (1994): 419–434.

32. For an indication of the kinds and degrees of having see my "Structural Justification," *Journal of Philosophical Research* 16 (1991), reprinted in my *The Structure of Justification* (Cambridge and New York: Cambridge University Press, 1993).

33. Hume did not, however, use the terms employed here. For discussion of Hume on this question, with attention both to the *Treatise* and to selected secondary literature, see Elizabeth Radcliffe, "How Does the Humean Sense of Duty Motivate," *Journal of the History of Philosophy* (forthcoming), and "Hume on Passion, Pleasure, and the Reasonableness of Ends," *Southwest Philosophy Review* 1994.

34. This is a rough characterization, in which 'substantive' is meant to allow instrumentalists to construe as irrational, desires for impossible states of affairs, especially those whose occurrence obviously entails a contradiction. Detailed treatments of the problem are given in my *Practical Reasoning*, esp. ch. 3, and "Autonomy, Reason, and Desire."

35. This partial defense of instrumentalism is not meant to answer the kind of objection to it that Korsgaard's paper cited in note 10 raises. More generally, it is arguable that if there are no non-instrumental reasons for action, then instrumental reasons cannot render action rational, in part because it would seem that the reason for action provided by the prospect of bringing about only ends that are subservient to further ends is like the guarantee of a promised good expressed by an infinite series of conditional promises: to give one *x* if *A* gives one *y*, which *A* promises to give one provided *B* gives one *z*, which *B* promises to give one provided *C* . . . etc. An account of this issue is given in ch. 11.

36. Did Hume himself have a problem? He does say that morals influence action and reason by itself does not, but he does not seem committed to saying that moral judgments provide even motivational reasons for action independently of non-instrumental desires.

37. The relevant distinction between a non-occurrent desire and a disposition to form one (which some might call a kind of hypothetical desire) is not easy to draw; a detailed account of it is given in my "Dispositional Beliefs and Dispositions to Believe," *Nous* 28 (1994): 419–34.

38. These actual desires might, but need not, include a second-order desire to act on desires one now lacks but would form on certain kinds of reflection; if they do not, then it might be argued that taking hypothetical desires to supply reasons is like allowing a hypothetical nature one might or would have to dictate to the nature one does have.

39. This is not an ordinary empirical 'could'; in any case, empirically one could be brain-manipulated to make some of the desires in fact impossible.

40. For direct criticism see Thomas Nagel's *The View from Nowhere* (Oxford and New York: Oxford University Press, 1986). Some of my critical discussion is in "Autonomy, Reason, and Desire" (ch. 9 above) and in "The Architecture of Reason," in *The Structure of Justification*.

41. For a textually detailed account of Humean practical rationality and of how Hume provides for the possibility of moral judgments figuring in practical reasoning, see Elizabeth Radcliffe, "Kantian Themes on a Humean Instrument: Why Hume is not *Really* a Skeptic about Practical Reasoning," *Canadian Journal of Philosophy* 27 (1997).

42. One notable approach is taken by Richard Fumerton in *Reason and Morality* (Ithaca and London: Cornell University Press, 1990). There are also powerful Humean strains in Bernard Williams's work, e.g. in his *Ethics and the Limits of Philosophy* (Cambridge: Harvard University Press, 1985). Cf. Donald C. Hubin, "Hypothetical Motivation," *Noûs* 30 (1996): 31–154 and "Irrational Desires," *Philosophical Studies* 62 (1991): 23–44. John Rawls, in *A Theory of Justice* (Cambridge: Harvard University Press, 1971), does not endorse instrumentalism in general but does try to derive his principles of justice from an instrumentalist conception of rationality, apart from the special assumption that rational persons do not suffer from envy. The relevant references and some discussion of his approach are given in chapter 9, "Autonomy, Reason, and Desire." For a detailed examination of autonomy and the role of reasons therein see Alfred R. Mele, *Autonomous Agents* (Oxford and New York: Oxford University Press, 1995).

11

Intrinsic Value and the Dignity of Persons

It is obvious that some things are good *for* certain purposes, others are good *of their kind*, and still others are good *as* one thing or another. But is anything good in itself, independently of its relations to anything else — intrinsically good, to use the most common term for this notion? Many philosophers have thought so, including most who are central figures in "the tradition." Others have denied this.[1] Many philosophers have also held not only that there is something good in itself but also that the intrinsically good is what makes life worth living.[2]

Even apart from the connection of purportedly intrinsic goodness with the "meaning of life," there is the question of how goodness of any kind is related to moral rightness and moral obligation. Are right actions, for instance, equivalent to those that it is in some way good to permit, and are morally obligatory actions those that it would be, in a certain way, bad not to perform? On one plausible view, these questions have an affirmative answer because the basic reasons for action, those constituting an independent normative basis for action, are grounded in intrinsic value conceived as including moral value.

Even if the intrinsically good (or intrinsically bad) does not provide the *only* basic reasons for action, and thereby a key both to living a good life and to understanding rightness and obligation, surely anything intrinsically good would provide *one* kind of basic reason for action.[3] To grant that pleasure, for example, is intrinsically good and then to deny that there is any reason to seek or promote pleasure would be at best inexplicable and would seem irrational.[4] Is there, however, a distinct kind of intrinsic value that provides *moral* reasons for action? And if the apparent reason-giving power possessed by moral considerations does not derive from intrinsic value, might moral considerations still provide reasons for action?

Both of these questions in turn are fundamental in understanding the dignity of persons. The notion of personal dignity has been important in moral philosophy, especially from Kant onward, but resists analysis. Is such dignity best understood as a kind of (intrinsic) moral value, or in terms of rights, or in some quite different way?

My aim here is to outline answers to all of these questions, drawing on and extending various points defended in previous chapters.

I. An Aristotelian Case for Intrinsic Goodness

Aristotle is the classical source of a certain kind of argument both for the existence of something intrinsically good and for the thesis that the basic intrinsic good is happiness. He says in a famous passage: "Suppose, then, that (a) there is some end of the things we pursue in our actions which we wish for because of itself, and because of which we wish for other things; and (b) we do not choose everything because of something else, since (c) if we do, it will go on without limit, making desire empty and futile; then clearly (d) this end will be the good, i.e. the best good."[5] Plainly, in the overall context Aristotle is arguing that there *is* an end of the kind described in (a). He thinks that we do not choose everything because of (for the sake of) something else; and in later passages it is clear that he takes only *eudaemonia* to fulfill the two criteria here set out for the good: being wished for (roughly, wanted) because of itself (for its own sake), and such that all else we want we want because of it. (Commonly 'eudaemonia' is translated as 'happiness', but it is also plausibly taken to be equivalent to 'human flourishing' in a special sense appropriate to the excellences whose exercise constitutes that flourishing.)

Among the striking elements of this passage is its apparent identification of the good, normatively conceived, with our psychologically final end, understood (at least chiefly) in terms of empirical facts about our motivational structure.[6] This apparently naturalistic identification is not surprising given Aristotle's teleological conception of nature as a realm in which each distinct kind of thing, including the human person, has a natural end whose achievement is its proper function (though that function is perhaps ascertainable without making irreducibly normative judgments of what is proper). It should also be noted, however (and is less often given sufficient weight) that the premise presented by (c) for one of Aristotle's central psychological assumptions suggests that he is thinking of a regress argument similar to the one he offers in *Posterior Analytics* 72b for a somewhat parallel conclusion in the theory of theoretical reason, a conclusion about the basis of knowledge. He is surely ruling out an infinite regress of choices — choosing A for the sake of B, B for the sake of C, and so forth — and presumably ruling out a circular chain as well — say, choosing A for the sake of B, B for the sake of C, and C for the sake of A — a kind of chain that is also endless and can "go on without limit."

Still another element in this passage should be stressed: the apparently normative presupposition that whatever the good is, it prevents desire from being endless and futile. This functionalistic presupposition is clearer in the *Nicomachean Ethics* as a whole: not only is the good — happiness — the ultimate psychological ground of desire; it also provides the basic kind of normative reason for desire and thereby for action. It provides both an *explaining* reason why we *do* want whatever else we want and a *normative* reason why we *should* want certain things.

Adding this point to the others about the passage, we can formulate a broadly Aristotelian argument regarding intrinsic goodness. The twofold strategy I suggest is, first, to take the intrinsically good as, whatever else it is, something that provides basic (normative) reasons for desire (and thereby for action, since there is at least some reason to do whatever promotes a state of affairs there is reason to desire) and, second, to assume that nothing can play this role regressively.

To be sure, Aristotle here assumes broadly psychological criteria for the good, whereas I am seeking an argument not dependent on any such naturalistic premise. But we can accomplish much by putting the good in place of the desired and making use of Aristotle's main raw materials. Where his argument is very roughly to the effect that since desire is not regressive, it has a basis in something wanted as (and only as) an end, we can construct an argument to the effect that since goodness is not regressive it has a basis in something good as an end (leaving aside the question whether it is good only as such, since there is no need, in the theory of value, to establish that negative conclusion that it is not good in any other way.)[7] More guardedly, if there is anything good at all, in the sense implying, as Aristotle surely takes the good to do, provision of basic (normative) reasons for desire and action — *basic practical reasons* — then there is something intrinsically good. Let us develop this line of argument.

Consider the existence of instrumental goods — something virtually anyone will grant, since it simply implies that some things are efficient in bringing about others. Could these be the only kind of good? Suppose for the sake of argument that (1) there is only instrumental (hence extrinsic) good, that is, good which is instrumental in some broad way, so that a good thing is, as such, a means to something else. Now consider the plausible view that (2) there are only four possible kinds of valuational chain: a thing, x, may be (a) *regressively good*, that is, good as a means (in the widest sense) to something else, y, which in turn is good as a means to z, and so on ad infinitum; (b) *circularly good*, that is, good only as a means to something which is ultimately good as a means to x; (c) *terminatingly good*, and hence merely instrumentally good, that is, good only as a means to something which, ultimately, is itself good only as a means to something that is not good in any sense, thus to something with which goodness in any sense ends;[8] or (d) *intrinsically good*, that is, good in itself.[9] Surely (3) in none of the first three cases — covering the categories of instrumental goodness — is there anything that provides a basic practical reason. Hence, (4) if there is anything good in the sense implying provision of a basic practical reason, there is something intrinsically good.

It is difficult to show that none of the first three kinds of valuational chain provides for any basic reason for action. It would be widely agreed, however, that if x is terminatingly good (hence merely instrumentally good) then it grounds no basic practical reasons. First, one could not always cite something or other as a reason for wanting x, as with cases (a) and (b) — with respect to which one could either continually regress or repeatedly circle. Second, on arriving at the termination, one could not say anything positive about the goodness of x as the terminal element, since x is by hypothesis not good in any sense.

Cases (a) and (b) are more difficult to rule out as sources of basic practical reasons. But let me suggest that in addition to Aristotle's plausible idea that in the regressive and circular cases, desire for the relevant goods would be futile, there is also reason to think that the motivational counterparts of these chains are not even psychologically possible for human agents. Because of the finitude of our minds, we cannot have an infinite chain of desires; and there is also good reason to doubt that we can have a circular chain of desires, in part because this would imply that a desire is partly caused by itself. If, for instance, I want A for the sake of B, then I want A in part *because* I want B; so if I have a circular motivational chain, say wanting A for the sake of B, wanting B for the sake of C, and wanting C for the sake of A, then (on the plausible assumption that this because-of relation is transitive, so that if I want A in part because I want B, and I want B in part because I want C, then I want A in part because I want C), we may conclude that my wanting C will ultimately be both partly caused by, and a partial cause of, my wanting A.[10]

Suppose, then, that the argument is sound. In this case its Aristotelian reasoning refutes its supposition that there is only instrumental goodness but falls short of entailing that there in fact *is* anything intrinsically good. The conclusion is conditional: *if* there is anything good (in a sense implying that there are reasons for action), there is something intrinsically good. Still, for all but skeptics about the existence of anything normatively good at all (where this implies providing a prima facie justificatory reason for action), the argument seems to show that there is something intrinsically good.

We know what Aristotle's candidate for the intrinsically good is: happiness. There are other plausible candidates (some soon to be discussed) for intrinsic goodness, and it may be that in the end only the unmistakable goodness of certain specific things, such as pleasure in playing one's favorite game, as opposed to any general arguments such as we have just considered, can convince those who doubt it that some things are intrinsically good.[11] What follows may bring intrinsic goodness into high relief. Ideally, we can then have intuitive confirmation of the conclusion we may also reach from the broad Aristotelian considerations just set out.

II. The Range of Purportedly Intrinsic Goods

Among the widest available lists of purportedly intrinsic goods is one constructed by William K. Frankena, who cited these candidates: life, consciousness, and activity; health and strength; pleasures and satisfactions of all or certain kinds; happiness, beatitude, contentment, and so forth; truth; knowledge and true opinion of various kinds, understanding, wisdom; beauty, harmony, proportion in objects contemplated; aesthetic experience; morally good dispositions or virtues; mutual affection, love, friendship, cooperation; just distribution of goods and evils; harmony and proportion in one's own life; power and experiences of achievement; self-expression; freedom; peace, security; adventure and novelty; good reputation, honor, esteem, and so forth.[12] This list may be subdivided in various ways. There are animate and inanimate items, for example consciousness and happiness versus truth and proportion; moral and non-moral ones, such as just distribution versus adventure; psychological and non-psychological ones, such as consciousness and pleasure versus proportion and just distribution; and, among the psychological, occurrent (experiential) and non-occurrent items, for instance consciousness and aesthetic experience versus true opinion and the virtues.

For the last category, the psychological, which is the most common, and probably the best, candidate to encompass the others, there is some important unclarity. Consider one of the psychological items, say pleasure construed as an intrinsic good. Is the primary bearer of intrinsic value (here intrinsic goodness) (1) the property of being pleased, or (2) the state of affairs, someone's being pleased, or (3) an instance thereof, such as Karen's being pleased, or (4) a genetic instantiation (or instancing) of one or the other of these, in the sense of the coming into being of (3)? I cannot provide an analysis of any of the (generally quite rich) concepts on Frankena's list (and will not offer a full-scale account of intrinsic value itself), but we can pursue the question of what *has* intrinsic value even without an analysis of what it is or even of any of the kinds of things that are candidates for its possession.

If we take seriously the enormous diversity of Frankena's list — which by no means exaggerates the variety of things people have called (intrinsically) good — virtually any kind of thing can be a candidate for a bearer of intrinsic goodness. Beauty is a candidate for such good, and it seems to be a property; tranquility is another candidate and it seems to be a state of affairs; pleasure is another, and it seems to be an experience (though the term can also designate pleasantness as a quality of an experience); and if truth can a candidate it is, perhaps, a relation between the abstract entity that has it, such as a proposition, and the reality that entity represents. We could probably go on into other categories, but like most who have written on the topic I find it more natural to try to understand some of the relevant ascriptions of intrinsic value in terms of more basic ones.

To achieve clarity about intrinsic goodness, one kind of question we should ask is how abstract the good can be. There is some plausibility in saying that beauty is an intrinsic good, but would this be plausible if there were no instances of beauty — no beautiful things? It appears that beautiful things are more basically good than the property of beauty, if that property in the abstract is intrinsically good at all. This point may be in part what leads some philosophers to say that the primary bearer of intrinsic value is the instantiation of a state of affairs: Michelangelo's *Pietà's* (actually) being beautiful may be thought to be such an instantiation (of beauty)— it instantiates a state of affairs that did not obtain until he created the sculpture, thereby realizing the state of affairs he might have only imagined before he began. In some terminologies, such as one suggested by Ross, this instantiation of beauty is an aesthetic fact.[13] (Elsewhere, however, Ross maintained that intrinsic goodness "is essentially a quality of states of mind,"[14] a matter pursued in detail later.)

This instantiation view in some form is plausible, but 'the instantiation of a state of affairs' is ambiguous: it can designate (1) the general fact that a property is instantiated, say the fact that there is something beautiful; (2) the event of a state of affairs' *being* (genetically) realized (say, the coming to be of the instance of beauty), which may take years; or, less commonly, (3) the instance itself, the beautiful thing. Regarding (1), the mere fact that beauty is instantiated may entail the *possibility* of something's having intrinsic value, but in itself this fact seems too abstract to be a bearer of such value. The fact that there is beauty would seem a good thing only on the basis of something connected with the goodness of the beautiful things in question, such as their enrichment of the lives of persons. As Ross might have put it, the intrinsic goodness associated with beauty is essentially a quality of state of mind constituted by properly experiencing beauty.[15] As to (2), the process of instantiation, say the coming into being of the beauty of the *Pietà*, does not seem to be a basic bearer of value: the goodness is in its product, not in the genesis of that (the genesis might even be an ugly process despite its beautiful product). Concerning (3), the instance of beauty is more like what people seem to have in mind in saying that beautiful things are intrinsically good (or that beauty itself is, where this is not meant to designate the property): the beautiful statue as such is surely a candidate to be an intrinsically good thing.

Perhaps we can capture the best intuitions underlying the value-as-instantiation view if we say that the primary bearers of intrinsic value are instances, conceived as concrete realizations, of certain kinds of states of affairs, and that these concrete items are intrinsically good in virtue of intrinsic (roughly, non-relational) properties of them.[16] A pleasurable experience, then, might be good in virtue of its felt qualities; a poem in virtue of its aesthetic properties, such as delicacy and musicality; a person's will in virtue of its (i.e., the agent's) intentions. The first is an instance of the state of affairs, someone's having a pleasurable experience, the second of the state of affairs, a poem's being beautiful, and the third of the state of affairs, someone's having good will.[17]

Even if we can find a category, such as that of state of affairs, broad enough to constitute the primary kind of bearer of intrinsic value, we may still want to reduce the number of types of bearer under that heading. It is natural when we find the kind of wide diversity of Frankena's list to look for a certain kind of unity and, in that light, to economize if possible. A plausible move to make in this spirit is to say (as Aristotle might have) that what is significant about intrinsic value is that its presence in our lives is what makes living worthwhile, and that the only irreducible bearers of it occur where it is truly realized: in experience. It is, after all, experience that constitutes our life in the most intimate sense. Subtract experiences from a life and the most that is left is the insensate organism whose experiences they were. On this view of intrinsic value, if there could be no experience of beauty, it could not be true that beauty has intrinsic value. And what good is truth in itself, one might ask, if no one ever contemplates it or otherwise experiences it?[18]

Another way to see the appropriateness of taking the bearers of intrinsic value to be experiential is to consider the different directions of mind-world fit of the practical and theoretical attitudes. As noted in chapter 3, whereas beliefs, which are paradigms of theoretical attitudes, properly reflect the world, practical attitudes, such as desire and intention, properly "aim" at changing it to reflect them. Now experiences, unlike substances, properties, and presumably facts, can be brought about: realizing experiences, say in enjoying a meal or expressing praise to a friend, can thus be a favorable change in the world, and they can figure (under an appropriate, at least normally prospective, concept) as the objects of practical attitudes such as desire and intention. We can want to enjoy a meal and intend to praise a friend. This realizability by action is a role the intrinsically good should be able to play. As belonging to experience, moreover, the intrinsically valuable can have both the motivational potential, as implied by its capacity to determine the object of desires and intentions, and the internal accessibility, as figuring in consciousness, that (as argued in chapter 10) apparently belong to normative reasons for action.

If these points are correct, then one would naturally think that ascriptions of intrinsic value to non-experiences are always explicable in terms of properties of experience. The indicated view might be called (axiological) *experientialism*: only states of experience have intrinsic value (or intrinsic disvalue), where these states are construed purely psychologically, roughly as mental states or processes.[19] They may be as phenomenally rich as the combined auditory and visual experience of hearing and seeing an opera, as powerful as the pain of a severe burn, and as faint as a silent recitation of a stanza from Emily Dickinson. I want to explore this experientialism, and indeed the general question of what has intrinsic value, by starting with the narrowest plausible version of such experientialism: hedonism.

III. Prospects for an Aristotelian Hedonism

To do justice to hedonism, we must first appreciate how broad it is. Hedonism at its best is not a monistic theory: on any plausible understanding of pleasure and the absence (or reduction) of pain, they are substantively different values: neither is simply the negation of the other. Moreover, if pleasure is understood in a broadly Aristotelian fashion, as (at least mainly) an activity concept, then it alone is as diverse as the multifarious activities that yield it. It is even more diverse construed as also arising in experiences in which one is not agent, but patient. As much as the pleasures of reading differ from those of viewing paintings, both may differ even more from the pleasures of swimming, and all three are quite different from the relatively passive pleasures of a sunbath, wherein the subject is not acting but only having an experience. (To his credit, Mill's examples of pleasures exhibit this kind of diversity; but although his hedonism is really pluralistic in content, he sometimes represents it as monistic, or at least dualistic, with the two basic elements of pleasure and pain.)

Is it not possible, however, for, say, a conversation to be intrinsically rewarding even if one does not take pleasure in it? Some conversations are engaging and interesting, but they are too much work or too fraught with tensions or problems to be enjoyable. A hedonist might say that if they are intrinsically rewarding but do not seem enjoyable, this is because the pleasure they give is mixed with discomfort and obscured by the labor of comprehension. Another possibility is that the rewarding quality is really instrumental: one learned something.

Certainly these points sometimes apply to a rewarding conversation, but I cannot see that intrinsic rewardingness *must* reduce to some kind of pleasure. Indeed, one can clearheadedly want to do something for its intrinsic interest or intrinsic intellectual challenge, even when one thinks it will not be enjoyable and may at times be positively unpleasant. (This is how some people view meetings with respected senior colleagues, editors, or dissertation advisers.) Such experiences share with pleasant ones the tendency to engage us, for example to keep us interested and to produce spontaneous attention. But they do not have the same tendency to make one smile or glow inside, and they may lack any visceral manifestations of the engagement with their objects, such as being moved by the power of a symphonic climax. Must a desire for such an experience be less than rational? Can it not be a desire for some kind of, say, intellectual good? This seems possible. If it is, hedonism is too narrow as an account of the nature of goodness and, so far as goodness is basic for rational desire, of the foundations of rational desire.

Even where something is wanted for qualities other than those conducing to pleasure, it may be wanted for qualities one experiences. We can go well beyond hedonism in broadening the objects of intrinsic value and still hold (axiological) experientialism, for which only experiences are bearers of intrinsic value. Experientialism, like hedonism, has the advantage, over egoistic views, of allowing that one can rationally want something for someone else's sake; but experientialism, unlike hedonism, allows this even if one knows the wanted thing will not bring anyone pleasure or reduce anyone's pain. On either view, one's own experiences are not the only bearers of intrinsic goodness, but for experientialism pleasure need not be the only intrinsic good.

Perhaps we can see in another way that there is a plurality of intrinsic goods: if, as seems plausible, the fact that doing something, say playing a game, will produce a rewarding experience for someone else can be a basic reason for action even if the experience is not pleasurable, then there is a strong presumption that the experience is to some degree intrinsically good. Hedonism seems, then, too narrow a theory of value and, correspondingly, to underestimate the range of basic rational grounds for action. This is not to say that intrinsic value provides the *only* basic reasons for action. That controversial thesis is plausible in the light of much that has been said, but it may be left open here.[20]

IV. *Axiological Experientialism*

Plausible though it is, even experientialism may be too narrow. It surely makes sense to say that the world could continue to contain beautiful things even if there were no one to experience them. Could wanting that it continue to have them even if there were no one to experience them not be rational, and indeed directed toward something of intrinsic value, namely the beautiful things in question? A natural reply is that anyone who reflectively believes these things is conceiving the beautiful things as valuable because experiencing them *would* be valuable — and clearly one cannot mount this objection at all without in some way thinking of such things, and thereby experiencing them "representationally" in thought.[21]

One alternative to giving up experientialism, then, would be to call such things as unexperienced beautiful objects *contemplatively valuable* to suggest that the intrinsic value they point to is really in the rewarding contemplation of them and not in their existence. One reason they seem intrinsically valuable, it might be argued, is that their value is (at least commonly) grounded in their intrinsic properties, in particular those that give the contemplation of the objects for their own sake intrinsic value. If, in addition, such contemplation of them would have intrinsic value owing to their qualities experienced therein, this would imply that they have *inherent* value, as distinct from both intrinsic and instrumental value: roughly, they are such that properly contemplating them for their own sake (say a painting for its beauty) or experiencing them in some other appropriate way (say in playing a good game) is intrinsically valuable. Thus, they are not valuable independently of their relation to contemplation (or experience), hence not intrinsically so, yet they are not means (in any ordinary sense) to the value of experiencing them, since they are partly constitutive of that experience.[22] A good game is not a means to the playing of it, nor a delectable good meal to eating it; but the intrinsic good is in the enjoyable recreational and gustatory experiences. Moreover, inherent goods are by their nature *necessarily* capable of being a component in intrinsic value, since they would be essential to any experience that is *of them*.[23] Hence, unlike things of instrumental value, they necessarily provide possible occasions for the realization of intrinsic value. Thus, by countenancing the inherently valuable, experientialism can do justice to a major reason Moore and others attribute intrinsic value to such things as beautiful paintings: they provide non-instrumental reasons for action, for instance for contemplating artworks. In a sense they *call* for action, even if they never actually figure in enriching anyone's experience.

The Hallucination Problem

It can help in thinking about the status of experientialism to imagine a serious challenge to it. Suppose a Cartesian demon — or a technology of the future — causes us to have experiences intrinsically just like those we find enjoyable or, in any other way, intrinsically valuable. If only experiences have intrinsic value, then it would seem that playing a Bach invention with great pleasure is no better, intrinsically, than a perfect hallucination of doing so with corresponding pleasure: from the inside, the experiences are indistinguishable. If one thinks that the veridical experience is, in itself, better, the readiest explanation is that one ascribes some intrinsic value to a non-experiential element such as truth (or veridicality)— or at least ascribes some negative intrinsic value to falsity (one would believe, or at least be disposed to believe, falsely, that one is playing the invention). If one thinks that the veridical experience is not better, then one should be ready to grant that the most practical ideal for human life might be to create such machines and find a safe way to have them produce the best lifelong experiences in us that they possibly can.

I do not take it as obvious that this kind of example undermines experientialism. The problem merits considerable analysis. To begin with, consider Moore's principle of organic unity — "*The value of a whole must not be assumed to be the same as the sum of the values of its parts*"[24]— or, positively expressed, the intrinsic value of a whole may be more or less than the sum of the intrinsic values of its parts. In this light, one might argue that the admixture of falsity affects the value of the whole hallucinatory experience even though falsity itself may have no intrinsic value or intrinsic disvalue, and that veridicality (a kind of truth) might make such a whole better without having intrinsic value itself. If, however, we work with Moore's notion of organicity as stated, this defense of experientialism fails; for truth and falsehood are not *parts* of the experience.

To get around this objection, we must reformulate the basic idea of the organicity of intrinsic value. Suppose that (as is independently plausible) we widen our conception of its organicity in such a way that the intrinsic value of the experience can be affected by the *properties* of the experience possessing that value whether or not they themselves have intrinsic value and, if they do, in a way that is not purely additive. Just as a color or line in a painting can affect its beauty without itself being beautiful, a property of an experience might affect its value without in itself having value. This wider conception of intrinsic value is preferable but still does not solve the problem: the falsehood (non-veridicality) of a hallucinatory experience is a relational or at any rate non-intrinsic property (a kind of miscorrespondence with the facts); hence — on the plausible assumption that the intrinsic value of a thing depends on its intrinsic properties — falsehood is not a candidate to affect that value.

It is still open to us to say, however, that although the falsity of a hallucinatory experience is neither an intrinsic property of it nor intrinsically bad, it is a bad-making characteristic in that it tends to produce such intrinsically bad experiences as dejectedly coming to believe one is only hallucinating, as where one is pained or deflated at finding out that one is not really playing a beautiful Invention. A serious difficulty with this claim is that even if it is true, there may not have to be any *intrinsic* property of a hallucination, such as instability, in virtue of which it has such effects.

We might make at least two points in response. First, there remains a *liability* to such bad effects, which arguably is an intrinsic property of a hallucination: by its very nature, a hallucinatory experience can be discovered to be so. Second, even if neither this liability nor instability is an intrinsic property, an intrinsically valuable experience must apparently have the second-order merit of its value's being *able* to survive the subject's recognition of the nature of the experience. The intrinsically good is, arguably, good in the contemplation of it as well as in the experiencing of it. Call this the *principle of second-order survivability*. Supposing this principle is true, however, even if the first-order experience produces distress at the thought of its falsity, it can retain its intrinsic value. That value is simply obscured by the distress of the second-order experience, which may, given the organic unity principle, in fact be bad on the whole despite the goodness of the pleasurable experience that is its object.

We might, however, argue from this very point about the possible overall badness of experiencing a hallucination as such for an equally plausible related principle — the *principle of the intrinsic preferability of the veridical*: other things equal, a veridical experience is intrinsically preferable to a qualitatively intrinsically indistinguishable hallucinatory one. This would be enough to derive the modest conclusion experientialism needs here: that the veridicality of an experience matters to its intrinsic desirability. Hallucinatory experiences, after all, have the bad-making property of a liability to an overall intrinsically bad second-order experience even if that might leave the intrinsic value of the hallucinatory one unchanged.

This point about hallucination shows something about the overall intrinsic value of experience but does not establish the preferability principle. In any case, even supposing that principle is true there remains the question whether it concerns only the *intrinsic* nature of the experiences whose value is in question. It is not clear that liability to being seen to be hallucinatory is an intrinsic property of hallucinatory experiences. To be sure, it would seem that hallucinatory experience is *essentially* liable to exposure given rigorous scrutiny, or at least given some possible conditions. But this claim may depend on how one conceives the power of a demon (or of a technology of the future) to make hallucinatory experiences steadfastly truthlike. This is a large issue I leave open.

If we pursue the basic issue in relation to inherent value, there is something further to be learned. The *inherent* value of an experience of hallucinating something perhaps can be affected by its veridicality. Consider one's hallucinatory experience of playing a beautiful Bach Invention. There seems to be less intrinsic value in the second-order experience of one's having that experience — say, in the contemplative consideration of the hallucinatory experience — than in the second-order experience of one's veridically experiencing one's playing the piece. If so, the inherent value of the veridical experience exceeds that of the hallucinatory one. Given the point that inherently valuable things can provide (non-instrumental) reasons for action, there would thus be better reason to realize the veridical musical experience than to realize the hallucinatory one. That would be a significant result. We would have a *principle of the inherent preferability of the veridical* (other things equal). This principle may be all experientialism needs to blunt the main force of the hallucination problem. There is, after all, no need to deny *all* intrinsic value to hallucinatory experiences; the problem is to account for the apparent intuition that in some way they are not as good as the real thing. That there is less reason to bring them about may be sufficient to account for what is sound in this thought.

This last line of defense of experientialism is vulnerable, as is the principle of the intrinsic preferability of the veridical, on the ground that the second-order experiences of a veridical and a hallucinatory performance need not differ *intrinsically*, as they would have to for the inherent values of the first-order, performative experiences to differ. This may be so; the question is whether the falsity of an experience implies that the second-order experiences *could* differ in intrinsic value owing to some essential aspect of the hallucination, since this would provide a ground of preference for the veridical. This is not entirely clear, though I think a good case can be made for the idea that in such cases, there is, always a possible difference in intrinsic value. It is clear that in the world as we take ourselves to know it, hallucinations provide at least contingent reasons to expect such second-order differences as are implied by discovering the falsity of a hallucination. For non-skeptics, this may be enough to sustain a version of the inherent preferability principle. Let us suppose, for the sake of argument, however, that there could be hallucinatory experiences with precisely the inherent value of their veridical counterparts. Is there any other resource available to experientialism to argue for the rational preferability of the veridical?

Experientialism might still appeal to the different *contemplative* values of the second-order experiences, where these are the values of contemplating the first-order experiences as having *both* the intrinsic properties they do and certain other important ones, including veridicality. If including veridicality seems insufficiently motivated, two points tend to offset that impression. First, as agents, and certainly as self-reflective beings, we are interested in this kind of veridicality and tend to respond affectively — in ways that have intrinsic value or disvalue by any plausible reckoning — to the sense of it. We tend to care more about actually enjoying a beautiful piece than about hallucinatory enjoyment of it. Second, insofar as what is intrinsically good must provide basic reasons for action, we should not only be able to aim at realizing it but should, insofar as we are rational and informed, tend to do so. We *can* aim at having enjoyable hallucinatory versions of all the kinds of experiences we enjoy, but normally we do not, and our preference for aiming at veridical experiences, other things equal — for example at really playing an Invention enjoyably rather than hallucinating it with the same subjective experience — seems rational.

In part, the rationality of preferring to aim at veridical experiences rather than comparable hallucinatory ones may be grounded in the realization that an experience of self-manipulation of the kind involved in causing oneself to have hallucinatory pleasurable experiences is intrinsically (perhaps morally) bad. Indeed, insofar as we can think of enjoyable hallucinatory experiences as natural and utterly spontaneous — gratuitous gifts, as it were — rather than self-induced or produced by an external manipulator, the comparison with veridical counterparts is less favorable to the latter. Still, the preference for the veridical seems rational. If it is not — indeed, if it is even equally rational to aim simply at having the enjoyable experience in question subjectively conceived — then perhaps it is not rational to doubt experientialism on the basis of the hallucination problem in the first place.

Intrinsic Value and the Mixture of Good and Evil

Whatever we conclude in the end about the hallucination problem, experientialism can account for the point that there are inappropriate objects even of experiences that embody an intrinsic good, such as pleasure. There is, for example, something intrinsically bad in taking pleasure in another's pain. One thing an experientialist may say here is that the pleasure a sadist might take in another person's suffering, even though good in itself and possibly greater in positive value than the suffering is in negative value, might, owing to its being pleasure taken in something intrinsically bad, fail to yield an experience that, *overall*, is intrinsically good. Intrinsic goodness may be ineradicable, but it is not indomitable: it may be quite insufficient to render good the whole to which it belongs. In the case at hand, even if the suffering were hallucinated, the property of suffering — which is a clearly bad-making characteristic — is essential to the content of the pleasurable experience and is thus intrinsic to it. We thus have an explanation of how *Schadenfreude* can generally be condemned by an experientialist view (even by a certain kind of hedonism).[25] Because of its content — what it is pleasure *in* — the pleasure cannot be expected to contribute as much to the value of the whole experience as it would if it were pleasure in something good.

One might object that pleasure can be bad even when taken in something innocent, such as a swim for exercise. As Kant said, "[A] rational and impartial spectator can never feel approval in contemplating the uninterrupted prosperity of a being graced by no touch of a pure and good will. . . . [G]ood will seems to constitute the indispensable condition of our very worthiness to be happy."[26] This point is consistent with construing pleasure (surely the central element in prosperity and happiness) as intrinsically good. Indeed, if pleasure is not so construed, it is hard to see what is so objectionable about the uninterrupted prosperity (including pleasures) of a person without good will. Surely the main point is that such people ill deserve the good their lives contain. If, on the other hand, intrinsic value is organic rather than additive, the complex state of affairs uninterrupted prosperity (or happiness or pleasure) on the part of someone without good will, can be considered intrinsically bad, overall.[27] Here, however, it is not pleasure as such, but its "unfittingness" to the character of the subject, that makes the overall experience intrinsically bad.

For my purposes here, there is no need to make a final determination in favor of experientialism. For one thing, the imagined hallucinatory scenario might by some philosophers be argued to be heaven on earth — at least if its content and stability could be determined by an omniscient, omnipotent, and omnibenevolent being. I do not endorse this line and am inclined to qualify experientialism rather than adopt the line. The main points I make about intrinsic value — concerning, for example, its plurality and its connection with reasons for action — could certainly survive a different account of its bearers, say a mixed account maintaining that both experiences and certain relationships have such value, for instance the relationships that are *experienced*, as in the case of one's actual relation to a piano one is enjoyably playing. But enough has been said to warrant tentatively accepting the account and briefly exploring its consequences. For one thing, if non-experiential items, such as beautiful things, have intrinsic value, they are surely such that the proper contemplation of them necessarily has it, so our axiological inventory would be expanded, not contracted. Moreover, if things that experientialism takes to have inherent but not intrinsic value are not basic sources of reasons for action, they are very close to that: since they can be objects of intrinsically valuable experiences, they are necessarily sources of *potential* reasons for action. Arguably, there is as much derivative reason to preserve or promote them as there is basic reason to preserve or promote the intrinsically valuable experience of them. In regard to reasons for action, then, an experientialism that countenances inherent value can posit as wide a variety of non-instrumental reasons for action as there are types of states of affairs worth contemplating (or otherwise experiencing) for their own sake. Despite initial appearances, experientialism is not a narrow theory of value.

Whatever else may be intrinsically valuable, then, it seems plain that if anything is of intrinsic value, certain states of experience, including certain pleasures, are. Moreover, it may turn out that important connections can be discerned between the good and the right even if we do not consider any non-experiential bearers of value there may be. The experiential goods, even if not exhaustive, may be so comprehensive that they still enable us to discern the main connections between goodness and rightness.

V. The Axiological and the Deontic

The way in which hedonists have tended to connect the good and the right is well-known. Mill is the historically most important theorist here. The question I want to pursue now is whether experientialism can countenance any *moral* intrinsic goods and thereby approach an axiological but still non-hedonistic account of how the right might be based on the good.

The Experimental Dimensions of Moral Value

A central question here is whether moral value can belong not only to, say, just laws or to virtues of character, which are not experiences, but (more basically, perhaps) to certain experiences of such moral elements. There are experiences both of doing and of receiving justice, say of establishing, and of being protected by, just laws. Why not say that these experiences can have moral (intrinsic) value? Is not experiencing an injustice capable of being morally bad in itself even if it is not unpleasant and happens to have no bad effects? And if justice and beneficence as virtues of character are (non-instrumentally) good, why not also regard certain kinds of experiences of acting from them and of being the beneficiary of their exercise as morally (intrinsically) good? Indeed, is beneficence intrinsically good at all as *un*exercised, say as a mere disposition of character? Does it not exist, morally speaking, for the benefit of others, who, apart from its exercise toward them, cannot benefit from it?[28] And can I benefit from something if neither I nor anyone I care about ever *experiences* anything good as a result of it?

It is very difficult to find a decisive basis for the experientialist reading of the facts here, on which it is moral experience — whether as agent or patient — that is the primary bearer of moral value (goodness or badness). Still, even apart from that, surely moral experience is *a* bearer of moral (intrinsic) value. Thus, we can at least plausibly take moral value, conceived as belonging primarily to experiences — and *inherently*, if derivatively, to persons and deeds — as potentially significant enough to warrant asking whether rightness and obligation can be grounded in moral value. Even if the *most* one could say is that moral value is inherent — for instance, that suffering injustice is inherently bad — the normative thrust, as opposed to the ontology, of one's moral theory, would be largely unaffected. Inherent value is simply a step further from warranting action than intrinsic value, but both do so non-instrumentally.

It may seem that although hedonically positive and negative experiences may be accompanied by moral beliefs about them, there are no specifically moral experiences. Granted, moral experience is not just pleasurable or painful experience combined with moral beliefs about it, such as the belief that it results from injustice. But it is also true that experiential states and processes are not limited to perceptual sensations, much less to focal bodily sensations or to pleasure and pain. Consider felt indignation. It is not merely anger that is in some way based on a belief that a moral wrong has been done: the qualitative content of one's emotional experience is affected by one's moral sensibility in a way that makes the experience moral. Similarly, granting that there is such a thing as doing justice to one's employees while simply believing one is doing it, there is also doing it with a conscious attitude of moral approval and a sense of being guided by duty. We can be sensitive to *why* we are doing something as well as to what we are doing, and to the moral character of the deed as well as to the proposition that it is moral. Experiences that manifest such sensibility can be intrinsically good or intrinsically bad.

To be sure, one need not have this sort of experience in doing justice. As Kant surely noticed, the experienced sense of doing duty is clearest when one is acting against inclination, though we need not take it to occur only then. There is a further experience one can have: that of one's sense of duty prevailing over some temptation one faces. This kind of experience is another candidate for intrinsic moral value. Perhaps a sense of the fittingness of one's conduct to the situation, or of a good motive prevailing over an "inferior" one, is a ground of the value here.

These points about moral value should not be thought to support the mistaken view that doing justice has no value apart from any sense of doing it; it surely has at least inherent value. My point here is that there can be a distinctively moral (positive) value in the experience of doing justice. As to negative intrinsic value, consider first someone who experiences the loss of an investment. Compare the experience of discovering that the stock has gone bad with that of discovering that the certificate one was sold is bogus. The financial loss and disappointment may be the same, but the experiential sense of injustice in the latter case makes the experience repugnant in a moral way: the feeling of being used, though not a kind of pain, is felt as an *injury*. In morally good people, furthermore, the sense of doing wrong can have intrinsic disvalue of a kind they seek to avoid as something bad in itself.

On the theory that any kind of intrinsic value provides basic reasons for action, we may assume that if there is moral value, moral considerations are reasons for action. They certainly seem to be that: an action's conducing to justice, for example, is a reason for performing it, as a deed's promoting the well-being of others is a reason for doing it. More generally, that experiencing the exercise of moral virtue is good is itself a reason for a policy of action: for endorsing the battery of behaviors conducive to exercising and nurturing the virtuous trait in question, thereby making such good experiences more likely. We might now hypothesize that an act is morally permissible provided no overriding moral reason weighs against it, and morally obligatory provided there is overriding moral reason against its non-performance, where reasons are understood in terms of moral value and disvalue.

To be sure, the question remains whether the reasons for action constituted by *moral* considerations must outweigh any conflicting ones that may be constituted by non-moral considerations. But this is a problem faced by any theory of practical reason that countenances both moral reasons and other, independent reasons. The problem is not peculiar to an experientialist grounding of moral reasons. (I return to it later.)

It should also be stressed that even if, as I am suggesting, moral value can ground moral rightness and obligation, it does not follow that the notion of moral goodness is *needed* for this grounding — at least if we follow Ross and other intuitionists. As argued in chapter 2, there can be independent sets of sufficient reasons for believing certain moral principles; and perhaps certain principles of (prima facie) obligation, such as Ross's principles of duty, are non-inferentially knowable and are sufficient to ground moral obligations independently of any sense we may have of obedience to them as promoting moral value.[29] It may be, then, that ethics is epistemically autonomous relative to moral value (or at least non-moral value) in a way that enables ethical theory to account for basic reasons for action apart from any dependence on connecting actions with intrinsic value. An account of such reasons that does not exhibit them as axiologically grounded may be theoretically unsatisfying, at least to those for whom intuitive principles of obligation cry out for some kind of systematization; but such an account may yet be true so far as it goes.

Human Dignity as a Higher-Order Value

There is still another way to see the relation between moral value and moral obligation. Consider the dignity of persons (sometimes taken as roughly equivalent to their worth), a key category of — largely — moral value stressed especially by Kant and later Kantians. Even this notion can be accommodated by experientialism (though perhaps not by hedonism). To have dignity might be roughly a matter of being a kind of creature capable of experiences having at least the following value properties and, especially, moral properties. (1) These experiences contain active realizations, say in the form of awareness, of moral value, though not necessarily under that description. For instance, one might have a felt sense of doing justice or an awareness of the sincere making of a judgment of obligation. These experiences are intrinsically good. There can be such awareness of similar experiences for at least the full range of basic moral duties. Such experiences are arguably most valuable when they contain a sense of acting *from* duty or, more broadly, *from virtue*, in the sense of that phrase characterized in chapter 9. (2) A value-bearing experience may also be one figuring in some way in others' experiences that actively realize moral value, say their experiences of doing one justice. Here one's experience is of being *done* justice; justice is realized in one's life, though one is not the active realizer of it but its beneficiary. If moral value is realized on both sides, the case is one of axiological reciprocity. (3) The experiences may be of suffering *in*justice (an essential liability for a being with dignity) or neglect. (4) Since there are non-moral virtues, such as aesthetic and intellectual ones, the sense of acting from these may also have value. (5) As the last point suggests, value-bearing experiences may also be experiences of realizing some "higher" intrinsic value, such as the appreciation of beauty, as opposed to the pleasures of a dull but adequate meal. Experiencing a "lower" value, such as that of a sunbath, is different on this score: it certainly does not imply *in*dignity, but it also does not imply dignity.

Dignity is not just a moral matter, and its non-moral side can also be understood along experientialist lines.[30] The broad idea, then, is that *dignity is a higher-order value*. It is an axiological property that depends on moral and other "higher" values, and it belongs to persons in virtue of their capacity for certain kinds of experiences.[31] These experiences are the primary bearers of such values and are the kind, such as conscious performances of virtuous deeds, constitutive of a life in which dignity is not merely possible, but realized. On this view, although dignity is not a basic category of moral value, it may still be a *central* moral category, even one capable of serving as a basis for an ethic. The possibility that it is grounded in other values does nothing to prevent it from playing a central role in framing moral principles.

It might be thought that dignity should instead be understood in terms of moral rights, but I doubt that this is as fruitful an approach. This is not to underplay the importance of the *connection* between dignity and moral rights. It may be that a being has dignity if and only if it has certain moral rights, but this equivalence does not bring out what dignity *is*. Dignity is more the ground of (moral) rights than vice versa: rights are reflections of the kinds of values constitutive of dignity, not grounds of those values. It is more nearly true that we have rights because without their observance our lives can be intrinsically bad in ways that constitute violations of our dignity than that we have dignity because observing our rights can show us respect, and violating them can cause us indignity.

The ethical significance of dignity from the point of view of the connection between value and obligation is that dignity is a plausible basis for respect for persons and, equally (or perhaps thereby), of the categorical imperative (and similar general moral principles). Consider Kant's emphasis on dignity. He says, "Suppose . . . something which as *an end in itself* could be a ground of determinate laws; then in it and in it alone would there be the ground of a possible categorical imperative."[32] He adds immediately after this that "every rational being *exists* as an end in himself, *not merely as a means*," and later he speaks of the intrinsic value in question as dignity.[33]

In the intrinsic end formulation of the imperative — Act in such a way that you always treat humanity, whether in your own person or in the person of any other, never simply as a means but always at the same time as an end[34]— the principle in effect affirms the centrality of dignity in determining moral obligation. Clearly, beings with dignity deserve respect; and the categorical imperative is as plausibly, though perhaps not as basically, groundable on the idea of deserved respect as on the idea of the dignity of persons itself (my interest, however, is more in whether dignity *and* respect are groundable in value than in which, if either, is more basic relative to the other). I would also argue (as in chapter 12) that human dignity (and with it respect for persons) is a possible unifier of the Rossian duties: they give an interpretation of it, even if they are not theorems derivable from the proposition that persons have dignity (or deserve respect).

Dignity, then, provides a bridge between the axiological and the deontic, between value and obligation. There are various ways to build this bridge: with deductive pathways from a rigorous specification of what constitutes dignity to a set of moral rules, or more loosely; as an essential supply route, with dignity serving as a necessary element connecting value and obligation, or as simply one among other adequate sources of obligation; and with dignity construed as capable of providing all or only some of the underpinnings of obligation. Moreover, the path can go through respect as an independently groundable moral notion or can treat deserving respect as equivalent to dignity or to a kind of autonomy or to both. On any of these interpretations of the relation between the axiological and the deontic, we can move in interesting ways from either side to the other.

VI. The Epistemology of Value

So far, I have defended the view that there is intrinsic value if there is any value at all in a sense implying the existence of reasons for action, set out an experientialist conception of the bearers of intrinsic value, suggested how this conception can be used to ground the ideas of human dignity and respect for persons, and prepared the way for a grounding of principles of rightness and obligation in axiological concepts, including moral ones such as dignity. In a way, my effort has been to demystify intrinsic value by associating it with familiar experiences that we all, in day-to-day life, seem to recognize as providing basic reasons for action and to connect intrinsic value with obligation. I now want to suggest that the epistemology of value, and ultimately of ethics, that we might bring to this framework is also plausible. I begin with some very broad epistemological and metaphysical considerations.

Intrinsic Value and Reasons for Action

If we seek a view that does justice to the data described in this essay (and indeed in this book as a whole), it might well be a moderate intuitionism, one on which, above all, both the intrinsic value of certain kinds of experiences and the truth of certain moral principles is non-inferentially knowable (or at least justifiedly acceptable) by those with sufficient maturity and adequate clarity of mind. I have defended this sort of view for selected moral principles in discussing Rossian intuitionism in chapter 2. Here I shall discuss (in outline) only the related epistemology of intrinsic value.

If we take an Aristotelian approach to determining what has intrinsic value, we may conclude from certain observations about the structure of human motivation and conduct that pleasure (among other things) is intrinsically good; and if we apply Aristotelian reasoning to natural avoidance behavior, it seems even more plausible to conclude that pain is intrinsically bad. If one is a certain kind of naturalist about value — if, for example, one takes goodness to be a functional property applicable to things in proportion to their facilitating a certain kind of harmonious social life for us — this line of argument may be appealing. But especially since Moore's *Principia Ethica*, many ethical theorists have been inclined to think that all such reasoning commits some kind of "naturalistic fallacy." Quite apart from whether Moore was correct,[35] I want to draw on another strain that seems at least implicit in Aristotle and can be common ground between naturalists and non-naturalists: the idea that intrinsic goodness (or intrinsic badness) entails (and perhaps is equivalent to) providing a basic reason for action.

Even Hume, famous for skepticism about the power of reason, grants that we do not ask people why they hate pain, and he goes so far as to call pleasure and pain good and evil.[36] He seems to be conceiving the experience of pain (in part) functionally, as providing some kind of basic reason for action. What I want to suggest is that there are certain kinds of experiences that are (in part) *constitutive* of basic reasons for action, and that when we have sufficiently wide and deep experience we can see their normative power through appropriate reflection. Imagine an adult native speaker of English saying, for example, 'I realize that the door's being closed on my finger is causing me excruciating pain, but that doesn't provide any reason for me to open it'. What could such a person mean by 'any reason'? Or is the point that pain does not provide *sufficient* reason for action — which is correct but not relevant? Compare 'I see that you enjoy singing, but what reason is that to do it?'[37]

Hedonists hold that apart from pleasure and pain, there are no basic reasons for action. I have argued that this is not so, for instance in countenancing the reason-giving experiences whose intrinsic rewards are non-hedonic. Now consider a moral case. Imagine someone who says that although cheating one's employees is an injustice, this is no reason to abstain from it. If this utterance seems intelligible, it may be because there are, in addition to moral reasons, conventional reasons and merely prudential reasons, either of which even a criminal syndicate might recognize as constitutive of its structure.[38] These can easily become confused with basic moral reasons in a way that undermines the perception of the normative force of the latter. But is it not clear, *in* contexts such as the one I am imagining, that even apart from prudence and convention, injustice provides at least some reason not to do the deed? Let us explore this.

Agreement in Reasons versus Agreement on Reasons

It is important to see that I am talking about what we might call *contextual denial*, denial of the reason-giving force of a consideration in a context where its nature is evident. The issue is not abstract, *general denial*, denial of the general proposition instantiated by such contexts, say the proposition that an action's being an injustice is a reason not to perform it. Contextual denial is first-order, concrete, and specific; general denial is second-order, abstract, and focused on some generalization. The former rejects a claim *of morality*; the latter merely rejects a claim *about morality*.[39] The latter is a decidedly different kind of thing: a general, second-order proposition that tends to have less grip on the mind, and perhaps to be in a sense less basic epistemically, since by and large we must appreciate the force of specific reasons in concrete contexts in order to acquire adequate grounds for accepting general propositions about the *kinds* of reasons instantiated by the more specific cases.

By contrast with contextual denial, denial of the abstract propositions in question often tells less about the conceptual comprehension of the speaker and is more easily attributed to, say, skepticism.[40] Sincere contextual denial would be at best difficult to square with the conceptual comprehension presupposed by any denial that can tell against the kind of normative connection we are considering. I have never known of anyone genuinely rejecting — contextually — the painfulness of something as a reason to avoid it. If anyone did, I would want to see independent evidence that the person had sufficient comprehension of the rejection to qualify it as counting against the basic reason-giving force of pain. Mere rejection of a sentence used to give a reason is not sufficient to count as a denial of the conceptually rich proposition such a sentence normally expresses.[41]

Another way to put the main point here is to say that agreement *in* reasons does not require agreement *on* reasons. For each of a huge range of reasons for action, such as reasons of pain and pleasure, reward and boredom, obligation and prohibition, we can, on the one hand, unquestioningly accept appeals to it as a ground for action, and can even agree on its force — in the sense that we agree on how good a consideration it is for or against the action in question — yet, on the other hand, disagree on the criteria for reasonhood and other theoretical matters such as the epistemic status of reason-giving claims. From our agreement in reasons it by no means follows that we agree on abstract characterizations of reasons, say on their objectivity or knowability or even on their range of content. For all that, skepticism about consensus *on* reasons has often led to underestimation of the consensus there is *in* reasons.

It does not follow from any of these points that we can be justified a priori in believing such propositions as that pleasure is intrinsically good. There are nonrationalist accounts of how reflection can yield justification, for instance through a kind of moral perception.[42] But once a rationalist account is freed of the dogmatism and infallibilism so often attributed to rationalism, there is far less to object to in a moderate version of it. In closing this section, however, I want to be more positive by drawing an analogy between the epistemology of goodness (and by implication rightness) and that of truth: broadly, between practical and theoretical reason.

An Analogy Between Practical and Theoretical Reason

Goodness as I have construed it seems to be in some measure knowable on an internal basis: by reflection on one's experience in relation to the concepts involved, such as that of pleasure and pain, of a reason for action, and of value, one can know (or at least justifiedly believe) some important propositions about the intrinsically good. Goodness is analogous to truth at least in this: truth is revealed by *believability*, goodness by *desirability*; and the relevant kinds of believability and desirability are both experientially, hence internally, grounded in qualities of experience.

Let us start with the question of how experience grounds propositions both about what (merely) is the case and about what is desirable. Propositions about my environment are believable (or not) on the basis of my sensory experience; many concerning my past are believable on the basis of my memorial experience; those concerning conceptual relations are believable on the basis of my reflections; and so forth. Propositions about what is intrinsically desirable are believable on the basis of my experiences of the kinds of things in question, such as pleasures and pains produced by a good conversation or a persistent headache; or on the basis of my reflections on the way certain deeds treat people, for example justly or unjustly, beneficently or respectfully. An experience of green justifies (renders believable) the proposition that there is something green before one, and it may justify an actual belief of that proposition (where I form one on the basis of what I see); an experience of pleasure in viewing a painting indicates the desirability of that viewing, and it may justify an actual desire one has to view it (where I want to view it for pleasure). The first kind of experience can render a belief justified; the second kind can render a desire rational. The first kind of experience is fundamental in providing grounds for believing, the second kind in providing grounds for acting. The former experience illustrates that not every ground of belief is inferential, the latter that not every ground of action is instrumental.

Granted, the same individual experiences in virtue of which a kind of experience is intrinsically desirable, for instance pleasures in viewing a painting, can render believable the proposition that experience of that kind is intrinsically good. Here a practical ground plays a theoretical role. Moreover, a ground for believing something to be intrinsically good can thereby count toward the rationality of wanting it for its own sake. Here a theoretical ground plays a practical role. But there is no need for an experientialist approach to deny that beliefs as well as experiences can provide grounds for desire and hence for action. Experience is still the crucial ultimate ground of reasons for action, as it apparently is of justification for beliefs: if, for instance, it could not be rational to want something for its own sake in the light of one's experience of its properties, it presumably could not be rational to believe that it is intrinsically good on the basis of its having those properties.

Another way to see how experience supplies practical reasons is to note *how* the intrinsic goodness of something provides a reason to pursue it. If intrinsic goodness supplies a reason for action — and thereby a practical reason — it must be possible to want what it is a reason for (in the wide sense of being motivated to realize it) *for* the properties in virtue of which it is good, say the aesthetic qualities of the desired kind of experience; and such desire is probably not possible for beings with no experiential sense of those properties. This connection between the normative power of the intrinsic good and the possibility of its producing intrinsic motivation holds, at least, on the plausible assumption that wanting in the widest sense is crucial for motivation and action.

To be sure, one could indirectly acquire a justified belief to the effect that an experience is desirable for the reason in question. Testimony that the experience is enjoyable might justify such a belief. But that testimony would itself be warranted only on the basis of someone's actual experience of the (kind of) enjoyment in question or of something similar. Moreover, if one were incapable of wanting something for enjoyment, the justification provided by the prospect of enjoyment could not intrinsically motivate, and in appealing to the prospect one would not know what one is talking about in a way that would enable the appeal to exhibit one's action as rational. Cognitive justification can, then, be a ground for reasons for action, but it seems to depend on experiential justification. In that dependence, desirability is like believability, and practical reason is parallel to theoretical reason.

This internalist experientialism is not necessarily rationalist; indeed, that experience is the (or an) ultimate ground of reasons for desire and action as well as for belief might be taken to reflect an empiricist emphasis on the importance of experience for justification and knowledge (even if the status of this principle itself is not easily made out as empirical). But internalist experientialism provides a good way of doing justice to experience within a rationalist perspective. This gives it an advantage over rationalist positions that are more abstract and less moderate.[43] There is also a serious question whether the intrinsic goodness of anything can be known empirically. Hume taught us to worry about this; Mill showed us one natural kind of empiricist solution that apparently fails. Contemporary empirical, naturalistic approaches exhibit other difficulties.[44] If empiricism is to provide a way to avoid skepticism about the existence of intrinsic value, this remains to be shown.

VII. *Problems for Valuational Pluralism*

So far, the emphasis on reasons for desire or action has concerned only prima facie reasons. But an adequate ethical theory must provide a way to move from those to overall reasons. It is one thing to say that we may by reflection (or through suitable experiences) achieve non-inferential knowledge of the intrinsically valuable and thereby of basic reasons for action and that we may derive an adequate theory of *prima facie* obligation from an adequate theory of value. It is (as brought out in chapter 3) quite another to say that we may in general achieve such knowledge of the *overall* value of experiences and of our overall obligations.

Overall value and overall obligation are not merely additive matters, as Moore and Ross clearly saw, and knowledge of them is, we might say, epistemically organic. In embodying this point, the pluralist view I have been developing contrasts with consequentialism: maximizing impersonally conceived good is not the criterion of either rational action or right action. The idea implicit in the organicity of overall value is one of proper balance or integration among the relevant intrinsic values, and sheer quantity of intrinsic value is necessarily relevant only where other things are equal. In the case of an opportunity to save (say) ten innocent people from a firing squad by killing one innocent scapegoat, then, the overall values, including the moral disvalue of using someone in this way as a means to save others, must be considered.[45] There is no formula that tells us that there is better reason for the single killing and multiple saving than for the avoidance of injustice with the consequent ten killings — particularly when each alternative is viewed in the context of the total relevant situation in the world — something of enormous complexity. This strategy can be applied to a famous example in Dostoevsky:

> "Imagine that you are creating a fabric of human destiny with the object of making men happy in the end . . . but that it was essential and inevitable to torture to death only one tiny creature — that baby beating its breast with its fist, for instance. . . . Would you consent to be the architect on those conditions?". . .
> "No, I wouldn't consent," said Alyosha softly.[46]

The total value of the relevant state of affairs need not be the sum of the intrinsic values of its elements, including the terrible deed and its good consequences. The problem is how to figure out why the relevant total is so immensely affected by a single intrinsic evil. Again the aesthetic analogy can help. Think of a clumsy, aesthetically clashing stroke in an otherwise fine painting: because of its relation to the ugly stroke, no part of the whole, even if beautiful in itself, can be appreciated as it should be.[47]

This kind of difficulty is not limited to ethics. Consider choosing scientific theories in the light of their ability to account for the relevant evidence. Neither in science nor in philosophy do the supporting data simply dictate the best choice. We may have considerations of predictive success on one side and of apparent explanatory power on the other. Coherence with other plausible theories may also pull one way and simplicity another. Even a hedonistic utilitarian like Mill saw no possibility of finding an intuitively cogent way of rigorously measuring the quality of pleasure against its quantity.[48]

Any theory of justification that admits a plurality of basic standards faces this kind of problem. Ross, like Aristotle, appealed to the need for practical wisdom in deciding how to balance competing intuitive considerations, such as those of fidelity and those of beneficence. Practical wisdom requires maturity and, admittedly, may not rule out all prejudice and subjectivity, even in experienced people. But there are nonetheless universally applicable standards and procedures for making reasonable decisions. Reflective equilibrium is available to us, both within our own system of cognitions and among our views and those of others: what we do today, for instance, should (prima facie) cohere with what we did yesterday and with what we intend to do tomorrow; and we should be able to explain each of these to others without inconsistency or mere rationalization.

What the pluralist experientialism I have outlined can offer as a check on prejudice and subjectivity is at least this: first, a series of necessarily relevant considerations — the kinds of things, such as pleasure and pain, that we are entitled to take to be of intrinsic value or disvalue; and second, a strong presumption that the totality of these considerations covers the entire territory in which relevant considerations occur. Pleasure and pain are in principle always relevant to what we should want and what we should do; and I believe that many non-hedonic experiences, moral, aesthetic, and intellectual, are also in principle relevant.

Perhaps non-experiential factors, such as truth about external matters, can also be relevant to determining overall values or obligations on balance. But perhaps their value can be taken into account by experientialists, since that value can be appropriately reflected *in* experience even if experience is not the bearer of any intrinsic value truth may have. It is less clear that *all* of the considerations providing basic reasons for desire and action are accessible to us by appropriate experience and reflection. But both our reasonings about what to do and our corrections of mistakes in action suggest that the realm of (overriders) is virtually the same as that of the original justifiers: defeat seems to be counter-justification coming from the same range of considerations, such as pleasure and pain, that provide positive practical reasons in the first place. Where a prima facie reason to do one thing is overridden by a better prima facie reason to do another, both are grounded in the same range of values, such as those constituting respect for persons.

Conclusion

Our experience reveals the good and the bad as basic practical reasons and counter-reasons — reasons for or against desire and action — much as it reveals justifiers and defeaters as theoretical reasons and counter-reasons — reasons for or against belief. Reflection in the light of experience can warrant our believing that certain kinds of experiences are valuable, as it can warrant our believing that certain kinds of experiences are justificatory. Experiences of pain and pleasure can apparently provide reasons for action as readily as sensory impressions of color and shape can provide reasons for belief. For those with sufficient experience and adequate maturity, both practical and theoretical principles of rationality can be justifiedly believed on the basis of reflection. Among the values in human life are apparently some that are moral; it is above all these that undergird human dignity and constitute the basis of respect for persons. When the notion of respect is adequately understood, we have a basis for a theory of moral obligation. Value can ground obligation, even if obligation can also be grounded independently, say in reasons for action that are derived from intuitive principles that can be seen to be true (or can at least be reasonably believed) without any deeper or more comprehensive basis.

If it is true that there is a plurality of basic values, then we face possible conflicts, sometimes resolvable at best in principle, regarding what to do. But this challenge does not prevent us from reaching reasonable decisions in concrete cases, any more than a plurality of theoretical considerations prevents us from ever justifiedly accepting a scientific theory. If, moreover, there is a plurality of basic goods and evils, and "the good life" is one rich in those goods relative to the evils, then it should be expected that such a life is heterogeneous, or at least that there is an indefinite variety of kinds of lives that are genuinely good. This is not meant to be a deeply relativistic conclusion: there are still universal standards, there are good and bad reasons for desire and action, and there are admirable and deplorable lives. That indefinitely many kinds of lives can be good does not entail that there are no universal standards for distinguishing those lives from the indefinitely many that are not good. Still, as autonomous agents we can choose from a vast range of options. There are myriad evils to be avoided, numerous goods to be sought, and a multitude of ways to combine them in lives of human flourishing.

Notes

Much of this essay was written for a symposium in memory of William K. Frankena held at the Central Division meetings of the American Philosophical Association in 1996, and I benefited from the discussion there as well as from other presentations. I thank the *Southern Journal of Philosophy* for permission to use material from "Intrinsic Value and Moral Obligation," which appeared slightly earlier, in vol. 35 (summer, 1977). For helpful comments on earlier versions I thank Lenn Goodman, Thaddeus Metz, Michael Meyer, Katherin Rogers, Michael Tonderum, and Michael J. Zimmerman.

1. The "tradition" I have in mind runs from Plato and Aristotle through Aquinas and other medievals, and (of course with exceptions in modern and contemporary philosophy) through the modern period and well into the twentieth century. For discussion of some dissenters, see Irwin Goldstein, "Pleasure and Pain: Unconditional Intrinsic Values," *Philosophy and Phenomenological Research* 50 (1989):255–75; and for both a historically detailed positive treatment of intrinsic value and discussion of skepticism concerning it see Panayot Butchvarov, *Skepticism in Ethics* (Bloomington: Indiana University Press, 1989).

2. Aristotle called happiness self-sufficient: "[W]e regard something as self-sufficient when all by itself it makes a life choiceworthy and lacking nothing; and that is what we think happiness does" (*Nicomachean Ethics*, trans. Terence Irwin [Indianapolis: Hackett Publishing Co., 1985], 1097b14ff).

3. A conditional I have argued for, in outline, and partially explicated in ch. 10.

4. Examples or other considerations making this plausible are given in chs. 2, 3, and 10.

5. *Nicomachean Ethics* 1094a.

6. The point that desire would be futile and endless if we chose everything for the sake of something else is, by contrast, not psychological but is also neither obviously normative nor a point of specifically ethical theory as opposed to the general theory of practical reason.

7. It would not matter if everything intrinsically good were also a means to something else, whereas if there is nothing wanted *only* as an end there is the psychologically repugnant conclusion (for one who rejects regresses) that even when one wants something as an end one must have a further want which that one subserves and then, by the same logic, a still further one, leading to a circle or infinite regress. (This can be avoided by allowing that some things, such as happiness, are *sometimes* wanted only as ends, but Aristotle apparently seeks foundations that cannot be wanted as means.)

8. We should allow as a limiting case something's being simply not good at all, in itself or in conducing to anything else: there is just one link, x being "a means" only to x. This third kind of chain corresponds to an epistemic chain terminating in belief that is not knowledge (or not justified if the argument is formulated to show that, if there is any justification, there is non-inferential justification).

9. I omit inherent and other kinds of good that will be discussed later; but these depend on the possibility of intrinsic good and do not independently provide reasons for action.

10. I offer an explanation of the problem here in *The Structure of Justification* (Cambridge and New York: Cambridge University Press, 1993), especially the Overview and chs. 1 and 4. Even apart from the difficulty of implying that something is a cause of itself, notice that at any point on a circular motivational chain, say wanting A, one might be said to want something *ultimately* for the sake of itself, since no matter how many links are in the circle one always "returns" to any point at which one starts. At that rate, however, it is hard to see why one should not be described as committed to wanting (as at least indirectly wanting) A for its own sake and thereby as prima facie committed to taking x to be intrinsically good. One may question the warrant for 'thereby'; this chapter as a whole is in part an attempt to show how it is warranted.

11. For detailed discussion of a parallel regress argument concerning not value but *valuing*— the psychological attitude of (roughly) taking something as in some way valuable — see my "Axiological Foundationalism," *Canadian Journal of Philosophy* 12, no. 1 (1982), pp. 163–82, reprinted in *The Structure of Justification*. This paper also explores how Aristotle understood valuing and motivation in general.

12. William K. Frankena, *Ethics*, 2nd ed. (Englewood Cliffs, N.J.: Prentice-Hall, 1973), p. 88. For other indications of the diversity of candidates for intrinsic goodness see Butchvarov, *Skepticism in Ethics*, esp. chs. 4–5.

13. See Noah Lemos, *Intrinsic Value* (Cambridge and New York: Cambridge University Press, 1994), for a detailed and systematic discussion of the nature and bearers of intrinsic value. His own candidate for basic bearer is a kind of obtaining state of affairs, which he identifies with a fact, as did W. D. Ross in *The Right and the Good* (Oxford: Oxford University Press, 1930), p. 113. I would not myself identify facts with obtaining states of affairs, but there is no need to go into that side issue here. For supporting discussion of Ross's view on bearers of intrinsic value see Michael J. Zimmerman, "Virtual Intrinsic Value and the Principle of Organic Unities" (forthcoming). An earlier systematic discussion of intrinsic value, also bearing significantly on Moore and Ross, is provided by E. J. Bond, *Reason and Value* (Cambridge and New York: Cambridge University Press, 1983).

14. *The Right and the Good*, p. 86.

15. This reflects the earlier quotation from *The Right and the Good*, p. 86; I add 'properly' because plainly not just any experience of beauty need have intrinsic value.

16. I take it that an intrinsic property need not be an essential one, i.e., one the thing in question has in any world in which it exists; but some have conceived intrinsic properties that way, and I leave open the possibility that properties of a *particular experience* in virtue of which it has (positive or negative) intrinsic value are essential to it.

17. Three points may help here. First, it is plausible to conceive the bearers of intrinsic value as experience *tokens* such as a specific enjoyment of a symphony by a given person at a time. Second, I believe the same substantive results can be achieved using property talk, but it does not seem as natural for the purpose, and I leave it aside to avoid making matters more complex. Third, the uniqueness attributable to God's goodness could be preserved: God might be said to be maximally *substantively good* (necessarily, omnitemporally, and perfectly): in no world and at no time would God lack experiences that are intrinsically good, or have a combination of them undermining his overall goodness.

18. I am not alone in suggesting that experiences are the primary bearers of intrinsic value. Frankena said, of the items on the list I quoted from him, "[A]ll of them may be kept on the list, and perhaps others may be added, if it is understood that it is the *experience* of them that is good in itself. Sidgwick seems to me to be right on this point. . . . [T]ruth is not itself intrinsically good. . . . [W]hat is good in itself is knowledge or belief in the truth." *Ethics*, p. 89.

Actually knowledge and belief are not experiences, and a page later Frankena corrects the apparent oversight here, saying that "knowledge, excellence, power, and so on are . . . valueless in themselves unless they are experienced with some kind of enjoyment or satisfaction."

19. There is of course a relational notion of experience in which, if one is hallucinating a tree, one is not experiencing one at all. But note the naturalness of saying, e.g., 'The experience was so vivid I expected to feel the lush foliage'.

20. Thomas Nagel seems to hold the equivalence view but does not try to show it systematically. See ch. 8 (on value) in *The View from Nowhere* (Oxford and New York: Oxford University Press, 1986).

21. It is interesting to note that on the assumption of God's existence everything is presumably in some way experienced (by God) and anything possible *can* be experienced (by God, at least, unless it is incompatible with his nature, such as the doing of evil by the omnibenevolent creator); and insofar as one takes God to exist in all possible worlds, one may have trouble thinking of something existing in any world at all yet absolutely unexperienced.

22. The term 'inherently valuable' was C. I. Lewis's term for things whose (proper) contemplation is intrinsically valuable. See *An Analysis of Knowledge and Valuation* (LaSalle, Ill.: Open Court, 1946), p. 391. I take it that inherent value is possessed on the basis of intrinsic properties and leave open whether *every* instance of proper contemplation (or experience) of them for their own sake has intrinsic value or whether there is simply a tendency for this to occur.

23. I assume that no candidate for inherent value is such that it cannot be contemplated, e.g. is such that on being contemplated it ceases to exist.

24. G. E. Moore, *Principia Ethica* (Cambridge: Cambridge University Press, 1903), p. 28. On p. 184 Moore adds that the value of an organic whole is not *proportional* to that of its parts. I this as also highly plausible.

25. See Frankena, *Ethics*; Lemos, *Intrinsic Value*; Goldstein, "Pleasure and Pain"; and Zimmerman, "Virtual Intrinsic Value," for helpful discussion of organic unities in relation to intrinsic value.

26. Immanuel Kant, *Groundwork of the Metaphysics of Morals*, trans. H. J. Paton (London: Hutchinson, 1948), sec. 393. In the same passage Kant places happiness in the same category as other items in being possibly "bad and hurtful," though the overall context does not warrant taking him to considering it *intrinsically* bad.

27. Lemos (*Intrinsic Value*, pp. 42–44) also defends the idea that the overall badness of the state of affairs is best understood on the assumption of the (essential) intrinsic goodness of the pleasure, but he sees this as preferring Moore's view over that of Kant and Ross, whereas I am suggesting that Kant, at least, is not best read as denying the value of the relevant pleasure taken by itself (not, at any rate, in the *Groundwork*). Another experientialist reading of the example would construe the overall experience as *inherently* bad; this could still satisfy the basic demand Kant articulates: that it merits disapproval.

28. Except incidentally, as where I benefit from an unintended result of someone's doing something good for a third party, this is not benefiting in a distinctively moral way. On the general question of the relation between the axiological and deontic, cf. Frankena's remark that "we do not have any moral obligations . . . to do anything that does not, directly or indirectly, have some connection with what makes somebody's life good or bad, better or worse . . . Morality was made for man, not man for morality." *Ethics*, p. 44.

29. I word this cautiously because it may be that from an action's being obligatory it *follows* (synthetically) that it is morally good and to that extent promotes moral value. I simply want to leave this open on the theory that someone could endorse principles of obligation, say from a noncognitivist perspective, and deny that there is any intrinsic value.

30. For a detailed discussion of dignity see Michael J. Meyer, "Dignity, Death, and

Modern Virtue," *American Philosophical Quarterly* 32 (1995): 45–55. An interesting constraint on dignity is that you can't increase your dignity by reducing someone else's. This is proposed by Margaret Pabst Battin in "Suicide: A Fundamental Right?," in Louis P. Pojman, ed., *Life and Death* (Boston: Jones and Bartlett, 1993), p. 221.

31. Thoughts (in the sense of thinkings) might be included here; mere belief states would not be: they are not only dispositional in nature, but candidates to be sharable with machines of a kind in which intrinsic value is not realized.

32. Kant, *Groundwork*, sec. 428.

33. Ibid., sec. 435. In sec. 436 Kant seems to regard autonomy as even more basic than dignity. I cannot attempt here to try to harmonize this and (and others of his major points) with the line of argument suggested here: it is meant to be broadly Kantian but is not necessarily the best interpretation of his overall intentions.

34. Ibid., p. 96.

35. On this matter William Frankena's critical work is probably as insightful as any there is. See especially "The Naturalistic Fallacy," *Mind* 48 (1939): pp. 464–77, and *Ethics*, esp. ch. 6.

36. In the *Enquiry Concerning the Principles of Morals* Hume says, "Ask a man *why he uses exercise*; he will answer *because he desires to keep his health.* If you then enquire, *why he desires health*, he will readily reply, *because sickness is painful.* If you push your enquiries further, and desire a reason *why he hates pain*, it is impossible he can ever give any. This is an ultimate end, and is never referred to any other object." *Enquiry Concerning the Principles of Morals*, ed. P. Nidditch (Oxford: Oxford University Press, 1975), p. 293. Calling this an ultimate end does not commit Hume to its being intrinsically good, but he often talks as if he conceived ultimate ends as such.

37. Marcus Singer has suggested to me that we *can* say 'I see that you are enjoying beating him, but what reason is that to do it?' I agree, but here the force of 'What reason is that?' is 'How does that give you a justification?'— for plainly the suggestion is that it is wrong to beat someone and, overall, bad to enjoy it. My view accounts for both the overall disvalue of enjoying someone's pain (in terms of the organicity of value) and for the apparent absence of any justification: even a minimal justification here would (at least normally) have to come from a different domain of reasons than pleasure. All this is quite compatible with saying that the pleasure itself provides a prima facie reason for action; but where a reason is overwhelmingly overridden — and especially where it provides no "justification" for an immoral deed — it can be quite odd to say it.

38. A prudential reason, say one grounded in avoiding pain, may be a basic reason, but prudence can also be based on mere desire, as where, for a thief, it could be imprudent not to kill someone who may reveal the location of the loot.

39. Compare Judith Jarvis Thomson's distinction between explanatory and object-level moral judgments, e.g. between the judgment that capital punishment is wrong because it is intentional killing of someone who poses no threat, and the judgment that capital punishment is wrong. See *The Realm of Rights* (Cambridge: Harvard University Press, 1990), p. 30.

40. This point about basicality may explain why Ross is a particularist in the sense indicated in ch. 2 and takes "intuitive induction," as did Aristotle, so seriously as an account of how we come to know intuitive propositions.

41. For a defense of a similar view, see Bernard Gert, *Morality: A New Justification of the Moral Rules* (Oxford and New York: Oxford University Press, 1988), and "Rationality, Human Nature, and Lists," *Ethics* 100 (1990): pp. 279–300.

42. There is some explanation of this possibility in ch. 2.

43. Consider, e.g., Alan Gewirth's approach using analytic propositions to show substantive moral results. His is a less moderate rationalism than the version suggested here. See his "Can Any Final Ends Be Rational?", *Ethics* 102 (1991): 66–95.

44. See, e.g., R. B. Brandt's A *Theory of the Good and the Right* (Oxford: Oxford University Press, 1979), which I have critically assessed in "An Epistemic Conception of Rationality," reprinted in *The Structure of Justification*.

45. For a very different conception of the organicity of intrinsic value see Robert Nozick, *Philosophical Explanations* (Cambridge: Harvard University Press, 1981), esp. pp. 418–46. For him, intrinsic value is an organic unity, whereas for Moore, and certainly on the view presented here, it is the overall value of a complex state of affairs with different intrinsically good (or bad) elements that is organic. I leave open that even a single element having intrinsically value, e.g. pleasure, may have organic unity as an important aspect; but unlike the unqualified view that intrinsic value is simply an organic unity of a certain structure, my position does not leave open whether certain specific kinds of thing, such as pleasure and pain, are good or bad.

46. *The Brothers Karamazov* (New York: Macmillan, 1923), p. 258.

47. This is not quite to say that the only rational alternative is to decline: arguably, it may depend in part on how bad a state the world is in, and Bernard Gert notes in this connection that it matters greatly whether we are considering eliminating evils or simply increasing pleasures. See his *Morality*, 2nd ed. Oxford University Press, (forthcoming). Another possibility is that the rational and the moral can diverge; the overall good to be served may still be organic but then might not be moral. There are still other problems, e.g. where, if I do not sacrifice one innocent person, ten will do just that, scapegoating in the same way, and the original ten will be killed in any case. Any theory will have some difficulty with certain trade-offs. For relevant discussion of one kind see Fred Feldman, "Justice, Desert, and the Repugnant Conclusion," *Utilitas* 7 (1995): 189–206 and Peter Vallentyne's critical discussion of his paper, "Taking Justice Too Seriously," immediately following it (206–16). Feldman is particularly concerned, as is Zimmerman, "Virtual Intrinsic Value," in part, with cases in which a bad state of affairs occurs when pleasure is undeservedly possessed. The organic conception of value sketched here can accommodate strategies similar to those they use.

48. He tells us whom to appeal to, but the "test" is at best rather loose. See *Utilitarianism*, ch. 2.

12

———
———

Conclusion

The Moral Justification of Actions and the Ethical Character of Persons

The ethical theory developed in this book is a moderate intuitionism that is epistemologically internalist, normatively objective, ontologically realist, valuationally pluralist, and qualifiedly naturalistic. This theory is not fully expressed in any one chapter. One aim of this one is to present a rounded though still less than complete account of the theory. But I also want to propose a normative ethical position that puts the theory in the context of a set of standards that can guide moral conduct and inform ethical character. I begin with a major unifying idea that controls much of what is said in the book.

I. Ethics and the Theory of Reasons for Action

Ethical theory may be viewed as a major branch — in some ways the major branch — of the theory of reasons for action. This perspective leads to an approach that can unify the main tasks of ethical theory without prejudging what kind of normative view we should hold, say a Kantian as opposed to utilitarian position. Certainly moral reasons for conduct are paradigms of reasons for action and are incalculably important both in everyday life and in philosophical inquiry. Insofar as ethics is understandable in terms of reasons for action, it can be fruitfully connected with other fields in which such reasons are central.

This book explores three major sources of reasons for action, the three that are perhaps most important in the history of ethics: desire, practical judgment — especially moral judgment as a major kind — and value. To illustrate, a desire for a new topic of conversation provides a motivational reason to change the subject; a (practical) judgment that the committee must move on to the business at hand provides a normative reason to change it; and the value of accomplishing the task provides a reason both to make that judgment and to act on it.

If desire, in the widest sense, has emerged as providing the basic motivational reasons for action, intrinsic value — including moral value — has emerged as the best candidate to provide the basic normative reasons for action. When desire does provide a normative reason for action, it may be viewed as an appropriate conative response to value or the sense of it, for instance to the pleasure of hearing a symphony or to the belief that hearing one would yield that pleasure. When practical judgment provides a normative reason for action, it may be seen as an appropriate cognitive response to value or the sense of it, as where one judges, on moral grounds, that a plan one is considering would be unfair.[1] Instrumental beliefs can also provide reasons for action, but the reasons they yield are not the basic kind. Believing, for instance, that my not stopping now will result in my running out of gas provides a reason for me to stop only insofar as there is reason for me to want to avoid that outcome.

It is in rational persons that we can best see how practical reasons emerge as responses to value or the sense of it. This applies both to motivational and to normative reasons. In a rational person, desires and practical judgments — especially moral judgments, which express normative reasons — tend to cohere both with one another and with one's sense of value. Aristotelian ethics can explain this coherence by appeal to the role of happiness as both motivationally and valuationally basic in human life. Utilitarianism as we have it in Mill is mainly Aristotelian in attributing this dual role to happiness, but Mill's hedonistic conception of happiness and its maximization requires a substantial departure from Aristotle. A Kantian view can explain the coherence by (among other resources) appeal to a rational being's response to the dignity of persons. The moderate intuitionism developed in this book can explain it in terms of mutually interacting cognitive and conative responses to the various kinds of value that are encountered in the experiences of normal rational persons.

This sketch of an approach to ethical theory as part of the theory of reasons for action is only that, though it is a sketch readily filled in by points made in earlier chapters and elsewhere.[2] In what follows I want both to develop this general approach to ethical theory and to formulate an associated normative ethical view. I shall do this by laying out some major points based on, and in some cases extending, positions defended in earlier chapters. I begin with moral epistemology.

II. Epistemology and Ethical Theory

Two influential views of justification in ethics have tended to divide philosophers and non-philosophers alike. One is that ethics is a cognitive domain in which there is truth and falsity and hence (setting skepticism aside) knowledge of true or false moral judgments. The other view is that ethics is basically not cognitive and thus not an epistemological subject matter. I find both of these views too stark. Ethics can be cognitive even if we never have moral knowledge as opposed to, say, some degree of justification insufficient to sustain knowledge. And even if ethics is not cognitive, epistemological considerations can be brought to bear in appraising the *rationality* of the attitudes (or other non-truth-valued elements) we express in making moral judgments.

My ethical theory is cognitivist, but much of what this book says can be applied to noncognitivist views. A judgment can be a response to a sense of value even if value is not "in the world," and hence in saying that, for instance, injustice is wrong, one is not attributing a property to it but expressing an attitude toward it. Such an attitude, moreover, can, like certain moral judgments conceived as truth-valued, be reasonable or unreasonable on the basis of a perception of the way the relevant action treats human beings.

I have not argued directly for cognitivism. My case in this book rests on the over-all plausibility of the ethical theories we can construct along cognitivist as opposed to noncognitivist lines. Here I refer not just to the moderate intuitionism developed in chapter 2 but to (at least) Aristotelian, Kantian, and utilitarian views; the best versions of these seem clearly cognitive. I have, however, argued in chapter 10 that one major argument for noncognitivism — the argument from the intrinsic motivating power of moral judgments — cannot be sustained.

Moral epistemology, like general epistemology, has exhibited a second divide, nearly as basic as the division over cognitivity but far less often noticed because the essential distinction has only recently come to the fore in general epistemology and is still not widely acknowledged in ethical theory. This is the distinction between (epistemologically) internalist theories, which take justification to be grounded in something accessible to reflection, and externalist theories, which take it to be grounded in something not thus accessible. Chapter 1 shows how this distinction applies to Kantian and utilitarian theories: the former take reflection guided by the categorical imperative to be capable of providing justified beliefs (and knowledge) as to what we kinds of things we should do; the latter take such justified belief (or knowledge) to require inductively grounded beliefs (such as beliefs about how one or another action will affect the general welfare) drawing on perceptual, and in that sense external, sources.

Among the reasons given in chapter 1 for preferring internalism is its avoiding a counter-intuitive *cleavage* between our intuitive assessments of character and the appraisal of it required by an externalist theory such as hedonistic utilitarianism. On that view, because it is a contingent matter what features of character optimally promote the good, the question of what constitutes good character is also a contingent matter, and justification for taking a trait to be a virtue of character is broadly inductive, whereas for internalism it is a non-contingent truth, justifiable by reflection, that (for instance) beneficence, veracity, and justice are traits essential to good character. Reflection on what right action and good character are shows that these traits are partly constitutive of good character. But only external evidence can show that having them optimally contributes to whatever kind of non-moral goodness a utilitarian view takes as fundamental for the rightness of action and the goodness of character.

There are also reasons of general epistemology for preferring an internalist account of justifiedness for beliefs in general;[3] but even apart from those considerations, the positive account of moral knowledge and justification (including the justification of actions) developed in chapters 2 and 3 supports an epistemically internalist view of their basic grounds. Moreover, the account of moral responsibility outlined in chapter 7 suggests that for that notion, too, normativity is an internal matter.

The wider position that normative concepts in general are epistemically internal is confirmed by the essays taken together. This applies particularly to the experientialist account of value and personal dignity given in chapter 11. Despite this internalist thrust, much of what is said in this book, even a good deal of its epistemology, is neutral with respect to epistemological internalism. My effort throughout is to present as definite a position as the data warrant while leaving open as many options as possible for those who may reject one or another element in my view. Let us proceed to a more definite characterization of the overall position proposed in the book, this time with emphasis on its implications for commonsense moral standards.

III. The Justification of Moral Judgments: A Kantian Intuitionism

Some of the major points I have made about intuitionism leave open the possibility of an empiricist version, but I have suggested that a moderately rationalistic intuitionism is both plausible and far more in accord with the historically important versions of the view, such as Moore's and Ross's.[4] The intuitionism presented in chapter 2 has at least these major characteristics: it accounts for the possibility of non-inferential justification that does not depend on a special faculty; it defends a principled rejection of the idea that intuitive justification or even intuitive knowledge is indefeasible; it presents a moral pluralism so understood that it does not produce valuational fragmentation or disunity among the positive moral principles; and, related to this last point, it establishes the possibility of integrating intuitive moral principles with major ethical theories, such as Kantianism.

These and other points are best seen as applied to a definite normative ethical theory, that is, the kind of theory that accounts for the sorts of deeds we ought (or ought not) to do. Chapter 2 takes Ross as a point of departure in developing a wider and more moderate intuitionism metaethically; I now take him as a point of departure for an intuitionist normative theory. Although he did not claim to have an exhaustive list of our basic duties, the ones he presented as our basic prima facie duties are highly comprehensive. They are the duties of fidelity (covering both promise keeping and truth telling), non-injury, reparation, justice, gratitude, beneficence, and self-improvement. He was keenly aware of conflicts both between duties in two or more of these categories and between duties in the same category, say between a promise to Peter and a promise to Paul. He maintained that there is no general ethical theory for satisfactorily dealing with these conflicts and that practical wisdom is our best resource for them.[5] I want to develop, and to some extent qualify, this view by making it clearer and integrating it with a Kantian perspective. We might start by outlining two ways in which an ethical view can be complete. Both are specially relevant to appraising the kind of normative theory in question.

Let us call an ethical position, such as intuitionism or utilitarianism, *normatively complete* provided it accounts for everything people (morally) ought (or ought not) to do, say to abstain from harming others, to keep our promises, and to render aid to those in distress when we readily can. For simplicity I assume that (as Ross apparently thought) everything we ought to do is in some sense a duty.[6] It is not clear whether Ross considered his position normatively complete, and it would take a major treatise to clarify in detail each of the wide-ranging duties on his list. We would do better to assume its completeness for the sake of argument and consider the pivotal question of how intuitionism can provide for resolving conflicts of duty. Two kinds of cases are crucial here.

Consider first a case in which a worthy charity approaches one for a donation. For Ross, one has a prima facie duty of beneficence here, grounded in the goodness one may promote. I propose to say that a normative theory has *first-order normative completeness* provided it accounts for every instance in which we have a prima facie duty and thus for all our basic duties. A theory having any significant degree of depth does this by accounting for all the grounds of duty. It does not just list them; like Ross's theory, it indicates, in some way, why we have them.

Now consider a different case, in which I break a promise to Peter because I have a stronger obligation (owing to sudden sickness in my child) which Peter will recognize as excusatory. I ought at least to give Peter an explanation, and the 'ought' seems moral — if I do not give it to him, I fail in some moral respect. But if I do not give it, which Rossian duty have I violated, as I must have done if at this level the view is normatively complete? Explaining my non-performance to Peter is not clearly a case of reparation, as would be my doing the promised deed doubly well later on. Perhaps an explanation is required by the duty of non-injury, if not by that of reparation. I see no reason why Ross could not say this, and I propose to say it for the sake of argument.

There is still a bar to the overall normative completeness of Ross's view: how is it to account for the finality of my duty to aid my child (thereby breaking my promise)? Ross himself has a rough *procedure* for doing this. But his theory does not provide a ground for finality of a duty, even though this is something we need to ascertain in some way whenever, as is common, there is a conflict of duties and we must act in fulfillment of one of them; and Ross denies that rival theories can provide a general account of overriding,[7] but he did not adequately consider how intuitionism might be extended to deal with the problem. Let us say that a normative theory that (like any plausible moral theory) countenances conflicts of duty has *second-order normative completeness* provided that it accounts for the finality of any duty that prevails in a conflict of duties (and for the equal stringency of two conflicting duties if they have equal stringency and one may therefore flip a coin).[8] How might we extend Rossian intuitionism to achieve both kinds of completeness and thereby overall normative completeness?

I believe that a broadly Kantian theory can provide for some extension and unification of Rossian intuitionism. To see how, consider the kind of deliberation appropriate to deciding the relative stringency of two conflicting duties. I might realize that my child could have a sudden rise in fever requiring immediate attention and that I am the only person who can keep watch; I might note that if I break the promise, my friend will only make a needless trip to the university and, finding me not there, phone me to see what is wrong. Now suppose that, following Kant's categorical imperative — though not his own interpretation of it[9] — I consider both the universality and the intrinsic end formulations of it.[10] Let us explore these in turn.

The universality formulation would require asking myself whether I can (rationally) universalize my maxim, which we may take to be roughly 'If the only way to keep my sick child safe is to break a promise to a friend at the cost of his inconvenience but in a way he would not (at least on careful reflection concerning the facts of the case) resent, then I will break it'.[11] Would universalizing this undermine the practice of promising? Surely not, since we regularly accept promises fully aware that things like this in fact do prevent their fulfillment in cases where non-fulfillment is not very serious. Would my doing it in such circumstances offend the promisee insofar as that person is reasonable? It would seem not — and one ground I can have for thinking so is that I would not myself be offended or resentful if the circumstances were reversed. To be sure, the universalizability in question implies only that I *may* break the promise. If, in addition, I determine that I cannot rationally universalize any maxim *preferring* my keeping the promise, then I *should* break it. The idea is that acts which accord with a universalizable maxim are permissible; if, in addition, *non*-performance of an act accords with no such maxim, the act is obligatory.

Now consider an appeal to Kant's intrinsic end formulation of the imperative: Always treat humanity, whether in your own person or in the person of any other, never merely as a means but always as an end. In risking serious illness to keep a promise of the relevant sort, I would seem to be failing to treat my child as an end in the relevant sense of that phrase, implying minimally that I value the well-being of the child for its own sake; yet arguably, in breaking the promise to care for the child I would not be using my friend "merely" as a means in the situation imagined. For one thing, I do not in any obvious way use the friend at all, as I would by lying to get the friend's car for a trip to the drugstore. For another, since my explanation of breaking the promise would be accepted by any reasonable person in the situation, it seems a mistake to say that the friend is used (at least in any objectionable way). The intuitive idea is roughly that we may not use someone *exploitively*, and Kant apparently thought that his view did not depend on any prior *moral* notion of exploitation (or on any concept of rationality that presupposes moral notions).[12]

Ross might of course say that we have no theory of conflict resolution here, only some rules of thumb to facilitate the use of practical wisdom. Certainly it is true that practical wisdom is required to apply the categorical imperative. But I cannot see that we do not derive some help from the principle beyond what we receive from just getting the facts and trying to make a wise decision apart from reliance on principles (I leave aside the important question whether forswearing such reliance is even psychologically realistic). Indeed, Ross himself would probably agree that in principle whatever we do should, if it is correct, be describable in a way that is generalizable, so that any moral agent could properly act on the same basis. For Ross regards moral properties as consequential upon natural ones, such as those involving the consequences of an action for pleasure and pain, approval and resentment.[13] Thus, the overall obligatoriness of staying with a child might be consequential (mainly) on its natural property of being necessary to save its life.

If we make the further assumption, as I believe Ross does, that in order to make a justified moral decision to act one needs a sense of the identity and bearing of the relevant facts, one could not reasonably deny that the categorical imperative yields a *test* even for judgments arrived at without its help. Ross might reasonably insist that one can be *guided* by facts without being able (at least apart from Socratic prodding) to *formulate* roughly how they bear; but his view implies no reason to deny that the effort to formulate this is appropriate and often successful. And he would surely grant that in a similar way the categorical imperative could at least be intelligibly, if not always decisively, invoked in cases of conflict of duties. If it can be, then if bringing it to bear yields a minimally satisfactory answer as to which of two (sets of) conflicting duties is final, the Kantian intuitionism we get by supplementing Ross's framework with the categorical imperative has second-order normative completeness.

The duty of beneficence poses special problems for this approach (as indeed for virtually any ethical view that takes the welfare of persons to imply weighty duties of beneficence). Why is it that my duty of beneficence does not always outweigh my ordinary fiduciary duties to, say, my family, as well as all of my duties of self-improvement whose fulfillment will not conduce to my doing more for humanity as a whole than I would do it I devoted my energies to other people?

This should suggest the more general question how a Kantian intuitionism can at once admit a general duty of beneficence and avoid requiring the same deeds as would act utilitarianism. I believe Ross heightened the problem by describing the duty of beneficence as resting "on the mere fact that there are other beings in the world whose condition we can make better in respect of virtue, or of intelligence, or of pleasure."[14] Still, he also stressed "the highly personal character of duty" and argued that other things equal the duty of fidelity outweighs that of beneficence.[15] A Rossian intuitionism can thus take it as clear on reflection that even a large contribution to the welfare of humanity does not necessarily outweigh all duties of fidelity or all duties of self-improvement, and that there is no quantitative criterion — such as a maximizing standard — which we can appeal to in deciding each case. There are at least two respects in which the Kantian approach outlined here can help with such cases. They correspond to the two parts of the intrinsic end formulation.

First, there is a sense in which, if one devotes one's life simply to maximizing the good of persons (or sentient beings), one is using oneself merely as a means; for instance, one's personal commitments and talents do not matter at all *independently* of their contribution to the general good in question. Similarly, even if one does not try to *maximize* the general good but always prefers large contributions to it over one's personal commitments and talents, one is likely to be often using oneself merely as a means. This suggests that a plausible application of the categorical imperative would at least block a large-scale preference for fulfilling the duty of beneficence over competing duties. In resisting that preference, moreover, one would not necessarily be using others merely (or in any intuitively inadmissible way) as a means: in not doing charitable deeds toward the poor, for instance, one need not be using them at all; and in doing *some* such deeds, even if falling far short of maximizing welfare in the world, one may be treating them as ends. Granted, this strategy does not provide a definitive standard for deciding each case — as opposed to implying that once a case is correctly decided there is a universalizable principle that can be extracted from it.[16] Intuitionism need have no commitment to the existence of more than rules of thumb available in advance for deciding the relevant conflicts of duty.

The second respect in which the intrinsic end formulation is instructive comes to light when we ask what it is to treat persons as ends. This can be given an impersonal reading, on which to treat people as ends is simply to promote their good for its own sake, something possible when one has no notion how this will occur, as where one contributes to a charity one simply knows is philanthropic. It can also be given a personal reading, on which it applies only to people to whom one has some personal relationship. The latter reading fits Kant's main illustrations of the imperative better, though his theory as he develops it may work best if one also allows at least indirect relationships, say where one either has a definite description adequate to provide a sense of who is in question, for instance children in a New York slum. Two points, at least, are clear. First, in failing to prefer duties of fidelity or self-improvement over those of general beneficence in the ways that are intuitively objectionable, one is not only likely to be using oneself merely as a means but will also fail to treat others, such as a promisee, or oneself, or both, as ends. Neglect or exploitation of others can contribute to the overall goodness of the world as well as neglect or exploitation of oneself. Second, where these two deficiencies under the intrinsic end formulation occur, one is justified in giving a very high degree of preference for duties of fidelity or self-improvement over that of beneficence (and much the same would hold for other duties that might conflict with beneficence).

There are at least two further considerations suggesting that a Kantian intuitionism is a good extension of the Rossian version. One concerns the kinds of normative considerations relevant to applying the categorical imperative to cases of conflicting duties. The other concerns the normative principles one will choose to live by in the first place if the categorical imperative is one's basic principle. I take these in turn.

First, it could well turn out that the *kinds* of variables relevant to applying the categorical imperative to conflicts of duty are all of the sort specified in the seven principles of duty we are provisionally taking as basic in a normatively complete first-order theory. The same kinds of variables that ground prima facie duty are, at the second level, determinants of final duty. This would make the Kantian intuitionism *homogeneously complete*, by contrast with a theory like (hedonistic) rule utilitarianism, which says roughly that our actions should conform to rules that, if conscientiously followed by all, would maximize goodness, and then specifies non-hedonic rules such as prohibitions of lying and theft. The second-order completeness of this view would invoke the principle of utility, and thereby the supreme considerations of pleasure and pain that are *not* essential in the theory's day-to-day normative principles, such as the principle requiring a prima facie duty to keep promises and possibly others parallel to Ross's. Rule utilitarianism would be complete only by invoking a hedonic principle for adjudicating conflicts between its first-order principles, and thereby relying on elements not figuring in (all of) its first-order principles. It would thereby exhibit a split-level completeness and might be called *heterogeneously complete*.[17] This would make it less unified, other things equal, than the Kantian intuitionism I am sketching.

A second reason to consider a Kantian intuitionism a fruitful extension of Ross's view is that the Rossian principles of duty may be argued to be just the general moral principles one would derive from a careful application of the categorical imperative to everyday life. For instance, if one set out to avoid treating people merely as means, one would recognize duties of non-injury, including avoidance of murder, brutality, and injustice; of reparation; and of fidelity (to promises and to one's word). Moreover, if one set out to treat people positively as ends, one would recognize duties of beneficence, gratitude, self-improvement, and justice (meaning, as Ross intended, rectification of injustice one discovers as opposed to avoidance of injustice, though arguably some cases of this Rossian duty would be recognized under the non-exploitation clause of the categorical imperative). This derivational strategy gives the categorical imperative a double role: it in some sense generates the Rossian duties — and possibly other basic duties (this possibly broader thrust is something I leave open); and, as illustrated with the case of the sick child, it provides a (non-quantitative) account of how to weight the factors associated with those duties in cases of moral conflict.

So viewed, the Kantian imperative also helps us to see a difference between positive and negative duties as well as associated differences in stringency often attributed to perfect as opposed to imperfect duties: roughly, the perfect duties are those whose violation treats someone merely as a means (roughly, in an exploitive way) and the imperfect duties are those whose violation does not necessarily do this but does fail to treat someone as an end (roughly with concern for the person's good for its own sake).

The suggested approach is also beneficial in understanding Kant at points where he is at best quite abstract. There are at least three significant places where the Kantianism and Rossian intuitionism are mutually clarifying. First, one can think of the Rossian duties as representing standards for treating people with respect. Second, one can conceive the basis of the appropriate respect as the dignity of persons, understood, for example, as in the previous chapter and taken to be typically undermined more by violation of a perfect duty like that of non-injury than by violation of an imperfect one like that of beneficence. Third, if we take dignity to be fundamental in a Kantian view, in the way outlined in that chapter, we can conceive it to underlie rights of autonomy and can take the proper sphere of personal moral autonomy to be that in which the Rossian duties, particularly the negative ones, are observed. On this account, they would be the constitutive first-order principles of self-government for autonomous moral agents.

Ross and other intuitionists who are epistemologically immoderate on the same points would likely object that because the prima facie duty principles are self-evident, they cannot be derived from or even inferentially justified by appeal to anything prior. In chapter 2 I argued that this restriction holds only for a small range of propositions that are strongly axiomatic — thus self-evident in a way the principles of prima facie duty, even on Ross's view, are not. Supposing, however, that Ross accepted this epistemological point, he might go on to say that his principles *specify* what the categorical imperative comes to, rather than being derivable from it in a way that gives it any justificatory power. There is a truth very close to this that I readily grant, but it does not seem to me to undermine the basic point that the imperative framework provides both support and unification to the Rossian duties — or, in principle, to any intuitively acceptable set of prima facie duties (I am not here making more than a provisional proposal that Ross's set is complete). Let me develop this point.

It must be granted that there is a sense in which any non-trivial derivation of substantive consequences from a proposition specifies what it comes to. Still, the categorical imperative has meaning independent of the Rossian duties. We have, for instance, a sense of what it is to treat someone merely as a means from our understanding of instrumental relations among both animate and inanimate things; people regularly use tools and far too often similarly use other people. Here, getting the job done is all that matters: what happens to the tool is of no concern — unless we need it for another job. We also have a sense of what it is to treat someone as an end. Consider love. Those who love people seek to do things for those they love, and they do them with no further end than some aspect of the good of the other.

The categorical imperative can also serve both to connect the Rossian duties with one another and (as already suggested) to provide a kind of rationale for them. Notice, for instance, how failures to fulfill duties of gratitude, beneficence, and self-improvement seem (to some degree) to fail to treat one or more persons (or perhaps other sentient beings) *as an end*, and failures to fulfill duties of fidelity, reparation, justice, and non-injury seem (to some degree) to treat one or more merely *as a means*. These points connect the duties as the standards enjoined on us in order to live up to the imperative's required treatment of persons, and the points provide a rationale for the duties by exhibiting their fulfillment as obeying its double-barreled injunction.[18]

It must be granted that our understanding of the categorical imperative may be affected by what we learn from using it to systematize such normative standards as the Rossian duties, just as our application of them and our resolution of conflicts among them may be affected by how we interpret the categorical imperative. This is in part a conceptual point, concerning moral concepts and their application. There is a related epistemological point: our justification for accepting the categorical imperative can be enhanced by our justification for accepting the principles of duty it systematizes; and our justification for accepting them may be enhanced by our sense of their support by the imperative, as well as by our sense of their being intuitively confirmed as applied to concrete moral cases about which we have clear convictions. Both points suggest that we may reasonably seek to bring a broadly Kantian theory and a Rossian intuitionism into reflective equilibrium. Each may clarify the content of the other; each may help in applying the other to concrete moral decisions; and each, in a different way, can provide evidence for the other or for one or another element therein.

Once we free ourselves of a narrow theory of self-evidence and the confinement of intuition to the self-evident, our overarching moral principle and the specific prima facie duty principles it generates can admit of justification both from above — in terms of leading to plausible consequences — and from below, in terms of inferential justification by more comprehensive principles (both kinds of justification are discussed and shown to be compatible in chapter 2). To be sure, in the case of the categorical imperative, it is arguable that we do not have any moral principle that is deeper. But if chapter 11 is correct, we can at least exhibit the imperative as a reasonable principle to hold if something like the dignity of persons is the primary value morality is to serve.

It may now seem that I have in effect suggested not just a Kantian intuitionism but an intuitionist Kantianism. There is much truth in that: I cannot see how a Kantian theory can be plausible without both a high degree of epistemic dependence on intuition and a normative dependence on secondary principles, as Mill termed them: call them categorical imperatives with a small *c*. But I also cannot see how anything important in Kant's theory is falsified by the account I am suggesting of how Kantian considerations can yield a more comprehensive intuitionism.[19]

It need scarcely be added that I am assuming here that skepticism about the foundations of ethics can be overcome. Chapter 3 defends this view, though I do not claim that skepticism is not a serious problem for ethical theory (even for noncognitivism, which must distinguish between reasonable and unreasonable moral attitudes). If, however, that chapter succeeds in showing the main similarities between practical and theoretical skepticism, and how both can be rationally resisted even if not vanquished, that is surely enough to warrant approaching ethical theory as I do.

IV. The Descriptive and Explanatory Powers of Moral Concepts

If the concern of part I of this book is primarily the epistemology of ethics — including construction of an intuitionist account of moral justification — that of part II is mainly the metaphysics of ethics. Are ethical concepts natural, and how, in any case, do they fit into the larger natural order? This question is central for understanding their descriptive and explanatory powers, which in turn are crucial for understanding the role of moral concepts and judgments in everyday life.

The tension between naturalism and non-naturalism in ethics is very old. Surely Plato may be seen as a non-naturalist, deriving his ethics from a theory of transcendent forms, whereas Aristotle is at least arguably a naturalist, deriving his ethics from a largely psychological and biological account of our nature.[20] Aquinas's natural law approach is a complicated compromise between Aristotle's naturalism and his own Christian theology. Hume is quite arguably a thoroughgoing naturalist, though there are passages in which he sounds like a reductive naturalist and others in which he at least foreshadows noncognitivism.[21] Kant is surely a non-naturalist, Mill quite plainly a naturalist. In the twentieth century we find naturalism strongly opposed by Moore, Ross, and others, but with a major concession: that moral properties supervene on natural ones (in the ways described in chapters 3 and 4).

This concession is of great significance. It may warrant speaking, as some philosophers do, of a *non-reductive naturalism*, since moral properties are determined by natural ones. Morally good will, for instance, is determined by intentions and other relevant psychological dispositions, and one might argue that all the basic moral properties are grounded in some set of natural properties.[22] If all basic moral properties can be shown to be so grounded, as for the sake of argument I have assumed can be shown, then a limited naturalism holds true. We might call it the *moral dependence view*.

It has been common, however, for naturalists to be empiricists, though this is not entailed by naturalism as a metaphysical position. Here, I have been unwilling to grant what many naturalists maintain. As argued in chapters 3 and 4, the relation between moral properties and their natural grounds is, in the basic cases, conceptual and a priori. It seems to me that the relation between, say, promising and incurring a prima facie obligation (a word that seems preferable to 'duty' in some cases) is a

priori. This is why the intuitionism I find most plausible is rationalist; but it is important to see that one could maintain both a non-reductive naturalism and some kind
of intuitionism even if one took this relation to be empirical.[23]

Whether the moral dependence view, which says in part that things possessing
moral properties have them in virtue of their natural properties, is considered a non-
reductive naturalism or not, it is a kind of realism. It entails that moral predicates,
such as 'unjust' and 'obligatory', express genuine properties of things. This contrasts
with noncognitivism, which takes such predicates to be only moral terms which
seem to represent properties of things, chiefly acts and persons, but instead express
something non-truth-valued, say attitudes. Now if there are moral properties, we
would expect them to have descriptive power. How can this be, if their primary role
is normative, say to evaluate and even motivate action?

This is where the moral dependence view is specially helpful. If I condemn a
deed as unjust, then even if my main purpose is to criticize it, I must also be taken to
describe it at least in some open-ended, indirect way. For I must be assumed to
ascribe injustice on the basis of some natural property such as unequal sentencing of
two offenders found guilty of the same crime under the same conditions, and if possession of that property implies injustice, then my moral statement commits me to
ascribing to the act some such natural property. If I know what I am talking about,
this property is precisely the kind of ground on which I will ascribe injustice, and I
can be expected to adduce it if queried. Moral judgments of individual deeds or of
people, then, are at least indirectly descriptive in the open-ended way this illustrates.
If, in addition, the crucial descriptive content is connected, in relation to something
of value, with the *ground* of the judgment, and if we can suppose that normally people who make moral judgments are motivated by the presence or prospect of value
or disvalue, we can see why the acceptance of such a judgment can be motivating as
well as descriptive. Injustice, for instance, is likely to be perceived as a bad thing,
and we expect a normal person who so perceives a deed to be averse to it in
prospect, disapproving of it at the time, and indignant about it in retrospect.

To some philosophers it seems clear that, say, the injustice of a government can
explain, in a broadly causal sense, such phenomena as uprisings by the people. But
if applications of moral concepts can be, as just illustrated, indirectly descriptive,
they can also be indirectly explanatory. This is because of a second aspect of moral
dependence: the *epistemic dependence* of moral on natural properties (described in
chapter 5). Roughly, the idea is that our knowledge and justification regarding the
application of moral properties depends on our knowledge or justification concerning their natural base properties. Thus, I cannot know that there is governmental
injustice unless I know that, for instance, there is seizure of lands. But this widespread seizure is just the kind of natural property that can plainly cause an uprising.
My suggestion, then, is that what looks like a moral explanation, in the sense of one
that ascribes a causal role directly to a moral property, is really a familiar kind of naturalistic explanation, presented *by way of ascribing a moral property*, as where the
causally explanatory element is some relevant base property, such as a resentment of
the sociopolitical conditions implied, in the context of the proffered explanation, to
be present in the situation of injustice.

If this is the correct account, we have naturalized moral explanations without naturalizing moral properties. I believe the account can accommodate the data at least as well as the reductive naturalist view that takes moral properties to *be* natural, and it is also a version of moral realism. Moral properties are real and indeed have as good a claim to be ineliminable as do the natural base properties that necessarily imply their presence. But the former are a different kind of property. They are irreducibly normative, as one would expect if they are ultimately grounded in intrinsic value, which is also irreducibly normative. Unlike Platonic normative realism, however, this realism is worldly, with moral properties firmly anchored in the natural order; it is also pluralistic, where Plato's (in *The Republic*, at least) is more nearly monistic.

V. Ethics in Action, Morality in Character

Suppose there is moral knowledge, or at least moral justification — justification for holding moral principles and certain moral judgments — and that such knowledge and justification are construed along the lines of a Kantian intuitionism. How do justified moral principles and, especially, justified self-addressed moral judgments guide our actions? How does our character properly reflect them? Mere words are not enough. But although actions speak louder than words, they are not enough either. An action might arise from self-deception, as where a husband does something to maintain an appearance of fidelity (say, helping his wife in a difficult task) when deep down he knows he is straying from fidelity. This kind of self-serving motivation tends to undermine or attenuate the moral significance the good deed might otherwise have.

Rationalization may cover up self-serving motivation, as where, asked why he is being so solicitous, the man notes that a holiday weekend is a good time for teamwork; and here he might speak the truth, but for a reason that prevents his doing so from being a manifestation of veracity. Indeed, a case like this suggests a self-manipulative person deficient in the ethics of belief as well as in the virtue of fidelity. If, in addition, he seeks (even if unconsciously) to deceive, the rationalization may bespeak dishonesty, and for that he may be morally responsible even if he is deceiving himself as well as his wife.

A natural view to take on how moral judgment should guide action and be represented in character is that our moral commitments should be deep enough so that when we make judgments in accord with them those judgments are highly motivating. Roughly, our moral character should be strong enough to enable us to subordinate our actions to our moral judgments. Chapters 6 and (to some extent) 7 and 10 bring out that this subordination of action to judgment cannot always be expected. The picture of normal persons as rational, responsible agents must be qualified by noting the possibility that we can be influenced by psychological forces of which we are unaware and that we may offer explanations that merely rationalize our behavior.

If, however, reason and morality do not always determine as much of our behavior as we might like to think, it also turns out that we can be morally responsible for some of our failures in this regard. If I am right about actions produced or influenced by self-deception or rationalization, they often come within the scope of moral responsibility. Imagine that my self-deception leads me to give a friend a gift of rare spices in a way that brings me no moral credit, since I am merely seeking to appear affectionate. Suppose further that I cause my friend indigestion because of an allergy I know about but conveniently underestimate in mixing the species. Here I am morally criticizable. A lack of understanding of why one wants to do something morally wrong is not automatically excusatory or even mitigating. This is in part a reply to Freudian and post-Freudian skepticism about the scope of moral responsibility, as chapter 1 is in part reply to epistemological skepticism about morality.[24]

So far, I have suggested that our moral commitments should be anchored in our character and that, largely because of how firm this anchoring should be, moral responsibility extends even to actions deriving from unconscious motivation. Does it, however, extend to elements of character themselves? Aristotle apparently thought so, and chapter 7 explores the nature and extent of our responsibility for our character. From the point of view of the Kantian intuitionism outlined earlier, we can say that our moral character should reflect an internalization of the basic duties, together with some appropriate dispositions concerning conflicts among them that go with using the categorical imperative framework. Moral character may of course be strong or weak; it may be well developed, as in conscientious, experienced adults; it may be rudimentary, as in small children; and it may be subtle or coarse. There is no need to go into detail here (much of relevance to such character is said in chapter 8); I simply want to bring out how responsibility for character may be accommodated by the Kantian intuitionism I have presented.

To see how a Kantian intuitionism may account for responsibility for character, at least two points are essential. First, we should distinguish, for traits as for self-deception, three cases of responsibility: *genetic* responsibility (for acquiring them); *retentional* responsibility (for retaining them); and *prospective* responsibility (for acquiring them in the future). Second, we should note that one basic duty bears quite directly on at least the second two cases: the duty of self-improvement. Indeed, suppose I have a bad trait, such as envy, that leads me to downgrade people. In addition to the duty to improve myself by reversing this tendency, I have at least an indirect duty of non-injury pointing in the same direction: I have a direct duty not to downgrade people (in damaging ways) and an indirect duty to change my tendency to do this (if only because I may not always be able to control it). A second point here is that even if one is not morally responsible for acquiring a trait, say as a child, it does not follow that one cannot later be responsible for retaining it. Our moral responsibility changes with our capacities; and as we become capable of improving ourselves, our duties in this direction are both more numerous and less easily overridden.

Pursuing the Kantian side of this intuitionist framework is suggestive in another way. Kant took good will to be the only unqualified good, and he insisted on the related point that only deeds done from duty have moral worth.[25] Given my view that there is moral intrinsic goodness and that it provides one kind of basic reason for action, together with the assumption that being or remaining morally good is clearly in the scope of the duty of beneficence or of self-improvement or of both, cultivating and retaining good will are among those of our duties that affect our own character. Moreover, on the highly plausible assumption that an action's having moral worth is a good thing for oneself or others or both, the duties of beneficence and self-improvement similarly imply a duty to cultivate a tendency to act from duty, not merely in accordance with duty (or to cultivate a stronger such tendency if one already has it). This in turn suggests that one should try to internalize the basic moral principles and their underlying values. Virtue as understood from the point of view of a Kantian intuitionism, then, is above all a state of character in which the basic moral principles and suitable second-order dispositions are internalized and, in relation to the categorical imperative, well integrated with one another. This idea brings us to the question of how actions should manifest such character — of what constitutes action from virtue.

VI. Virtue in Character and Moral Worth in Action

To say that we can be responsible for our character traits, including especially virtues and vices, is not to say what virtues or vices are or how they lead to action of the kind appropriate to them — the kind I am calling actions from virtue. I have already suggested that virtues are features of character and that they can result from and (in some cases) be viewed as internalization of the appropriate moral principles. This is not to deny Aristotle's point that they can result from habituation. Habituation is a highly commodious category. I am more concerned with their structure and with how they *can* be acquired than with the genetic question of how they in fact are acquired, important though that is for moral education.

As argued in chapter 8, we can understand virtues largely in terms of six variables, corresponding to situational, conceptual, cognitive, motivational, behavioral, and teleological dimensions of action from virtue: first, the *field* of a virtue, roughly the kind of situation in which it characteristically influences conduct; second, the characteristic *targets* it aims at, such as the well-being of others in the case of beneficence; third, the agent's *understanding* of that field, say in taking fidelity to others to be essential to respecting them; fourth, the agent's *motivation* to act in that field in a certain way, where that way is appropriate to the virtue, as where (from honesty) one wants to tell friends how much one fears the failure of their plan; fifth, the agent's acting on the *basis* of that understanding and motivation (rather than, say, from mere self-interest); and sixth, the *beneficiaries* of the virtue, above all (and perhaps solely) the person(s) who properly benefit from our realizing it: for beneficence, other people in general; for charitableness, the needy; for fidelity, family and friends; and so forth.

If we view virtues in this light, then some of the points about how a Kantian intuitionism can accommodate the moral importance of virtues become clearer. First, a virtue can be an internalization of one or more basic moral principles together with an appropriate second-order understanding of how to deal with conflicting moral considerations. Take the duty of beneficence. Above all, one may have a suitably deep, long-standing desire to promote the good of others, an understanding of how and when to do it, a tendency to do it on that basis, and a sense of what duties, under various conditions, override it. Second, none of this requires rehearsing a moral principle in the context of acting beneficently; an internalized principle can guide without being called to mind. This even applies (as explained in chapter

1) to using the categorical imperative framework: one can work appropriately with the ideas of universalizability and of means and ends without reciting, or even being readily able to formulate, the imperative that guides one. Third, the suggested conception of a virtue and how we act on it (developed in detail in chapter 8) is quite harmonious with the idea that we have at least retentional and (sometimes) prospective responsibility for our virtues. If a series of misfortunes makes me bitter and self-protective, my duty of beneficence may impose on me a special responsibility to resist losing the corresponding disposition — to reach out to others as best I can. If I fail, both the duty of beneficence and that of self-improvement would imply a duty to cultivate a minimally beneficent character once again.

A fourth point emerges when we ask how virtue ethics, with which I am in many respects sympathetic, squares with the moral epistemology of this book. If we distinguish the moral rightness of action types — which I have argued is knowable intuitively — from moral worth of concrete deeds (action tokens), which requires grounding in good character and hence is not knowable without genetic information, than we can see that the proposed conception of a virtue accords well with the idea that we can be guided in exercising virtue by the basic moral principles understood along the lines of Kantian intuitionism. Indeed, it is difficult to see how one could ultimately arrive at a warranted conception of good character without independent moral or axiological knowledge or justification, such as we have of the Rossian principles.

Still, if ultimately the *moral constitution* of our character is based on some set of principles or standards that are grounded outside character but internalizable in it, the *moral exercise* of that constitution in deeds requires at least some degree of good character, such as appropriate intentions and dispositions. No amount of moral knowledge gives moral worth to actions that are merely in accordance with that knowledge; actions having moral worth must be done from the right sort of motivation. Virtue is thus absolutely central in the theory of moral worth, even if it is secondary in the theory of moral obligation.

A good intuitionist view, then, will have a major aretaic component: it will seek, as a Kantian theory should, to account for how its principles may best be internalized in a virtuous character and will insist that the moral worth of actions be grounded not in their mere conformity with its principles but in their proper motivation by the associated elements of character. When they are so motivated, moreover, the agent tends to have a sense of their moral grounding, say of acting in fulfillment of a commitment. The sense of that grounding can be among the kinds of experiences that have intrinsic moral value.

VII. Reason and Motivation

A major issue in the theory of practical reason concerns the relation between reason and desire. Which is — or should be — master? The topic of autonomy is an excellent focus for this question. As one would expect, if we take the Humean view that reason is and ought only to be the slave of the passions, then we should understand autonomy as (roughly) a condition of self-government in which one's basic desires, guided in some way by reason, control one's conduct. If we take an objectivist view on which there are some things worth wanting — things of intrinsic value, for instance — then we should understand autonomy as (roughly) a condition in which our basic desires, if not directed toward what is actually worth wanting, are at least rational in the light of whatever access we have to such proper ends of action.

I have challenged the Humean, instrumentalist view. Chapter 9 argues that by contrast with an objectivist position, it does not give a good account of autonomy, and, more positively, chapter 11 defends an objectivist account of value and thereby of reasons for action. Here I mainly want to bring out how the ethical theory proposed in this chapter bears on autonomy.

If the suggested basic moral principles belonging to a Kantian intuitionism are knowable, then it would surely be a mistake to think that for someone who knows them, autonomy could be defined simply by appeal to basic desires. This is so, at least, if I am correct (in chapter 10) in arguing that holding a moral belief does not entail overriding motivation to act accordingly. If I know the Rossian principles, surely my being autonomous requires my acting broadly in accordance with them. They are meant to cover life as a whole. If I do not generally abide by them, then far from being a self-governing agent under their proper guidance, I would be like someone who makes major resolutions and cannot follow them unless motivated to do so by independent desires. My desires would be my real governing constitution; the moral principles would be at their service.

The picture so far painted of an autonomous moral agent suggests that autonomous agents must operate, as it were, under a moral constitution containing regulative principles of action, such as the Rossian duties. This would be too narrow a picture. A major lesson of the account of acting from virtue given in chapter 8 is that moral action, in the full-blooded sense of action from moral virtue, need not be rule-following conduct or performed under the conception of the virtue in question or indeed under any explicitly moral concept, such as that of (moral) duty. Moral autonomy is roughly a capacity for self-government under moral standards; those standards may be more or less explicit and may be either internalizations of principles learned through moral education or aretaically encoded habits of action. Autonomous agents may be guided by an adherence to principles or by a largely non-propositional sense of duty or even by an intuitive responsiveness to the properties of action and circumstance — the kind Ross calls grounds of duty — that are basic to both principles of duty and the sense of it. A good account of moral autonomy should be neutral among plausible normative theories.

To say, however, that moral principles are normatively central to the autonomy of those who hold them, and that a mature, rational autonomous agent who accepts moral principles has an appropriate degree of motivation to abide by them, is not to say that *just* in virtue of holding a moral principle or moral judgment one must have such motivation. Motivation is not intrinsic to the mere holding of such principles or judgments.

Autonomy, by contrast with moral judgment, is an intrinsically motivational notion, and one reason some philosophers have taken motivation to be intrinsic to holding moral judgments may be that those judgments are normally — and most prominently — held by autonomous agents and, when held by *them*, do normally imply a significant degree of motivation to act accordingly. A major question in moral psychology is whether some significant degree of motivation is also in some way implied by, or otherwise follows from, one or another kind of acceptance of moral principles and judgments. Broadly, the issue is in what way, and to what extent, reason is "practical." This is the central problem for chapter 10.

It is essential to distinguish two ways in which reason can be practical: motivationally, by providing motivational reasons for action — reasons actually inclining one to act — and normatively, by providing normative reasons for actions — reasons why one ought to act. My moral epistemology implies that reason is normatively practical: through its exercise we have knowledge of, or at least can have justified beliefs regarding, both moral principles and intrinsic value, and each kind of knowledge or justified belief provides basic (normative) reasons for action. But I hold that it is only in a qualified way that reason is motivationally practical. It may, through such self-addressed moral judgments as that I must keep a promise, produce desire; indeed, it will do so in an adequately rational person. Still, such judgments (cognitively construed) are not intrinsically motivating. Here, then, I accept objectivism about morality and value and endorse the normative practicality of reason, while denying its motivational practicality in the strong sense implying the intrinsically motivating power of self-addressed moral judgments. I stand with Kant and most other major moral philosophers on the objectivity of the grounds of normativity, but (except insofar as he is a noncognitivist) I am closer to Hume in the theory of motivation.

If we had no ready access to experiences that motivate us in the direction of rational and, more specifically, moral conduct, a motivational externalist view would make it seem just good fortune that we so often are motivated not only to act in accord with our practical judgments but also to act on them. This is where the internalism of my epistemology and the related experientialism of my theory of value have a special bearing. Quite early in life, we are acquainted with such non-moral goods as pleasure, with moral goods like fair treatment, and with such evils as pain and unfair treatment. These elements are often memorably experienced and, for people with a normal psychological makeup, often naturally motivating. Given a normal intellectual makeup, as we mature they appear as plainly normative considerations, weighing positively and negatively in favor of the relevant deeds or states of affairs.

In the genetic order, of course, motivation is prior to normative understanding; children recoil from pain before they come to see it as a reason to avoid its causes. There may be naturalists, including certain Humeans, who claim that pain only seems self-evidently to count as a reason to avoid the painful because we naturally *do* avoid the painful. Granting that a psychologically natural connection can seem self-evident when it is not, I do not see how we can adequately explicate normative reasons for actions apart from such apparently a priori connections. (It is an interesting question how Hume might have explicated his own apparently normative 'ought' in "[R]eason is and ought only to be the salve of the passions.")

None of this is to deny that a virtuous person is habitually motivated by moral judgments. The point is that apart from some kind of internalization of moral standards, the mere intellectual acceptance of even a self-addressed moral judgment is not intrinsically motivating. There is no such direct path from intellect to will. But in normal lives there are also no bars to the many normal paths, by way of moral education, from teaching and role modeling of moral standards to their internalization in the character of receptive individuals — above all, children growing up in moral environments.

VIII. The Place of Value in the Foundations of Ethics

The good — the intrinsically good — has played a major role in ethical theory at least since Plato. For him it is fundamentally transcendent; for Aristotle, immanent in our nature; for Aquinas, both natural and theological; for Kant, deontological; for Mill, hedonic; and for Moore and Ross, intuitive and pluralistic. As the notion functions in most of these philosophers, it is natural to take action and desires as properly aimed — though often indirectly — at some aspect of the good. It is also natural to think that the more good there is, the better, and this easily leads some philosophers, such as utilitarians, to a maximizing theory of obligation, on which our basic obligation is to contribute as much as we can to the balance of good to evil. If Mill is, as he appears, committed to such a view, he nonetheless recognized qualities as well as quantities of what is good (pleasure) and so would have us maximize goodness only when other things are qualitatively equal. In my view, even that kind of maximizing theory is a mistake, and I have presented a more pluralistic view.[26]

In addition to maintaining that there are irreducibly different kinds of intrinsic goods, I have argued that intrinsic value is organic, both in the sense that the intrinsic value of a whole need not be equivalent to that of its parts and in the sense that non-value properties of a thing can affect its overall value, as a part of a painting that it not itself beautiful can affect the beauty of the painting. This point is connected with moral theory in several ways. What I want to stress here is that just as practical wisdom is required to determine which of two sets of conflicting duties prevails, it is often required to determine the value of a complex whole, either absolutely or as compared with another.

There is a direct relation between the organicity of value and a kind of *moral incommensurability* that holds among certain duties. Just as we cannot assign numbers to the weight of every duty and must consider the duty of, say, self-improvement as in a way incommensurable with that of fidelity, we must regard the moral disvalue of, say, sacrificing an innocent person as incommensurable with that of saving other innocent persons who could be spared through the sacrifice. If *some* kind of commensurability is implied by the possibility of using practical wisdom, aided by the categorical imperative, to deal with such difficult cases, there is still nothing like hedonic units, or even a hedonic comparison, that can be brought to the decision as Mill might have to do when the qualities of pleasure and pain in question are equal. If, as suggested in chapter 11, duty may be derived from moral and other intrinsic values only when these are organically conceived, it should be no surprise that where there are conflicts of prima facie duty there is no single value, nor non-organic plurality of values, in terms of which all conflicts of duty may be resolved.

A good life, then, cannot be described as a maximization of some one kind of value or even of all the kinds additively combined. Some combinations will yield what is an overall bad result; others, possibly with value constituents that individually seem less weighty, will be better or good overall. The overall goodness of a state of affairs depends on how its constituents combine. We can generalize about good and bad combinations; but (with at most some special exceptions) the generalizations, even when guided by principles bearing on the composite value of various combinations, must be based on experience.

The ontology of value I have (provisionally) proposed is experientialist; but although it takes the bearers of intrinsic value to be concrete experiences — the kinds of things that constitute a life *as lived* — these are not the only non-instrumental values. There are also inherent goods. A beautiful thing, or a good moral character, can be by their very nature such that contemplating them in an appropriate way is an intrinsically valuable experience. They are thus potential non-instrumental sources of reasons for action. These reasons are normatively external, in the sense that they do not depend on actual desires, yet they are epistemically internal in the sense that there is access to them through reflection or introspection. They are, then, both objectively grounded and subjectively accessible. This objectivity does not entail realism, but it goes well with that view. That is in part because value supervenes on natural properties, such as being pleasant or painful, and so is no more eliminable than they are. The broad axiological grounding of moral principles possible on this approach, then, anchors moral principles in the world without positing a reductive naturalism, as is so tempting for moral realism.

To say that ethics can be grounded axiologically is not to say that moral principles do not have an important kind of autonomy — epistemic autonomy. Ross was surely right in saying that the basic moral principles are — as I would put it — mediately self-evident: roughly, knowable by adequately informed, suitably mature, and sufficiently extensive reflection on their content. To say that something can be known, or at least to some degree justified, by appeal to something else is not to say that it cannot be known directly. Even if we cannot unify or ground moral principles in considerations of intrinsic value or in any other way, we can have moral knowledge and justification, we can be motivated by moral judgments, and we can develop ethical character.

These central achievements of the moral life do not even require our mutual agreement on any ethical theory. One could live by a theory such as the Kantian intuitionism proposed here without ever formulating it, and in everyday life we can agree with others *in* reasons for action even if we diverge *on* such reasons the moment we begin to philosophize about their nature or status. Agreement in moral practice does not require agreement in ethical theory. We can, moreover, be guided by a conception of human good even if we do not explicitly take aim at it as such, but simply pursue it through one or another of its many aspects, sometimes piecemeal, sometimes with a more organic sense of how our lives should be shaped. In the everyday framework of grounds for action, the normativity of moral principles is accessible to reason, appropriate to eliciting desire in rational persons, and internalizable in anyone fortunate enough to be brought up in a minimally civilized community.

Notes

For valuable discussion of some of the issues raised in this chapter I am grateful to Hugh McCann and, especially, Mark van Roojen.

1. As ch. 10 brings out in emphasizing moral experience as a possible source of evidence for moral judgment, I do not take the sense of value, say of fairness, to be reducible to *beliefs* about the relevant value.

2. For instance, the dual motivational and normative role of happiness for Aristotle is described in detail in ch. 1 of my *Practical Reasoning* (London and New York: Routledge, 1989); much concerning how practical judgment is a response to what is good is noted in ch. 10; and ch. 11, on intrinsic value, presents intrinsic value as a basic source of reasons for action and sketches (along the lines of ch. 2) an epistemology that accounts for the possibility of justified beliefs, and thereby justified judgments, about value and obligation.

3. I offer support for this kind of internalism in *The Structure of Justification* (Cambridge and New York: Cambridge University Press, 1993), esp. chs. 10–12. I also argue for a partly externalist account of knowledge, but that externalism does not significantly aid the case for an overall externalism in moral epistemology.

4. Among the important views in the contemporary literature that seem broadly intuitionist are those of Thomas Nagel and Judith Jarvis Thomson. See esp. his *The View from Nowhere* (New York and Oxford: Oxford University Press, 1986) and her *The Realm of Rights* (Cambridge: Harvard University Press, 1990), particularly its "Introduction and Metaethical Remarks," where she contends that there are moral truths that are necessary, are non-trivial, and (as I would put it) do not need proof from prior premises to be seen to be true. See esp. pp. 12–20. For a valuable discussion of her position that takes it to commit her (as I think intuitionism need not be committed) to our having a "moral faculty," see M. B. E. Smith's review of the book in the *Hastings Center Report* 22 (1992).

5. These points are in ch. 2 of *The Right and the Good* (Oxford: Oxford University Press, 1930). More specific references relevant to them are given in ch. 2 of this volume.

6. What we ought to do *seems*, however, to go beyond our duties. For instance, although in some cases I ought (and it would be virtuous) to help a guest of my daughter with a flat tire even though I am busy, it is not clearly any kind of a duty. There is no need to settle this. Cf. Bernard Gert's view that the so-called positive duties (at least of beneficence) represent moral *ideals*. See *Morality* 2nd ed. (forthcoming).

7. Ross, *The Right and the Good*, ch. 2.

8. Since I am only sketching a normative theory, I largely ignore the point that one may have conflicting *sets* of duties, say two pulling one way and two pulling another. Third-order and even higher-order conflicts are also possible.

9. I refer to Kant's widely known view, suggested in the *Foundations of the Metaphysics of Morals* and other works of his, that a perfect duty, such as the duty to keep a promise, always outweighs an imperfect duty, such as the duty to help someone in distress. Since perfect duties can conflict, even if Kant were right about the former case, he would presumably need to appeal to the categorical imperative, in the way suggested in the text, to deal with those conflicts.

10. Kant apparently regarded these as equivalent, even if not *identical*, in content. I provisionally assume that if only because the intrinsic end formulation provides the main materials needed to guide interpretation of the universality one (which is highly schematic), the equivalence claim is plausible. The falsity of this claim would not, however, substantially affect my project here.

11. I insert 'rationally' to capture Kant's intention and because it is in any case not plau-

sible to think the requirement concerns either psychological or strict logical possibility; as is well-known, in the *Groundwork* Kant grants that there is no inconsistency in universalizing the maxims corresponding to failure to do good deeds and to develop one's talents. In the application at hand we could be more cautious and say 'could not reasonably resent', but this may not be necessary for a sound maxim in such cases. The notion of what is reasonable in such a case is by implication clarified in many parts of this book. A similar notion is illuminatingly discussed by T. M. Scanlon in connection with contractarian justifications. See, e.g., his "Contractarianism and Utilitarianism," in Amartya Sen and Bernard Williams, eds., *Utilitarianism and Beyond* (Cambridge: Cambridge University Press, 1982).

12. I leave open the prospects for developing such prior notions from a Kantian perspective. My own approach in ch. 11 allows taking certain moral values as basic and using them to clarify the content and application of both the categorical imperative and the Rossian duties. As will be apparent shortly, this approach also allows that our axiological and deontic concepts may be mutually clarifying.

13. This is a reference to the supervenience of moral properties, discussed especially in chs. 4 and 5. The relevant passages in Ross are mainly in chs. 2 and 4 of *The Right and the Good*. See esp. pp. 33, 105, and 121–23.

14. Ross, Ibid., p. 21.

15. Ibid., pp. 21 and 17–18.

16. One worry is that in practice we can only extract such vague principles as 'In cases like this, prefer spending money on educating one's children over saving children abroad', where at best we can be specific by listing so many circumstances that the principle is unlikely to reapply. As suggested earlier, moral decision is often guided by discriminations that are both readily generalizable and, on reflection, can be roughly formulated. But there is no need to deny that there is a problem of formulation in such cases. It seems, however, to confront any plausible comprehensive ethics.

17. Without implying that Mill is best read as a rule utilitarian, we should not take lightly his point that "only in cases of conflict between secondary principles is it requisite that first principles [notably the principle of utility] should be appealed to. *There is no case of moral obligation in which some secondary principle is not involved*; and if only one, there can seldom be any doubt about which one it is" (emphasis added). See *Utilitarianism*, (Indianapolis: Hackett, 1979), p. 25.

18. I leave open whether some non-moral concept of treating people as means and ends may be devised from a Kantian perspective, so that application of the categorical imperative does not require independent moral standards. If this is not so, then the Kantian framework in question needs supplementation by, for instance, an intuitionist perspective such as the one presented here.

19. I distinguish between the theory Kant presented and his pronouncements in interpreting it. I cannot, e.g., see that anything fundamental in the categorical imperative framework makes all suicides immoral, as Kant is commonly read as holding.

20. See, e.g., Plato's characterization of the Form of the Good in *The Republic*, 508 (where he says, "This, then, which gives to the objects of knowledge their truth and to him who knows them his power of knowing, is the Form or essential nature of Goodness"), and Aristotle's derivation of happiness as the good from considerations about the structure of motivation, in *Nicomachean Ethics*, e.g. in the passage quoted in ch. 11, sec. I, p. 249. For a detailed account of Plato's moral theory, with numerous comparisons of it to Aristotle's, see Terence Irwin, *Plato's Ethics* (New York and Oxford: Oxford University Press, 1995).

21. See the *Treatise* (Oxford: Oxford University Press, 1888), esp. pp. 467–69.

22. One might argue that the *content* of the relevant intentions or dispositions must be moral, so that the psychological properties in question are not purely natural. Even if having

such content implies that the properties are not themselves natural, if in ch. 8 I am right about acting from virtue, it is at least possible to exercise moral virtue without depending on moral concepts, and (on plausible assumptions) this implies that there is at least one kind of person of good will who need not have moral concepts figuring in the crucial intentions and dispositions.

23. Ch. 2 argues for the compatibility of a generic intuitionism with empiricism, and at least by implication defends the claim that none of the varieties of intuitionism it considers is incompatible with the dependence of moral on natural properties.

24. John Hospers is a clear case of a philosopher who has taken unconscious motivation to be automatically undermining of responsibility. See his "What Means This Freedom?," in Sidney Hook, ed., *Determinism and Freedom in the Age of Modern Science* (New York: New York University Press, 1958), esp. sec. I. I have tried to block that threat in chs. 7 and 10 of *Action, Intention, and Reason* (Ithaca and London: Cornell University Press, 1993).

25. See the *Foundations of the Metaphysics of Morals*, Lewis White Beck trans. (New York: Liberal Arts Press, 1959), ch. 1, especially secs. 393 and 399.

26. There have been many plausible attempts to deal with apparently counterintuitive consequences of a maximizing utilitarianism. For some of them, see Samuel Scheffler, ed., *Consequentialism and Its Critics* (Oxford and New York: Oxford University Press, 1988). Particularly relevant is Amartya Sen's effort in "Rights and Agency." For contrasting views see Scheffler's treatment of agent-centered restrictions (ch. 11) and the chapters by Thomas Nagel (7) and T. M. Scanlon (4).

Index

accessibility. *See* internalism, epistemological; internalism, normative

Alston, William P., 62n. 29, 87n. 30, 110n. 23, 155n. 6, 171n. 5

anti-realism, 74–75, 78. *See also* eliminativism

a priori, the, 28, 102–3. *See also* rationalism; self-evidence

Aquinas, Thomas, 68, 271n. 1, 286, 294

aretaic conflict, 186

aretaic connectedness, 179–85

aretaic grounding, 182–85

Aristotle, 7, 36, 62n. 31, 73, 170n. 1, 171n. 11, 174–80, 186–87, 249–51, 253, 271n. 1, 271n. 2, 271n. 7, 272n. 11, 277, 286, 290, 294, 296n. 2, 297n. 21

Armstrong, David, 172n. 20

autonomy, 165, 195–216, 264, 284, 291–93
and second-order attitudes, 201–2, 211
as self-government, 196–205
scope of, 203–4

Bach, Kent, 155n. 5, 155n. 13

Baier, Kurt, 190n. 12, 244n. 14

basic act, 158

Battin, Margaret Pabst, 274n. 30

Beehler, Rodger, 213n. 3, 214n. 5

belief, ethics of. *See* ethics of belief

belief rationalization, 143

Bond, E. J., 215n. 23, 243n. 14, 272n. 13

Bosley, Richard, 155n. 12

Brandt, R. B., 60n. 13, 64n. 42, 65n. 53, 86n. 20, 110n. 28, 113, 171n. 5, 215n. 17, 275n. 44

Brink, David O., 109n. 11, 109n. 19, 127n. 13, 127n. 17, 243n. 14

Broadie, Sarah, 190n. 5, 190n. 8, 191n. 14, 191n. 21

Butchvarov, Panayot, 108n. 9, 126n. 8, 271n. 1, 272n. 12

categorical imperative, the, 25, 26–27, 48, 189n. 4, 264, 280–85, 296n. 10, 297n. 18

character, 4, 5, 6, 24–26, 160, 288, 289. *See also* virtue

Clifford, W. K., 147

cognitive dissonance, 151

cognitivism. *See* noncognitivism

Cohen, Joshua, 214n. 5

coherentism, 63n. 37, 207. *See also* foundationalism

Cohon, Rachel, 244n. 14, 246n. 29

compatibilism, 169

completeness, normative. *See* normative completeness

conditional duty, 34

consequentialism, 23

control, 164–65, 197–98, 201, 204, 214n. 6. *See also* voluntariness

Cooper, John M., 191n. 21

cooperating motives. *See* motivation, cooperating

Copp, David, 110n. 23

Dahl, Norman O., 214n. 7

Dancy, Jonathan, 51n. 1, 244n. 14

Darwall, Stephen L., 213n. 2, 214n. 9, 243n. 14

Davidson, Donald, 242n. 6

Deigh, John, 155n. 7, 243n. 14, 244n. 18

deliberation, 177. *See also* practical reasoning

delusion, 134, 144

Dennett, Daniel, 173n. 24